SHORT STORIES
for Students

Advisors

Jayne M. Burton is a teacher of secondary English and an adjunct professor for Northwest Vista College in San Antonio, TX.

Klaudia Janek is the school librarian at the International Academy in Bloomfield Hills, Michigan. She holds an MLIS degree from Wayne State University, a teaching degree from Rio Salado College, and a bachelor of arts degree in international relations from Saint Joseph's College. She is the IB Extended Essay Coordinator and NCA AdvancEd co-chair at her school. She is an IB workshop leader for International Baccalaureate North America, leading teacher training for IB school librarians and extended essay coordinators. She has been happy to serve the Michigan Association for Media in Education as a board member and past president at the regional level, advocating for libraries in Michigan schools.

Greg Bartley is an English teacher in Virginia. He holds an M.A.Ed. in English Education from Wake Forest University and a B.S. in Integrated Language Arts Education from Miami University.

Sarah Clancy teaches IB English at the International Academy in Bloomfield Hills, Michigan. She is a member of the National Council of Teachers of English and Michigan Speech Coaches, Inc. Sarah earned her undergraduate degree from Kalamazoo College and her Master's of Education from Florida Southern College. She coaches the high-ranking forensics team and is the staff adviser of the school newspaper, *Overachiever*.

Karen Dobson is a teen/adult librarian at Plymouth District Library in Plymouth, Michigan. She holds a Bachelor of Science degree from Oakland University and an MLIS from Wayne State University and has served on many committees through the Michigan Library Association.

Tom Shilts is the youth librarian at the Okemos branch of Capital Area District Library in Okemos, Michigan. He holds an MSLS degree from Clarion University of Pennsylvania and an MA in U.S. History from the University of North Dakota.

SHORT STORIES
for Students

**Presenting Analysis, Context, and Criticism
on Commonly Studied Short Stories**

VOLUME 44

Kristin B. Mallegg, Project Editor

Foreword by Thomas E. Barden

GALE
CENGAGE Learning·

Farmington Hills, Mich • San Francisco • New York • Waterville, Maine
Meriden, Conn • Mason, Ohio • Chicago

Short Stories for Students, Volume 44

Project Editor: Kristin B. Mallegg

Rights Acquisition and Management:
Moriam Aigoro

Composition: Evi Abou-El-Seoud

Manufacturing: Rita Wimberley

Imaging: John Watkins

Product Design: Pamela A. E. Galbreath,
Jennifer Wahi

Digital Content Production: Edna Shy

For product information and technology assistance, contact us at
Gale Customer Support, 1-800-877-4253.
For permission to use material from this text or product,
submit all requests online at **www.cengage.com/permissions.**
Further permissions questions can be emailed to
permissionrequest@cengage.com

While every effort has been made to ensure the reliability of the information presented in this publication, Gale, a part of Cengage Learning, does not guarantee the accuracy of the data contained herein. Gale accepts no payment for listing; and inclusion in the publication of any organization, agency, institution, publication, service, or individual does not imply endorsement of the editors or publisher. Errors brought to the attention of the publisher and verified to the satisfaction of the publisher will be corrected in future editions.

Gale
27500 Drake Rd.
Farmington Hills, MI, 48331-3535

ISBN-13: 978-1-4103-2856-4
ISSN 1092-77355

This title is also available as an e-book.
ISBN-13: 978-1-4103-2861-8
Contact your Gale, a part of Cengage Learning sales representative for ordering information.

Printed in Mexico
1 2 3 4 5 6 7 20 19 18 17 16

Table of Contents

Why Study Literature At All?

Short Stories for Students is designed to provide readers with information and discussion about a wide range of important contemporary and historical works of short fiction, and it does that job very well. However, I want to use this guest foreword to address a question that it does *not* take up. It is a fundamental question that is often ignored in high school and college English classes as well as research texts, and one that causes frustration among students at all levels, namely why study literature at all? Isn't it enough to read a story, enjoy it, and go about one's business? My answer (to be expected from a literary professional, I suppose) is no. It is not enough. It is a start; but it is not enough. Here's why.

First, literature is the only part of the educational curriculum that deals directly with the actual world of lived experience. The philosopher Edmund Husserl used the apt German term *die Lebenswelt*, "the living world," to denote this realm. All the other content areas of the modern American educational system avoid the subjective, present reality of everyday life. Science (both the natural and the social varieties) objectifies, the fine arts create and/or perform, history reconstructs. Only literary study persists in posing those questions we all asked before our schooling taught us to give up on them. Only literature gives credibility to personal perceptions, feelings, dreams, and the "stream of consciousness" that is our inner voice. Literature wonders about infinity, wonders why God permits evil, wonders

what will happen to us after we die. Literature admits that we get our hearts broken, that people sometimes cheat and get away with it, that the world is a strange and probably incomprehensible place. Literature, in other words, takes on all the big and small issues of what it means to be human. So my first answer is that of the humanist we should read literature and study it and take it seriously because it enriches us as human beings. We develop our moral imagination, our capacity to sympathize with other people, and our ability to understand our existence through the experience of fiction.

My second answer is more practical. By studying literature we can learn how to explore and analyze texts. Fiction may be about *die Lebenswelt*, but it is a construct of words put together in a certain order by an artist using the medium of language. By examining and studying those constructions, we can learn about language as a medium. We can become more sophisticated about word associations and connotations, about the manipulation of symbols, and about style and atmosphere. We can grasp how ambiguous language is and how important context and texture is to meaning. In our first encounter with a work of literature, of course, we are not supposed to catch all of these things. We are spellbound, just as the writer wanted us to be. It is as serious students of the writer's art that we begin to see how the tricks are done.

Seeing the tricks, which is another way of saying "developing analytical and close reading skills," is important above and beyond its intrinsic literary educational value. These skills transfer to other fields and enhance critical thinking of any kind. Understanding how language is used to construct texts is powerful knowledge. It makes engineers better problem solvers, lawyers better advocates and courtroom practitioners, politicians better rhetoricians, marketing and advertising agents better sellers, and citizens more aware consumers as well as better participants in democracy. This last point is especially important, because rhetorical skill works both ways when we learn how language is manipulated in the making of texts the result is that we become less susceptible when language is used to manipulate us.

My third reason is related to the second. When we begin to see literature as created artifacts of language, we become more sensitive to good writing in general. We get a stronger sense of the importance of individual words, even the sounds of words and word combinations. We begin to understand Mark Twain's delicious proverb "The difference between the right word and the almost right word is the difference between lightning and a lightning bug." Getting beyond the "enjoyment only" stage of literature gets us closer to becoming makers of word art ourselves. I am not saying that studying fiction will turn every student into a Faulkner or a Shakespeare. But it will make us more adaptable and effective writers, even if our art form ends up being the office memo or the corporate annual report.

Studying short stories, then, can help students become better readers, better writers, and even better human beings. But I want to close with a warning. If your study and exploration of the craft, history, context, symbolism, or anything else about a story starts to rob it of the magic you felt when you first read it, it is time to stop. Take a break, study another subject, shoot some hoops, or go for a run. Love of reading is too important to be ruined by school. The early twentieth century writer Willa Cather, in her novel *My Antonia*, has her narrator Jack Burden tell a story that he and Antonia heard from two old Russian immigrants when they were teenagers. These immigrants, Pavel and Peter, told about an incident from their youth back in Russia that the narrator could recall in vivid detail thirty years later. It was a harrowing story of a wedding party starting home in sleds and being chased by starving wolves. Hundreds of wolves attacked the group's sleds one by one as they sped across the snow trying to reach their village. In a horrible revelation, the old Russians revealed that the groom eventually threw his own bride to the wolves to save himself. There was even a hint that one of the old immigrants might have been the groom mentioned in the story. Cather has her narrator conclude with his feelings about the story. "We did not tell Pavel's secret to anyone, but guarded it jealously as if the wolves of the Ukraine had gathered that night long ago, and the wedding party had been sacrificed, just to give us a painful and peculiar pleasure." That feeling, that painful and peculiar pleasure, is the most important thing about literature. Study and research should enhance that feeling and never be allowed to overwhelm it.

Thomas E. Barden
Professor of English and Director of
Graduate English Studies, The
University of Toledo

Introduction

Purpose of the Book

The purpose of *Short Stories for Students* (*SSfS*) is to provide readers with a guide to understanding, enjoying, and studying short stories by giving them easy access to information about the work. Part of Gale's "For Students" Literature line, *SSfS* is specifically designed to meet the curricular needs of high school and undergraduate college students and their teachers, as well as the interests of general readers and researchers considering specific short fiction. While each volume contains entries on "classic" stories frequently studied in classrooms, there are also entries containing hard-to-find information on contemporary stories, including works by multicultural, international, and women writers.

The information covered in each entry includes an introduction to the story and the story's author; a plot summary, to help readers unravel and understand the events in the work; descriptions of important characters, including explanation of a given character's role in the narrative as well as discussion about that character's relationship to other characters in the story; analysis of important themes in the story; and an explanation of important literary techniques and movements as they are demonstrated in the work.

In addition to this material, which helps the readers analyze the story itself, students are also provided with important information on the literary and historical background informing each work. This includes a historical context essay, a box comparing the time or place the story was written to modern Western culture, a critical overview essay, and excerpts from critical essays on the story or author. A unique feature of *SSfS* is a specially commissioned critical essay on each story, targeted toward the student reader.

To further help today's student in studying and enjoying each story, information on audiobooks and other media adaptations is provided (if available), as well as reading suggestions for works of fiction and nonfiction on similar themes and topics. Classroom aids include ideas for research papers and lists of critical and reference sources that provide additional material on the work.

Selection Criteria

The titles for each volume of *SSfS* were selected by surveying numerous sources on teaching literature and analyzing course curricula for various school districts. Some of the sources surveyed include: literature anthologies, *Reading Lists for College-Bound Students: The Books Most Recommended by America's Top Colleges*; *Teaching the Short Story: A Guide to Using Stories from around the World*, by the National Council of Teachers of English (NCTE); and "A Study of High School Literature Anthologies," conducted by Arthur Applebee at the Center for the Learning and Teaching of Literature and sponsored by the National Endowment for the

Arts and the Office of Educational Research and Improvement.

Input was also solicited from our advisory board, as well as educators from various areas. From these discussions, it was determined that each volume should have a mix of "classic" stories (those works commonly taught in literature classes) and contemporary stories for which information is often hard to find. Because of the interest in expanding the canon of literature, an emphasis was also placed on including works by international, multicultural, and women authors. Our advisory board members—educational professionals—helped pare down the list for each volume. Works not selected for the present volume were noted as possibilities for future volumes. As always, the editor welcomes suggestions for titles to be included in future volumes.

How Each Entry Is Organized

Each entry, or chapter, in *SSfS* focuses on one story. Each entry heading lists the title of the story, the author's name, and the date of the story's publication. The following elements are contained in each entry:

Introduction: a brief overview of the story which provides information about its first appearance, its literary standing, any controversies surrounding the work, and major conflicts or themes within the work.

Author Biography: this section includes basic facts about the author's life, and focuses on events and times in the author's life that may have inspired the story in question.

Plot Summary: a description of the events in the story. Lengthy summaries are broken down with subheads.

Characters: an alphabetical listing of the characters who appear in the story. Each character name is followed by a brief to an extensive description of the character's role in the story, as well as discussion of the character's actions, relationships, and possible motivation.

Characters are listed alphabetically by last name. If a character is unnamed—for instance, the narrator in "The Eatonville Anthology"— the character is listed as "The Narrator" and alphabetized as "Narrator." If a character's first name is the only one given, the name will appear alphabetically by that name.

Themes: a thorough overview of how the topics, themes, and issues are addressed within the

story. Each theme discussed appears in a separate subhead.

Style: this section addresses important style elements of the story, such as setting, point of view, and narration; important literary devices used, such as imagery, foreshadowing, symbolism; and, if applicable, genres to which the work might have belonged, such as Gothicism or Romanticism. Literary terms are explained within the entry, but can also be found in the Glossary.

Historical Context: this section outlines the social, political, and cultural climate in which the author lived and the work was created. This section may include descriptions of related historical events, pertinent aspects of daily life in the culture, and the artistic and literary sensibilities of the time in which the work was written. If the story is historical in nature, information regarding the time in which the story is set is also included. Long sections are broken down with helpful subheads.

Critical Overview: this section provides background on the critical reputation of the author and the story, including bannings or any other public controversies surrounding the work. For older works, this section may include a history of how the story was first received and how perceptions of it may have changed over the years; for more recent works, direct quotes from early reviews may also be included.

Criticism: an essay commissioned by *SSfS* which specifically deals with the story and is written specifically for the student audience, as well as excerpts from previously published criticism on the work (if available).

Sources: an alphabetical list of critical material used in compiling the entry, with bibliographical information.

Further Reading: an alphabetical list of other critical sources which may prove useful for the student. Includes full bibliographical information and a brief annotation.

Suggested Search Terms: a list of search terms and phrases to jumpstart students' further information seeking. Terms include not just titles and author names but also terms and topics related to the historical and literary context of the works.

In addition, each entry contains the following highlighted sections, set apart from the main text as sidebars:

Media Adaptations: if available, a list of audio-books and important film and television adaptations of the story, including source information. The list also includes stage adaptations, musical adaptations, etc.

Topics for Further Study: a list of potential study questions or research topics dealing with the story. This section includes questions related to other disciplines the student may be studying, such as American history, world history, science, math, government, business, geography, economics, psychology, etc.

Compare and Contrast: an "at-a-glance" comparison of the cultural and historical differences between the author's time and culture and late twentieth century or early twenty-first century Western culture. This box includes pertinent parallels between the major scientific, political, and cultural movements of the time or place the story was written, the time or place the story was set (if a historical work), and modern Western culture. Works written after 1990 may not have this box.

What Do I Read Next?: a list of works that might give a reader points of entry into a classic work (e.g., YA or multicultural titles) and/or complement the featured story or serve as a contrast to it. This includes works by the same author and others, works from various genres, YA works, and works from various cultures and eras.

Other Features

SSfS includes "Why Study Literature At All?," a foreword by Thomas E. Barden, Professor of English and Director of Graduate English Studies at the University of Toledo. This essay provides a number of very fundamental reasons for studying literature and, therefore, reasons why a book such as *SSfS*, designed to facilitate the study of literature, is useful.

A Cumulative Author/Title Index lists the authors and titles covered in each volume of the *SSfS* series.

A Cumulative Nationality/Ethnicity Index breaks down the authors and titles covered in each volume of the *SSfS* series by nationality and ethnicity.

A Subject/Theme Index, specific to each volume, provides easy reference for users who may be studying a particular subject or theme rather than a single work. Significant subjects from events to broad themes are included.

Each entry may include illustrations, including photo of the author, stills from film adaptations (if available), maps, and/or photos of key historical events.

Citing Short Stories for Students

When writing papers, students who quote directly from any volume of *SSfS* may use the following general forms to document their source. These examples are based on MLA style; teachers may request that students adhere to a different style, thus, the following examples may be adapted as needed.

When citing text from *SSfS* that is not attributed to a particular author (for example, the Themes, Style, Historical Context sections, etc.), the following format may be used:

> "How I Met My Husband." *Short Stories for Students.* Ed. Sara Constantakis. Vol. 36. Detroit: Gale, Cengage Learning, 2013. 73–95. Print.

When quoting the specially commissioned essay from *SSfS* (usually the first essay under the Criticism subhead), the following format may be used:

> Dominic, Catherine. Critical Essay on "How I Met My Husband." *Short Stories for Students.* Ed. Sara Constantakis. Vol. 36. Detroit: Gale, Cengage Learning, 2013. 84–87. Print.

When quoting a journal or newspaper essay that is reprinted in a volume of *SSfS*, the following form may be used:

> Ditsky, John. "The Figure in the Linoleum: The Fictions of Alice Munro." *Hollins Critic* 22.3 (1985): 1–10. Rpt. in *Short Stories for Students.* Vol. 36. Ed. Sara Constantakis. Detroit: Gale, Cengage Learning, 2013. 92–94. Print.

When quoting material from a book that is reprinted in a volume of *SSfS,* the following form may be used:

> Cooke, John. "Alice Munro." *The Influence of Painting on Five Canadian Writers.* Lewiston, NY: Edwin Mellen Press, 1996. 69–85. Rpt. in *Short Stories for Students.* Vol. 36. Ed. Sara Constantakis. Detroit: Gale, Cengage Learning, 2013. 89–92. Print.

We Welcome Your Suggestions

The editorial staff of *Short Stories for Students* welcomes your comments and ideas. Readers who wish to suggest short stories to appear in future volumes, or who have other suggestions, are cordially invited to contact the editor. You may contact the editor via E-mail at: **ForStudentsEditors@cengage.com.** Or write to the editor at:

Editor, *Short Stories for Students*
Gale
27500 Drake Road
Farmington Hills, MI 48331-3535

Literary Chronology

1822: Edward Everett Hale is born on April 3 in Boston, Massachusetts.

1863: Edward Everett Hale's "The Man without a Country" is published in *Atlantic Monthly*.

1886: Wilbur Daniel Steele is born on March 17 in Greensboro, North Carolina.

1908: Ann Petry is born on October 12 in Old Saybrook, Connecticut.

1909: Eudora Welty is born on April 13 in Jackson, Mississippi.

1909: Edward Everett Hale dies on June 10 in Roxbury, Massachusetts.

1914: Bernard Malamud is born on April 26 in New York, New York.

1920: Wilbur Daniel Steele's "Footfalls" is published in *Pictorial Review*.

1922: José Saramago is born on November 16 in Azinghaga, Portugal.

1924: James Baldwin is born on August 2 in Harlem, New York.

1937: Bessie Head is born on July 6 in Pietermaritzburg, South Africa.

1938: Joyce Carol Oates is born on June 16 in Lockport, New York.

1940: Bobbie Ann Mason is born on May 1 in Mayfield, Kentucky.

1943: Eudora Welty's "The Wide Net" is published in *The Wide Net and Other Stories*.

1945: Ann Petry's "Like a Winding Sheet" is published in *Crisis*.

1948: Leslie Marmon Silko is born on March 5 in Albuquerque, New Mexico.

1955: Gish Jen is born on August 12 New York, New York.

1960: James Baldwin's "This Morning, This Evening, So Soon" is published in *Atlantic Monthly*.

1963: Bernard Malamud's "The Jewbird" is published in *Reporter*.

1966: Joyce Carol Oates's "In the Region of Ice" is published in *Atlantic Monthly*.

1966: Bessie Head's "Looking for a Rain God" is published in *The New African*.

1966: Sherman Alexie is born on October 7 in Spokane, Washington.

1967: Bernard Malamud is awarded the Pulitzer Prize for Fiction for *The Fixer*.

1969: Leslie Marmon Silko's "Tony's Story" is published in *Thunderbird*.

1970: Wilbur Daniel Steele dies on May 26 in Essex, Connecticut.

1973: Eudora Welty is awarded the Pulitzer Prize for Fiction for *The Optimist's Daughter*.

1973: Anthony Doerr is born in Cleveland, Ohio.

1982: Bobbie Ann Mason's "Detroit Skyline, 1949" is published in *Shiloh and Other Stories*.

1986: Bernard Malamud dies of heart failure on March 18 in New York, New York.

1986: Bessie Head dies of hepatitis on April 17 in Serowe, Botswana.

1987: James Baldwin dies of stomach cancer on December 1 in Saint-Paul-de-Vence, France.

1997: Ann Petry dies after a brief illness on April 28 in Old Saybrook, Connecticut.

1997: José Saramago's "The Tale of the Unknown Island" is published in Portuguese as "O Conto da Ilha Desconhecida." It is published in English in 1999.

1998: José de Sousa Saramago is awarded the Nobel Prize for Literature.

1999: Gish Jen's "Who's Irish?" is published in *Who's Irish?*.

2001: Anthony Doerr's "The Hunter's Wife" is published in *Atlantic Monthly*.

2001: Eudora Welty dies of pneumonia on July 23 in Jackson, Mississippi.

2003: Sherman Alexie's "What You Pawn, I Will Redeem" is published in *New Yorker*.

2010: José Saramago dies of Leukemia on June 18 in Tías in the Canary Islands, Spain.

2015: Anthony Doerr is awarded the Pulitzer Prize for Fiction for *All the Light We Cannot See*.

Acknowledgements

The editors wish to thank the copyright holders of the excerpted criticism included in this volume and the permissions managers of many book and magazine publishing companies for assisting us in securing reproduction rights. We are also grateful to the staffs of the Detroit Public Library, the Library of Congress, the University of Detroit Mercy Library, Wayne State University Purdy/ Kresge Library Complex, and the University of Michigan Libraries for making their resources available to us. Following is a list of the copyright holders who have granted us permission to reproduce material in this volume of *SSfS*. Every effort has been made to trace copyright, but if omissions have been made, please let us know.

COPYRIGHTED EXCERPTS IN SSfS, VOLUME 44, WERE REPRODUCED FROM THE FOLLOWING PERIODICALS:

Antioch Review, Vol. 62 (3), Summer, 2004, p. 581. Copyright © Antioch Review. Reproduced by permission.—*Ege University*, Vol. 15 (2), Fall 2006, p. 165. Copyright © 2006 Ege University. All rights reserved. Reproduced with permission.—*Guardian News Service Limited*, April 22, 2015. Copyright © 2015 Guardian News Service Limited. Reproduced by permission.—*Guardian News Service Limited*, November 22, 2002. Copyright © 2002 Guardian News Service Limited. Reproduced by permission.—*January Magazine*, March, 2002. Copyright © 2002 January Magazine. Reproduced by permission.—*Publishers Weekly*, Vol. 246 (17), April 26, 1999, p. 52. Copyright © PWXYZ, LLC. Reproduced by permission.—*Publishers Weekly*, Vol. 248 (48), November 26, 2001, p. 39. Copyright © PWXYZ, LLC. Reproduced by permission.—*Kirkus Reviews*, Vol. 69 (22), November 15, 2001, p. 1566. Copyright © 2001 Kirkus Media. All rights reserved. Reproduced with permission.—*Prairie Schooner*, Vol. 87 (23), Summer 2013, p. 166. Copyright © 2013 Prairie Schooner. Reproduced by permission.—*World Literature Today*, Vol. 74 (3), Summer 2000, p. 686. Copyright © 2000 World Literature Today.

COPYRIGHTED EXCERPTS IN SSfS, VOLUME 44, WERE REPRODUCED FROM THE FOLLOWING BOOKS:

Berglund, Jeff. From *An Introduction to Sherman Alexie*. University of Utah Press, 2010. Copyright © 2010 University of Utah Press. All rights reserved. Reproduced with permission.—Grassian, Daniel. From *Ten Little Indians*. University of South Carolina Press, 2005. Copyright © 2005 University of South Carolina Press. All rights reserved. Reproduced with permission.—Hernton, Calvin C. From *The Significance of Ann Petry*. Praeger, 2005. Copyright © 2005 ABC-CLIO. All rights reserved. Reproduced with permission.—Johnson, Joyce. From *Dredging the River: 'The Collector of Treasures'*. University of Delaware Press, 2008. Copyright © 2008 Associated University Press. All rights reserved. Reproduced with permission.—Johnson, Greg. From *Early Feminism.*Twayne Publishers, 1994. Copyright © Gale/Cengage Learning. All rights reserved. Reproduced with permission.—Johnson, Greg. From *The Short Stories (I): 'The Wheel of Love'*. University of South Carolina Press, 1987. Copyright © 1987 University of South Carolina Press. All rights reserved. Reproduced with permission.—Morel, Pauline. From *Counter-Stories and Border Identities: Storytelling and Myth as a Means of Identification, Subversion, and Survival in Leslie Marmon Silko's 'Yellow Woman' and 'Tony's Story'*. Peter Lang, 2005. Copyright © 2005 Peter Lang. All rights reserved. Reproduced with permission.—Pollack, Harriet. From *On Welty's Use of Allusion: Expectations and Their Revision in 'The Wide Net,' 'The Robber Bridegroom', and 'At the Landing'*. Greenwood Press, 1994. Copyright © 1994 ABC-CLIO. Reproduced with permission.—Pratt, Louis H. From *The Fear and the Fury*. Twayne Publishers, 1978. Copyright © Gale/Cengage Learning. All rights reserved. Reproduced with permission.—Price, Joanna. From *Shiloh and Other Stories*. University of South Carolina

Press, 2000. Copyright © 2000 University of South Carolina Press.—Ruoff, Lavonne Brown. From *The Critics: LaVonne Brown Ruoff*. Twayne Publishers, 1998. Copyright © Gale/Cengage Learning. All rights reserved. Reproduced with permission.—Salzberg, Joel. From *Parody as Exorcism: 'The Raven' and 'The Jewbird'*. G.K. Hall & Co., 1987. All rights reserved. Reproduced with permission.—Silko, Leslie Marmon and Laura Coltelli. From *Leslie Marmon Silko*. University of Nebraska Press, 1990. Copyright © 1990 University of Nebraska Press. All rights reserved. Reproduced with permission.—Solotaroff, Robert. From *Idiots First*. Twayne Publishers, 1989. Copyright © 1989 Robert Solotaroff. All rights reserved. Reproduced with permission.—Wilhelm, Albert. From *Travelers and Pilgrims: Looking for Love, Purpose, and Fulfillment in Many of the Wrong Places*. Twayne Publishers, 1998. Copyright © Gale/Cengage Learning. —Williams, Blanche Colton. From *Wilbur Daniel Steele*. Books for Libraries Press, 1922.Copyright © Books for Libraries Press. Reproduced by permission.

Contributors

Susan K. Andersen: Andersen is a writer and teacher with a PhD in English literature. Entries on "What You Pawn I Will Redeem" and "The Wide Net." Original essays on "What You Pawn I Will Redeem" and "The Wide Net."

Bryan Aubrey: Aubrey holds a PhD in English. Entry on "The Man without a Country." Original essay on "The Man without a Country."

Cynthia A. Bily: Bily is a professor at Macomb Community College. Entry on "Looking for a Rain God." Original essay on "Looking for a Rain God."

Rita M. Brown: Brown is an English professor. Entry on "Tale of the Unknown Island." Original essay on "Tale of the Unknown Island."

Klay Dyer: Dyer is a freelance writer specializing in topics relating to literature, popular culture, and the relationship between creativity and technology. Entry on "In the Region of Ice." Original essay on "In the Region of Ice."

Kristen Sarlin Greenberg: Greenberg is a freelance writer and editor with a background in literature and philosophy. Entry on "Who's Irish?" Original essay on "Who's Irish?"

David Kelly: Kelly is a writer and instructor of literature. Entry on "Detroit Skyline, 1949." Original essay on "Detroit Skyline, 1949."

Amy L. Miller: Miller is a graduate of the University of Cincinnati, and she currently resides in New Orleans, Louisiana. Entry on "Tony's Story." Original essay on "Tony's Story."

Michael J. O'Neal: O'Neal holds a PhD in English. Entry on "Footfalls." Original essay on "Footfalls."

Jeffrey Eugene Palmer: Palmer is a freelance writer, scholar, and high school English teacher. Entry on "Like a Winding Sheet." Original essay on "Like a Winding Sheet."

William Rosencrans: Rosencrans is a writer and copy editor. Entry on "The Hunter's Wife." Original essay on "The Hunter's Wife."

Bradley Skeen: Skeen is a classicist. Entry on "The Jewbird." Original essay on "The Jewbird."

Kathy Wilson Peacock: Wilson Peacock is a freelance writer specializing in literature criticism. Entry on "This Morning, This Evening, So Soon." Original essay on "This Morning, This Evening, So Soon."

Detroit Skyline, 1949

BOBBIE ANN MASON

1982

"Detroit Skyline, 1949," by Bobbie Ann Mason, tells the story of a nine-year-old girl who travels by bus with her mother from their Kentucky milk farm to see Detroit, one of the biggest and most thriving industrial cities in America. They stay with relatives in a Detroit suburb but find their plans to see the city foiled when a transit strike leaves them unable to go the few miles they need to reach downtown. At her aunt and uncle's home, feeling alienated from the other children around because of her rural background, Peggy Jo finds comfort when she discovers an engrossing new invention, television. She spends that summer happily learning about the characters and actors on television, listening to the adults in the house whisper nervously about people suspected of Communist sympathies, and waiting for her chance to see the marvelous Detroit skyline. When her mother is rushed to the hospital, she ends up briefly alone, far from home, in a mysterious, threatening environment.

This story was published in Mason's very first short-story collection, *Shiloh and Other Stories*. With that book, Mason established a name for herself as one of the funniest, most moving, most readable writers of her generation, a voice of the New South and of ordinary people trying to make the best of their lower-middle-class lives. Mason's people are people who enjoy television without irony, who gossip and know the brands of groceries, and who might aspire to see big buildings. This story is unusual for Mason, who usually

After her rural upbringing, Peggy Jo finds the city of Detroit overwhelming (*©LouLouPhotos / Shutterstock.com*)

writes about the world the way it is today, but the sense of familiarity she gives 1949 is as fresh as any current fiction.

AUTHOR BIOGRAPHY

Mason was born in Mayfield, Kentucky, in 1940. She grew up on her family's dairy farm. She wrote for the local newspaper, the *Mayfield Messenger*, while she attended the University of Kentucky, earning her bachelor of arts degree in 1962. In 1966, she was awarded her master's degree from the State University of New York at Binghamton, and then she went on to obtain her doctorate from University of Connecticut in 1972.

In the 1970s, Mason worked part-time as an assistant professor of journalism and literature at Mansfield State College in Pennsylvania while working on her fiction writing. Her first short stories were published in the *New Yorker*, one of the most prestigious magazines in the world for fiction writers, in the late 1970s. She came to

national fame with her first collection of short stories, published in 1982. This collection, *Shiloh and Other Stories*, which includes the story "Detroit Skyline, 1949," won the PEN/Hemingway Award and was nominated for the American Book Award, the PEN/Faulkner Award, and the National Book Critics Circle Award. Mason went on to earn an Arts and Letters Award for Literature from the American Academy of Arts and Letters.

Throughout her career, Mason has published five books of short stories: *Shiloh* (1982), *Love Life* (1988), *Midnight Magic* (1998), *Zigzagging down a Wild Trail* (2002), and *Nancy Culpepper* (2006), which is a series of intertwined stories focused on the title character, based on Mason herself, as well as people from her real life. She has also published five novels: *In Country* (1985), *Spencer and Lila* (1988), *Feather Crowns* (1993), *An Atomic Romance* (2005), and *The Girl in the Blue Beret* (2011). Her 1998 book, *Clear Springs*, traces her family's background, leading up to her childhood on the family farm. In 2003, Mason published a short biography of Elvis

Presley, using her insight into southern sensibilities to give readers an understanding of the singer's mind. She has also published an analysis of girl detectives in young-adult fiction, like the Nancy Drew books that she loved as a child, in her 1975 book *The Girl Sleuth: A Feminist Guide*.

PLOT SUMMARY

"Detroit Skyline, 1949" takes place when its first-person narrator, Peggy Jo, is nine years old. She lives on a farm in Kentucky, and her mother is taking her up to Detroit, Michigan, to visit relatives. Her mother, who has been there before, is looking forward to showing Peggy Jo the huge buildings of the one of the country's most thriving metropolitan centers. When her Aunt Mozelle and Uncle Boone Cashon meet them at the interstate bus station in suburban Detroit, however, they give Peggy disappointing news: the buses into the city are not running because of a strike by the drivers, so there is no way for them to go into the city. Boone complains that the union is on strike because it is run by Communists, or "reds." Still, Peggy Jo is amazed by suburban Detroit, which is much different from rural Kentucky.

At the Cashon house, Peggy Jo meets her cousin, Betsy Lou. Betsy Lou is older, a teenager, and more interested in dating boys than in spending time with a younger girl, so the Cashons have asked a girl who is about Peggy Jo's age, Sharon Belletieri, to come over and play with her. Sharon mocks Peggy Jo's southern accent and teaches her to roller-skate—where Peggy Jo comes from, they do not have sidewalks.

Uncle Boone introduces Peggy Jo to television, which in 1949 was not available in rural areas. She watches wrestling with her uncle and later, by herself, watches children's programs and then anything that comes on. She becomes increasingly hooked on television because she prefers to spend time alone: Sharon does not interest her, and Betsy Lou has an active social life.

They are visited sometimes by Lunetta Jones, a young war widow who is also from Kentucky. When television reception is bad, Peggy Jo sits on the porch with her aunt's scrapbooks while her mother, Aunt Mozelle, and Lunetta talk in the kitchen. The scrapbooks contain newspaper clippings of articles that Aunt Mozelle has kept to remind herself that other people's lives are worse than her own.

MEDIA ADAPTATIONS

- "Detroit Skyline, 1949" is one of the stories included in *American Short Stories: 1920 to the Present*, an audio CD released in 2003 by Recording for the Blind & Dyslexic of Princeton, New Jersey.

One day, the newspaper carries a story about a supervisor for a power plant who was accused of being a Communist. The women try to conceal their worries about how this could endanger Boone's job. That evening, Peggy Jo watches television by herself while the adults talk in serious tones out on the porch.

As she is preparing for Sharon's birthday party, Peggy Jo notices that her mother looks pale and has vomited, but she soon forgets about it because the party distracts her. At the party, she feels alienated, being the only stranger. To impress the other children, she tells them that there are no "reds" in Kentucky. Sharon confides that she has heard her parents say that a man who works with Boone is a red. That night, while the grown-ups are playing cards, Peggy Jo tells them about the gossip she heard. The adults become frightened and tell her to keep quiet, that her uncle could lose his job if anyone heard about this.

The next morning, Peggy Jo, still upset that she has been silenced about the secret she knows about Communist sympathizers, angrily points out that her mother has had trouble digesting her food. As the adults drift into a discussion about divorce, Peggy Jo's mother doubles over with pain. She is taken to a hospital in a taxi.

Peggy Jo tries to keep from worrying about her mother by looking through the papers for an article to put in Aunt Mozelle's scrapbook of odd stories, eventually cutting out one about a haunted house in Wisconsin. Mozelle and Boone come home and try to reassure her. That afternoon they take her to the hospital to see her mother, who explains that she has lost the baby she was carrying. She says that she did not even know that she was pregnant.

In the evening, while her mother is resting, the rest of the family watches television. Peggy Jo eventually grows bored and goes to her room to work on writing a jingle for a soap competition, but her aunt calls her to the television because they are broadcasting images of the Detroit skyline. She promises to take Peggy Jo downtown to see the buildings, but by this point in her trip, Peggy Jo says she is not interested in going.

That night, Peggy Jo pieces together the things she has experienced lately. She imagines that the "reds," who are always the enemies in family stories, have taken the baby her mother was carrying and fears that her guardian angel might have failed to stop it because she has not had enough faith. She makes up a line for her soap jingle that involves the Communists, which she realizes later is entirely inappropriate.

Peggy Jo and her mother leave Detroit a few days later, taking a bus back to Kentucky. She never did go to see the downtown buildings, but she is still fascinated with television. The bus lets them off on a rural road a half mile from their house. Because of her recent miscarriage, her mother decides it would be best to not carry her suitcase, so she leaves it in a ditch, and they start walking.

Her mother tells Peggy Jo a story about a time, years ago, when she took a bus trip by herself. Peggy Jo was two years old at the time. When her mother came home she walked up this same road, carrying her suitcase. Peggy Jo, playing in the yard, looked up and saw her but did not recognize her. Peggy Jo thinks that her father and brother will similarly have a hard time recognizing them now, indicating that their experience has changed them.

They reach the top of a hill and look down on their little house, the inverse view of looking up at the tall city buildings of the Detroit skyline. The biggest thing on their farm is a barn, which is practically hidden by trees from where they stand.

CHARACTERS

Sharon Belletieri

While Peggy Jo is staying with them, her Aunt Mozelle and Uncle Boone have arranged for Sharon, a local girl, to play with her. They know that their own teenage daughter, Betsy Lou, is not interested in having to entertain her nine-year-old cousin.

Having grown up in suburban Detroit, Sharon's experiences are nothing like Peggy Jo's. For example, she roller-skates, whereas living in a rural area with dirt roads, Peggy Jo has never had the occasion to try roller-skating. Sharon finds Peggy Jo's southern accent strange and makes fun of it, which does not make her a pleasant person for Peggy Jo to be around (later, with southern-born Uncle Boone, Peggy Jo comments that Sharon's way of speaking seems strange to her).

Peggy Jo would rather be alone or watch television than spend time with Sharon Belletieri. Peggy Jo does attend Sharon's birthday party, but almost as soon as she arrives Sharon makes her uncomfortable by drawing attention to the fact that Peggy Jo is from Kentucky, ostracizing her. When she is blindfolded and spun around to play pin the tail on the donkey, Peggy Jo feels that all of the other children are laughing at her.

Betsy Lou Cashon

Betsy Lou is Peggy Jo's older cousin, the daughter of Aunt Mozelle and Uncle Boone. She has a pronounced fear of polio, mentioning it when she first meets Peggy Jo and then later when Peggy Jo's mother has been admitted to the hospital.

Peggy Jo looks up to her older cousin, who dates a number of different boys, sometimes several boys on the same day. Peggy Jo watches her older cousin with rapt attention and is able to list in detail the names of her boyfriends, the songs she listens to, and the places where she goes on her dates. Betsy Lou is too urbane for her, though: she finds the nine-year-old from the country too young and naïve to interest her. She tries to limit her time with Peggy Jo and is sarcastic toward her when they are together.

In some ways, Betsy Lou is still as naïve as her relatives from the country. She has a greater fear of the polio epidemic than anybody else in the story, bringing it up any time Peggy Jo mentions going to a public place, such as a pool or a birthday party.

Boone Cashon

Peggy Jo's Uncle Boone, married to her Aunt Mozelle, is a war veteran who works for one of the Detroit automobile companies, putting bumpers on cars. He makes a good living in the postwar economy and can afford luxury goods, such as the television set that he watches often.

Boone is usually in a good mood, making jokes about things that his wife and sister-in-law take seriously. He comments on the family friend Lunetta's being "man-crazy," and he playfully pretends that he would torture his wife with tickling if he found out she were a Communist. He is, however, very conscious of and worried by how vulnerable his position at the auto plant is.

Like everyone else in the story, Boone suspects that there are Communists, or at least people who are sympathetic to the Communists, working at the plant with him; he fears that someone might mistakenly think that he agrees with their political position, and he knows that even being suspected of such a thing can put his job in jeopardy.

Mozelle Cashon

Aunt Mozelle is the sister of Peggy Jo's mother. She and her husband, Boone, live in a Detroit suburb with their daughter, Betsy Lou. Coming from rural Kentucky, Mozelle is impressed with the big urban area she lives in now and the many modern conveniences that they can buy for a household like theirs, such as electric appliances. She tells her sister that when she thinks about her life she has to pinch herself, implying that it all seems like only a dream to her.

One of Aunt Mozelle's most notable characteristics is the scrapbook she keeps. It is full of newspaper articles she has cut out. It contains things that an average suburban housewife would want to save, such as sewing tips and recipes, but for the most part it contains articles that describe unusual facts and events from exotic places around the world. Mozelle tells Peggy Jo that she keeps these news articles as a constant reminder of how unusual life can be and to remind herself of how good her own stable life is.

Lunetta Jones

Lunetta is seventh-grade teacher whose husband, a sailor, died while fighting in World War II. Lunetta dresses elaborately and takes great pride in listing the details of her clothes to the other women. She does not talk to Peggy Jo, who pays careful attention to her way of dressing and her way of talking. Both Mozelle and Boone think that their friend Lunetta is so particular about the way she dresses because she is desperate to attract a new man.

Lunetta lives in fear for her job. She knows that, in the current political climate, she could be fired if there were even a hint that she was involved with or sympathetic toward Communists. Her interest in expanding her social life is balanced against her fear that new people she meets could leave her vulnerable if they were Communists, whether she knew it or not.

Peggy Jo

Peggy Jo is the narrator of the story. Her last name is never given. At the time of the story, Peggy Jo is nine. She has traveled to suburban Detroit with her mother from the family farm in rural Western Kentucky to visit relatives. Her mother wants to show Peggy Jo the huge buildings of the Detroit skyline, which she knows will amaze the girl, who has never seen anything like them; unfortunately, even though they are close to the city, they cannot make it downtown because the bus drivers that they need to take them there are on strike.

Thrust into the strange and potentially hostile environment of the city, Peggy Jo is awkward. Other children make fun of the way she talks and of her general cultural ignorance. She has never seen television. She does not know about Communists or polio. Still, she feels secure in knowing that she is protected by her guardian angel. Because she is socially awkward, Peggy Jo spends much of her time in Michigan engrossed in the television. She memorizes shows and actors and schedules. She tries to make a name for herself by thinking up a jingle for a detergent to win a competition she heard about on television.

As the adults talk about the threat of Communism, Peggy Jo's sense of security fades. She hears them say that Communism, like disease, can attack unseen and ruin a person's life. When her mother suddenly becomes ill and has a miscarriage, Peggy Jo associates her illness with an attack by Communists and thinks that her guardian angel has failed to protect her. The last line she writes for her soap jingle shows that she is afraid of the invisible but ever-present Communist threat.

Before returning home, the buses start running again: Peggy Jo could go to see the city of Detroit, which is what brought her here, but she refuses. Her Aunt Mozelle and Uncle Boone promise that she will be able to visit the city during her next trip north, but Peggy Jo says that she is not interested. She rejects the fast-paced urban life.

Back in Kentucky, after the interstate bus has left her at the crossroads, Peggy Jo approaches her home and looks down on her house from above. She has not seen the Detroit skyline, but when she is in her element, she stands over the tallest building on the farm. She is not the simple girl she was when she left home.

Peggy Jo's Father

Peggy Jo's father has little to do with the story. He stays back home in Kentucky while Peggy Jo and her mother leave for Detroit. Before they go, he jokes with an ethnic slur about the Polish people they might meet in the city, indicating that he has a narrow, defensive worldview.

Peggy Jo's Mother

The story's narrator, Peggy Jo, travels from rural Kentucky to a Detroit suburb with her mother to stay with her mother's sister, Mozelle, and Mozelle's husband, Boone. The stated motivation for their trip is that the mother wants Peggy Jo to see the Detroit sky-line, which she herself saw on a trip when Peggy Jo was too small to accompany her. The mother is trying to expand her daughter's cultural range, to show her what the world is like beyond their small family farm.

While they are in Michigan, Peggy's mother suffers a miscarriage. When Peggy Jo talks to her later, she says that she did not even know that she was pregnant before falling ill.

As they walk the country road toward their house at the end of the story, Peggy Jo's mother tells her a story about a time that she went on a trip by herself, when Peggy Jo was just two years old: as she approached the house, young Peggy Jo looked up and did not even recognize her mother. After this trip to see the wonders of the world together, a bond has been formed between mother and daughter.

THEMES

Postwar Society

People today look back at the years after World War II as a kind of golden age for the American

working class. Most of Europe had been directly affected by the fighting of the war, while America still had its manufacturing base intact. During the war, American factories had been churning out materials, from steel and rubber to vehicles, clothes, and food—whatever was needed for the war effort. After the war was over, places like Detroit, the unchallenged center of American automobile manufacturing, flourished. The strong manufacturing base made Americans financially stable enough to buy goods manufactured in America, promoting the country's strong economy.

Millions of people, like the story's Uncle Boone, moved from rural areas to urban centers, where they could get steady, well-paying jobs. To some, this migration tore families apart, but, as this story shows, it also helped connect sections of the country that had once been mysteries to one another: more people knew and visited with friends and relatives in areas that they might never even have given a thought to before. In the postwar years, America remained a country of distinct regions, each with dialects and practices that had been handed down for generations, but the vibrant economy made relocation and travel more possible, while friendships made during America's massive military action introduced many men and women who had served in the armed forces to people from other areas of the country.

Suburban Life

One of the hallmarks of the booming postwar society was the rise of suburbia. With American manufacturing expanding, people were drawn to cities for the well-paying jobs they offered. Many of these workers who found stable employment in cities preferred to live under less crowded, less hectic conditions than those the cities had to offer. Many cities experienced "suburban sprawl," as suburbs that existed grew with unprecedented building booms while new suburbs were built farther and farther from the city centers on land that had been forest or farm.

As depicted in this story, suburban living was less isolated than life on a farm, but it still could be a lonely existence. There were neighbors within walking distance, but the big city that was nearby could be an insurmountable distance away: in "Detroit Skyline, 1949," Peggy Jo never actually sees the city because her family relies on mass transportation, which is shut down for a strike. Television, which was invented before the war but did not really become popularized until

TOPICS FOR FURTHER STUDY

- Today, few people fear polio the way the people in this story do, because the polio vaccine practically erased the disease from America by the end of the twentieth century. In recent years, however, some people have come to think of vaccines as so dangerous that they feel safer leaving their children unvaccinated. Create a chart showing why vaccines for various diseases such as polio, measles, mumps, and tetanus are considered dangerous by some people and why the dangers are considered overstated by others.

- Peggy Jo says that wrestling is one of Uncle Boone's favorite things to watch on television. Research the role that wrestling played in the early rise of television. Create a video report showing important wrestlers and behind-the-scenes organizers who helped make the sport an early favorite on the new medium.

- Do you think a mass hysteria like the "Red Scare" is more possible or less possible in the Internet age, when people are able to constantly question each other's claims? Using research into psychology and sociology, write a report that helps you argue whether we are or are not equally susceptible today to that kind of hysteria and paranoia.

- Peggy Jo says that her father stays home to milk the cows. How big could a farm run by one family's labor be? How much money could it have made in 1949, compared with the median income of the time? Create a chart that shows the smallest and largest number of cows and acres of land you think Peggy Jo's family could have had, based on your research into the historical economics of dairy farming.

- Prepare a slide show of Lunetta Jones's clothes, described in detail in this story. Include descriptions about material, special sewing, or anything else that would not be visible in pictures.

- Interstate bus travel has fallen off since the 1940s, replaced by air travel and private cars: still, many people think that it would be good for the environment to have fewer cars on the road. Create an ad campaign to persuade people to travel by bus. Your campaign can create new amenities that are not currently available on buses, if you think they are possible and are necessary to attract riders.

- When it was a booming industrial town in the postwar years, Detroit attracted hundreds of thousands of African American families from the South: today, according to the 2010 census, the population of the city is over 80 percent African American. Research how the migration of African Americans from the South to the North after the war changed the racial structure of the country. With maps, show where the greatest number of people left and where they ended up. Then write an essay about one aspect of culture (such as literature, theater, or music) that was affected by this huge population shift.

- Katherine Paterson won numerous awards for her 1978 young-adult novel *The Great Gilly Hopkins*, including the National Book Award, the Newbery Honor medal, and the Jane Addams Book Award. The protagonist, an eleven-year-old girl placed in a foster home who imaginatively schemes to reconnect with her birth mother in California, has a worldview similar to that of Peggy Jo in "Detroit Skyline, 1949." Read Paterson's book and write a short story that reverses the characters' situations, either putting Peggy Jo in Gilly's foster home or putting Gilly in suburban Detroit with Peggy Jo's relatives for a summer. At the end of your story, write a self-critique, explaining what personality traits you think your work highlights and how they are presented in the original work.

Peggy Jo is bored and confused by adult conversations about politics (©holbox / Shutterstock.com)

the war was over and home ownership spread, had a further effect of isolating suburbanites from one another. As depicted in the story, children and adults alike found themselves more fascinated by the characters they watched on the small television screen than in the people who lived nearby.

Malaise

Malaise is an indefinable sense of uneasiness. It is considered a condition that affects an entire society, not just an individual. In this story, Peggy Jo suffers from a sense of malaise that is a bit like disappointment and a bit like fear. For one thing, she has been told that she will see amazing sites: her mother recalls the first time she herself saw the majesty of the Detroit skyline and wants to share that same sense of wonder with her daughter. Peggy Jo is also promised summer companionship with Sharon Belletieri, a girl her own age who can show her what life is like in suburban Detroit. In addition, Peggy Jo is introduced to the new magic of television during her trip, with great fanfare: "This will ruin her," her aunt says, bracing her for a life-changing experience. Finally, she believes she can make herself famous by writing a jingle for

detergent soap that would, if it won a competition, be sung on radio and television. All of these experiences turn out to be much less engaging than Peggy Jo was led to believe, leaving her to stumble about without a good feel for whether life is good, bad, or indifferent. Even her mother's pregnancy is anticlimactic. Peggy Jo does not find out about the possibility of having a little sister or brother until that possibility is gone. She spends her time in Michigan in a malaise, a dreamlike fog of uncertainty.

Her one attempt to shake some excitement, some sense of vitality, into her life comes when she hears gossip about a presumed Communist who carpools to work with her Uncle Boone. She is not allowed to share her exciting news, though: as soon as she mentions it, the adults force her to bottle her secret up again, in the same way she bottles up every other chance for excitement in her life. They all live in fear of life; life in suburban Detroit is lived in a constant state of malaise.

Rural Life

In the end, Peggy Jo returns to her family's Kentucky farm. She feels that she has been changed by her experience—that her father and her brother, Johnny, will not recognize her when they see her. The sense of being a stranger to the farm does not last very long.

In the Detroit suburb she has been visiting, Peggy Jo is clearly a country girl. Her cousin, Betsy Lou, and the neighbor Sharon Belletieri make fun of her for the way she talks and the clothes she wears, as children generally do. What really makes Peggy Jo a stranger in the city, though, is her interest in the things that the city people take for granted, such as television, Communism, communicable disease, and her cousin's dating life. When she returns to the farm, she knows that what she has learned about these things will not be relevant to her life anymore. At first, she seems to resent going back to what she knew, but as the farm's silo comes into view she realizes that this is her world, equating the silo with the Detroit skyline that she had looked forward to seeing.

STYLE

Child's Point of View

Although this story is told from an adult perspective, it is funneled through the eyes of nine-year-old Peggy Jo. Readers experience suburban Detroit the way that she experiences it, and they are mystified by the things that mystify the child. For instance, modern readers who know how seriously Communism was taken in the 1940s and 1950s may not appreciate the sense of fear that all of the characters lived with if they were to experience the story through an adult, rational perspective, but instead they have the feeling of something big and unknown that Peggy Jo has. Similarly, readers can interpret the signs and assume that Peggy Jo's mother is pregnant before the nine-year-old has that idea explained to her.

By keeping the point of view so tightly focused on the mind of a child, Mason makes readers see the world as Peggy Jo sees it. Suburban Detroit of several decades ago might not seem that interesting to modern readers when viewed historically, but it is the world that Peggy Jo lives in, and readers are drawn in to figuring out what is going on, piecing the elements of her world together while Peggy Jo does.

Parallel Characters

Mason is able to give more depth to her characters by showing them in relation to other, similar characters. Peggy Jo's mother, for instance, does not talk much in this story, possibly because she has been living in isolation on a farm and is not used to having anyone to talk to. Readers get to know her better by seeing her interact with Aunt Mozelle, who, as her sister, shares a common background with her. The two sisters have lived in different circumstances, city and country, for years, giving readers a chance to compare their two perspectives.

On the other hand, Peggy Jo is almost entirely different from her cousin, Betsy Lou, who is just a few years older than she and is focused on boys, clothes, and a fear of polio. Betsy Lou's comfort with her home helps readers appreciate how uncomfortable Peggy Jo is, even though she does not talk about her discomfort. Sharon Belletieri's comfort with her own life also offers a contrast to Peggy Jo's discomfort about staying in a house so far from her own home, while Boone and Lunetta's shared fear of being accused of Communist sympathies combine to give a feeling of what that time was like.

Quest Narrative

This story relates many of the interesting things that Peggy Jo and her mother experience while visiting their relatives, but their experiences are all shaped around a quest narrative. They are on a quest to see the impressive city skyline that her mother saw on a visit long ago, a sight that she wants her daughter to experience. They arrive with that specific goal in mind and are reminded of it throughout the story. In the end, they are not able to fulfill their quest. They are disappointed, but they are consoled by the fact that their quest led them to other experiences. Readers are disappointed on their behalf but are equally consoled by the fact that the quest to see the skyline has brought them into the world of Peggy Jo and her mother.

A quest narrative is often a literary device to keep the story moving, which is what it is here. The object of the quest is not as important as where the search for the object takes the protagonist. In this case, the failure to see the Detroit skyline is itself a success: what is important is the lesson that Peggy Jo learns about the complexities of city life, which she would never have gotten if she had not gone seeking that look at the skyline.

COMPARE
&
CONTRAST

- **1949:** America is still affected by World War II, which ended in 1945. Factory workers like Uncle Boone enjoy a booming economy, while war widows like Lunetta Jones struggle to regain control of their lives.

  1982: America still recalls the Vietnam War, which ended after years of growing hostility from the general public, who became less and less confident that the war was for a good cause.

  Today: The country's involvement in oversees conflict is out of the view of many Americans because many people do not know anyone in the all-volunteer armed services.

- **1949:** Broadcast television is a stunning new form of entertainment. Broadcast towers have been built in concentrated urban areas, but people out in the country have trouble getting reception.

  1982: Videocassette recorders (VCRs) are a new and growing technology. For the first time, viewers do not have to be in front of their televisions at the time a show is broadcast in order to watch it.

  Today: Most television programs are available through cable systems that offer on-demand viewing. Streaming services like Netflix carry both old and original programs to be watched anywhere at any time.

- **1949:** The country is at the height of anti-Communist panic. Comparisons are made to the Salem witch trials of several centuries earlier because lives can be destroyed by a hint that they have not conformed to society's standards.

  1982: Americans are still concerned about the country's "Cold War" competition with the Soviet Union. Few suspect that the Soviet Union will be disbanded in approximately another decade.

  Today: Since the terror attacks in New York and Washington, DC, in 2001, Americans have been less fearful of Communist takeover and more fearful of a war between competing religious ideologies.

- **1949:** Some communities are in the grips of fear about polio, a crippling disease for which there is no cure.

  1982: Vaccines developed in the 1960s have practically eradicated polio in the United States, but a new, untreatable virus is starting to show up in urban areas: HIV.

  Today: There is no cure for AIDS, the disease caused by HIV, but proper treatments can often keep symptoms under control for years. Quick and cheap worldwide travel has medical communities all over the world on the lookout for the next epidemic outbreak, which could spread globally before any treatment can be developed.

- **1949:** Workers in manufacturing plants, like Uncle Boone in the story, can support their families comfortably with the union-negotiated wages they make at manufacturing jobs.

  1982: The decline of the powerful labor unions has begun. In 1981, President Ronald Reagan fires eleven thousand air traffic controllers whose union had voted to go out on strike, signaling the rise of hostilities between the government and the unions.

  Today: America has lost much of its manufacturing capacity to other countries with lower wage structures. The majority of households in Boone and Mozelle's economic class survive with at least two wage earners.

- **1949:** Scrapbooking is a popular way for people to keep records of things that interest them, such as the news stories that Mozelle collects in "Detroit Skyline, 1949."

  1982: People still need to cut out things that they want to save or copy them on publically available copy machines. The first image scanners, to let people import newspapers and pictures into their home computers, will not go on sale until the middle of the 1980s.

  Today: People can post articles about things they find interesting to Facebook, Twitter, or any number of other social media.

HISTORICAL CONTEXT

The Red Scare

American suspicion of Communism extends back to the early decades of the twentieth century, well before the 1949 date given in this story's title, though by the late 1940s and early 1950s, it had reached what some consider its peak. In 1917, the imperial government of Russia fell after two sweeping revolutions and was replaced by the Soviet Union, the first major Communist nation. Fighting World War I distracted the world's attention from rise of the Soviet Union, but it also led to a panic once that war ended in 1918. Americans feared that the Soviets could easily use the chaos the war had wrought across Europe as an opportunity to expand their empire. Laws that had been passed in the United States to protect the country during the war, such as the Espionage Act of 1917 and the Sedition Act of 1918, were used to prosecute people who supported Communist ideals.

In 1919 and 1920, the country experienced what historians have dubbed the first Red Scare. Attorney General A. Mitchell Palmer and his deputy, J. Edgar Hoover, oversaw programs to deport hundreds of US citizens on charges of treason. They initially focused on members of the American Communist Party, but they expanded the range of their investigations to include union members, Socialist politicians, and people affiliated with or friendly toward Communists.

The country's anti-Communist fever flared up again at the end of World War II, under similar circumstances. Once again, chaos in Europe raised the notion that the Soviet Union might move in to take control of established democracies. The Soviet Union's involvement in the Chinese Civil War from 1945 to 1949, culminating in China's becoming a Communist state at the end of the war in 1949, heightened fears that America was in the path of a global conspiracy bent on worldwide dominance. This led to what became known as the second Red Scare, a time of political tension that was dubbed the "Cold War" because, like a war, it had two clear opponents (the United States and the Soviet Union), but there was no actual fighting between them.

The political mood at the start of the Cold War is the aura of suspicion that readers see in "Detroit Skyline, 1949." Politicians built upon the country's apprehension to further their careers. The most well known of these was Joseph McCarthy, a senator from Wisconsin who came to national prominence when he declared himself to be in possession of a list of secret Communists working in the US government. He successfully blocked a Senate Foreign Relations Committee panel that tried to make him reveal the names on that list, which many at the time felt was fictional, and then he worked himself into a position of influence in the Senate Permanent Subcommittee on Investigations. For four years, McCarthy's committee investigated and accused people of affiliation with Communists. Whether their accusations were true or not, people's careers were ruined as they became "blacklisted" by employers and were unable to find jobs.

Political support for McCarthy eroded as the public saw that he was ruining lives, often unfairly. He lost his chairmanship in 1954 and died of severe alcoholism three years later. Although the government's "witch hunt" against suspected Communists subsided, the United States and the Soviet Union continued to vie for power in regional conflicts (such as Korea and Vietnam), maintaining the Cold War mentality until the collapse of the Soviet Union in 1991.

Kmart Realism

In the early part of her career, including the time of the release of *Shiloh and Other Stories*, which contained "Detroit Skyline, 1949," Mason was categorized by literary critics as a member of the "Kmart realism" school of fiction writing. In the late 1970s and the early 1980s, the trend among short-story writers was to write about lower-middle-class American life with a minimalist style. The most famous of these writers were Raymond Carver and Ann Beattie, but the movement also included Tobias Wolff, Frederick Barthelme, Joy Williams, and others.

To be considered "Kmart realism," stories had to project a bleak mood, lacking in self-awareness or emotional connections. They usually did this with short declarative sentences that had few descriptive adverbs and adjectives: characters seldom "explain" or "claim" or even "ask" what is on each other's mind, because the most common dialogue tag is the bland,

The variety of things available for purchase in stores amazes Peggy Jo (©hxdyl | Shutterstock.com)

disaffected word "said." When this writing style is applied to people working at low-wage jobs (when they work at all), living in rented rooms and trailers, drinking heavily and remembering better times in their childhood, it creates a culture that was identified with Kmart chain stores: featureless and impersonal venues for buying mass-produced products inexpensively to satisfy bland necessity.

Kmart realism made a huge impression on American fiction, but its influence was brief: critics felt that many of the writers who glorified people from social classes lower than their own were just being patronizing and that their conspicuous style was an insincere affectation. The term *Kmart realism* itself, coined in the mid-1980s, was meant as a negative comment on the style. Many of the writers from that era went on to write longer, more involved works. Though Mason's early works did not fit into this literary subgenre in terms of style, her subject matter, focused as it was on rural Kentucky and working-class suburbs, assures that her name will come up whenever Kmart realism is discussed.

CRITICAL OVERVIEW

Mason was already a formidable force when she first arrived on the literary scene. Her first collection of short stories, *Shiloh and Other Stories*, was nominated for the National Book Critics Circle Award and the PEN/Faulkner Award. It won the PEN/Hemingway Award and the American Book Award. The website for Penguin Random House, which publishes reprints of the book, quotes literary giant Raymond Carver as presciently saying of this collection, "These stores will last." Joanna Price, in her book *Understanding Bobbie Ann Mason*, notes that upon the publication of her first book, "Anne Tyler recognized Mason as already 'a full-fledged master of the short story.'" While that first book was almost universally lauded, Albert Wilhelm, in a literary book about Mason's career published in 1998, pointed out that "Detroit Skyline, 1949" is "an anomaly": most of Mason's stories were set in the present, in the South, but this reflection on childhood took a unique perspective. Looking back from years after its first publication,

Wilhelm took a literary critic's approach to the story, considering it a variant on the "initiation story" pattern that is familiar in literature: by that date, Mason was already clearly, solidly established as an important element in late-twentieth-century fiction.

As her career continued, Mason retained her place in American literature. Her first novel, 1985's *In Country*, about a veteran of the Vietnam conflict, was made into an acclaimed film directed by legendary director Norman Jewison and starring Bruce Willis. Her 2005 novel, *An Atomic Romance*, was lauded as one of her best works by Mary Ann Gwinn, who, in her review for the *Chicago Tribune*, noted that "Mason has the uncanny ability, possessed by a few virtuoso novelists, to create the layers and textures of her characters' world." Gwinn gives a few examples of characters from the novel before concluding, "We need to be reminded that people are so dauntingly and delightfully complex. Bobbie Ann Mason creates such characters, vivifies them and allows us a peek into their hearts."

Some critics find Mason's most recent novel, *The Girl in the Blue Beret*, published in 2005, to be slightly cold, lacking the kind of humor and fondness that characterize most of Mason's works, but almost every critic attributes that shift in tone to a shift in locale: Mason is writing about events in France, not her familiar territory of the American South. Even with this novel's perceived weaknesses, Mason is still considered to be a masterful fiction writer who, after a long career, is surprisingly willing to go outside of her comfort zone in pursuit of a good story.

CRITICISM

David Kelly

Kelly is a writer and instructor of literature. In the following essay, he looks at "Detroit Skyline, 1949" as the story of a woman who plans on running away from her husband, taking her daughter to a new state and a new life.

Mason's early short story "Detroit Skyline, 1949" tells the tale of Peggy Jo, a nine-year-old girl who accompanies her mother on a trip from rural Kentucky to the title city for a summer stay with relatives. The stated purpose of the visit is that the mother wants Peggy Jo to see

ALTHOUGH THERE IS NOT ENOUGH EVIDENCE TO BELIEVE THAT MASON ACTUALLY MEANT TO INCLUDE A HIDDEN MESSAGE ABOUT PEGGY JO'S PARENTS BREAKING UP, THERE IS GOOD REASON TO CONSIDER WHETHER THE STORY COULD BE READ FROM THIS ANGLE."

the huge skyscrapers of the city. One can easily assume that the mother is trying to broaden the girl's understanding of what humanity is capable of and that, the Great Pyramid of Giza and the other Seven Wonders of the Ancient World being unavailable, she feels that jaw-dropping amazement is still in their reach in the American Midwest. Their adventure does not turn out the way they hope, of course. Their trip is not awful—they are not exposed to the urban hellscape so many other writers have subjected simple country folk to when they go to the big city. There is suffering and disappointment in "Detroit Skyline, 1949," but, as in so much of Mason's work, it is moderate. It is just enough to make readers assume that Peggy Jo and her mother, in the end, find out that their farm at home is just the right place for them.

On the surface, there are plenty of signs to support this simple, often-covered lesson. The city does not present the country people with the sort of wonderment that city dwellers probably feel their land offers to country people—instead, it offers them a core of anxiety wrapped tightly in a coating of sarcasm, with the consolation prize of their first exposure to television thrown in. Peggy Jo does not get along well with the suburbanites her own age: the neighbor girl she is paired up with, Sharon Belletieri, wants little to do with her, and when she meets more kids at Sharon's birthday party, they openly mock her. Dressing like Sharon is an attempt to assimilate that does not spare Peggy Jo from rejection.

Her mother does not fail at urbanizing herself because she does not have to assimilate. They are staying with her sister, Mozelle, and Mozelle's husband, Boone, people who moved

WHAT DO I READ NEXT?

- In chapter 2 of her memoir, *Clear Springs,* Mason tells the story of a trip she and her mother made to see the huge buildings of Detroit in 1949, when they stayed with her mother's sister, Mary, and Mary's husband, Rudy. Interesting comparisons can be made between the actual events in Mason's life and the events that she chose to add to "Detroit Skyline, 1949." *Clear Springs* was published by Random House in 1999.

- In 1975, before her first collection of short stories was published, Mason published *The Girl Sleuth.* The book is aimed at a young-adult audience. Written as a mixture of memoir, literary criticism and how-to book about growing up to be a writer, it focuses on Mason's memories of reading series of girl detective novels when she was young, including Trixie Belden, Judy Bolton, nurse Cherry Ames, and, of course, Nancy Drew. The current 1995 edition of Mason's extended essay was published by University of Georgia Press.

- In his book *Once in a Great City: A Detroit Story* (2015), Pulitzer Prize–winning journalist David Maraniss, a native of Detroit, published an engrossing nonfiction account that traces the city's collapse from the height of its greatness in the early 1960s to the standard of poverty and urban blight it is known for today. This meticulous study of modern history has as much to say about the changes that have overcome America in the past half-century as it does about the specific city he and Mason write about.

- In this story, suburbia is viewed with wonder, a place with television and electric appliances and home ownership, where cars were showing up as quickly as the auto industry could pump them out. Over the years, though, suburbia has come to represent a place where dreams die. In 1995, sociologist Robert Putnam captured the inherent isolating effect of suburbia with the simple metaphor of how league bowling has given way to a lost sense of community in *Bowling Alone: The Collapse and Revival of American Community.* This popular and critically acclaimed book covers all aspects of suburban life in the modern age.

- Hanif Kureishi's 1990 novel *The Buddha of Suburbia* takes place in a suburb of London, but it captures many of the issues that would be relevant to suburban Detroit. Written with a sort of deadpan humor that echoes Mason's, it concerns a bored punk rocker, the son of a British mother and an Indian father who, in the course of the novel, becomes a religious figure. His punk approach to life highlights the emptiness of suburban life that Mason's Peggy Jo avoids, while the father's "Buddha" stature shows that spirituality, though unlikely, can be found. Winner of the Whitbread Prize in 1990, the book is published by Penguin.

- There are many books written about the early days of television, but Tim Kiska's *From Soupy to Nuts!: A History of Detroit Television* focuses specifically on the shows that Mason mentions in the story, offering readers background to the world of imagination that this story's protagonist loses herself in each day. This story of the wrestling and children's programs that filled the airwaves in the late 1940s was published in 2006 by Momentum Books.

north and have carved out a life for themselves. Adults and siblings have very little trouble finding a society for themselves when compared with the frantic, hypercompetitive lives of adolescents, who have not yet established their own individual identities.

In addition to the obvious dramatic tensions this story carries on its surface, there are also some underlying mysteries. One of the greatest of these is why they are in Michigan to begin with. Peggy Jo's mother does indeed seem sincere about wanting her daughter to look up to the skies in wonderment, but she does not try very hard in the weeks they are there to get to the city—by taxi, for instance, or borrowed car. At the same time, the story gives a lot of details about life over the child's head, things going on with the adults that Peggy Jo senses but does not understand. These unnamed details might not even be things that Peggy Jo's mother herself is conscious of, but looking more closely at her can give readers a better sense of how Mason establishes the story's ominous mood.

Although it is not necessarily what the author intended, it could help to consider whether, rather than simply offering her daughter a view of the Detroit skyline, her mother might be considering living in the city. The evidence for this kind of reading is entirely circumstantial, but taking an extreme view of the mother's actions might help readers better understand the effects these events have on the story's young protagonist.

One of the most conspicuous elements that could steer readers toward this interpretation is the absence of Peggy Jo's father. The story does not begin with mother and daughter leaving home and, in fact, drops the father only briefly into the third paragraph to show small-minded provincialism as he associates Detroit with "the Polacks," who, he jokingly tells his daughter, will "get you." Almost immediately, Peggy Jo and her mother are arriving at their relatives' suburban town.

The father's absence becomes even more notable, however, when, by the end of the story, Peggy Jo and her mother approach home but do not actually arrive there. Throughout the story, there is no mention of the father, even in situations where a husband and father would naturally come to mind, such as when the woman carrying his child has a miscarriage: Peggy Jo wonders what her mother will tell him about this turn of events but does not give any thought to what he will have to say about it. Even accounting for the way farm people might cope with the hardships of life by repressing emotions, the absence of any conversation or (if the farm has

no phone in 1949) even any mention of alerting her husband to the loss of this unexpected child is eerie. Whatever is going on in the mind of Peggy Jo's mother, she is either not thinking of the father or is consciously trying to steer around the subject of him.

If she really is thinking of leaving the farm with Peggy Jo and starting a new life, it would make sense to gravitate toward Mozelle and Boone. They already know how to take care of a single woman from Kentucky. Lunetta Jones, the daughter of one of Mozelle's old friends from back where she grew up, is a significant presence in the story. She seems to serve little function in this story, unless one reads her as a template for the type of life Peggy Jo's mother might have planned.

Lunetta has been widowed by World War II. Her husband apparently died young—Peggy Jo, reflecting what she has heard from the adults, calls him "her sailor-boy husband." Lunetta works as a schoolteacher, one of the few professional careers available to women at the time; she may be on her own, but that does not stop her from personal growth. Widowhood has not put an end to Lunetta's social life, either. Most likely she is not promiscuous by modern standards, given that one of her dates is to go to church and that she is working at a job that would be very aware of her moral standing. By the standards of suburban Detroit in 1949, however, she is at least interested enough in men for her friends to comment on it. Her clothes are viewed as exotic and flamboyant, meant to capture the attention of men. Regarding her clothes, Aunt Mozelle tells nine-year-old Peggy Jo, "Lunetta's man-crazy." Uncle Boone calls her lipstick "man bait."

In a story about the colorful characters in the neighborhood, Lunetta might have just been another example of the sort of people trying to put their lives back together after the war. This, however, is not that story. There are only two adults hovering around Mozelle and Boone's house: Lunetta Jones and Peggy Jo's mother. And there is one quasi-adult, teenaged Betsy Lou, who is just as focused on her social life as Lunetta is. Even if she did come to Detroit to show her daughter the skyscrapers, Peggy Jo's mother might eventually bend to the local customs if she were to stay around this environment for weeks or months.

Whether she is consciously planning to look for a new life in Michigan or Mason has simply put her into an environment that encourages dating, the possibility that Peggy Jo's mother will turn into her own kind of war widow in a northern industrial city is still quite slim. It is not her unmentioned husband that keeps her from assimilating into this culture. It is the crush of other people that eventually drives her back to Kentucky.

There are two existential threats in this Detroit suburb. The first is polio. It was the plague of its time, a communicable disease that was so prevalent before the Jonas Salk vaccine that Franklin Roosevelt, scion of a prominent, wealthy family and four times elected president of the United States, could not be protected from it. Betsy Lou is petrified of polio, warning Peggy Jo about swimming pools and birthday parties, where she might contract it. As with any communicable disease, physical relationships are always suspect, feared as opportunities for infection.

The other thing that Peggy Jo's mother learns to fear catching in suburban Detroit, though it is not a threat back home, is the social stigmatization associated with accusations of Communist sympathies. The shame of being talked about in this context is so strong that the adults in the story fall quiet when the subject comes up, and they encourage silence from Peggy Jo, lest she bring the social curse upon herself or her family. Boone, an otherwise light-hearted man, turns grim when the subject comes up, as does the one other adult in this story who has a job, Lunetta. Lunetta is so frightened of being vulnerable to the Red Scare, of losing her job and future employment prospects to the intangible hint of Communism in her vicinity, that she has tried to vaccinate herself by willingly signing a Loyalty Oath.

Literary interpretations often speculate about meanings that can be found in works whether the author intended to put them there or not. Although there is not enough evidence to believe that Mason actually meant to include a hidden message about Peggy Jo's parents breaking up, there is good reason to consider whether the story could be read from this angle. Reading the story in this context explains the disconnect between the mother and the father, even when they lose a baby. It explains why the skyline of Detroit simultaneously is and is not the focus of the trip. It explains Lunetta's role. Most likely, "leaving her husband" would be an overstatement of the mother's sense of independence. However, "Detroit Skyline, 1949" is a story full of unexplained elements; sometimes it helps understanding motives and behaviors to look at them symbolically.

Source: David Kelly, Critical Essay on "Detroit Skyline, 1949," in *Short Stories for Students*, Gale, Cengage Learning, 2017.

Joanna Price

In the following excerpt, Price summarizes critical reception of the collection that includes "Detroit Skyline, 1949."

Mason's first collection of short stories, *Shiloh and Other Stories*, was generally well-received by critics. Robert Towers observed that Mason "is one of those rare writers who, by concentrating their attention on a few square miles of native turf, are able to open up new surprisingly wide worlds for the delighted reader." Anne Tyler recognized Mason as already "a full-fledged master of the short story." Tyler applauded Mason's compassionate treatment of her characters who, although feeling "bewilderment" at the changes that confront them, nevertheless try to adapt to them with an "optimistic faith in progress." Tyler observed that "it is especially poignant that the characters in these stories, having led more sheltered lives than the average reader, are trying to deal with changes that most of us already take for granted." Mason herself has reflected that the "strength of my fiction has been the tension between being from there and not from there" and has commented that "My work seems to have struck a chord with a number of readers who have left home and maybe who have rejected it, and I think it startles them because they thought they were rid of it." Andrew Levy points out that in Mason's own view, the appeal of her stories to the lower-upper-class or upper-middle-class readership of such magazines as the *New Yorker* lies in the fact that "reading her stories, like writing them, constitutes an act of reconciliation with the home that is left behind." Moreover, Levy continues, "the 'home' that is left behind is not just rural Kentucky, but the popular culture that is repudiated (or diluted) by a rising middle class, or an entrenched upper class." According to Levy, Mason's stories, therefore, appeal to an audience that is largely "displaced out of its

MASON'S ADULT CHARACTERS GENERALLY
ADJUST TO THE INTRUSION OF THE UNFAMILIAR IN
THEIR LIVES BY ASSIMILATING IT TO THE FAMILIAR,
WHICH INVOLVES A DENIAL OF DIFFERENCES."

class of origin" through the "reconciliation" of class differences that they represent.

Other reviewers argued that the stories in *Shiloh* epitomized the limitations of "minimalist" writing. Robert Dunn, for example, commented that the stories are an example of "private interest fiction" in that their characters, lacking a sense of history, focus their anxieties about cultural change exclusively through a diminished world of private relationships. Similarly, John Barth and Ben Yagoda, while recognizing that this fiction aspires to give a realistic representation of a consumer culture dominated by television, lamented its perceived failure to offer a broader, historicized interpretation of that culture. Yagoda concluded that writers of such fiction, including Mason, "give us random and unimaginatively chosen details and events, signifying nothing."

As the reviewers observed, the most initially striking quality of the short stories collected in *Shiloh* is Mason's evocative rendering of the details of the daily lives of her characters. The central theme of the stories is the way in which Mason's characters respond to the changes effected by contemporary culture on formerly rural life in western Kentucky. Mason generally renders the narrative perspective on these changes either through a working-class character who is trying to adjust to the cultural shifts through which he or she is living or through an educated, newly middle-class woman character who is reflecting on some of the changes in order to interpret her past and present life.

. . . In each of these stories, Mason's protagonists are adapting to the changes that occur as familiar traditions of rural life in western Kentucky are being replaced by the images and ideology introduced by consumer culture. In the stories Mason shows how the process of

adaptation is a gradual one, attained through moments of recognition in which the past is brought to bear on the interpretation of the present. This process is inscribed with a sense of what is being lost and often generates anxiety and fear, but, as Mason shows, individual and cultural identities may be tentatively renewed through it. The characters' assimilation to an "Americanizing" consumer culture is imitated by Mason's style, with its naturalization of references to consumer products. In some of the stories, however, consumer culture retains its strangeness as Mason uses defamiliarizing techniques to emphasize the apparently incongruous juxtaposition of the values embedded in past traditions with the ideology imparted by the images and artifacts of consumer culture. Linda Adams Barnes has suggested that Mason's revelation of the incongruity of this juxtaposition adds an element of the grotesque to her work, which locates it in a tradition of Southern grotesque descending from Flannery O'Connor. She argues that although inherent in O'Connor's use of the grotesque is a faith that assumes "the possibility of grace," a faith that has largely disappeared from the world evoked by Mason, Mason's stories also imply a moral vision through the "instructiveness" of her "dramatization" of the conflict between "traditional Southern life and encroaching modern life." This effect of grotesqueness that unsettles the spare surface created by the precise, literal details of dirty realist writing has also been described as "a kind of surrealism of the everyday."

One story that emphasizes the strangeness of the everyday is "Detroit Skyline, 1949." This story is an anomaly in the collection in that it is told by a first-person narrator ("Residents and Transients" is the only other example of this) and the events of the story take place in a Northern industrial city in 1949 rather than in Mason's usual setting of contemporary Kentucky. The narrator is recalling a journey she made as a nine-year-old girl to visit relatives in Detroit. Mason's use of a first-person narrator allows her to create an impression of interiority that contrasts with most of the stories, where she allusively infers her characters' states of mind through the evocation of their perception of external details, as recounted by a third-person narrator. Her use of a child's point of view also enables her to defamiliarize the "reality" to which adults become inured. By setting the story in the post–World War II period, Mason historicizes some of the changes that her other stories represent, particularly as much of her narrator's sense of wonder and disorientation is aroused by the commodities that she is encountering for the first time. The narrative frame of a journey from western Kentucky to Detroit (a reversal of most of the journeys undertaken in Mason's stories) focuses the conflict between rural and urban culture that is to become more complex and pervasive in the contemporary world of Mason's other stories.

Peggy Jo learns from fragments of her aunt's and uncle's conversation that the Detroit in which she has arrived with her mother is darkened by people's fear of "reds" and immobilized by a bus strike caused by "trouble with the unions." Against this backdrop, Peggy Jo is fascinated by such "strange" manifestations of consumer culture as a "toaster, a Mixmaster," an advertisement of "a fabulous life with Fab," and a "Toni doll . . . with a Play Wave, including plastic spin curlers and Toni Creme Rinse." Most fascinating and astonishing of all, she finds, is the television, which begins to permeate her imagination. The cultural collision between North and South evinced by the child's response to these commodities is immediately interpreted by her Detroit relatives as a class difference, the result of being "raised with a bunch of country hicks." The child's sense of the strangeness of the everyday reality of life in Detroit is amplified by her aunt's scrapbooks of newspaper clippings, which "included household hints and cradle notes, but most of the stories were about bizarre occurrences around the world—diseases and kidnappings and disasters." Her aunt explains: "Life is amazing. I keep these to remind me of just how strange everything is." To the adult, in contrast with the child, the defamiliarization of the quotidian only occurs when extremity or anomaly reveals its "bizarreness." Mason's adult characters generally adjust to the intrusion of the unfamiliar in their lives by assimilating it to the familiar, which involves a denial of differences. Mason's mimetic representation of this process through a preponderance of similes and metonymy over metaphor creates the "flattening" effect of her writing. The stories invented by Peggy Jo, however, exemplify a child's desire to find narratives that explain both the differences and the connections between things. These narratives necessarily become metaphoric as layers of

"reality," imagined and literal, cultural and "natural," are interpreted through each other. For example, Peggy Jo's familiar world is further unsettled when her mother, who has been taken to hospital, explains to her that she has "lost" a baby. The child forms a narrative to try and understand what has happened: "That night, alone in the pine-and-cedar room. I saw everything clearly, like the sharpened images that floated on the television screen. My mother had said an egg didn't hatch, but I knew better. The reds had stolen the baby. They took things. They were after my aunt's copper-bottomed pans. They stole the butter. They wanted my uncle's job. They were invisible, like the guardian angel, although they might wear disguises. You didn't know who might be a red. You never knew when you might lose a baby that you didn't know you had." Peggy Jo's explanatory narrative is a bricolage of fragments of overheard adults' gossip, other children's lore, and the images she has received from the television, radio, and children's books.

On her return journey to the South, the child is seized by the sense of wonder that Mason's adults have largely lost: "I felt—with a new surge of clarity—the mystery of travel, the vastness of the world, the strangeness of life." Momentarily the child fears that her father and brother will not recognize her and her mother when they return, but she is reassured by seeing that "our little white house was still there." To Mason's adults, however, the concept of "home" is always destabilized by departure and return. . . .

Source: Joanna Price, "*Shiloh and Other Stories*," in *Understanding Bobbie Mason*, University of South Carolina Press, 2000, pp. 20–21, 43–47.

Albert Wilhelm

In the following excerpt, Wilhelm traces the theme of incompleteness in "Detroit Skyline, 1949."

. . . Among Mason's collected stories, "Detroit Skyline, 1949" is an anomaly. Mason's settings are usually Southern and contemporary but, as the title implies, the setting here is the industrial North several decades earlier. More commonly Mason's characters are adults experiencing midlife crises like divorce or senior citizens confronting retirement or debilitating illness. The central character in "Detroit Skyline, 1949" is a nine-year-old girl

"BECAUSE PEGGY CANNOT UNDERSTAND THE ADULT CODES, SHE OBVIOUSLY HAS FACTS GARBLED, BUT HER ASSERTIONS CAPTURE IMPORTANT TRUTHS."

about to emerge from childhood into adolescence. Mason uses first-person narration infrequently, but here this point of view allows a revealing double perspective. It displays firsthand the naive behavior of the child, but, since time has elapsed and the narrator is now more mature, it also permits bemused detachment.

Mason has commented that this travel story was motivated by her faint recollection of a trip she took with her mother as a child. On that trip from rural Kentucky to the home of relatives near Detroit, Mason "was captivated by the television set, and the story was originally called 'The Television Set.'" Because her memories of the summer of 1949 were fuzzy, Mason read "two weeks worth of microfilm of the *Detroit Free Press*" and discovered stories about polio epidemics, the city bus strike, and the pervasive Communist scare. Then she "invented the story about the mother's miscarriage" and worked all these strands into her narrative. With these enriching additions the story became much more than an account of a young girl's first exposure to television.

According to the taxonomy suggested by Mordecai Marcus, "Detroit Skyline, 1949" is a tentative initiation story. It brings the protagonist to a threshold of understanding and maturity but does not allow her to cross. Although Peggy Jo's rite of passage remains incomplete, the story includes many motifs typical of initiation stories. One common initiation pattern restricts the protagonist to a limited, familiar environment but subverts innocence by introducing an interloper representative of the larger world. Such is the case for Seth in Robert Penn Warren's "Blackberry Winter" and for Sylvia in Sarah Orne Jewett's "A White Heron." In keeping with her emphasis on travelers and pilgrims, Mason chooses an inverse but equally common pattern of initiation. Peggy's primary

action is a journey from the country to the city—from the safely familiar to the mysteriously ominous. She travels with a mature guide, her mother, but this guide is not always able to protect her from hurt or answer troubling questions. As in many initiation stories Peggy confronts the mysteries of adult sexuality, sickness, and death. Because she is only nine, however, such confrontations usually leave her more bewildered than enlightened. Indeed, Peggy is the same age as Sylvia in "A White Heron" and Seth in "Blackberry Winter," and like these two characters she is frequently puzzled by intimations of mortality all around her.

In traveling to Detroit, Peggy follows the path of relatives who have left the more innocent agrarian South for jobs in the industrial North. Such migrations are not entirely successful, and thus they foreshadow the incompleteness of Peggy's passage. Her Uncle Boone now works in an automobile factory and has acquired a comfortable house. Instead of finding himself, however, he leads a decidedly fragmented life. He can never build a complete car because all he knows is bumpers. Unable to afford the automobiles he helps to assemble, Boone is left stranded by a public bus strike. Boone Cashon's two names (one the surname of a famous pioneer and the other an echo of the cliché "cash on the barrel-head") probably suggest a conflict between his frontier heritage and the crass world where he now works.

A further suggestion of separation from and nostalgic longing for the agrarian ideal surfaces in the reading material of Boone's daughter, Betsy Lou. Surrounded by the factories of Detroit, she reads Louis Bromfield's *Pleasant Valley*. This idyllic account of Malabar Farm, established in rural Ohio in 1939, is far removed from her urban life, and the allusion suggests another failed or sharply truncated journey. Betsy Lou can hardly realize Bromfield's pastoral vision, just as Peggy will not complete her journey of initiation.

Many initiation stories move from darkness to light—from symbolic sleep to harsh awakening. Accordingly, after an all-night bus trip Peggy steps off into a Detroit suburb and wakes up to a strange and confusing world. Here, if she leaves the house of Aunt Mozelle and Uncle Boone, she risks being stricken with polio. Even within the house she reads in her aunt's scrapbooks about bizarre occurrences such as kidnappings, diseases, and disasters all around the world. Peggy's teenaged cousin, Betsy Lou, has three dates in one day, and these mature courting practices mystify Peggy. Lunetta, an unmarried friend of Mozelle's, introduces more bizarre hints of adult sexuality. Her elaborate costumes and thick lipstick function as "man bait" (*S*), and she tells complicated stories about adulterous relationships. All the adults around Peggy discuss Communist infiltration of labor unions and the danger that any worker who even knows a Communist will be fired. In Peggy's new environment even playtime is frightening. Sharon Belletieri, a new playmate from down the street, zooms along the sidewalk on her roller skates and laughs at Peggy's clumsiness. Peggy has never skated before and has as much difficulty keeping her physical balance as she does maintaining her psychological equilibrium.

In several other scenes Peggy's physical acts objectify her confusion. At a children's birthday party, for example, the game of pin the tail on the donkey becomes a dramatic enactment of her inner state. Immediately after Sharon has neatly pinned a label on Uncle Boone's coworker by asserting that he is a Communist, Peggy finds herself blindfolded and being spun in circles. She becomes dizzy and attaches the donkey tail to a flower on the wallpaper instead of to the elusive animal. Peggy's blindness and disorientation in the game are comparable to her intellectual and emotional confusion in this strange new world.

Just as Peggy's eyes fail her in the party game, her powers of speech and aural comprehension frequently prove deficient to meet the challenges of her new environment. In a realm where people speak a new or coded language, the initiate is sometimes both deaf and dumb. Peggy's speech is that of the rural South, and her playmate Sharon cannot understand her pronunciation of simple words like "hair." On the other hand, when Sharon says Peggy's name it comes out sounding like "piggy." Peggy cannot communicate easily even with her own cousin. To Betsy Lou's greeting of "Hey," Peggy responds timidly with "Corn." This country joke bewilders Betsy Lou, and she stares at Peggy as though she were "some odd sort of pet allowed into the house" (*S*). Such verbal misunderstandings provide incidental humor, but they also reinforce the story's major theme. In her initiation Peggy must expand her vocabulary and absorb new idioms as mechanisms for ordering this strange new world. Her adult relatives expose her to unfamiliar words like "reds" but offer no clarification of the code. In fact, the adults proclaim that such terms "don't concern younguns." Scorned by the neighborhood children because she doesn't speak or comprehend their language, Peggy is not yet accepted into adult conversation. She knows the terms appropriate to this discourse but does not understand their signification.

The decisive event in Peggy's rite of passage is her mother's miscarriage. Already puzzled by earlier events and unable to understand the adult talk she overhears, Peggy becomes terrified. Peggy's mother miscarries without even knowing she was pregnant, and this totally unexpected development makes her role as mother and guide especially difficult. Like Nick Adams's father in the Hemingway story "Indian Camp," she must clarify for her child the mysteries of life's beginning as well as its ending. The complicated circumstances force her to explain how the potential for birth has been abruptly displaced by the reality of death. In her attempt she first tells Peggy that she was going to have a baby brother or sister. Then she hastily retracts and says, "I'm trying to tell you there wasn't really a baby. I didn't know about it, anyway" (*S*). Retreating to a rural analogy (suggesting perhaps the lost order and simplicity of an agrarian culture), she compares her situation to that of a hen that failed to hatch some of its eggs. Throughout this halting conversation Peggy's mother seems as confused about proper idioms as Peggy. Even if she understands the coded discourse of adults, she cannot share it with her daughter.

With its disturbing conjunction of sexuality and mortality, this scene recalls one of the Miranda stories by Katherine Anne Porter. In "The Grave" another nine-year-old girl must face the mysteries of birth and death as she examines the body of a dead rabbit with babies in its womb almost ready to be born. These fetal rabbits are obscured by a thin red veil (presumably the amniotic sac), but in her struggle toward mature awareness Miranda wants desperately to break through this symbolic veil so she can see and know all. Since this action takes place in an abandoned cemetery, the echoes of mortality become even more strident.

Just as Peggy's mother's pregnancy and that of the rabbit in "The Grave" are abortive, Peggy's initiation is incomplete. Her journey is supposed to take her from the farm to the big city, but, in fact, she never gets close enough to see even the skyline of Detroit. Peggy merely glimpses the tall buildings on a television newscast, and there she sees only "some faint, dark shapes, hiding behind the snow, like a forest in winter" (*S*). The television (literally, vision from afar) provides a semblance of truth but obscures more than it reveals. Thus, Peggy's exposure to the big city is indirect just as her experience of the story's sharpest pain—her mother's miscarriage—is vicarious. Like the mysteries of life in "The Grave," the city remains hidden behind a veil.

In her room alone after watching the fuzzy television newscast, Peggy experiences a vision of truth in which she claims to see "everything clearly" (*S*). This vision (much like Bob's mock epiphany in "The Secret of the Pyramids") presumably explains all the mysteries of her time away from home: "My mother had said an egg didn't hatch, but I knew better. The reds had stolen the baby. They took things. They were after my aunt's copper-bottomed pans. . . . They wanted my uncle's job. They were invisible . . . although they might wear disguises. You didn't know who might be a red. You never knew when you might lose a baby that you didn't know you had. I understood it all." These musings of a precocious nine-year-old are both charmingly naive and brilliantly insightful. Because Peggy cannot understand the adult codes, she obviously has facts garbled, but her assertions capture important truths. Although the specific labels she assigns to the forces of evil may be erroneous, she is correct in perceiving that it can be both immanent and imminent. Since she cannot escape its influence, she must be prepared at any moment.

Although Peggy's initiation is incomplete, the journey does change her profoundly. She returns to Kentucky with an acute appreciation of "the mystery of travel, the vastness of the world, the strangeness of life" (*S*). The bus drops Peggy and her mother at an intersection half a mile from their home. As they walk toward the farm, Peggy sees their white house and tin-roofed barn amid tall oak trees. In the final sentence of the story, however, this Kentucky skyline is still in the distance. Just as

Peggy never traveled all the way to Detroit, the story ends without her ever returning all the way home. Having experienced so much that was new, Peggy cannot easily return to her old self and remains in limbo. . . .

Source: Albert Wilhelm, "Travelers and Pilgrims: Looking for Love, Purpose, and Fulfillment in Many of the Wrong Places," in *Bobbie Ann Mason: A Study of the Short Fiction*, Twayne Publishers, 1998, pp. 28–33.

SOURCES

"About Bobbie Ann Mason," Bobbie Ann Mason website, http://www.bobbieannmason.net/bio.htm (accessed February 25, 2016).

"About Shiloh and Other Stories," Penguin Random House website, http://www.penguinrandomhouse.com/books/108765/shiloh-and-other-stories-by-bobbie-ann-mason/9780375758430/ (accessed February 25, 2016).

Gwinn, Mary Ann, "Mason Is at Her Best in *An Atomic Romance*," in *Chicago Tribune*, September 9, 2005, http://articles.chicagotribune.com/2005-09-09/features/0509090117_1_nuclear-plant-reed-futrell-bobbie-ann-mason (accessed February 25, 2016).

Jacques, Kathy, "Bobby Ann Mason's Biography," http://rimstead-cours.espaceweb.usherbrooke.ca/ANG341_FALL2007/kathy%20jacques%20-%20ANG34103.htm (accessed February 25, 2016).

Kim, Walter, "Up from Kmart," in *New York Times*, August 19, 2001, http://www.nytimes.com/2001/08/19/books/up-from-kmart.html?pagewanted=all (accessed February 14, 2016).

Maus, Derek C., Introduction to *Living Through the Red Scare*, Greenhaven Press, 2006, pp. 9–19.

Price, Joanna, *Understanding Bobbie Ann Mason*, University of North Carolina Press, 2009, p. 20.

"QuickFacts: Detroit City, Michigan," United States Census Bureau, U.S. Department of Commerce, http://www.census.gov/quickfacts/table/PST045215/2622000 (accessed March 4, 2016).

Wilhelm, Albert, *Bobbie Ann Mason: A Study of the Short Fiction*, Twayne's Studies of Short Fiction, No. 75, Twayne Publishers, 1998, pp. 28–29.

FURTHER READING

Alsen, Eberhard, *Romantic Postmodernism in American Fiction*, Rodopi, 1996.
    This scholarly survey of literature at the time when this story was published covers the labels of "Kmart realism" and "dirty realism" that

are often affixed to Mason's writing. Alsen gives a good overview of late-twentieth-century fiction.

Eckard, Paula Gallant, *Maternal Body and Voice in Toni Morrison, Bobbie Ann Mason, and Lee Smith*, University of Missouri Press, 2002.

The Mason works Eckard focuses on here are her novels, but the insights that she has about the position of mothers in the author's longer works are equally relevant to the central relationship in "Detroit Skyline, 1949."

Fariello, Griffin, *Red Scare: Memories of the American Inquisition*, W.W. Norton, 1995.

There are many books available analyzing the social climate that allowed the fear of Communism to spiral out of control in the late 1940s and early 1950s. This book gives readers a series of interviews with people whose lives were affected by the Red Scare, from prosecutors to Communists to laborers who were swept up in the hysteria, as the characters in Mason's story fear they will be.

Fine, Laura, "Going Nowhere Slow: The Post-South World of Bobbie Ann Mason," in *Southern Literary Journal*, Vol. 1, 1999, pp. 87–97.

Mason is often categorized as a "southern writer," a label that is more appropriate for writers of a generation or two earlier. In this study, Fine looks at how the southern tradition affects Mason's writing, though it does not define it.

Marín, Candela Delgado, "An Interview with Bobbie Ann Mason," in *Transatlantica*, Vol. 2, 2014, http://transatlantica.revues.org/7141 (accessed March 19, 2016).

This recent interview gives the author's ideas, in her own words, about her aesthetic theories of fiction, as well as a long and detailed biography.

Pollack Harriet, "From *Shiloh* to *In Country* to *Feather Crowns*: Bobbie Ann Mason, Women's History, and Southern Fiction," in *Southern Literary Journal*, Spring 1996, pp. 95–116.

While many literary studies have been written about the short story "Shiloh," this is one of the few to consider the whole collection by that name (which includes "Detroit Skyline, 1949"). The volume gives readers a good way to consider themes recurring in Mason's writing at that time.

SUGGESTED SEARCH TERMS

Bobbie Ann Mason

Bobbie Ann Mason AND "Detroit Skyline, 1949"

Bobbie Ann Mason AND Kentucky

Detroit AND postwar

Shiloh and Other Stories AND "Detroit Skyline, 1949"

Detroit AND communism

Red scare

fiction AND early television

Kmart realism

Footfalls

WILBUR DANIEL STEELE

1920

"Footfalls" is a short story written by American author Wilbur Daniel Steele. The story was first published in October 1920 in the periodical *Pictorial Review* and was subsequently selected as an O. Henry Prize story for that year. It first appeared in book form in a 1929 collection of Steele's short stories, *Tower of Sand and Other Stories*.

Steele's career spanned five decades. In addition to writing ten novels and several plays, he wrote more than two hundred short stories and enjoyed a reputation as one of the chief practitioners of the short-story form in America, particularly during the 1920s and 1930s. His stories appeared in many of the leading popular periodicals of the time, including *Atlantic Monthly*, *Harper's*, *Collier's Weekly*, *Scribner's Magazine*, *Good Housekeeping*, *Ladies' Home Journal*, *Cosmopolitan*, and *Pictorial Review*. "Footfalls" is in many respects typical of the kind of short story Steele wrote because of its reliance on melodrama, ironic twists, and coincidences. It has remained a favorite among the many short stories he wrote for its atmosphere and suspense and for the surprising revelation at its climax. In 1946 the publishing firm Doubleday included "Footfalls" among the twenty-four stories it selected for *The Best Stories of Wilbur Daniel Steele*.

"Footfalls" can be found in *A Book of Modern Short Stories*, edited by Dorothy Brewster (Macmillan, 1928) and in *The Best Stories*

The story takes place in a New England fishing village (©cnkdaniel / Shutterstock.com)

of *Wilbur Daniel Steele* (Doubleday, 1946). The story is available online at the *O. Henry Memorial Award Prize Stories of 1920* website at http://www.fullbooks.com/O-Henry-Memorial-Award-Prize-Stories-ofx11877.html.

AUTHOR BIOGRAPHY

Steele was born on St. Patrick's Day, March 17, 1886, in Greensboro, North Carolina—incidentally, the birthplace of short-story writer William Sydney Porter, better known as O. Henry. He was the third child of the Reverend Wilbur Fletcher Steele and Rose Wood Steele. Although he was born in the South, he was not a southerner; the family lived briefly in Greensboro while Steele's father served as principal at the Bennett Seminary, a Methodist Episcopal school for African American girls. When Steele was four years of age, the family left for Germany, where his father continued his graduate studies and Steele attended kindergarten.

In 1893 the elder Steele completed his PhD and took a position at the University of Denver as a professor of biblical studies. His son completed his bachelor's degree in history and economics at the University of Denver in 1907, but he believed his true calling was that of an artist, so he enrolled at the Boston Museum School of Fine Arts. He later studied painting at the Académie Julien in Paris, but his interests turned to etching, which he studied in Italy in 1909. In 1910 he returned to the United States and settled in Provincetown, Massachusetts, on Cape Cod, determined to become a writer. In Provincetown he shared quarters with novelist Sinclair Lewis and was friends with playwright Eugene O'Neill; he and O'Neill were among the original playwrights for the famed Provincetown Players. Although he regarded Provincetown as his home base, he traveled widely, taking trips to Ireland, England, France, Switzerland, Tunisia, the Caribbean, and South America, which provided him with varied settings for his stories.

Steele published his first short story in 1910, but his career gained momentum in 1912 with the publication of "White Horse Winter" in *Atlantic Monthly*. That year he began a flirtation with the bohemian lifestyles and literary trends of Greenwich Village in New York. He also married Margaret Orinda Thurston, whom he had met at the Museum of Fine Arts, in 1913. The couple would have two children. He found the life of a bohemian artist not to his liking, however, so he returned to Provincetown. By the end of 1914 Steele had published his first novel (*Storm*) and several short stories. In 1918 he published his first collection, *Land's End and Other Stories*; several of the stories, like the later "Footfalls" (published in *Pictorial Review* in 1920), are set in Portuguese American seacoast towns, similar to the ones on Cape Cod. His next collection, *The Shame Dance and Other Stories* (1923), features stories with exotic settings in the South Seas, the Caribbean, North Africa, and the Middle East, and one story in the collection, "The Anglo-Saxon," was an O. Henry Award winner. Later collections include *Urkey Island* (1926); *The Man Who Saw through Heaven and Other Stories* (1927), whose title story, first published in *Harper's* in 1925, is regarded by many readers as among his finest; *Tower of Sand and Other Stories* (1929), which contains the first book publication of "Footfalls"; and *Full Cargo: More Stories by Wilbur Daniel Steele* (1951).

In addition to writing short stories, Steele produced novels, among them *Taboo* (1925), *Meat* (1928), *Undertow* (1930), and *That Girl from Memphis* (1945). He was also a playwright; his best-known dramatic works include *Post Road* (1934), which he wrote with his second wife, the actress and playwright Norma Mitchell (whom he married in 1932 after the death of his first wife), and *How Beautiful with Shoes* (1935), which he wrote with Anthony Brown.

In 1955 Steele published the novel *The Way to the Gold* (which was turned into a movie by Twentieth Century-Fox in 1957), but he published very little in the final years of his life. In the late 1950s and the 1960s, he became increasingly frail and was losing his hearing. He and Norma bought a home in Old Lyme, Connecticut, where Steele came to be regarded as an eccentric shut-in. He tried to write, but deepening senility made writing next to impossible. In 1965 the couple, needing special care, entered a convalescent facility in Essex, Connecticut, where Norma died in 1967 and Steele lingered

until his death from the effects of advanced age on May 26, 1970.

PLOT SUMMARY

"Footfalls" is set in an unspecified town along the Eastern Seaboard where significant numbers of Portuguese immigrants and their families settled. The protagonist is Boaz Negro, an exuberant man who works day and night as a cobbler (shoemaker), even though he is completely blind. Accordingly, he relies heavily on his other senses: his sense of touch enables him to make shoes, and his acute sense of hearing enables him to identify people by the sound of their "footfalls." His cobbler's shop has become a gathering place for locals, who meet there to socialize.

Boaz is a widower, having lost his wife, Angelina, and three of his four sons. He has a surviving grown son, Manuel, whom he describes by saying he "wasn't too stout" but also describes as a "good boy." He spoils Manuel, giving him spending money and not requiring him to work. The only person who ever speaks to Boaz about his laxity is Campbell Wood. Wood, an officer at a local bank, is a "rising" man in town, described as incorruptible, a little "ruthless," and an eligible bachelor. One day, Wood appears at the shop to speak to Boaz about Manuel. He has with him a large sum of money, which he describes as government money. He says that believes the money is not secure in the bank's antiquated safe, so he is taking it home for safekeeping overnight. While he is in the shop, he drops the bag, which, because it is filled with coins, makes a noticeable clink. Boaz is horrified, because he is aware that Manuel has appeared, heard the clink of the falling gold, and might be tempted to steal it.

Boaz owns his shop, along with his living quarters behind it. His son lives in the house with him, and Wood rents rooms on the upper floor. That night, Boaz hears footfalls in the house, both on the lower floor and on the upper floor. He then hears a brief conversation between Manuel and Wood, during which the latter invites Manuel to play euchre in Wood's room. After a while, Boaz hears the sound of footfalls around the corner of the shop from the house, as if someone is fleeing. Soon, passers-by

MEDIA ADAPTATIONS

- In 1921 a silent film version of "Footfalls" was released by the Fox Film Corporation. The film was directed by Charles Brabin and starred Tyrone Power Sr. as Boaz Negro.

- "Footfalls" was adapted for radio by Alvin George and Robert L. Richards. William Spier produced and directed. J. Carrol Naish starred. This episode first aired on July 12, 1945. The broadcast can be downloaded at the "Escape and Suspense!" website at http://www.escape-suspense.com/2010/08/suspense-footfalls.html.

- On July 7, 1955, ABC broadcast a television version of "Footfalls" as an episode in its *Star Tonight* series. The lead role was played by actor Theodore Bikel (best known for creating the role of Captain von Trapp in the original stage production of *The Sound of Music*).

in the street raise the alarm because the house is on fire. The fire destroys the house, and searchers discover the charred body of a man; the victim, dressed in Wood's clothing, including his watch, his cuff buttons, his collar studs, and other items a professional would wear, died from a severe blow to the head. Another banker, Asa Whitelaw, appears and asks the question everyone has in mind: Where is Manuel? The townspeople all conclude that Manuel murdered Wood, stole the money, and set fire to the house to cover his crime as he fled. Boaz is distraught and vows revenge on what he repeatedly and consistently refers to as the "*cachorra*," or dog.

Nine years pass. Efforts to locate the fugitive have been unavailing. Boaz has not rebuilt the house, and he has lost his zest for life. The amount of work he has as a cobbler has been dwindling. He continues, however, to listen for the footfalls of the fugitive. One evening, during the Festival of Menino Jesus, he hears them as a man enters his shop. He traps the person in the shop by pulling a cord that closes the shop's

doors and latches them. The fugitive remains perfectly silent in the dark, so the blind Boaz is unable to pinpoint his location. Finally, the intruder has to exhale, producing a sound that causes Boaz to leap from his chair and, with his powerful cobbler's hands, strangle the man to death. Passers-by hear a scream, and when they investigate, they find Boaz shaving a beard off the body of the man. Boaz was puzzled by the beard and wants to ensure that he has killed the right man.

In a final ironic twist, the man is identified not as Manuel but as Wood, who killed Manuel, dressed Manuel in his clothing, set the fire, and fled with the money, growing a beard to disguise his identity. He has returned to the town for reasons that are unclear but probably out of a desire to determine what, if anything, Boaz knows about the murder. All along, Boaz has known that the "*cachorra*" was Wood, not Manuel, but he had long been suspicious of "the Law," so he did not report what he knew. Boaz is not prosecuted for killing Wood, he begins to rebuild his house, and his exuberance starts to return.

CHARACTERS

Boaz Negro

Boaz is of Portuguese descent; his last name is Portuguese/Spanish for "black" and has no racial connotations. He works as a cobbler, or shoemaker, and is totally blind, forcing him to rely on his other senses to navigate his world. He is described as a man of unquenchable exuberance, despite having lost his wife and three of his four sons. He spoils his surviving son, Manuel, by constantly giving him pocket money and not requiring him to work. Located just behind Boaz's cobbler shop is his house, where Manuel lives and where Campbell Wood, a local banker, rents rooms on the upper floor. One night, Boaz hears pacing on both floors of the house. Shortly thereafter, a fire breaks out. The house is destroyed, and the body of a man is found in the bed on the upper floor. Boaz vows revenge on the murderer, who, everyone assumes, was Manuel, who is believed to have robbed Wood of a sum of money he had brought home from the bank for safekeeping. Boaz, however, never reveals to the townspeople that he knows that the body was that of

Manuel and that the criminal was Wood. After the passage of several years, Wood reappears, and Boaz strangles him to death. Having achieved his revenge, Boaz rebuilds his house and reclaims his zest for life.

Manuel Negro

Manual is the sole surviving son of Boaz. The reader learns little about him other than what his father says of him—that he is not very stout but that he is a good boy and the last surviving link Boaz has with his deceased wife. Manuel does not work, and he gets by with pocket money his father provides him. One night, he agrees to play euchre with Wood in Wood's room on the upper floor of the Boaz house. There he falls victim to Wood's murderous plan to abscond with the bank money he has brought home for safekeeping.

Asa Whitelaw

Whitelaw is a bank employee who appears on the scene after the fire destroys Boaz's house. It is he who asks the key question: Where is Manuel?

Campbell Wood

Wood is a local banker. He is described as a "rising" young man, and he is said to share with Boaz a quality of "incorruptibility." He is also described as "a little ruthless" and a good-looking, "eligible" man. One day, he removes a quantity of money from the bank, claiming that the funds were not secure in the bank's antiquated safe. In Boaz's shop he drops the bag containing the coins, creating a clink that Manuel hears. Later, he is heard inviting Manuel to his room on the upper floor of Boaz's house to play euchre. A fire breaks out, and a badly charred body is discovered. Because the victim is dressed in Wood's clothing, it is assumed that Manuel murdered him, stole the money, and fled. In reality, the reader learns that Wood is the murderer and that he killed Manuel and set the fire to cover his crime. After the passage of some nine years, he is unable to resist returning to the scene of his misdeeds, where Boaz exacts his revenge and kills him.

THEMES

Revenge

A key theme of "Footfalls" is revenge. Because of his acute sense of hearing, particularly his ability to distinguish individuals by the sound of their footfalls, Boaz Negro knows that the perpetrator of the crime in his house is Campbell Wood, not his son, Manuel. Following the murder, Boaz is alone, having already lost his wife and his three other sons. After the townspeople conclude that Manuel is the fugitive, Boaz hints at his intent:

> "Now I have lost everything. My house. My last son. Even my honour. You would not think I would like to live. But I go to live. I go to work. That *cachorra*, one day, he shall come back again, in the dark night, to have a look. I shall go to show you all. That *cachorra!*"

Later, when the townspeople assure him that the criminal will return to hang, Boaz shakes his head and says, "No, you shall not catch that *cachorra* now. But one day—."

The narration goes on to describe the change that takes place in Boaz. His spirit becomes "an entrenched camp, lying silent, sullen, verdureless, under a gray sky." Further, much is made of the fact that Boaz seems to be building up the strength in his hands and arms: "Storing it up. Against a day!" The reader learns, too, that Boaz spends much of his time listening to the sound of footfalls. All of these details suggest that Boaz is patiently planning his revenge. One day, after nine years, he hears the fatal footfalls he has been waiting for as a man enters his shop. He is prepared, for he has rigged a device that enables him to close both the front and back doors to the shop by pulling a rope hanging before him. When the intruder finally makes a sound, Boaz springs and strangles the man to death. At first he has doubts; the man's beard initially leads him to worry that he might have killed the wrong man. But as he shaves off the beard, one of the townsmen identifies the body as that of Wood. Boaz has achieved his revenge, allowing him now to rebuild his house and restoring his "priceless and unquenchable exuberance."

Father-Child Relationships

"Footfalls" depends for its overall effect on the relationship between Boaz Negro and his surviving son, Manuel. Early on, it is clear that Boaz has great affection for his son, the sole survivor of four sons. He is frequently heard to say that Manuel "wasn't too stout," which is the father's explanation for why he does not require Manuel to work. Further, the reader

TOPICS FOR FURTHER STUDY

- Although the setting of "Footfalls" is never precisely specified, reference is made in the second paragraph to "one of those old Puritan sea towns" that "has become an outpost of the Portuguese islands." Steele settled in Provincetown, a Cape Cod, Massachusetts, community that was a sea town with a large Portuguese community. Conduct research into the history of Portuguese settlement along the East Coast of New England. Present your findings to your classmates in a PowerPoint or similar presentation.

- An important custom among Portuguese Americans on the Eastern Seaboard at the time was the Blessing of the Fleet. Conduct research into this custom and describe it for your classmates in an oral presentation.

- Conduct research into the O. Henry Prize. Who was O. Henry, and why was the prize named after him? Who have been some of the prominent recipients of the prize? Present the results of your findings in a visual chart for your classmates.

- Read a story by O. Henry. One of the most popular ones is the widely available "The Gift of the Magi" (contained in *The Best Short Stories of O. Henry*, published by Modern Library in 1994). In a written essay, compare O. Henry's use of the ironic, surprise ending with Steele's.

- Research the history of blindness in literature, starting perhaps with *Oedipus Rex*, a play by the ancient Greek author Sophocles. What are some prominent works that use the motif of blindness? Is blindness used as a metaphor or symbol for a state of mind? Prepare an oral report on blindness in literature and share your findings with your classmates.

- *Mirror, Mirror on the Wall: The Diary of Bess Brennan*, by Barry Denenberg (Scholastic, 2002), is a young-adult novel

set in 1932. It tells the story of a twelve-year-old girl who lost her sight in an accident. She maintains a diary, recorded by her twin sister, in which she describes life at Perkins School for the Blind in Watertown, Massachusetts. Read the novel, then write a report comparing Denenberg's use of blindness as a thematic device with Steele's.

- Conduct research on the Provincetown Players, a prominent theatrical group on Cape Cod from 1915 to 1929. (The Provincetown Playhouse survives and continues to stage plays.) Who were some of the playwrights who participated? What contributions did the players make to modern American drama? Prepare a written report in which you present the results of your research.

- Convert the text of "Footfalls" into a dramatic script. With willing classmates, perform your version of the story for the remainder of your class. Record your performance and upload the audio to a free audio hosting site such as Upload-MP3, Tindeck, or MySpaceFileHosting. Invite your classmates to comment.

- Join a group of your classmates in conducting a courtroom "trial" of Boaz Negro for the murder of Campbell Wood. Imagine that the rest of the class is the jury. When you have concluded the trial, invite the class to render a "verdict" on Boaz.

- *Blindness* (1995) is a novel by Portuguese author José Saramago; in the original Portuguese, the title is *Ensaio sobre a cegueira*, or "Essay on Blindness." The novel, was published in English translation in 1997 by Harcourt Brace. Read the novel, then perform an oral interpretation of a key passage of your choosing for your classmates.

Boaz Negro makes his living as a cobbler (©*frankie's | Shutterstock.com*)

learns that Boaz frequently provides Manuel with pocket money:

> And there was always something for his son, a "piece for the pocket," a dollar-, five-, even a ten-dollar bill if he had "got to have it." Manuel was "a good boy." Boaz not only said this; he felt that he was assured of it in his understanding, to the infinite peace of his heart.

(It is worth noting that $10 in 1920 would be worth nearly $120 in 2016.)

Manuel stands in contrast to Campbell Wood. Wood, who appears to be roughly the same age as Manuel, is a "rising" young man and an eligible bachelor. He holds a responsible position at the bank where he works. He apparently has enough money to dress professionally and with great care. Boaz is said to have "reverence for the young man's position," although that very position induces in Boaz a feeling of "vague distrust," and that distrust deepens when Wood calls Boaz's parenting views into question. In a sense, the story frames the two young men as contrasting sons, one of whom is a "good boy" who is victimized by the other.

Greed

Greed, or the lack of greed, plays a key role in "Footfalls." The story makes a great many references to money. The reader learns that Boaz has a thriving business as a cobbler, but one never senses that he is overly concerned about money. Indeed, he is generous with his money, often giving pocket money to his son, and the reader is told that Boaz had an inherent distrust of finance. He has worked hard, enabling him to purchase his own house, yet he fails to insure the house, again out of distrust for finance. Campbell Wood is a banker, so he deals with money on a daily basis. Setting the plot of the story in motion is the bag of money that Wood takes from the bank, apparently for safekeeping in his rooms. Manuel hears the clink of the coins in the bag when Wood drops it in Boaz's shop, setting in train the events that follow. Ultimately, the reader learns that it was not Manuel who stole the money, murdered Wood, set the fire, and fled; rather, Wood was the criminal, staging events so that he could flee with the money and make it appear as though Manuel committed the crime.

STYLE

Plot

In literary criticism, *plot* refers to the pattern of events in a narrative. Typically, plots exhibit causality and unity and have a beginning, a middle, and an end. "Footfalls" includes all of the basic elements of a well-constructed plot. It begins with *exposition*, the "scene setting" that orients the reader; in this case, the reader learns about the New England community in which the story is set, about Boaz Negro and his work as a cobbler, and about his relationship with his son. *Rising action* refers to the introduction of complications and *conflict*; these elements include the appearance of Campbell Wood, the revelation that he has with him a large sum of money, Manuel's awareness that Wood has money in his possession, and Boaz's realization that Manuel has been invited to Wood's room to play euchre. The chief complication, however, is the murder, the fire, and the flight of the criminal, followed by the nine years during which Boaz plans his revenge. The plot reaches a *climax* when a man enters Boaz's shop and Boaz knows—or thinks he knows—that the intruder is the criminal, for he recognizes his "footfalls." In a climactic scene, Boaz strangles the intruder to death. Much of the interest of the story derives from the *dénouement*, or unraveling, when it is revealed that the dead man is Wood, not Manuel, and that Boaz has known all along that Wood was the fugitive. The story's *falling action* in the final paragraphs notes that Boaz was never held accountable for his crime.

Suspense

Suspense is the literary device by which an author maintains the audience's attention through the buildup of events that are intended—but may fail—to result in a specific outcome. In "Footfalls," Steele builds suspense from the very first words: "This is not an easy story; not a road for tender or for casual feet. . . . Let me warn you, it is as hard as that old man's soul and as sunless as his eyes." These words create a sense of anticipation, of foreboding, that sustains the story through to the final page. As the story proceeds, suspense is built through a number of implied questions: What role will Boaz's blindness play in the story? Why are "footfalls" important to the plot? How will Boaz's "laxity" toward his son contribute to the unfolding of events? If

Campbell Wood is "a little ruthless," how will that ruthlessness manifest itself? Suspense builds further when Wood drops the bag of money and Boaz realizes that his ne'er-do-well son has heard the clink of gold—"*and Boaz wished that he had not!*" As Boaz listens to the footfalls in his house, the reader knows that something dramatic is going to happen—as indeed it does, as the house burns and the criminal flees. The tension of the story relaxes as the narration skims over the next nine years, but it builds once again when the intruder enters Boaz's shop and the reader knows that Boaz knows that the intruder is the criminal he has been waiting for. Suspense reaches its peak as silence and darkness envelope the two men—until the sough of the intruder's exhalation enables Boaz to spring.

Irony

Many of Steele's short stories depend for their overall effect on highly ironic outcomes. "Footfalls" is no exception. The reader becomes, in effect, one of the townspeople, convinced that the charred body in the ruins of Boaz's house is that of Campbell Wood, that the murderer is Manuel, and that Manuel has fled with the bag of money Wood had in his possession. In the wake of the crime, Boaz never refers to the perpetrator by name; he is always the "*cachorra*," or dog. The irony becomes apparent after Boaz exacts his revenge and shaves the beard off of the intruder in his shop, allowing the townspeople to recognize him as Wood, not Manuel. The story, then, relies on ironic misdirection, with readers led to draw a conclusion that turns out to be false.

HISTORICAL CONTEXT

Although "Footfalls" makes no specific reference to historical events, the story takes place in the context of Portuguese immigration to the United States, specifically to the Eastern Seaboard, including Cape Cod. Early on, the narration mentions that Boaz lived "in one of those old Puritan sea towns. . . . Except that the town is no longer Puritan and Yankee. . . . It has become an outpost of the Portuguese islands." The narration further specifies that Boaz was a Portuguese from St. Michael, "in the Western Islands."

The "Western Islands" are the Azores, a group of islands in the Atlantic Ocean that were

COMPARE
&
CONTRAST

- **1920:** Although the process of making shoes became increasingly industrialized in the nineteenth century, traditional cobblers like Boaz continue to make shoes by hand, using such tools as lasts (forms), pegs, and awls and by hand stitching.

  Today: Although cobblers can still be found in traditional cultures, most shoes are manufactured by means of mass industrial processes.

- **1920:** Since the end of the nineteenth century Cape Cod has become a summer retreat for city dwellers, particularly those from Boston; many New England entrepreneurs and industrialists build vacation cottages on Cape Cod.

  Today: Cape Cod remains a summer retreat for New Englanders; Provincetown continues

to garner fame as an artists' colony and has attracted large numbers of gays and lesbians.

- **1920:** Relatively large numbers of Portuguese immigrants have come to the United States, most from the Azores. Portuguese immigration to the United States peaked between 1910 and 1920, with more than eighty-nine thousand arriving in the United States.

  Today: The number of Portuguese immigrants to the United States increased sharply after the passage of the Immigration and Nationality Act of 1965, with eleven thousand to twelve thousand entering each year, although the number later dropped off; about 1.4 million Americans are of Portuguese ancestry, with a large percentage coming from the Azores.

---

discovered and settled by the Portuguese in the fifteenth century and remain Portuguese territory. The archipelago consists of three clusters of islands. The island of St. Michael, or São Miguel (also known as the Green Island), is located in the southeastern-most group and is the largest island in the Azores. The earliest Azoreans who came to the United States did so in whaling ships, settling in the New Bedford area of Massachusetts, then moving into the surrounding region. Most of these immigrants were young men looking for work. As the whaling industry declined, many moved inland to work in New England's textile mills; others remained behind to work in the fishing industry.

Portuguese immigration to the United States occurred in three waves. The first was from about 1820 to 1870. A second wave took place from about 1870 to 1930. A more recent wave took place after 1960, largely as a result of devastating volcanic eruptions in 1957. In the decade before the initial publication of "Footfalls" (1910–1920), more than eighty-nine thousand Portuguese immigrants arrived in the

United States, and during the preceding decade (1900–1910), the number was more than sixty-nine thousand. One impetus behind Portuguese immigration was the fall of the Portuguese monarchy in 1910. Many Catholics believed the new government was hostile to their religion, so they left Portugal and the Azores for the United States. Further, immigrants from St. Michael found their passage to the United States easier after the US consulate moved to the island in 1917, bringing with it direct shipping between the island and the United States.

The impact of Portuguese settlers in such places as Provincetown, Massachusetts (where Steele settled in 1910), was captured by Wallace Nutting in a 1923 book, *Massachusetts Beautiful* (quoted by Karen Christel Krahulik in *Provincetown: From Pilgrim Landing to Gay Resort*):

> Provincetown itself has of late, indeed, been seized by a new band of Pilgrims, the Portuguese, who succeeded the Yankees in the fisheries, and who now themselves are finding other lines of effort more attractive. . . . There is something good to be said for the Portuguese which is not

Although Boaz is blind, he recognizes his neighbors by their footsteps (*©racorn | Shutterstock.com*)

so marked in the natives of Cape Cod. [The Portuguese] are rather notably courteous and lively and have added a note of joyousness and vivacity which may be more superficial than the sturdy graces of the English character but is, nevertheless, agreeable as met by the traveler.

"Footfalls" makes reference to one Portuguese custom. The narration notes that the intruder who appears in Boaz's shop does so at the time of the "Festival of *Menin' Jesus*," a variant of Menino Jesus, meaning "boy Jesus" or "baby Jesus." In effect, the festival is the Portuguese version of Christmas. Typically, the holiday was celebrated by attending Mass, decorating an altar in honor of the Menino Jesus, and, in particular, visiting one another's homes—ironic, given that the "visit" Campbell Wood pays to Boaz leads to his just punishment.

CRITICAL OVERVIEW

In his profile of Steele for *American Short-Story Writers, 1910–1945* (part of the *Dictionary of Literary Biography* series), Mel Seesholtz

summed up the rise and fall of Steele's reputation:

> During the first third of the twentieth century Steele was popularly and critically regarded as one of America's premier short-story writers. Exaggerated caricatures as characters, melodramatic plots in lavish settings of intrigue, narratives which tried to "reduce to writing" the unity of oral tradition, the values and beliefs of pre–World War I America: Steele's formulas for fiction, which had led to such popular success, never evolved and led inevitably to his short stories' literary extinction. However, it is that rapid rise to the top and equally rapid plunge into virtual extinction that signals Steele's key role as a transitional figure in the history of the modern American short story.

Seesholtz further points out that even as early as 1929 "Steele's formulaic stories were still favorites among popular magazine audiences, but the American short story and modern literature were going in other directions."

Writing in 1926 for the *Bookman*, Frank B. Elser confirmed the widely held view at the time that Steele was a major literary figure, suggesting that he "might be critically appraised as the master technician in America of the short story form." Edward J. O'Brien, in his introduction to Steele's first collections, *Land's End and Other Stories*, wrote: "The rich, human embodiment of the stories collected in his volume assure them a permanence in our literature for their imaginative reality, their warm color, and their finality of artistic execution. Almost without exception they represent the best that is being accomplished in America today by a literary artist."

The O. Henry Prize committee agreed. In *Our Short Story Writers*, Blanche Colton Williams noted:

> In 1922 Mr. Steele first came into extraordinary recognition when the O. Henry Memorial Committee [of which Williams was a member] awarded him a special prize for supremacy in story writing from the year 1919 to 1921, inclusive. They summed up his abilities as lying in an individual temperament that invests the real with the color of romance, in a sense of correct architecture, in the happy knowledge of unique situations, in the climactic development of struggle or complication, in the power to move the reader's emotions, and in a satisfactory dénouement. All these characteristics are manifest in tales marked by a distinctive style, a style dependent upon seizure and conveyance of atmosphere.

Martin Bucco, in *Wilbur Daniel Steele*, backed this point of view:

> Educated contemporaries found in Steele not only escape from the everyday, but—more important—entrance into another place, another culture, another way of looking at life. Whether set at home or abroad, his stories embody a kind of unschematized history of certain values prevailing in America before and, to a lesser extent, following World War I.

Bucco added that "today Steele appears old-fashioned and reactionary, not because he lacks fantastic literary skill, but because fictional statements now in vogue are so different." Commenting on "Footfalls," however, Bucco called Boaz Negro "one of Steel's great story figures," adding that "a Steele feat of psychological motivation and blindman's buff, the story ends with Boaz' violent revenge. The weird fusion of introspective hero, commenting chorus, scheming villain, and sensational murder makes 'Footfalls' a type of Senecan or Elizabethan tragedy."

Paul Allen, in a review of *Tower of Sand* (the collection in which "Footfalls" appeared in

1929) in the *Bookman*, was not impressed by Steele's efforts, writing that "what one takes at first for genius seems on second thought to be merely a trick of writing." Allen further referred to the collection as consisting of "machine-made stories"—the notion that in Allen's view Steele hit on a formula and used it to crank out stories. In contrast, Dorothy Brewster, in her note on "Footfalls" in her collection *A Book of Modern Short Stories*, praised the story for its "vivid portrayal of the motives for revenge. It is a story in which there seems to be no author, in which you feel your way through the events and the years of waiting from some place within the father's own mind and heart."

Later, however, a strong reaction set in. In a 1951 *Time* magazine review of Steele's collection *Full Cargo* (quoted by Seesholtz), the reviewer, commenting generally on Steele's work, called him a "reactionary and flavorful old fogy," adding: "At his best, Author Steele can stir a jigger of irony, a dash of adventure, a sprig of the exotic and a pinch of mystery into a tippling good yarn. At his worst, he makes the tricks of Fate look like the hoked-up tricks of the trade."

CRITICISM

Michael J. O'Neal

O'Neal holds a PhD in English. In the following essay, he examines the role of the chorus in "Footfalls."

In discussions of modern fiction and drama, reference is often made to "choric characters." The term derives from the word *chorus* and alludes to the use of the chorus in ancient Greek drama. In that drama, the role of a group of undifferentiated actors was to describe and comment on the action, providing the spectator with commentary, interpretation, and insight. Usually they did so through song, dance, and recitation—and, indeed, ancient Greek tragedy had its origins in choral performances during which groups of fifty men danced and sang lyric hymns to the god Dionysius. Later, such playwrights as Aeschylus and Sophocles added individual actors to the performance and reduced the size of the chorus and limited its role to that of commentary on the action and on the motivations of the

WHAT
DO I READ
NEXT?

- One of Steele's most highly regarded stories is "The Man Who Saw through Heaven," which tells the story of a missionary whose wife searches for him in Africa; her harrowing story is told by the narrator, who accompanied her. The story is available online at http://people.eku.edu/sicar/saw.through.heaven.htm.

- One of Steele's highly regarded ghost stories is "The Woman at Seven Brothers," which can be found in *Fifteen Ghost Stories: Famous Modern Ghost Stories*, edited by Emily Dorothy Scarborough (Peruse Press, 2013).

- A story that echoes "Footfalls" in some of its particulars is "A Retrieved Reformation" by O. Henry (*The Best Short Stories of O. Henry*, Modern Library, 1994). It tells the story of Jimmy Valentine, a safecracker who cases a town bank but unexpectedly falls in love with the banker's daughter. Jimmy abandons his life of crime and becomes a shoemaker, but a lawman recognizes him. As a child gets accidentally locked in the airtight bank vault, Jimmy springs into action.

- Wilkie Collins's nineteenth-century novel *Poor Miss Finch* (1872; Oxford University Press, 2009) has been praised for its sensitive—and

medically accurate for its time—depiction of its blind heroine, Lucilla Finch.

- Readers interested in nonfiction examinations of visual impairment and its cultural implications might start with *Diversity and Visual Impairment: The Influence of Race, Gender, Religion, and Ethnicity on the Individual*, a collection of scholarly essays edited by Jane N. Erin and Madeline Milian (AFB Press, 2001; "AFB" stands for American Foundation for the Blind).

- Two novels by African Americans that incorporate blind characters and motifs having to do with blindness and sight are Ralph Ellison's *Invisible Man* (1952; Vintage, 1995) and Richard Wright's *Native Son* (1940; Harper Perennial, 2014).

- An account of one aspect of Portuguese immigration to the United States can be found in *In Pursuit of Their Dreams: A History of Azorean Immigration to the United States*, 2nd ed., by Jerry R. Williams (Tagus, 2007).

- *Tales from Gold Mountain* (Groundwood, 1999), by Paul Yee, is a collection of eight short stories for middle-school readers about the Chinese immigrant experience. Like "Footfalls," some of the stories deal with greed and vengeance.

---

characters. In comedy, the chorus was eventually replaced by interwoven songs whose purpose was largely decorative.

The concept of the chorus, however, did not die out entirely. During the Renaissance, the function of the chorus was often taken over by a single character; the actor who recites the prologue to *Romeo and Juliet* is a good example of a choric character who comments on the action. In the twentieth century, Eugene O'Neill used a chorus in *Mourning Becomes Electra*, as did T. S. Eliot in *Murder in the Cathedral*. Sometimes, individual characters take on the

role of chorus; good examples are the characters Cathleen and Nora in John Millington Synge's play *Riders to the Sea*. German playwright Bertolt Brecht achieved many of his dramatic effects by projecting on a screen captions and illustrations that served a choric function.

In modern literature, however, the choric function has more frequently been woven into the actions, behaviors, and words of the larger community in which the narrative is set, often an undifferentiated set of "townspeople." In this regard, "Footfalls" makes effective use of the concept of the chorus to advance the action,

'FOOTFALLS' MAKES EFFECTIVE USE OF THE
CONCEPT OF THE CHORUS TO ADVANCE THE ACTION,
CONTRIBUTE TO THE SUSPENSE AND THE SURPRISE
OF THE DÉNOUEMENT, AND INVOLVE READERS BY
MISDIRECTING THEM WITH A NARRATIVE SLEIGHT
OF HAND."

contribute to the suspense and the surprise of
the dénouement, and involve readers by misdirecting them with a narrative sleight of hand.

The choric role of the Portuguese community in which the story is set is established in the
opening paragraphs, which explain the role of
Boaz's cobbler's shop in the community:

> In that town a cobbler's shop is a club. One
> sees the interior always dimly thronged. They
> sit on the benches watching the artizan at his
> work for hours, and they talk about every-
> thing in the world. A cobbler is known by
> the company he keeps.

Noting that Boaz "kept young company,"
the narration goes on to describe the "lusty and
valiant" men who frequent the shop and drink,
revel, laugh, and sing but also work hard. By the
time the reader arrives at the details concerning
Boaz's work and family, the story has been
firmly entrenched in a community that sur-
rounds Boaz and his shop. Further, it is made
clear that Boaz can identify the people who pass
his shop by the sound of their footfalls, enabling
him to greet them by name. Boaz is constantly
surrounded by sound and by people.

The townspeople's choric function begins
to take shape when they comment on Boaz's
leniency as a parent. The people of the town are
said to be "joining . . . in the general condemnation of that father's laxity—'the ruination of
the boy!'" Further quotations are provided:
"He should have put him to work, that's what."
"He should have said to Manuel, 'Look here, if
you want a dollar, go earn it first.'" What is
significant is that these snippets of what appear
to be dialogue are not attributed to a particular
person. Instead, they are presented as the kinds
of things that are *generally* said about Boaz and

his relationship with his son. In this sense, the
words become commentary, and the townspeople function as a chorus.

The town's function as a chorus recurs after
the fire destroys Boaz's house. The narrative
notes an "appalling discovery" that "began to
be known. Slowly. By a hint, a breath of
rumour here; there an allusion, half taken
back." Again, the reference is not to a particular character but to a generalized sense of the
town—what the townspeople were saying and
thinking in response to events. Steele thus
presents information not through the narrative
voice of the story but through the voice of the
town, which witnesses the events and comments
on the action.

The town as chorus then takes up the issue
of who the criminal was. After the charred body
is found in the ruins of Boaz's house, a member
of the public, Asa Whitelaw, appears on the
scene to ask the question that other witnesses
have in mind: "Where is Manuel?" Whitelaw
goes on to question Boaz about when he had
last seen his son and to ask whether Boaz and
Manuel knew about the money in Campbell
Wood's possession. He further asks Boaz about
what he heard. Although this dialogue is attributed to a particular character, Steele uses the
words "they" and "them" in connection with
Boaz's responses: "He went on to tell *them*
what he had heard." "Having exhausted his
monosyllabic and superficial evidence, *they*
could move him no farther. . . . He sat before
them. . . . His lack of visible emotion impressed
them." Additionally, the narration states, "Only
once did *they* catch sight of something beyond."
This statement, which foreshadows Boaz's act
of revenge ("something beyond"), again reflects
the insight of the town functioning as a chorus,
commenting on Boaz and on events.

The town's choric function continues in the
aftermath of the crime. Boaz loses his zest for
life. He has become sullen. For a while the
townsmen continue to come to the shop, laughing and boasting, but in time they drift away,
leaving Boaz alone because of his unresponsive-
ness and the lack of cheerfulness that formerly
suffused the shop. Again, rather than telling the
reader about these developments, Steele
describes them as the reactions of the chorus.

During the climactic scene that takes place
when Campbell Wood enters Boaz's shop, the
presence of the community continues to be

made clear, for Boaz can hear feet outside, "ringing on the frozen road; voices were lifted." After Boaz exacts his revenge and attacks Wood, the narration states: "On the road outside, up and down the street for a hundred yards, merrymaking people turned to look at one another." Snippets of dialogue are given as people inquire about the scream they had heard coming from the shop, but again the dialogue— "What was that?" "God's sake! What was that? Where'd it come from?"—is not attributed to anyone in particular. These queries represent the voice of the community as it responds to what they heard. Boaz is puzzled by the beard on the man he attacked and worried that he has wreaked vengeance on an innocent man. As he is shaving off the beard, the townspeople act on their curiosity and break down the door to Boaz's shop. They are then able to confirm that the dead man is Campbell Wood, not Manuel. Again, no one identified by name makes the story's key observation: "Say now, if it don't look like that fellow Wood, himself. The bank fellow—that was burned—remember?" In effect, the reader becomes a member of the town, convinced by partial evidence that the crime that earlier took place in Boaz's house was committed by Manuel and that Wood was the victim. Steele misdirects the reader in just the same way that the townspeople are misdirected, creating in this way the ironic dénouement of the story.

The town as chorus continues its role during the falling action of the story's final paragraphs. It is to point out that "no one ever touched Boaz Negro for that murder. . . . Their minds and imaginations in that town were arrested by the romantic proportions of the act. Simply, no one took it up." Although the Law is circumvented, the chorus renders a verdict. Justice is served, and community norms prevail. Order is restored as Boaz regains his zest for life.

Source: Michael J. O'Neal, Critical Essay on "Footfall," in *Short Stories for Students*, Gale, Cengage Learning, 2017.

Blanche Colton Williams

In the following essay, Williams provides a broad overview of Steele's life and work.

By a pleasant coincidence the American who has received two prizes from a memorial to O. Henry shares with the older writer the birthplace of Greensboro, North Carolina. On

Boaz fears he has not taught his son Manuel the importance of work (©ARENA Creative | Shutterstock.com)

March 17, 1886, four years after Will Porter left his native city, arrived Wilbur Daniel Steele. But whereas O. Henry's parents were at home in the South, and he was throughout his life essentially a Southerner, Mr. Steele's forebears belong to the East and he is himself a citizen of the world. His father, the Rev. Wilbur F., Professor of Biblical Science at the University of Denver, is in turn the son of the late Rev. Daniel, known within and without Massachusetts as a Greek scholar. Wilbur Daniel was born while his father was principal of Bennett Seminary (Greensboro), a position he occupied from 1881 to 1888.

From 1886 to 1907 Mr. Steele profited by the advantages of careful training at home and in the school room. When three years of age, he accompanied his parents to Berlin, at the University of which the Rev. Wilbur pursued his post-graduate studies. Young Steele was placed in the kindergarten of Fräulein Froebel, niece of the great educator. His memory of this

> ALTHOUGH A TRIED DEVICE OF THE STORY-
> TELLER IS THAT OF CREATING A CHARACTER WHO
> GRASPS THE EXTERNAL WORLD THROUGH FEWER
> THAN THE USUAL FIVE SENSES, YET MR. STEELE HAS
> NOT EMPHASIZED THE TRICK IN *THE OTHER SIDE OF
> THE SOUTH*. HE HAS DONE SO IN *FOOTFALLS*."

period is justifiably hazy, nor is it surprising that it has to do not with work but wholly with the fact of his aversion to the fat in the luncheon soup. In 1892 his father was called to the University of Denver, where he still remains, and it was, therefore, in the Western city that Wilbur Daniel received his academic education, attending successively grammar and preparatory schools and the university. As he says, himself, since his ancestors had been theologians it was ordained somewhat inconsequentially that he must become an artist. So it was, partly by choice, partly by coöperation with a sense of destiny, that he began his studies at the art school in Denver, making use of the night school and summer sessions.

After proceeding to his A.B. degree from the university in 1907, he went to the Boston Museum of Fine Arts, where he studied in the life class of Philip Hale, son of Edward Everett; in 1908–1909 he continued at Julien's, in Paris; in 1909–1910 he was a member of the Art Students' League of New York City. Although his taking a number of prizes may be regarded as indicative of ability in the field of pictorial art, Mr. Steele gradually turned to the story form of expression. In this preference he was encouraged by his friend, Mary Heaton Vorse. With only his third attempt at narrative, he achieved the printed page: *Success* accepted *On the Ebb Tide*. He believes, however, that his real start lay in *A Matter of Education* (*Harper's*, 1911). When in 1912 *A White Horse Winter* was published in the *Atlantic Monthly*, it was at once realized, says Edward O'Brien in his introduction to Mr. Steele's first collection of stories, *Land's End*, "that a new talent of great promise had appeared in American short-story literature."

After *A White Horse Winter* followed a series of five narratives set in the imaginary island of Urkey, lying off the North Atlantic coast. Since these were brought out at various times and places they may be recalled here as *White Hands*, *Ching, Ching, Chinaman*, *Wages of Sin*, *Out of Exile*, and *Crocuses*. These and his Provincetown stories, stories wherein the native and the Portuguese divide interest of author and reader, may be put down tentatively as constituting the work of Mr. Steele's first period. A descendant of the *Mayflower* pilgrims, he had turned to the land of the Puritans for his material, and he had found there an unexpected character contrast afforded through the old stock and the new. It is recorded that Longfellow was stirred by the memories of "Spanish sailors with bearded lips," aliens in Portland harbor; it is no less true that Joseph C. Lincoln and Wilbur Daniel Steele have been moved by the juxtaposition of the Latin race and the English in Cape Cod.

To the analyst, these early stories reveal the author's inheritance; his own genius for depicting color, form, mood; and his skill in narrative structure. A strong theological flavor is manifest in the choice of certain of his characters, for example, Minister Malden, of *Ching, Ching*; in biblical references and allusions throughout a number of the stories, as in the title *For They Know not What They Do*, in fragments of church scenes and in echoes of the thunder rolling voice of the Puritan God. But this spirit is tempered and combined with the artist's love for vivid pictures, preferably pictures of the sea in storm. His sympathy with the unrest of nature has further witness in the title of his one novel (*Storm*, 1914). Since, however, our present concern is with his short stories, it need be remarked only that he has not succeeded, as yet, with the longer story, despite prognostications of certain critics, and that his characteristics are best exemplified in his briefer tales.

All the Urkey Island stories are told, logically, as if by "the Means boy" grown to manhood; for as they are of the past they seemed to the author best unfolded by one still living and familiar with that past. Through this boy, then, Mr. Steele delights in recalling the shouting of the Round Hill Bars, a shouting that filled the bowl of the invisible world and rumbled in tangled reverberations: "I could see the outer bar only as a white, distorted line athwart the gray, but the shoreward shallows were writhing, living things, gnawing at the sky with venomous teeth of spume. . . . " In this instance, also, is apparent that fine modulation or harmony whereby the real and the imagined perfectly merge. Says the narrator: "My mother used sometimes to sing a little Portuguese song to my brother Antone, the baby. It had a part which ran—

> The herd of the King's White Horses
> Comes up on the shore to graze . . .

And so well has the author combined the boy's fancy of the ocean in frenzy as that of an animal gnawing with venomous teeth, the reader is hardly aware of the transition whereby the white horses of the bar pass into the splendid white steed that, washed ashore from the wreck, staggered up the face of the dune and stood against the sky. Further, the same tale illustrates the author's sense of structure. The salvation of the white horse would hardly be sufficient for a well rounded tale. With it, therefore, is inwoven the love story of the boy's sister, Agnes Means, and Jem Hodges, the owner of the white stallion. The narrative is not illustrative of Mr. Steele's procedure in composition; for though based on an actual occurrence, it stands alone in this regard. One other story may be excepted, in that the hero of *A Devil of a Fellow*, Va Di, reflects a man of Mr. Steele's acquaintance.

Since in only these two instances has the author drawn upon life immediately, the conclusion is inevitable that he relies almost altogether upon imagination. Place or locale is the usual basis, but the evolution of the building process is confined to the cerebrations of Mr. Steele. He says with too great modesty that this evolution is a matter of mechanics. He determines to write a story and gives himself up to meditation. The story comes. He cannot recall its genesis, save that he develops a mood from which the whole fabric seems to take shape. In former days this manner of creation would have been termed inspirational, a word of more exact application here than the word mechanical, but having always back of it—except in the assertions of literary mediocrity—hard work and knowledge of technique. If his method is in the least mechanical, it is because of the author's reliance upon mood, a mood which he from resolution or perhaps now with the ease of practice rigidly maintains. In 1920

I wrote in the Introduction to *O. Henry Memorial Prize Stories*, Volume I, "The tale predominantly of atmosphere, revealing, wherever found, the ability of the author to hold a dominant mood in which as in a calcium light characters and acts are colored, occurs so rarely as to challenge admiration when it does occur. *For They Know not What They Do* lures the reader into its exotic air and holds him, until he, too, is suffused, convinced." Stevenson practised this procedure, notably in *The Merry Men*, as he has told in one of his essays, nor is the work of Mr. Steele so reminiscent of any other author in this respect. Since he cannot recall following the example of the Scotch writer, however, Mr. Steele resembles him, out of doubt, only because of similar approach in workmanship.

Not Stevenson but Lafcadio Hearn is the writer for whose works Mr. Steele expresses enthusiasm. Between the author of *A Japanese Miscellany* and *Some Chinese Ghosts*, and the author of Provincetown and Urkey Island stories exists no obvious kinship, save in the apprehension and delicate use of the fanciful. Rather will *Down on Their Knees* and *A Devil of a Fellow* demand comparison with the fiction of Mr. Joseph C. Lincoln. Yet this challenge is met in a brief enumeration: Mr. Lincoln writes of another neighborhood in Cape Cod, both men relish the salt of locale and atmosphere, neither draws portraits—if they know it—of the living. Their styles are far apart. If Mr. Steele should ultimately settle upon a particular foreign soil and should emphasize his handling of the fantastic, he would afford reasons for the conclusion that he has, to a degree, profited by study of Hearn. His second period has inaugurated the possibility of such later deduction. As he was moved by the Portuguese of the Massachusetts coast, so he has reflected his visit to Bermuda in *At Two in the Bush*, has written of *Both Judge and Jury* in the West Indies, has forecast a trip to the South Sea Islands in *The Shame Dance*, and has interpreted to readers at home the Arab in Africa.

The Shame Dance, titular story of his second collection, entertains by suggesting the origin of a dance popular toward the close of the second twentieth century decade. It illustrates, further, the grip in which Mr. Steele is held by the magnetizing influence of place, even from afar. It offers an etymology, interesting if not philologically correct, "Shame dance, Shemdance, Shimmie dance."

Perhaps the war had something to do with Mr. Steele's change of locale as a setting, though admittedly he has "finished with Provincetown," to the extent of selling his home there. After the United States entered the conflict Mr. Steele, asked to write articles on the American Naval participation, visited the North Sea, Dunkirk, Brest, and North Ireland. The results he utilized in *Contact!* published in *Harper's*, September, 1919. This work excited provocation among critics who like to consider the question, "What, anyway, is a short story?" Three out of five declared that its finely imagined situation and its maintenance of the struggle placed it in the fiction class and that of the short story in particular. But the editors, when questioned, wrote: "It is a faithful portrayal of the work done by our destroyers and therefore falls under the category of 'articles.'" And the author: "I am not quite sure what to say. *Contact!* was, in a sense, drawn from life, that is to say, it is made up of a number of impressions gained while I was at sea with the U.S. destroyers off the coast of France. The characters are elaborations of real characters, and the 'contact' told of was such a one as I actually witnessed. Otherwise, the chronology of events, conversations, etc., were gathered from various sources and woven to the best of my ability so as to give a picture of the day's work of our convoying forces in the war."

No better instance can be adduced than this for showing the reorganizing habit of the fictionist by which the record of fact is imbued with the feeling and coloring of fancy.

The Dark Hour, a conversation centered on the meaning of the struggle among the nations, was reprinted in O'Brien's anthology of 1918 as one of the best twenty stories of the year. Although it possesses literary merit, it is not a story; moreover, it displays its author in a philosophic rather than artistic state of mind. On his way home from France, Mr. Steele received news of the armistice. Its timeliness having departed, the rest of his war material was lost, temporarily at least, to the world.

In recent years, as has been indicated above, Mr. Steele has left far astern the curving peninsula of Cape Cod. Among the countries he has visited, and which have been summarized in preceding paragraphs, he has found North Africa fertile for his imagination. "Kairwan the Holy lay asleep, pent in its thick walls.

The moon had sunk at midnight, but the chill light seemed scarcely to have diminished; only the lime-washed city had become a marble city, and all the towers turned fabulous in the fierce dry needly rain of the stars that burn over the desert of mid-Tunisia." The story, *A Marriage in Kairwan*, presents the crisis in the life of an Arabian lady who elects for herself her lover's standard of morality, a standard, as the outcome tragically reveals, one for his sex alone. The thread of the narrative may be a trifle thin, though somewhat strengthened by the terminal shock (nowise dulled because the reader is subtly prepared for it), and it runs through a warp and woof Orientally splendid, heavy as cloth of gold.

Akin to this story are *The Anglo-Saxon*, *East and West*, *He That Hideth His Secret*, and *The Other Side of the South*. Tales of Arabian nights and days, they have in common with his preceding stories the elements of the strange and the fanciful. As in *The Woman at Seven Brothers* the ghost became for the author the best possible form of fairy tale, as in *Guiablesse* the jealousy of a ship for a woman constitutes the cause for conflict, so in *The Anglo-Saxon* the vision of the sands and the palm trees is the flotsam of memory by which the Anglo-Saxon recovers all his past.

He That Hideth His Secret brings together the Arabian and New York City, as *The Other Side of the South* performs a *tour de force* in a Civil War story. Over in Africa survives a blind one-time slave, whose story is told by the nephew leading him from place to place. It is the more diverting as a Steele story, in that the author has never revisited, in all his wanderings, the land of his birth; it apprehends the South of slavery through the author's interest in North Africa. A mighty compass, but he has fetched it round.

Although a tried device of the story-teller is that of creating a character who grasps the external world through fewer than the usual five senses, yet Mr. Steele has not emphasized the trick in *The Other Side of the South*. He has done so in *Footfalls*. Boaz Negro lived in one of those old Puritan sea-towns, which has become of late years an outpost of the Portuguese Islands. When in spite of blindness he relies on his ability to distinguish footfalls, he sets up suspense which is terminated only at the redemption of his son's name. Boaz's killing of the villain who had brought about the dishonor of that son is perhaps the best instance of surprise in all the narratives, if *For They Know not What They Do* is excepted. The latter story presents a most poignant instance of sacrifice: a mother, lovely and virtuous, recognizes that the curse of insanity obsesses her son. He has discovered that his father and his father's father committed crimes, knowing not what they did. His own life seems doomed. To save him from himself the mother avers that her dead husband was not his father. Of course, he learns long after that she had lied gallantly; but, then, his mother, from whom he had withdrawn himself, was dead.

Ordinarily, surprise is a tool this author handles with not more than casual concern for its incisiveness. His management of a single vivid moment is frequently more compelling. For instance, in *A Man's a Fool*, the narrator is rehearsing the struggle he and his brother Raphael endured with the *Flores*, and he has reached the point where the boom had broken Raphael's back: " . . . I get down beside my brother and I give him a kiss, and I see tears running down his face, and they was mine. And I says to him:

"'Wait! You're all right, Raphael boy. You'll be all right and you ain't hurt bad. It's all right, Raphael boy. Only you wait here quiet a second while I heave over that anchor and I'll be back.'

"I give him another kiss on the cheek, and then I tumble up forward and heave that anchor over. It never take me no time. I was back like that. But yet what little sea there was had shift him a mite on the deck, and I see my brother was dead."

The passage is rescued from the sentimentality, which might be otherwise charged to it, by the previous long struggle between the two brothers over a woman. This is the resolution of the problem.

In 1922 Mr. Steele first came into extraordinary recognition when the O. Henry Memorial Committee awarded him a special prize for supremacy in story writing from the year 1919 to 1921, inclusive. They summed up his abilities as lying in an individual temperament that invests the real with the color of romance, in a sense of correct architecture, in the happy knowledge of unique situations, in the climactic development of struggle or complication, in the

power to move the reader's emotions, and in a satisfactory dénouement. All these characteristics are manifest in tales marked by a distinctive style, a style dependent upon seizure and conveyance of atmosphere. . . .

Source: Blanche Colton Williams, "Wilbur Daniel Steele," in *Our Short Story Writers*, Books for Libraries Press, 1922, pp. 372–84.

SOURCES

Allen, Paul, Review of *Tower of Sand and Other Stories*, in *Bookman*, December 1929, pp. 448–49.

Brewster, Dorothy, ed., *A Book of Modern Short Stories*, Macmillan, 1928, p. 478.

Bucco, Martin, *Wilbur Daniel Steele*, Twayne Publishers, 1972, pp. 17–39, 111, 160, 163.

"Chorus," in *Merriam Webster's Encyclopedia of Literature*, Merriam-Webster, 1995, p. 239.

Elser, Frank B., "Oh, Yes . . . Wilbur Daniel Steele," in *Bookman*, February 1926, pp. 691–94.

Krahulik, Karen, *Provincetown: From Pilgrim Landing to Gay Resort*, NYU Press, 2007, pp. 58–59.

Matos, Carolina, "Portuguese Americans Are Organized and Well," in *Portuguese American Journal*, April 13, 2011, http://portuguese-american-journal.com/portuguese-americans-are-organized-and-well-connected/ (accessed February 16, 2016).

Motawi, Wade K., *How Shoes Are Made: A Behind the Scenes Look at a Real Shoe Factory*, CreateSpace, 2015.

Norden, Ernest E., "Portuguese Americans," in *Countries and Their Cultures*, http://www.everyculture.com/multi/Pa-Sp/Portuguese-Americans.html (accessed February 16, 2016).

O'Brien, Edward J., Introduction to *Land's End and Other Stories*, by Wilbur Daniel Steele, Harper & Brothers, 1918, p. xiii.

"Ponta Delgada, Azores: History of the Consulate," Consulate of the United States website, http://azores.usconsulate.gov/history.html (accessed February 21, 2016).

Santos, Robert L., "Azorean Immigration into the United States," http://www.library.csustan.edu/bsantos/immigr.html (accessed February 16, 2016).

Seesholtz, Mel, "Wilbur Daniel Steele," in *American Short-Story Writers, 1910–1945: First Series*, edited by Bobby Ellen Kimbel, Gale Research, 1989.

Steele, Wilbur Daniel, "Footfalls," in *A Book of Modern Short Stories*, edited by Dorothy Brewster, Macmillan, 1928, pp. 356–77.

Thomas, June, "Do We Still Need Gay Resorts like Provincetown?," in *Slate*, July 30, 2014, http://www.slate.com/

blogs/outward/2014/07/30/provincetown_fire_island
_asbury_park_rehoboth_beach_do_we_still_need_gay.
html (accessed February 16, 2016).

Walser, Richard, "Steele, Wilbur Daniel," in *NCpedia*,
1994, http://ncpedia.org/biography/steele-wilbur-daniel
(accessed February 16, 2016).

Williams, Blanche Colton, *Our Short Story Writers*,
Moffat, Yard, 1922, pp. 383–84.

FURTHER READING

Bucco, Martin, *Wilbur Daniel Steele*, Twayne Publishers, 1972.

> This volume, part of Twayne's U.S. Authors Series, is the only book-length treatment of Steele and his work. Readers will find extensive biographical information, along with commentary on most of Steele's published work.

Daley, James, ed., *The World's Greatest Short Stories*,
Dover Publications, 2006.

> Readers interested in an international perspective on the short story will find this compact collection useful. The volume contains selections from the nineteenth and twentieth centuries, and although it includes some American authors (Herman Melville, John Updike, Ernest Hemingway, and others), it also includes numerous selections from South America, Europe, Africa, and Asia.

Thomas, James, Robert Shapard, and Christopher Merrill, eds., *Flash Fiction International: Very Short Stories from around the World*, Norton, 2015.

> A contemporary form the short story has taken is that of "flash fiction," that is, very short stories—usually no more than 750 words—that tend to be highly experimental in form. This collection contains eighty-six examples of flash fiction by authors from around the world, including Israeli writer Etgar Keret, Zimbabwean writer Petina Gappah, Korean screenwriter Kim Young-ha, Nobel Prize winner Czeslaw Milosz, and Argentinian "Queen of the Microstory" Ana María Shua, among many others.

Updike, John, and Katrina Kenison, eds., *The Best American Short Stories of the Century*, Mariner Books, 2000.

> To compile this collection, Updike and Kenison sifted through some two thousand stories, ultimately providing this chronological arrangement of short stories spanning the years 1915 to 1999. Among the stories included are those by Ernest Hemingway, William Faulkner, Willa Cather, F. Scott Fitzgerald, Tennessee Williams, J. F. Powers, and Eudora Welty, along with more recent stories by Philip Roth, Saul Bellow, Donald Barthelme, Raymond Carver, Tim O'Brien, Bernard Malamud, Cynthia Ozick, John Cheever, Vladimir Nabokov, and others.

SUGGESTED SEARCH TERMS

American short story

Azores

Menino Jesus

O. Henry

O. Henry Prize

Portuguese Americans

Provincetown, Massachusetts

Steele AND "Footfalls"

Wilbur Daniel Steele

The Hunter's Wife

ANTHONY DOERR

2001

"The Hunter's Wife" is a short story by Anthony Doerr. It was first published in *Atlantic Monthly* in 2001 and was reprinted a year later in Doerr's short-story collection *The Shell Collector*. The story concerns a hunter living in Montana who falls in love with and marries a magician's assistant. Over the course of several brutal winters in the hunter's cabin, the woman develops psychic abilities, which leads to their separation. "The Hunter's Wife" is Doerr's first published work, written while he was living in the mountains of Telluride, Colorado, two years after finishing college. It brought him immediate recognition and was an O. Henry Prize Story in 2002. Doerr's fiction is known for its rich and carefully accurate detail, the result of his love of research. "The Hunter's Wife" demonstrates this attention to detail and marks it as a feature of Doerr's work from the beginning of his career.

AUTHOR BIOGRAPHY

Doerr was born in Cleveland, Ohio, in 1973 and raised in the nearby township of Novelty. His mother was a high school science teacher, and his father ran a small printing company. "In my parents' house," Doerr states,

> books tower atop pretty much every piece of furniture: on the toilet tanks, inside kitchen cabinets, even on Dad's workbench in the basement. . . . So I grew up in a world where books

Anthony Doerr *(©Ulf Andersen / Getty Images)*

were both totemic and ubiquitous: On Wednesday nights, my brothers and I were allowed to bring books to the dinner table and read while we ate.

Despite this, books come last in his description of a youth spent "riding bikes, fishing, wandering through the woods, burning ants with a magnifying glass (sorry, ants). And reading." The young Doerr's room was decorated with maps and pictures of mountains and deserts. Travel and rock climbing were early passions, and his mother encouraged an interest in nature and science, quizzing him, for example, about the mollusks he found on trips to the beach. At a private school for boys, Doerr was introduced to literary classics, and he was writing at the age of nine. In college, he majored in history and English, earning a master of fine arts degree, but he also

> prioritized travel and as soon as I started working, I started saving money for trips. My first job was on a horse farm when I was 14: $5 an hour. Then a busboy. Then a cook. Then I worked in a salmon processing facility in Alaska—that sort of stuff.

Doerr started writing in earnest in high school, keeping a journal for a class in his junior year:

My friends would make fun of me—you're doing your man diary again. . . . But I didn't start writing seriously until I was 22, writing at night after work. It wasn't until I was 26 or 25 when I started sending work out to magazines. . . . It wasn't instantaneous, at all. I was getting a lot of rejections.

With the publication of "The Hunter's Wife" in *Atlantic Monthly* in 2001, Doerr began earning widespread public recognition. Since then, Doerr's work has earned multiple awards, including the 2015 Pulitzer Prize for Fiction for his novel *All the Light We Cannot See*, the 2010 Story Prize, and the 2011 *Sunday Times* EFG Short Story Award. Four of his stories have won the O. Henry Prize. His short stories and essays have been anthologized many times.

PLOT SUMMARY

"The Hunter's Wife" opens as the hunter of the title is flying into Chicago, having left Montana for the first time in his life. He is going there to see his wife, whom he has not seen in twenty years. From the airport, he is driven to the local university and dropped off at the chancellor's residence, a mansion, where a gathering of some sort is about to begin. He meets Bruce Maples, the director of the university athletics program. Maples points out a thin elderly man in the room with them, President O'Brien, and refers to (but does not describe) a terrible tragedy that has befallen the president.

The story then flashes back to a winter evening in Montana in 1972. The season is marked by unusually strong winds. As the hunter makes his way through the town of Great Falls, an especially powerful gust forces him into an alley and presses him against the window of a church, where he sees a magic show in progress. The magician is helping his assistant, a young woman, into a plywood coffin and saws the coffin in half. When the halves are wheeled apart, the assistant is able to wiggle her toes.

The hunter is struck by the assistant's beauty and begins to court her, following her and the magician from town to town for several days until she agrees to eat with him at a hotel restaurant. During the meal, he tells her that he hunts and when not hunting dreams about it. She tells him that she dreams about magic. She returns to Great Falls to be sawed in half again the next year and the year after that. On both occasions, the hunter takes her out to eat.

After she turns eighteen, the young woman accompanies the hunter to his remote cabin. They arrive at the beginning of winter. It is twenty degrees below zero, and soon the roads will be impassable. Once they have settled in, the hunter takes her on snowshoes to see a grizzly bear hibernating in a hollow cedar. They listen to the bear breathing. The hunter carefully pulls away the snow to expose the bear's fur, warning the woman to be very quiet. To his shock, she touches the fur and buries her face in it. When she pulls her face away, she describes the bear's winter dreams to the hunter. Back at the cabin, the hunter is struck by how out of his element he is in their budding relationship.

The story returns to the mysterious gathering at the chancellor's mansion. The hunter studies the increasing number of guests, wondering "what strange curiosities and fears" have driven them there. He and Bruce Maples continue talking, but there is no real understanding between them.

In a second flashback to their initial winter together, the young woman describes the hunter's own forgotten dreams to him, telling him that he is a wolf in every dream. One morning they go skating along the river and discover a dead heron standing upright in the ice, its beak frozen open in death. She lays her hands on the bird and goes into a sort of trance. That evening she tells the hunter that she "saw where [the bird] went when she died," describing an afterlife consisting of a lake where a hundred herons in the shallows watch the sunrise together. The hunter is worried that winter and isolation are affecting her mental state, so he takes her out one evening to look at the atmospheric phenomenon known as the northern lights. She sees an image of a hawk in the lights. The hunter explains that the lights are caused by charged particles in a solar wind interacting with nitrogen and oxygen in the earth's atmosphere, but she stands by her impression.

Throughout that winter, the hunter takes the woman out every day. He shows her hibernating ladybugs, frogs asleep in the frozen mud, and a "globe of honeybees," which he pulls from its hive and places in her hands. This triggers another trance in which she sees the bees' dreams, and over the rest of the winter, she explores and refines her ability to see the dreams of sleeping animals and the afterlives of newly dead ones by touching them. The hunter's perceptions of the world that winter consist of wolf tracks, owls hunting, and other physical details while the woman sees "burrowed dreamers nestled under the roots against the long twilight," but he loves her, and in the spring, they marry.

The story returns to the present. The hunter's wife arrives at the gathering, and he notes how she has changed since he last saw her twenty years ago: "refined, less wild, and somehow, to the hunter, worse for it." Everyone in the room marks her arrival; she is the guest of honor. The hunter senses her isolation from the others, but when she notices him over dinner, she looks at him warmly for a moment.

A third flashback introduces the hunter's profession: a hunting guide to lawyers, politicians, and other clients. He loves the valley and his life there, but his wife finds herself bored now that winter is over and she can exercise her newfound abilities only occasionally, as when he teaches her to clean trout and she sees their "final, ecstatic visions." He continues hunting with his clients through the fall, while she sleeps as much as possible.

The next winter is especially bitter. Everywhere the hunter sees animals dying in the cold; every night he dreams of being a wolf. In February, coyotes break in to the crawl space under the cabin, where the hunter stores food for the winter. The hunter, hearing them, rushes to the crawl space entrance and fires an entire quiver of arrows into the darkness. When the coyotes charge him, he draws a knife and fights back as they bite and claw.

When the confrontation is over, the hunter, wounded and desperate, digs his truck out of the snow for a trip to Great Falls to replace the food the coyotes have raided. But the crust of ice over the snow is too thin to drive on for more than a few miles before the truck breaks through. The hunter digs the truck free, drives, and again sinks into the snow several more times before finally abandoning the truck. He builds a fire and attempts to rest next to it but realizes that he may fall asleep and freeze to death. He makes the journey back to the cabin, occasionally crawling on his hands and knees from exhaustion. When he gets there, he discovers his wife kneeling on the floor with ice in her hair "lost in some kind of hypothermic torpor."

The couple manages to survive the rest of the winter on a meager diet of fish, squirrel, hare, and ultimately the roots of cattails. During this time, emaciated and starving, the wife continues to develop her mysterious gift. When the roads are passable once again, the hunter takes her to town to buy groceries, eat at the diner, and go to the library, where she checks out twenty books.

This begins her research into the paranormal. Every week the hunter goes to the post office to pick up "essays about sorcery, primers on magic-working and conjury that had to be mail-ordered from New Hampshire, New Orleans, even Italy." When they find a bull elk frozen to death in November, she lays her hands on it and tells the hunter she can see where the elk has gone. The hunter denies that this is possible.

A few months later a snowplow driver slides off a bridge in Great Falls and crashes into the river forty feet below. The driver dies before a group of would-be rescuers can save him, but the hunter's wife is among them and touches the dead body. She has a vision of the dead man riding a bicycle down a tree-lined lane, his son in a child's seat behind him,

touching his hair. Several men in the crowd who touch the woman during the rescue share the vision: "All you had to do was *touch* her, a barber said, and you saw it too." Word about her gift spreads rapidly through the town.

The gossip eventually reaches the hunter, who believes his wife has worked a trick of some kind and does not accept her explanations that she has not. People begin calling to ask that she demonstrate her ability for them. At first the hunter hangs up on them, but eventually he agrees to drive her to a funeral parlor to visit a grieving father. These trips become routine, though the hunter maintains his disbelief in his wife's psychic talents. Families begin giving her money for a session with her, and throughout the following year, the hunter and his wife feel increasingly disconnected from each other. She receives more and more calls and now drives herself to visit people, occasionally fantasizing about leaving her husband. His business suffers as his loneliness distracts him from hunts and makes him short-tempered with his clients.

While the wife is away, the hunter discovers six thousand dollars in her boot. He angrily confronts her on her return. He insists that she is taking advantage of people and calls her gift a con. She tells him he is wrong, and he responds by again accusing her of being a swindler. He throws the money out of the cabin, where a wind scatters it across the snow. She hits him and laments, "You, of all people, should understand. You who dream of wolves every night."

The next evening, she follows him in secret to his deer stand and waits until he fires an arrow at a doe. She then follows him as he tracks it. When the hunter slits the deer's throat, the wife comes out of hiding and grabs his wrist and the doe's foreleg. This enables the hunter to see the wife's vision of the doe's afterlife: fifty deer wading in a sunlit brook. The hunter struggles to free himself from her grip but is overwhelmed by this "world washed in amber" before he breaks loose and runs home. When she returns to their cabin, hours later, he warns her to stay away from him. Over the next few months, she is gone more and more frequently, until one day she drives away from him forever, after five years of marriage.

Watching a diner television twenty years later, the hunter sees his wife being interviewed. She has become famous, a world traveler in demand everywhere for her talent, and has written two books. The next morning he buys both of her books. After reading them, he writes her a letter. In response, she sends him a plane ticket to Chicago and a brief letter inviting him to come if he likes.

The story returns to the chancellor's mansion for the last time. The guests are ushered into the reception room, where three caskets rest on the carpet. The hunter's wife enters and motions for President O'Brien to sit beside her. As she begins talking about life and death, beauty and loss, the guests join hands, and when the vision begins, the hunter participates in it, finding himself on a beach where two girls are building a sand castle while their mother lies nearby, drinking iced tea. They are the president's wife and daughters. When the vision ends, many people are crying, including O'Brien.

The hunter slips out a side door and makes his way through the falling snow to a pond. His wife joins him there, and though he has thought of many things he would like to say to her, he refrains from speaking. They stand in silence for some time, and the story ends as he reaches for her hand.

CHARACTERS

Chancellor's Wife
The hunter has a brief interaction with the chancellor's wife when he arrives at the mansion for his wife's performance at the beginning of the story.

Dumas
The hunter's last name, Dumas, is mentioned twice near the beginning of the story, but he is otherwise referred to only as the hunter.

The hunter has lived his entire life in Montana and makes his living as a hunting guide in a remote valley near the town of Great Falls. Hunting, the wilderness, and survival, especially in the winter, are the most important elements of his life, and in these areas, he is extremely capable. His skill, strength, and determination are well illustrated in his confrontation with a pack of coyotes. Though badly wounded, he kills or maims many of them with arrows and a knife. His subsequent journey through the snowbound wilderness marks him as a man who occupies the boundary between life and death.

The hunter is an acute observer of even the smallest details in the woods around his home. He recognizes and appreciates natural beauty; however, he is also a realist, unable, for example, to see or appreciate the image of a hawk in the northern lights that his wife tries to point out to him. These two qualities—vulnerability to beauty and an exclusive focus on the world of concrete physical detail—lead him to fall in love with, and lose, the magician's assistant.

The woman's beauty strikes the hunter so deeply that he pursues her across Montana, almost as if she were an animal he was hunting, and after a winter's romance, he marries her. Although she can appreciate his relationship to the world and his motivations, he fails to appreciate hers, growing increasingly suspicious of her developing psychic abilities, to the point of calling her a swindler. Even when their relationship ends, however, he cannot let go of her. Over the twenty years between her departure and their reunion in Chicago, he never becomes involved with another woman. Only in Chicago, after two decades, is he finally able to allow himself to see the world through her eyes.

Bruce Maples
Bruce Maples is the athletics program director at the university where the hunter's wife has been invited to demonstrate her paranormal abilities. He and the hunter meet at the chancellor's mansion and engage in small talk, but he has little understanding of or interest in the hunter's life.

President O'Brien
President O'Brien, a "tall, remarkably thin man," appears "as if he were visiting from some other, leaner world" when he is first pointed out to the hunter. His wife and two daughters have died recently in a terrible but undescribed tragedy, and the hunter's wife has been invited to use her gift to enable him to see them briefly and share in their afterlife.

Mary Roberts
The name Mary Roberts, like that of the hunter, is mentioned only twice; otherwise, she is referred to as the hunter's wife, she, or her.

The hunter first meets the woman who becomes his wife when she is a sixteen-year-old magician's assistant. This young woman already shows an interest in worlds beyond the visible one: when the hunter tells her, on their first date, that he dreams about hunting, she responds that she dreams about magic. Her sensitivity to other worlds is apparent early in their relationship when, ignoring the hunter's frantic warnings, she buries her face in the fur of a sleeping bear and describes what the bear is dreaming and when she describes to the hunter his own forgotten dreams about being a wolf. As the story progresses, her ability develops to the point of seeing the various "heavens" to which animals and even people go after death, which she can perceive simply by laying her hands on a recently dead body.

Her focus on these other worlds makes the woman at first completely dependent on the hunter for survival in their isolated cabin. But with time, her gift brings her to the attention of the outside world, and she gains a measure of independence as people pay her for sharing her gift with them. They can see the afterlives of their loved ones simply by touching her as she touches the bodies of the dead. This increasingly alienates her from her husband, who accuses her of swindling emotionally vulnerable people.

In the face of his unwillingness to believe in her, the wife leaves to pursue her own life. After two decades, during which she has achieved fame and fortune through her gift, she is able to bring the hunter to Chicago. By doing so she turns the story of their initial courtship inside out: instead of being pursued as in a hunt, she draws him to her.

Marlin Spokes

Spokes is the snowplow driver who dies in an accident. When the hunter's wife touches his body, she has a vision of him bicycling with his son. People in the crowd who are touching her also see the vision.

Tony Vespucci

Vespucci is the magician for whom the hunter's wife works as an assistant.

THEMES

Marriage

At its core, "The Hunter's Wife" is the story of a marriage and the causes of its destruction. The hunter and his wife are two very different people living in close quarters under conditions of isolation and extreme hardship, but these facts by themselves do not necessarily threaten their marriage. To survive the hardships they endure over several winters, they rely on each other for love and protection. She seems to appreciate both the life he has carved out of the wilderness for himself and his skill at navigating its dangers. He is fascinated both by her different approach to this same life (as when she buries her face in the sleeping bear's fur) and by her physical beauty.

What leads to the end of the relationship are the different stages of personal growth of both characters when they meet and the difficulty those stages pose for the hunter. He has never left Montana, and for the entirety of the narrative—which spans twenty-seven years—he occupies the same small valley. He has reached a high degree of both self-mastery and mastery over his environment, but anything beyond the boundaries of that world provokes his discomfort or suspicion. The young woman he marries, by contrast, is still in the process of discovering herself and her place in the world, which leads her to test and see past the mere physical realities of northern Montana. Her future as a celebrity and world traveler is forecast by her development in their little cabin in the woods, and that development proves too difficult for the hunter to cope with.

The more fundamental dynamic of people at odds with one another is illustrated at many points in the story. When the hunter briefly meets the chancellor's wife, she tells him that her husband is busy knotting his bow tie "and laughed sadly to herself, as if bow ties were something she disapproved of." Bruce Maples, the director of the athletics program, fundamentally misunderstands the nature of the hunter's profession and does little to hide his waning interest in their conversation. The hunter's wife, when she first appears at the chancellor's mansion, appears anxious about touching anyone or anything.

Nevertheless, the story's time line is framed by the hunter's need for connection with the title character, opening with his instant and intense attraction to her from the other side of a window and ending almost thirty years later as he reaches for her hand.

Tolerance

The story's major theme of the end of a relationship hinges on the subtheme of the hunter's

TOPICS FOR FURTHER STUDY

- In one passage, the hunter experiences a vision of a doe's afterlife when his wife grasps his arm while it dies. This passage does not appear in the story as originally published in the *Atlantic Monthly*; it is a later addition in Doerr's short-story collection *The Shell Collector*. Changes to an already published work are uncommon. Write an essay exploring how this addition changes the reader's perceptions of the hunter and his wife, and explaining why Doerr may have felt compelled to add it.

- One of the hunter's clients wounds but does not kill an antelope. When the hunter angrily tells him that wolves will harass it to death, the client responds that there have not been any wolves in the area for twenty years. Write a paper about the wolf and its place in the American imagination. Include information relevant to "The Hunter's Wife." How and why has the wolf population changed in Montana over the last hundred years? What cultural significance does the wolf have, and what particular significance might it have for the hunter? Include the place of the wolf in the Native American and Latin American worldviews.

- The passage detailing how the hunter and his wife survive winter after coyotes destroy their supplies of food illustrates Doerr's love of research, as when they eat rose hips and cattail roots, with which experienced foragers of wild edibles are well acquainted. Write your own short story of survival in which you describe your use of the wild edibles available in your region (and any other survival tips you wish to include, such as the best local materials for a primitive shelter). A number of websites describe the edible and medicinal plants of different regions; https://www.trails.com/outdoor-survival.html is one possible starting point.

- The hunter loses his wife but is unable to move on from her. She leaves him, on the other hand, to console others who have suffered loss and to help them move on. Research and write a paper on the psychology of bereavement, which is the period of grief and mourning after a death. In what ways does the death of a loved one leave friends and family members vulnerable? In what ways can it strengthen them? What are some of the methods by which people come to terms with such a loss and move forward from it?

- The relationship at the heart of the story begins in 1972. Over the next twenty-seven years the hunter watches as civilization slowly changes his beloved wilderness. Using an application such as PowerPoint, create a slide show of the changing environment of a region significant to you: your town, the area your family emigrated from, a favorite camping spot, or a place you would like to visit. Track the changes from around the time of your birth to the present day. Include maps, before-and-after photographs, time lines, and any other graphic information you think would be useful.

- The hunter's wife, though her story is radically different, shares certain characteristics with a woman from another era: Joan of Arc. Both are young female visionaries who are mistrusted by the men around them. Read *Beyond the Myth: The Story of Joan of Arc* (1999), a biography of Saint Joan for young adults by Polly Schoyer Brooks. In an essay, compare the two central characters in terms of their position in a male-dominated world, their separate journeys toward self-realization, and the two very different outcomes of their lives.

narrow-mindedness. His abilities as a hunter and survivor and his appreciation for the beauty of his dangerous world contrast starkly to his inability to appreciate his wife's talents as a visionary. These are two sides of his earthbound nature, and they result in both the marriage at the heart of the story and its failure. The images she sees in the northern lights are invisible to him, merely a puzzling flight of fancy, one more thing about his wife that makes him feel out of his element. But what starts as a simple difference in perception grows more and more troublesome for him: he sees her paranormal abilities first as evidence of mental disorder and later as dishonesty and outright fraud. "The Hunter's Wife" ends on a note of personal redemption whereby the hunter eventually overcomes his narrow-mindedness to accept and appreciate his wife's abilities.

Self-realization

The hunter's wife is only sixteen when the hunter first glimpses her through a window. She is remarkably self-possessed for her age, but she has yet to discover who she really is. Her journey toward self-realization sets the narrative in motion and lays the groundwork for the conflict at the center of the story. In contrast to the hunter, the woman is wide-eyed and open to the world in all its aspects, including those invisible to most people. Over the course of the five winters the couple lives together, her talents mature, her receptive nature is refined, and she invests more and more of her time pushing the limits of her abilities. This process leaves the hunter by turns baffled and frustrated and eventually antagonistic toward her. His resentment is not enough, however, to turn her away from the path she is on. Reaching her full potential is important enough to her that when her husband's narrow-mindedness becomes an obstacle to it, she makes up her mind to leave him. Her abandonment of the relationship is critical to her self-realization.

STYLE

Imagery

The term *imagery* refers to descriptive language used to appeal to the reader's senses, and critics have widely admired Doerr's precise, vivid imagery. For example, when he describes the terrible wind that blows across Montana one winter, Doerr does not merely tell the reader that

The hunting guide first spies his future wife through the window of a church (©ThelmaElaine | Shutterstock.com)

it is powerful. He illustrates its force by writing that it "flung thrushes screaming into the gorse and impaled them on the thorns in grotesque attitudes." The young woman's visions frequently feature light and its treasure-like qualities. Of one deer wading through a brook in the afterlife, Doerr writes, "A silver bead of water hung from its muzzle, caught the sun, and fell."

These are visual images, but Doerr makes sure to gratify the other senses as well, as when the title character encounters a hibernating bear. It smells

> like wet dog, like wild mushrooms. . . . She felt the soft silver tips of fur brush her cheeks. Against her nose one huge rib flexed slightly. She heard the lungs fill and then empty. She heard blood slug through veins.

Point of View

Point of view is the narrative perspective from which a literary work is presented to the reader. Doerr wrote this story using the third person, largely from the perspective of the hunter but sometimes from that of the wife. The technique allows the reader to experience both the hunter's skewed perceptions of his wife and her actual motivations, as when she agonizes over her inability to explain her experiences to him: "How could she tell him? How could she ask him to understand such a thing? How could anyone understand?" But her point of view in the narrative is rare. For the most part, the story is told through the hunter's eyes, so that she remains a mystery to the reader almost as much as to the hunter.

Metaphor

A metaphor defines one object in terms of a second object to express an idea. For example, on the hunter's flight to Chicago, he observes "the long braids of a river gleaming at the bottom of a canyon." This metaphor gives the water the quality of a woman's hair. It is an especially fitting metaphor, because the purpose of his journey is to see his wife for the first time in twenty years. Later in the story, when Doerr describes their first evening together sitting by the fireplace, he writes, "The hunter watched the fire, the flames cutting and sawing, each log a burning bridge." The expression *to burn one's bridges* suggests cutting off ties to something in one's past. The hunter has been anticipating this day for three years, but the day's events, and the young woman's nature, have been nothing like his expectations, so the metaphor of the burning bridge is a particularly appropriate one.

Simile

Closely related to a metaphor, a simile is a comparison, usually with the word *like* or *as*, of two essentially dissimilar things. Writing about the chancellor's wife, Doerr describes "her hand, a pale bony thing, weightless, like a featherless bird," suggesting powerlessness or loss. Of the hunter's experience of the wind just before seeing the magician's assistant, Doerr writes, "Like a wrestler the wind held him against the window." Doerr ends the story with a simile much like this one, as the hunter and his wife stand next to a pond "where their own reflected images trembled like two people trapped against the glass of a parallel world."

Motifs

A motif is a theme, character type, image, metaphor, or other verbal element that recurs throughout a work of literature. Winter, snow, and ice are dominant motifs in "The Hunter's Wife": the story begins and ends with them and is filled with images of snow and ice. Warmer seasons are described very briefly by comparison and are boring to the hunter's wife. "In winter," Doerr writes, "in that valley, life and death were not so different," and both she and the hunter live most fully on the line between life and death—she through her visions and he through his instinct for survival. Other motifs include the difficulty or inability of people to establish meaningful connections with one another and the constant juxtaposition of life and death.

Flashback

"The Hunter's Wife" is structured around a series of flashbacks. The time and place at the beginning of the story (Chicago in 1999) change after only three pages to an earlier time and different place (northern Montana in 1972). This jumping back in time is called a flashback. In this story, the purpose of the hunter's presence at a mysterious gathering in Chicago is slowly made clear through four lengthy flashbacks chronicling the evolution of the relationship between him and his wife.

Foreshadowing

Foreshadowing is a device used to create expectation or to set up an explanation of later developments. When the hunter first sees the young woman whom he will later marry, she is a magician's assistant and is sawed in half as part of an act, remaining alive as if by miracle. This foreshadows her later ability to move back and forth between the world of the living and the world of the dead. Several evenings later, when the hunter persuades the woman to have dinner with him, he says he understands how the illusion is performed. Doerr writes, "She laughed. Is that what you do? she asked. Follow a girl to four towns to tell her her magic isn't real?" This exchange foreshadows the fatal challenge to their marriage when the hunter cannot accept the reality of her visions.

HISTORICAL CONTEXT

"The Hunter's Wife" was published in May 2001, while Doerr was living in Telluride, Colorado, soon after finishing college. Of his college course load, he says that he

COMPARE
&
CONTRAST

- **1970s:** America's counterculture has created the back-to-the-land movement, which focuses on a deeper connection to nature. The era also marks the dawn of the New Age and its focus on varieties of spirituality, including practices such as astrology and channeling.

  2001: Rural communities begun in the 1970s still exist, but the environmental movement has turned its attention to sources of green energy and other ways to combat climate change. The New Age increasingly shows a political dimension with a focus on ethics and their application to everyday life.

  Today: Urban populations in the United States are growing faster than rural ones, a trend that has held steady overall for decades. The term *New Age* has somewhat negative connotations for many; its adherents focus increasingly on both personal development and improving the general state of the world.

- **1970s:** The United States is undergoing a time of intense political turmoil. An oil crisis and gas shortage, protests against the war in Vietnam, the Watergate scandal, and socially progressive movements like feminism and environmentalism transform the political landscape.

  2001: The dawn of the twenty-first century is a rocky period. George W. Bush is sworn into office after an extraordinary electoral controversy, months before the terrorist attacks of September 11, which trigger the signing of the Patriot Act and other transformative moments in US government.

  Today: America is living with the aftermath of September 11 and its military engagements in the Middle East, inherited by President Barack Obama. Terrorism is an overriding concern for many, matched closely by a broad sense of financial insecurity. There is a wide distrust of government and concern across the political spectrum over civil liberties, including gun rights and voting rights.

- **1970s:** In contrast to the back-to-the-land movement, the so-called space race between the United States and the Soviet Union is winding down. Genetic engineering makes its first appearance, and the era is regarded as the dawn of modern computing; VCRs, microwave ovens, and cell phones are developed.

  2001: Work on genetic engineering and mapping makes huge strides. Computers and cell phones are becoming standard items in American households, aided by the advance of nanotechnology. The first artificial heart is implanted in a human being. Space programs in the United States and Russia are working together.

  Today: Concern about climate change increases in the scientific community. Medical developments include the creation of human muscle in a lab, an HIV vaccine, and the first new antibiotic in thirty years, of special interest because of antibiotic-resistant bacteria. Space exploration continues, marked by a satellite fly-by of Pluto, the confirmation of water on Mars, and the discovery of a so-called second Earth fourteen hundred light-years away.

---

managed to sneak in Russian and constitutional law and architecture and environmental science 101. All of which meant that when I graduated, my friends went and got jobs and I drove to Telluride, Colo., and cooked calamari in a deep fryer and skied moguls every day for 80 days straight.

Telluride was once a silver-mining camp and is still surrounded by old mines, along with steep mountain slopes, cliffs, and forests. Mining remained its sole industry until the 1970s, when it began developing a reputation as a destination for skiers. At this time its

The beautiful woman works as a magician's assistant, and the guide follows her to several performances to woo her (©*Andrey_Popov / Shutterstock.com*)

population changed, becoming younger and more idealistic, largely opposed to economic expansion and growth. It has remained a small town—the population in 2001 was just over twenty-three hundred—while managing to become a well-known ski resort and home to a world-famous film festival.

In January, Telluride's temperature drops to an average of two degrees above zero Fahrenheit, and the area typically sees over fourteen feet of snowfall every winter. These winters, coupled with a visually dramatic wilderness, provide the backdrop against which Doerr wrote "The Hunter's Wife." Of the process itself, he says that "it was a solid half-year, six to seven hours a day of rewriting."

Doerr's brief residency in Telluride coincided with the town's much longer fight to preserve a nearby 857-acre wetland known as the Valley Floor. Preservationists opposed development plans that would have included draining the wetland and building a large hotel complex, golf course, condominiums, and retail stores. The fight over the Valley Floor, which pitted the town against the industrialist owner of the wetland, spanned two decades.

This contest between preservationists and developers is mirrored in the hunter's distaste for the world outside his pristine wilderness:

> There is no order in that world, he told her once, waving vaguely toward Great Falls, the cities that lay to the south. . . . But here there is. Here I can see things I'd never see down there, things most folks are blind to.

Little more than twenty years later, however, "The valley had diminished slowly but perceptibly: roads came in, and the grizzlies left, seeking higher country. Loggers had thinned nearly every accessible stand of trees."

CRITICAL OVERVIEW

"The Hunter's Wife" won widespread praise from critics, especially after its publication in *The Shell Collector* brought it to the attention of a wider audience. Reviews noted the quality of Doerr's prose, in particular. For example,

Nancy Willard writes in the *New York Times* that "Doerr's prose dazzles, his sinewy sentences blending the naturalist's unswerving gaze with the poet's gift for metaphor;" Margaret Gunning, in her review for *January Magazine*, remarks on "the neatly telescoped economy of expression crucial for the short fiction form and a great gift for the beauty and primal power of language." These and other reviewers took special note of Doerr's almost scientific eye for detail and his writing style.

Doerr's use of the natural world as a setting attracted the admiration of his reviewers. A *Publishers Weekly* review begins:

> The natural world exerts a powerful, brooding presence in this first collection; it's almost as much a main character as any of the individuals the 26-year-old Doerr records. Nature, in these eight stories, is mysterious and deadly, a wonder of design and of nearly overwhelming power.

Bernadette Murphy, in a review for the *Los Angeles Times*, suggests the broader relevance of Doerr's settings when she suggests that his writing "illuminates both the riotous dangers of the natural world and the rocky terrain of the human heart, thrusting us into environments we can only hope to control."

Nancy Willard, however, despite her overall admiration for "The Hunter's Wife" and the collection as a whole, took issue with several aspects of the story. "The characters in Doerr's stories," she notes, "often line up neatly (perhaps too neatly) on both sides of the divide between the natural and the so-called civilized worlds." She takes particular issue with the collection's presentation of women:

> A woman seen only in the context of a man's needs is not really seen at all. To Doerr's credit, he gives the female characters in his stories lives of their own, although the idealized woman is never far from the real one.

Willard went on to use "The Hunter's Wife" as an example of this androcentric (that is, specifically masculine) viewpoint. Nevertheless, "The Hunter's Wife" and Doerr's work in general have garnered considerable respect and admiration from the literary establishment as a whole.

CRITICISM

William Rosencrans

Rosencrans is a writer and copy editor. In the following essay, he examines "The Hunter's

> " THE HUNTER BELONGS TO THIS WORLD OF THE UNSEEN MORE THAN HE HIMSELF REALIZES. HE HEARS WOLVES AND SEES THEIR TRACKS, EVEN THOUGH THERE ARE NONE IN HIS AREA. HE DREAMS OF RUNNING WITH THE WOLVES EVERY NIGHT BUT DOES NOT REMEMBER THOSE DREAMS ON WAKING."

Wife" as a tragedy and analyzes Doerr's use of mortality to move the story forward and force its characters' development.

"The Hunter's Wife," Doerr's literary debut, won praise from many quarters for its fine-tuned style: it showcases vivid prose, thoroughly rendered settings, and striking imagery. The failed marriage at the heart of the story, seen from the point of view of a flawed character with unreliable perceptions, engaged critics as well. But beneath all of this, the story is powered by the juxtaposition of the world of the living with the world of the dead, and the collision of these worlds gives the story elements of a classic tragedy.

Tragedy, in its strictest definition, requires a misfortune brought about by a character's flaws or frailties and not by external circumstances. It also entails a revelation for that same character. In this context, the hunter-protagonist of the story is a definitive tragic hero.

For most of the story, the hunter is not an especially sympathetic character. He almost never engages in self-reflection, and so he never grows or changes; he lives in a peculiar stasis. He is able to navigate a dangerous and austere world, and he is ready to put his own life on the line for those close to him, but these are qualities common to many animals, such as the wolves with whom the hunter has a close bond. Nevertheless, the hunter engages a reader's sympathies in various ways, sometimes precisely because of his flaws.

Chief among the flaws, and the one that causes the hunter's downfall, is his inability to see the world from any perspective but his own. His wife remains an utter mystery to him for the five years they live together, and there are times

WHAT DO I READ NEXT?

- *All The Light We Cannot See*, a novel published by Doerr in 2014, won the Pulitzer Prize the following year. The novel is set in Europe during World War II and concerns a young blind French girl and an orphaned German boy. The novel follows their lives over a ten-year period, from childhood to their eventual meeting as teenagers in occupied France.

- The Canadian writer and environmentalist Farley Mowat spent a summer observing wolves in subarctic Canada and wrote about his experiences in his best-selling *Never Cry Wolf* (1963). The book is credited with redeeming the wolf's reputation in the twentieth century. It has been criticized for crossing the line between neutrality and advocacy under the guise of science, but many of those critics found it good reading nonetheless.

- *Julie and the Wolves* (1972), a novel by Jean Craighead George, also shares with "The Hunter's Wife" a chilly northern setting and a fascination with wolves. The protagonist is a young Eskimo girl who, like the hunter's wife, flees a marriage. Unlike the hunter's wife, Julie retreats farther into the wilderness. She is able to survive the rigors of winter on the Alaskan tundra only by establishing a relationship with a wolf pack.

- An authentic account of life in rural Montana, *This House of Sky: Landscapes of a Western Mind* (1977) is Ivan Doig's autobiographical tale of childhood on a remote ranch and his journey to adulthood. Doig's writing, like Doerr's, has won accolades for its style and descriptive power.

- Hunting and hunters have inspired much famous fiction. William Faulkner, a giant of American literature, wrote four short stories about hunting, and they appear in the collection *Big Woods: The Hunting Stories* (1955). These stories are regarded as some of Faulkner's most enjoyable and accessible work.

- For a classic woman's perspective on divorce and its aftermath, readers can turn to *Out of Africa* (1937), by Karen Blixen (also known by her pen name, Isak Dinesen). This memoir covers Blixen's seventeen years as a coffee plantation owner in colonial Kenya. Blixen was unusual for her sympathetic relationships with native Kenyans, for being a woman landowner and farm manager, and for her frank portrait of a failed marriage.

---

when his perplexity borders on sheer thickheadedness. It is one thing not to believe in the afterlife or psychic abilities, but the passage in which the hunter corrects his wife's perception of a hawk in the northern lights with a dry scientific definition is another thing altogether. Still, his bafflement and the powerlessness it makes him feel can arouse a reader's pity, as on the couple's first night together:

> Three years he had waited for this. Three years he had dreamed this girl by his fire. . . . But this felt different. . . . It was exactly as if he was still three years younger, stopped outside the Central Christian Church and driven against a low window by the wind or some other, greater force.

As long as he stays within the limits of his experience, the hunter is anything but weak. He loves the unforgiving world of the wilderness, knows its tiniest secrets by virtue of long and careful observation, and moves through its hardships with grace and skill. Death is a constant, almost intimate threat, and he endures that threat with remarkable stamina. When this hard-won mastery over his environment proves useless in maintaining a relationship with his wife, he reacts with arrogance and cruelty; but the careful reader can see the fear and weakness behind his reactions.

The immediate misfortune this tragic hero suffers is his abandonment by his wife, but that misfortune is followed by a remarkable self-imposed hermitage of twenty years. Doerr leaves the details of that twenty-year isolation to the reader's imagination. He lets the reader know only that the hunter was never with another woman and that civilization has steadily encroached on the wilderness the hunter loves. One can safely assume that he has spent much of that time experiencing regret and crushing loneliness. That assumption is borne out at the story's end, which brings the hunter to a humbled and broader perspective. It is in the final lines that he truly succeeds as a character:

> He wanted to tell her that although the wolves were gone, may always have been gone, they still came to him in dreams. That they could run there, fierce and unfettered, was surely enough. She would understand. She had understood long before he did.

That shift in the hunter's outlook resolves a difficulty not only on the part of the hunter but also in the story itself. Most of the story is perceived through his eyes. Nancy Willard of the *New York Times* takes this as a potential literary misstep. The story is indeed one-sided. The reader inhabits the wife's point of view to such a limited degree and on such rare occasions that it can seem almost superfluous, and those passages (except the ones concerning her visions) are not as engaging as the rest. It may be that even if the story had been told entirely from the hunter's perspective, the wife's actions and motivations would still be clear enough to the discerning reader and that without the sense of a token gesture the tale would actually seem less one-sided.

The story's title is a harbinger of the one-sided perspective. It is not called "Mary Roberts" (her name, almost never used) or "The Evolution of a Magician's Assistant." The title defines the woman in terms of her relationship to her husband. "The Hunter's Wife" is his story more than hers, even though she occupies the central place in his life. And that place is the crux of the story. Much has been written about Doerr's treatment of nature, its harshness and cruelty and beauty, and the various ways in which it threatens to overwhelm his characters. Less has been written about the counterpoint to

this in "The Hunter's Wife," which is the other world, the afterlife, to which his wife gains access, and the ways in which it permeates the natural world.

The psychic elements introduce a note of the fantastic. The contrast between this otherworldliness and the gritty reality of northern Montana is less striking than the reader may expect, because the various afterlives the woman sees are rooted so firmly in the Montana reality. The soul of the doe the couple sees together does not occupy an alien dimension; the doe wades in a brook with other deer. Doerr describes these realms as a jeweler would (the light in these other worlds is almost always tinted with gold or silver), and many elements are idealized to some degree, but they exist in a recognizable world, a perfected world of the living.

Contact with the other worlds is, at first, a source merely of fascination for the hunter's wife. But when she begins using her talent to help others see the afterlives of their loved ones, that contact is marked by grief and a certain obligation, and the failure of her marriage (the hunter's great tragedy) is set in motion. Her clients are suffering, and her help is crucial for them. She can no more keep from helping them than the hunter can keep from hunting. When he refuses to recognize the validity of that world, the couple's bond is doomed.

The hunter belongs to this world of the unseen more than he himself realizes. He hears wolves and sees their tracks, even though there are none in his area. He dreams of running with the wolves every night but does not remember those dreams on waking, at least until after his wife leaves him. In a sense, he suffers two tragedies. The pain of his wife's leaving him is almost secondary to the absence of these totemic animals in his life. At the end, her gift has made her "refined, less wild," and this is, of course, another disappointment for the hunter with his single-minded love of the wild. But he is already learning to pull himself out of his customary realm, to finally bridge his world and hers.

Ultimately, death and the afterlives the woman sees are mirrored in the death and afterlife of their relationship. At the story's conclusion, as he reaches for her hand, the tragedy has been completed, and the hunter has been given the revelation he always needed.

When the hunter's wife touches the animals, from deer to snakes, she has a glimpse of their visions
(©Bruce MacQueen | Shutterstock.com)

Source: William Rosencrans, Critical Essay on "The Hunter's Wife," in *Short Stories for Students*, Gale, Cengage Learning, 2017.

Michelle Dean

In the following interview, Doerr cites reading the Chronicles of Narnia as sparking his interest in writing.

It was Anthony Doerr's wife Shauna who saw the news first. She was the one who was secretly streaming the Pulitzer ceremonies on YouTube in another room of their Paris apartment. He was in the kitchen with their son Owen, eating mint chocolate chip ice cream. She came in shaking and the phone started ringing, because he'd just won the Big Kahuna of American literary prizes: the Pulitzer for fiction.

"I'd sort of known it was the day," Doerr said on the phone to the *Guardian* on Tuesday. But he was trying not to think about it, or expect the win. He had enough to be grateful for: even before the prize was announced he was already enjoying the greatest success of his career with *All the Light We Cannot See*.

The book has spent most of the last year on the *New York Times* bestseller list, and Doerr tells me now his readings are stuffed with a much wider variety of people than he used to draw. Doerr is the kind of writer who when asked about his influences readily cites Anne Carson and Cormac McCarthy. "Sometimes my readers ask me what else they should read," he told me, "and I recommend Sebald." But he's never sure if the sort of reader this new book has attracted will enjoy Sebald as much as he does.

All the Light We Cannot See follows two children whose fates are entwined by the second world war. One, a French girl named Marie-Laure, is blind. The other, a German boy named Werner, is a whiz with radios. Without giving much away, these complementary qualities lead them on a clear path towards each other. The novel has been praised in, among other publications, the *Guardian* as a "page-turner."

But Doerr's book is not like your average great American novel, in part because it is a very lyrical piece of work. It is not sprawling or maximalist; its pleasures come from how carefully and artfully Doerr commands plot and language. Doerr's sentences are short and spare; the chapters brief too. This gives the impression of simplicity, and indeed the book was sometimes criticized for it. In a review in the *New York Times*, for example, the novelist William T Vollmann called the book "more than a thriller and less than great literature." Vollmann found the book full of "flimsy types," particularly when it came to the Nazis.

The thing about lyrical prose and tight plots is that they have a habit of hiding the work they took to produce. It took Doerr 10 years to write *All the Light We Cannot See*, and in between, he told me, he "procrastinated" by writing two other books. (One was a collection of short stories, the other a memoir of fatherhood.) The problem that kept leading him away from the book, he said, was the research.

But it is research which allowed him to include details about the radios used in Nazi Germany: "Even the poorest pit houses usually possess a state-sponsored Volksempfänger VE301, a mass-produced radio stamped with an eagle and a swastika, incapable of shortwave, marked only for German frequencies." And it is the accretion of such details that makes the novel seem so intricate, beautiful and, on some level, magical.

Doerr acquired an interest in this kind of magic early on. He grew up outside Cleveland, "where to call yourself a writer would be precocious. Or pretentious." He became interested in books in the ordinary way: his mother read to him. He remembers, particularly, the *Chronicles of Narnia*. Even as a small child he asked her: "How did they do that?" His mother had to inform him that actually, just one person had written the story. And that's when he learned that was a thing people could do.

After a few years bumming around Telluride, Colorado, Doerr's first success was a short story he placed in the *Atlantic* in 2001. "I was paid maybe $3,000 for it," he said, "and the hourly wage on it was very small." But it generated a huge response, and led him to sell his first book of stories to Scribner. The short stories won him acclaim, but this is his first experience of mainstream popularity.

I ask Doerr if he knows what drew people to *All the Light We Cannot See* in particular. It can be dangerous to ask a writer to speculate about his own writing's appeal but he's game, and offers me a few theories. One has to do with the weight of the themes that the second world war raises, which he admits does draw a lot of interest. Another has more to do with his use of fable. At the beginning of the book, Marie-Laure is enraptured by a tale of a stone called the Sea of Flames. "It's a way of letting readers into the story," he says, of those elements. We talk about the way writers like Karen Russell and Kelly Link have used magical elements in their work. He talks about admiring Link, who he says, unlike himself, is confident, convinced that the inclusion of such elements "doesn't make her writing any less serious."

But Doerr also offers one, slightly more practical explanation for the appeal of his style. When he was writing *All the Light We Cannot See*, he said, he was busy with new fatherhood, not sleeping a lot. He found writing sparingly, with a lot of "white space," to suit the new-parent lifestyle. "Maybe," he said, "for readers, that helps too."

Source: Michelle Dean, "Anthony Doerr: 'I Grew Up Where to Call Yourself a Writer Would Be Pretentious'," in *Guardian*, April 22, 2015.

Margaret Gunning

In the following review, Gunning points out some of the weak stories in The Shel Collector.

Described by one reviewer as "a gifted and fearless new writer," at the relatively tender age of 28, Idaho-based Anthony Doerr is creating quite a stir with his short stories. His work has appeared in the likes of the *Paris Review* and the *Atlantic Monthly*, and already he has won the Black Warrior Review Literary Prize. (Note: though Doerr is not black, he does have a decided propensity for African locales.)

Doerr's first collection is made up of a mere eight stories, some of such quality as to inspire amazement, and others seriously off the mark. This makes me wonder if *The Shell Collector* wasn't rushed into print in the wake of his literary prize. Might he have produced a finer, more consistent collection if he had waited just a few more years?

But such are the mysteries of the publishing world. Flawed or not, there is much to admire in this slender, cream-colored volume with its exquisite shell drawings from the Museum of Natural History. Doerr has the neatly telescoped economy of expression crucial for the short fiction form and a great gift for the beauty and primal power of language.

The book leads off with one of its strongest entries. "The Shell Collector" reveals many of the elements Doerr favors: exotic locales, characters with strange gifts, nature threatened by human ruthlessness and a hungry searching which represents a larger, near-mystical quest. The title character, a blind old man living in a hut in Kenya, is washing a bucketful of shells in his kitchen sink when he hears a water taxi land:

> He cringed to hear it, its hull grinding the calices of finger corals and the tiny tubes of pipe organ corals, tearing the flower and fern shapes of soft corals, and damaging shells . . . . It was not the first time people tried to seek him out.

The unwanted visitors are two obnoxious reporters from New York, both named Jim, sniffing out what they think is a very hot story. It seems that the old man, a retired marine biologist originally from northern Canada, has accidentally stumbled on a miracle cure:

> This all started when a malarial Seattle-born Buddhist named Nancy was stung by a cone shell in the shell collector's kitchen . . . . Or maybe it started before Nancy, maybe it grew outward from the shell collector himself, the way a shell grows, spiraling upward from the inside, whorling around its inhabitant, all the while being worn down by the weathers of the sea.

The cone shell "cure" is completely serendipitous, nearly killing Nancy in the process, but nevertheless the shell collector now faces a most unwelcome celebrity. Doerr carefully fills in his backstory, demonstrating that remarkable telescopic technique:

> Four books, three Seeing Eye shepherds, and a son named Josh later, he retired early from his professorship and moved to a thatched-roof kibanda just north of Lamu, Kenya.

The shell collector's uneasy relationship with his well-intentioned but obtuse son Josh and its bitterly ironic ending points up certain existential ambiguities that Doerr wisely does not seek to resolve. Rather he illuminates the mysteries with sighingly beautiful prose:

> He dreamed of glass, of miniature glass blowers making cone teeth like tiny snow-needles, like the thinnest bones of fish, vanes on the arms of a snowflake.

Similar themes of wildness and mysticism run through "The Hunter's Wife," which is really a story of psychological captivity. Dumas, a hunter and guide in the wilderness of Montana, marries Mary, a teenager he barely knows:

> She was a magician's assistant, beautiful, sixteen years old, an orphan. It was not a new story: a glittery red dress, long legs, a traveling magic show performing in the meeting hall at the Central Christian Church.

Winters in their isolated cabin drive them to the brink of starvation, if not madness. Dumas' hold over his vulnerable young wife begins to seem like nothing more than an act of pure male selfishness. Mary sleeps 20 hours a day, but during this near-hibernation begins to develop strange powers:

> With her stomach empty and her body quieted, without the daily demands of living, she felt she was making important discoveries . . . . More clearly than ever she could see that there was a fine line between dreams and wakefulness, between living and dying, a line so tenuous it sometimes didn't exist.

Reduced to her bare essence by deprivation, Mary becomes a sort of shaman figure, able to connect eerily with the spirit realm. This bizarre gift frightens the unbending Dumas into retreat. But 20 years after their parting he returns to her as she demonstrates her powers to a group of university professors. Their halting, tender reconciliation is deeply poignant:

> But he was afraid to speak. He could see that speaking would be like dashing some very fragile bond to pieces . . . . So instead they stood together, the snow fluttering down from the clouds to melt into the water where their own reflected images trembled like two people trapped against the glass of a parallel world, and he reached, finally, to take her hand.

If only all these stories reflected such grace. "For A Long Time This was Griselda's Story" is a rather silly and superficial yarn about a high school volleyball queen in Boise, Idaho who runs away with the carnival, eloping with a strange little man who swallows large chunks of metal. Griselda's letters home reveal her unlikely travels to exotic places all over the world. When she returns (return being one of Doerr's obsessions), she assists her husband while he eats a suit of armor. Whatever Doerr is trying to do here, it misfires into shallow cartoonishness.

This is not the only clanger. "July Fourth," about a fishing contest between Americans and Brits, never rises above the level of glib entertainment. Similarly, "A Tangle by the Rapid River" (yet another fishing story, about an old man cheating on his wife) lacks real depth, coming across as empty writer's card tricks.

Fortunately, the penultimate entry "The Caretaker" pulls up the standard once again. Full of power and poignancy, it recounts the grueling ordeal of Joseph Saleeby, a Liberian civil war survivor trying to make a life for himself as a refugee in Oregon.

This story illustrates just what is meant by the clinical term "post-traumatic stress disorder" as we are forced to see what Joseph saw:

> In a place where the market sign once hung between two iron posts, a man has been suspended upside-down. His insides, torn out of him, swing beneath his arms like black infernal ropes, marionette strings cut free.

In his new home in Oregon, Joseph works as a caretaker for a wealthy couple with a deaf daughter. But the horrors of the past dog him. One day he is psychologically undone by the sight of six beached whales by the ocean and compulsively buries their hearts, as if to try to lay his own demons to rest:

> For Joseph it is as if some portal from his nightmares has opened and the horrors crouched there, breathing at the door, have come galloping through.

His near-telepathic relationship with the deaf daughter, Belle, whom he rescues from suicide, is Doerr at his most sensitive and effective.

But the last story, "Mkondo," misses the mark due to sheer repetition of themes. When an American paleontologist named Ward Beach travels to Tanzania to look for a fossilized bird, he meets a beautiful, wild young woman named Naima running through the forest. He takes her home, marries her and subjects her to a sort of psychological captivity. She begins to sleep for most of the day, but out of the depths of her ordeal arises an unusual gift. The parallels to "The Hunter's Wife" continue even up to the end, where Ward returns to Tanzania many years later for yet another halting, tender reconciliation. This time it plays a bit threadbare, almost as if we are being manipulated.

Given his enormous potential as a fiction writer and his relative youth, it seems strange and a bit disturbing that in a collection of only eight stories, Doerr is already repeating himself. There are other pitfalls he must watch out for. Premature celebrity has ruined many a creative gift. It is my hope that Doerr can resist the seductive trap of fame as resolutely as his most intriguing character, the shell collector.

Source: Margaret Gunning, "Many Happy Returns," in *January Magazine*, March 2002.

Alfred Hickling

In the following review, Hickling stresses the importance of the natural world in the collection that includes "The Hunter's Wife."

The American guitar player and big-game hunter Ted Nugent notoriously divides his time between cutting albums and culling animals. The philosophy behind this is explained in his newly published cookbook, *Kill 'Em and Grill 'Em* (Regency Publishing Inc), from which hard rockers with a strong stomach can try out Ted's toothsome recipe for sweet-and-sour antelope. I am not recommending that you read it; but the psychological profile of Nugent came to mind while flipping through Anthony Doerr's extraordinary debut collection of stories.

Doerr's obsessions appear to be hunting, fishing and itinerant life on the fringes of show-business. His stories stretch out across a vast terrain marked with natural phenomena and studded with tiny pockets of humanity. His characters are mostly misfits and outsiders—blind beachcombers, burly huntsmen and spurious mountebanks. And though there are no big-game-hunting rock stars, it would be quite within his compass to invent one.

The style of *The Shell Collector* is one part science to two parts showmanship. The opening pages of the title story throw up a welter of crustaceous research as Doerr's precise, economical prose traces the geometry of exoskeletons, the chemistry of calcium and the evolutionary development of whorls and folds.

Finally he introduces his anti-hero, the small but lethally poisonous cone snail, whose microscopic fangs resemble "tiny translucent bayonets, the razor-edged tusks of a miniature ice-devil."

Allowing oneself to be bitten by a cone is a bad idea, but Doerr's stories are full of irrational impulses. A disillusioned Seattle housewife discovers Buddhism, abandons her family and stumbles into the beach shack of an elderly shell collector; a near-fatal cone sting so closely resembles an enlightening acid trip that she immediately wants to do it again.

In another story, an awol magician's assistant hooks up with a Montana woodsman, determined to plunge her hands and face into the hot belly-fur of a hibernating grizzly. And in another, a high-school prom queen abandons her budding career in Boise, Idaho, to experience the world with a travelling freak-show.

The highlight, however, is the concluding story, "Mkondo," which draws together all of Doerr's themes of geographical displacement, disappointed love and lack of spiritual fulfilment. An American museum employee named Ward Beach is dispatched to Tanzania to acquire the fossil of a prehistoric bird. As he drives to the site, Naima, an impulsive native girl, leaps out and clings to the bonnet of his truck. Ward is smitten and he returns to Ohio with a guileless child-bride as well as his bag of bones.

The grey Ohio climate saps the life out of Naima, however. She tries to take an interest in ants, bees and a despondent pair of zebras at the zoo, but finds them scant consolation for the loss of her beloved rainforest. "She was learning that in her life everything—health, happiness, even love—was subject to the landscape. She heard a pulse inside her ear, a swishing cadence of blood, the steady marking of every moment as it sailed past, unrecoverable. She mourned each one."

Everything about Doerr's fiction is subject to the landscape—from Naima's sense of paradise lost to the desolate intimation of an Idaho housewife that there is "a world glimmering beyond Boise, outside the cracked and sinking bungalow in the North End." Doerr sees both Boise and the great beyond: his stories are filled with the vastness of the natural world pressing against human insignificance.

Whether he can realise his ambition and sustain these themes over a larger span remains to be seen, but for now he stands unchallenged as a great American malacologist.

Source: Alfred Hickling, Review of *The Shell Collector*, in *Guardian*, November 22, 2002.

Publishers Weekly

In the following review, the anonymous reviewer points out that Doerr uses subtle humor in his work.

The natural world exerts a powerful, brooding presence in this first collection; it's almost as much a main character as any of the individuals the 26-year-old Doerr records. Nature, in these eight stories, is mysterious and deadly, a wonder of design and of nearly overwhelming power. This delicate balance is evidenced by the title story, about a blind man who spends his days collecting rare and beautiful shell specimens. Self-exiled to the coast of Kenya, he discovers that a certain poisonous snail has the power both to kill and to effect a rapid recovery from malaria. This discovery brings him much attention but little joy, disturbing the carefully ordered universe that he has constructed to manage both his blindness and his temperament. A naturalist's perspective also informs the other stories. In "The Hunter's Wife," Doerr catalogues winter in Montana as "a thousand ladybugs hibernating in an orange ball in a riverbank hollow; a pair of dormant frogs buried in frozen mud." But Doerr can play it funny, too: in "July Fourth," a group of American fishermen endure a hilarious litany of woes in a fishing contest across Scandinavia and Eastern Europe. Their troubles include much drinking, few fish and losing their shirts (and all their tackle) to a Belorussian basketball team. The title story could well appear in the next Best American or O. Henry anthologies, and the others make a fine supporting cast.

Forecast: With blurbs from the likes of Rick Bass, this debut collection should do better than most, especially if reviewers take note.

Source: Review of *The Shell Collector*, in *Publishers Weekly*, Vol. 248, No. 48, November 26, 2001, p. 39.

SOURCES

"Anthony Doerr: By the Book," in *New York Times Sunday Book Review*, July 2, 2015, p. 8.

Caldwell, Erin, "Anthony Doerr," in *Superstition Review*, No. 9, Spring 2012, https://superstitionreview. asu.edu/issue9/interviews/anthonydoerr (accessed January 28, 2016).

Dargan, Michele, "Novelist Embraces 'Childhood Love' of Many Things in Best-seller," in *Palm Beach Daily News*,

March 19, 2015, http://www.palmbeachdailynews.com/news/news/local/novelist-embraces-childhood-love-of-many-things-in/nkZ5z (accessed January 18, 2016).

Doerr, Anthony, "The Hunter's Wife," in *The Shell Collector*, Scribner, 2002, pp. 40–72.

Gunning, Margaret, "Many Happy Returns," in *January Magazine*, March 2002, http://www.januarymagazine.com/fiction/shellcollector.html (accessed January 28, 2016).

Hickling, Alfred, "Where the Wild Things Are," in *Guardian*, November 23, 2002, p. 26.

"Interview with Anthony Doerr," in *Goodreads*, December 2014, http://www.goodreads.com/interviews/show/995.Anthony_Doerr (accessed January 18, 2016).

Liebrum, Martha, "Anthony Doerr: Diverse & Unpredictable," in *Sun Valley Magazine*, Winter 2009, http://www.sunvalleymag.com/Sun-Valley-Magazine/Winter-2009/Anthony-Doerr (accessed January 28, 2016).

Long, Karen R., "Anthony Doerr Wins Lucrative Short-Story Prize," in *Plain Dealer*, April 9, 2011, http://www.cleveland.com/books/index.ssf/2011/04/anthony_doerr_wins_lucrative_s.html (accessed January 28, 2016).

Murphy, Bernadette, "Matters of Nature and the Heart Intertwine in Remarkable Debut," in *Los Angeles Times*, January 15, 2002, http://articles.latimes.com/2002/jan/15/news/lv-books15 (accessed February 4, 2016).

"Off the Page: Anthony Doerr," in *Washington Post*, October 14, 2004, http://www.washingtonpost.com/wp-dyn/articles/A24073-2004Oct11.html (accessed February 4, 2016).

Prentice, George, "Anthony Doerr," in *Boise Weekly*, April 9, 2011, http://www.boiseweekly.com/boise/anthony-doerr/Content?oid = 2174021 (accessed January 18, 2016).

Review of "The Shell Collector," in *Publishers Weekly*, January 14, 2002, http://www.publishersweekly.com/978-0-7432-1274-8 (accessed February 4, 2016).

"Valley Floor Timeline," in Valley Floor Preservation Partners website, http://www.valleyfloor.org/timeline.html (accessed February 4, 2016).

Willard, Nancy, "Rivers Run through It," in *New York Times*, March 3, 2002, p. 7.

Gilbert, Sandra M., *Death's Door: Modern Dying and the Ways We Grieve*, W. W. Norton, 2007.
> The death of Gilbert's husband in 1991 prompted the creation of this book, a personal and insightful study of dying and bereavement that combines memoir, history, and social science. *Death's Door* examines the ways in which grieving has changed over time and the ways in which it is unchanging.

Howard, Joseph Kinsey, *Montana: High, Wide, and Handsome*, Yale University Press, 1959.
> Howard's book, an overview of Montana that includes its history, ecology, notable personalities, and landscape, is widely recognized as a classic. It has been praised both for its beautiful, engaging prose and for its wealth of information.

Krakauer, Jon, *Into the Wild*, Anchor Books, 1997.
> This international best seller chronicles events leading to the death of Christopher McCandless, a young man who in 1992 attempted to survive alone in the Alaskan wilderness, bringing with him only some rice, a rifle, and a field guide to edible plants. His experiences, some recorded in a private journal, are recaptured in detail.

Woodcock, Eldred Nathaniel, *Fifty Years a Hunter and Trapper*, A. R. Harding, 1913.
> One of America's legendary hunters, Woodcock (who killed his first bear at the age of thirteen) writes his memoir in simple, folksy language. He relates his adventures hunting and trapping in rural Pennsylvania in the late nineteenth and early twentieth centuries. The book is out of print, but Project Gutenberg at http://www.gutenberg.org/files/34063/34063-h/34063-h.htm has it available for download or reading online.

Woolf, Virginia, *A Room of One's Own*, Penguin Classics, 2002.
> First published in 1929, Woolf's argument that women must have financial freedom and personal liberty to create art is a seminal feminist work. The essay was provocative when it appeared, and Woolf's case for women's independence remains relevant.

SUGGESTED SEARCH TERMS

Anthony Doerr

Doerr AND "The Hunter's Wife"

Montana

Montana AND winter

visions AND afterlife

bereavement

hunting

marriage AND communication

FURTHER READING

Coontz, Stephanie, *Marriage, a History: How Love Conquered Marriage*, Penguin Books, 2006.
> Some early languages lacked even a word for love; in later years, love came to define (or was expected to define) marriage. Coontz's book explores the modern institution of marriage and its difficulties by studying the many kinds of marriage through the ages and across the world.

In the Region of Ice

JOYCE CAROL OATES

1966

Originally published in *Atlantic Monthly* in August 1966, the often anthologized story "In the Region of Ice" is considered by many critics to be one of Joyce Carol Oates's finest. It explores a familiar theme in her writing: the struggle for meaningful connections. The story focuses on Sister Irene, a nun and teacher whose worldview is challenged when a brilliant but emotionally disturbed student enters her life. Struggling to find a balance between the mysteries of her faith and the very real demands on her time and empathy, Sister Irene is forced to make a decision that is at once reassuring to her and profoundly disappointing. As Oates herself notes in an interview with Leif Sjöberg published in *Contemporary Literature*, many of her stories, including this one, are

> explorations of the contemporary world interpreted in a realist mode, from what might be called a tragic and humanistic viewpoint. Tragedy always upholds the human spirit because it is an exploration of human nature in terms of its strengths.

"In the Region of Ice" won Oates her first O. Henry Award in 1967, and it has been adapted into an award-winning short film. The story appears in *High Lonesome* (2006).

AUTHOR BIOGRAPHY

Oates was born on June 16, 1938, in Lockport, New York, the eldest of three children of

Joyce Carol Oates (©*Pako Mera / Alamy*)

homemaker Carolina Oates and tool-and-die designer Frederic James Oates. Her siblings are Fred Jr. (born 1943) and Lynn Ann (1956). The family moved eventually to the farming community of Millersport, where Oates spent most of her childhood. An avid reader, she often cites Lewis Carroll's *Alice's Adventures in Wonderland* (1865) as especially influential reading, along with the writings of Henry David Thoreau, whom she discovered as a teen.

Graduating from Williamsville South High School in 1956, Oates earned a scholarship to Syracuse University. She graduated as valedictorian with a degree in English in 1960, before heading for a master's degree to the University of Wisconsin–Madison, where she met and married her first husband, the scholar, editor, and publisher Raymond J. Smith. Oates was enrolled in the doctoral program at Rice University when she decided to dedicate herself to writing as a full-time profession, as well as partnering with her husband on a number of publishing ventures.

Her decision paid dividends almost immediately, with the publication of her first book,

the story collection *By the North Gate*, in 1963. She followed with a novel, *With Shuddering Fall*, in 1964, which was followed in 1966 by the frequently anthologized stories "Where Are You Going, Where Have You Been?" and "In the Region of Ice" (in *Atlantic Monthly*). The latter won Oates the first of her two O. Henry Awards in 1967; she won her second for the story "The Dead" in 1973.

Since these early publications, she has produced a body of work that includes more than forty novels as well as dozens upon dozens of plays, short stories, poetry, and works of nonfiction. Some of her most popular titles are *Them* (1969), *Black Water* (1992), *Wonderland* (1971), and *Blonde* (2000). Her critically acclaimed collection of essays *On Boxing* (1987) is still considered by many readers to be the best writing ever about the sport. But as an anonymous reviewer in *Publishers Weekly* observed in 2006: "However much is made of her prodigious output, it's the consistent quality of the work that lifts Oates into the literary pantheon."

Following the death of her husband in 2008 from complications associated with pneumonia, Oates struggled deeply with the loss. Eventually, though, she met Charles Gross, a professor at Princeton, and married for a second time in 2009.

Oates's work has been well recognized by award committees from around the world. She has won, for instance, the National Book Award (in 1970 for *Them*), two O. Henry Awards, the Bram Stoker Award (*Zombie*, 1996), the PEN/ Malamud Award for Excellence (1996), the Chicago Tribune Literary Prize (2006), the National Humanities Medal (2010), and the Norman Mailer Prize, Lifetime Achievement (2012). She has also been nominated for the Pulitzer Prize for *Black Water* (1992), *What I Lived For* (1994), *Blonde* (2000), and the story collections *The Wheel of Love and Other Stories* (1970) and *Lovely, Dark, Deep: Stories* (2014).

Oates continues to write productively from her home in Princeton, New Jersey, where she is Professor Emerita of Humanities at Princeton University.

PLOT SUMMARY

Sister Irene is a nun and teacher in her early thirties who is praying for the energy and resolve to get through her first semester of teaching at the Jesuit university at which she has just recently arrived. It

MEDIA ADAPTATIONS

- "In the Region of Ice" was adapted into a thirty-seven-minute short film of the same title in 1976. Directed by Peter Werner, it won the Oscar for Best Live Action Short.

is not the classroom that has her struggling; indeed, in that setting she feels fully confident and capable. It is the world outside the classroom that has her anxious, especially "the cynicism of her colleagues, the indifference of many of the students, and, above all, the looks she got that told her nothing much would be expected of her because she was a nun."

Two weeks after the semester begins, a new and apparently impetuous young man turns up in her class. His questions are frequent, dramatic, and often well off topic to the point of appearing irrelevant to the discussion. He argues passionately for what he calls "a logical consistency" to a world that appears illogical, chaotic, and unclear in its direction. He is equally vigorous in pushing for permission to attend her lectures despite the fact that he already has a degree from another university (Columbia) and is a Jew trying to enroll late in a course at a Catholic university.

Despite being confrontational, rude, and arrogant, the new student, Allen Weinstein, is also passionate about ideas and possesses an active though undisciplined mind. He gains Sister Irene's sympathy, and she allows him to join her Shakespeare class despite the fact that she recognizes that it is "a mistake to let him in."

Soon after allowing Allen to join her class, Sister Irene notices that her excitement about her Shakespeare class is heightened. She is forced to acknowledge that "until he had enrolled, she had not understood what was lacking, a mind that could appreciate her own." At the same time, she begins to recognize that Allen has a quick mind fueled by a knowledge that he "used . . . like a weapon" and that isolates Allen from those around him.

Gradually Sister Irene puts Allen on a kind of pedestal of expectations, so when he fails to meet his first paper deadline, she finds herself disappointed and even a touch angry that she has been deceived by his enthusiasm and determination. When he shows up with a paper that is twice as long as assigned and a day late, she makes an unusual concession and accepts it. With his paper on the "Erotic Melodies in *Romeo and Juliet*" accepted, Allen begins a long, disconnected monologue as the two walk along the campus paths. He presses her to read a long and rambling poem he could show only to her. Her realization terrifies her as she reads through the poem with its focus on such words as "life," "darkness," and "love": "She was terrified at what he was trying to do—he was trying to force her into a human relationship." She thanks him for sharing the poem and walks away without continuing the conversation.

Allen's emotions turn suddenly after sharing the poem, and he becomes dismissive and disdainful. Sister Irene, whose cloistered life has left her unprepared to deal with such raw and undigested emotion, is forced to consider her own life in deeper ways. Is he, she thinks, "a kind of crystallization of her own loneliness" or something else? The conflicts within her deepen. She does not like Allen but is fascinated by him. She feels embarrassed for him, but she also wants to protect him.

Sister Irene's struggles deepen, leading to a vigorous reflection upon her place in the world, her work as a nun, and her daily engagement with what she understands as "the mystery of Christianity." She questions her own understanding of Christian charity, her role as a teacher, and her life as a woman.

For a while this deep questioning is almost irrelevant, as Allen does not return to class to pick up his assignment or his graded paper or to invigorate the classroom discussion with his passionate defenses of humanism. Just as Sister Irene is beginning to return to her familiar routine, she receives a letter from Allen, who has been placed in a local sanatorium, Birchcrest Manor. In the letter, Allen makes a subtle suicide threat through careful references to Shakespeare's play *Measure for Measure*, specifically to Claudio's speech to his sister, Isabella.

Sister Irene believes that the reference is a clear message that Allen wants her to risk some small part of herself to answer his overwhelming need for a sustaining human connection.

Her initial step is to arrange a visit with Allen's parents, attempting to explain to them the depth of their son's despair at Birchcrest Manor, where he is being given shock treatments. Allen's father's frustration at her visit and his overwhelming confidence that his son is in need of treatment give Sister Irene a more complete sense of the chronic problems the young man brought to her classroom. Sister Irene leaves the family home with sadness and a deep sense of fragility and defeat.

A month after this home visit, Allen comes back into Sister Irene's life one last time with yet another awkward request: to borrow money so that he can escape to Canada. She is emotionally distant from him, unwilling to support his plan in any way. His scornful mocking of her is fueled by anger and resentment, and he insults her and storms out her office.

Months later, when she hears of his suicide by drowning in Quebec, Sister Irene allows "a part of herself" to drift off to thoughts of his reaching out to her and her inability or unwillingness to respond. As the story ends, Sister Irene regains her composure, reasserts to herself the belief that she is a person who has made a decision to commit to her faith and values and that she feels no guilt in the knowledge of Allen's death because, sadly, she cannot feel any real emotions at all.

CHARACTERS

Sister Carlotta

Sister Carlotta is the one colleague with whom Sister Irene discusses Allen, and that is only briefly and superficially. She also accompanies Sister Irene on her visit to Allen's parents, offering her emotional support and her critical opinion of the family dynamic that she witnesses.

Sister Irene

Sister Irene is "a tall, deft woman in her early thirties." She is described as a "serious" woman with "hard gray eyes, a long slender nose, [and] a face waxen with thought." Having spent her entire life as a teaching nun, she approaches the world rationally and unemotionally. Meeting Allen Weinstein, Sister Irene is forced to confront the limitations of her faith, her naïveté as a woman, and her misconceptions of the power of her teaching. She struggles throughout the story to find a balance in her life, not sure how to integrate her faith with the challenging realities

of Allen's situation or how to live fully in a world that she does not understand in many ways.

When Sister Irene sets out to talk with Allen's parents about his desperate plea for help, for instance, she feels in that moment an intense closeness to what she understands as the mysteries of Christianity and, more directly, with the sufferings of Christ. Her reaction to this moment is not an act of arrogance but a statement of her own insecurity and her inability to move beyond it to engage the world in an intimate way.

Allen Weinstein Jr.

Allen Weinstein is a "slight and fair-haired" student who joins Sister Irene's undergraduate class despite the fact that he has already completed a degree elsewhere. A bright young Jewish student with intense emotional problems, he sweeps into Sister Irene's contained, controlled world like a hurricane, challenging her ideas about faith, humanity, and the powerful need for human connection. Unable to bring Sister Irene to the depth of connection that he desires, Allen suffers a breakdown and is hospitalized by his parents, who give permission for shock therapy treatment to be given to their son.

Once discharged, Allen makes one final attempt to connect with Sister Irene, only to see his efforts fail miserably. He heads north to Quebec, Canada, where he later commits suicide by drowning.

Allen Weinstein Sr.

Allen Weinstein's father is a loud man with very strong opinions about what is wrong with his son and the treatment he should receive. He seems to value money over the health of his son, but he also describes to Sister Irene how difficult it was having Allen, with his behavioral problems, live at home with them.

Libby Weinstein

Libby Weinstein is Allen's mother, a woman overwhelmed by her son's emotional troubles.

THEMES

Connectedness

As Alan Cheuse notes in a review of *High Lonesome* in *World Literature Today*, many of Oates's best-known stories, including "In the Region of Ice," highlight "the desperate search for kinship of one kind or another." In other words, Oates's

TOPICS FOR FURTHER STUDY

- Writing in the *New York Times*, Cathleen Schine states that "Oates examines the way people disappear from one another—the dull, aching distance between mothers and daughters, between sisters, between lovers, between predators and prey—with laconic precision." In an essay that draws extensively on evidence from the story, discuss why (or why not) "In the Region of Ice" can be read as a story about disappearing.

- When asked by Sjöberg what makes great literature, Oates answered thoughtfully and specifically: "Standards of greatness must encompass depth of vision; a breadth of actual work; a concern for various levels of human society; a sympathy with many different kinds of people; an awareness of and concern with history; a sense of the interlocking forces of politics, religion, economics, and the mores of society; concern with aesthetics; perhaps even experimentation in forms and language; and above all a 'visionary' sense." In an essay that takes this statement as its starting point, make the case for or against "In the Region of Ice" being included in a list of great American stories.

- You have been asked to adapt "In the Region of Ice" into a short film for modern audiences. Create a sample soundtrack of five songs that you think should be built into the film. For each song choice, develop a thoughtful rationale for how it relates to key themes or crucial moments of the story.

- Develop a detailed and professional-looking poster to promote a film adaptation of Oates's story for a modern audience. Think carefully about color, design elements, and wording in order to connect your final product to the story's themes in as many ways as possible. Present your work to the class and explain your choices.

- Read David Owen's *Panther* (2015), a young-adult novel that examines the impact of mental health issues (most notably depression) on a family. Design and build a poster that compares Owen's and Oates's stories of the effects of mental illness on those who suffer from it and those who suffer alongside them. Remember this is a poster that is designed to raise awareness of the issue of depression, not to retell the stories.

---

stories very often explore the theme of connectedness (or disconnectedness) in a contemporary world stripped of much of the infrastructure that traditionally facilitated a strong sense of community and kinship. As Oates herself noted in a 1982 interview with Sjöberg, as people

> we *believe* we exist in terms of other people, our surroundings, our activities, our environment. If these are altered or denied us—what then? Is there a personality that is, to quote Dickinson, a "zero at the bone?" Or is personality nearly all cultural—external trappings?

Allen is a powerful example of what happens when a sense of disconnection takes hold of an already fragile life. As Sister Irene observes almost immediately upon his arrival in her classroom, "though he sat in the center of the class, [Allen] seemed totally alone, encased by a miniature world of his own" owing, in part, to his acute intelligence and, in larger part, to a personality that spins wildly through waves of paranoia and anger. Allen becomes a kind of self-fulfilling prophecy, distancing himself from the college community, his own family, and, inevitably, from Sister Irene. Heading north to Canada in order to escape the possibility of future hospitalization and treatment, Allen commits suicide as a final, tragic statement of his own disconnection from reality and from those around him.

Faith

Sister Irene's struggle throughout the story is very much a personal crisis of faith, both religious faith and, in a broader sense, faith in her

The story is set on the campus of a small Catholic college (©*Noah Strycker / Shutterstock.com*)

own humanity and skill as a teacher. When confronted by the challenges that Allen brings into her life, Sister Irene turns, naturally, to the values and skills that have always served her well in the past: detached empathy, logic, reason, and avoidance of emotional closeness. None of these strategies work when dealing with Allen, however, and Sister Irene is asked to confront the limitations to her faith and values that are suddenly unable to provide support or solace to a deeply troubled young man or his family.

In the end, Sister Irene gradually slips back into her life, allowing her experiences with Allen to fade into a memory that is touching but not life-changing. She returns to the world of books, prayer, and classroom teaching, using each as a barrier from the doubts and questions that Allen introduced into her world.

Female-Male Relations

Like much of Oates's writing, "In the Region of Ice" studies how ideas of femininity and femaleness collide with ideas of masculinity and male power. As Oates notes in an interview with

Sjöberg, it is not coincidence that this focus reappears in her writing:

> Since approximately 1965 I have set myself the task, in both novels and short stories, of exploring contemporary society on many levels. My focus has been a close examination of the sources of power. The political and economic milieu; professions like medicine, the law, and most recently education and religion; and, to some extent, the predicament of the young and of women—all these have fascinated me.

Allen proves a direct challenge to Sister Irene's understanding of how power is realized in a world beyond the classroom walls. His overbearing style and his unwillingness to adhere to social expectations leave Sister Irene at a distinct disadvantage throughout their relationship. He consistently makes demands of her that she is unable to refuse. He asks her to change her policy on late assignments in order to accommodate him, and she does. The underlying hint of sexual tension that he introduces into her life is in direct challenge to her vows as a nun. Allen is a powerful male personality that pushes Sister Irene in directions that she does not wish to go and is, ultimately, unprepared to deal with.

At the same time, because Allen is totally unaware of the social norms governing the power relationship between men and women (as well as between students and teachers) he never tries to use his power to any real advantage until late in the story when he attempts to borrow money in order to escape to Canada. Interestingly, when Sister Irene says no to this request, Allen responds in an unusually predictable way: his outburst is driven by anger. This anger, in turn, allows Sister Irene to step away from the relationship once and for all and return to the more comfortable (and predictable) relationships that have defined her life previously.

STYLE

Intertextuality

"In the Region of Ice" is a story that is greatly enriched by direct references to Shakespearean plays, which build stylistically on the sophisticated literary device of intertextuality. This device refers to the use of direct references within one work to another work (most often by another author) in ways that extend beyond a simple nod of appreciation in order to become a richer, fuller merging of themes, ideas, language, or governing concepts. One famous example is James Joyce's use of Homer's *The Odyssey* in order to guide the narrative structure and content of his own novel *Ulysses* (1922).

In her story, Oates builds in direct and substantial references to three Shakespearean plays that have the same basic theme as "In the Region of Ice": the terrible, and sometimes fatal, risks involved in human relationships. More specifically, the references to *Romeo and Juliet* illuminate the dangerous, although unrequited, sexual subtext to the interaction between Sister Irene and Allen. It is also a reference suggesting that such connections between men and women, when fulfilled, might have precisely the tragic outcomes that Sister Irene so vividly fears.

Oates's references to *Measure for Measure* are also fraught with the dangers of human interaction as the play unfolds with a series of paired characters being forced to negotiate the unsafe waters of personal and political relationships. Allen's first question ever to Sister Irene refers to *Hamlet*, a play in which human relationships are plagued by a variety of potentially fatal problems, most notably the protagonist's inability to

act in spite of the tremendous pressures of emotional and moral obligations.

Third-Person Limited Narrator

A common form of narration in which the teller of the tale (not to be mistaken for the author of the story) assumes a position of limited omniscience, which means that the narrator has access to the private, unspoken thoughts of some characters but not all. The narrator describes Sister Irene's thoughts and feelings, but Allen's remain a mystery throughout the story. This position allows the narrator to dive into private thoughts in order to understand motivations and struggles, to narrate otherwise secret events, or to jump effortlessly through space and time to change the order in which events are recounted. This stylistic decision provides "In the Region of Ice" with what Cheuse describes as "a dense infusion of details both physical and psychological, which sometimes reveals her kinship with D.H. Lawrence at his most psychologically intense."

HISTORICAL CONTEXT

"In the Region of Ice" first appeared in 1966, an era in American cultural history that was defined, in part, by a growing dissatisfaction on the part of younger people with the traditional institutions of power and decision making. Key to this unrest was the fact that domestic inflation continued to grow as the expanding conflict in Vietnam demanded more and more money. From September 1965 to January 1966, more than 170,000 young American men had been drafted and another 180,000 enlisted voluntarily. By January 1966, another two million men had reportedly secured college deferments, which allowed them to avoid the draft. Regular deployments of American troops into the region were announced throughout the year, with eight thousand troops landing in January. By April, the total number of American troops deployed reached 250,000, and protests were spreading across college campuses and American cities. Public resistance to the conflict reached a new height in 1966 when professional boxer Muhammad Ali (formerly known as Cassius Clay) refused to go to war following a series of controversial public statements that likened military actions in Vietnam

COMPARE & CONTRAST

- **1966:** When Allen is sent to Birchcrest Manor, he claims to be submitted to electroconvulsive therapy (ECT), often referred to colloquially as shock therapy. Popular in the United States in the 1940s, ECT is seen by doctors and patients as a promising new technology to help resolve complex emotional problems. Whereas the traditional and intensely invasive practice of lobotomy reduces patient functioning dramatically, ECT is seen as improving mood and everyday functioning in patients, especially those suffering from severe depression.

  Today: Although ECT is still popular, the machines used in delivering treatment have been reclassified as a class III (high risk) medical device by the Food and Drug Administration. Research is still under way today into both the effectiveness of ECT and the short- and long-term impacts on health associated with it. Contemporary concerns are still fueled, in part, by depictions of ECT in such popular films as *One Flew over the Cuckoo's Nest* (1975) and *Requiem for a Dream* (2000).

- **1966:** Catholic sisters and nuns in the United States play a major role in American religion, education, nursing, and social work, as they have since early in the nineteenth century. The number of nuns working in American institutions peaks in 1965, at nearly two hundred thousand.

  Today: By 2014, the number of nuns working in American schools and related institutions has fallen to fewer than fifty thousand, continuing a decade-long trend of decline.

- **1966:** In many ways the myths of the 1960s are remembered more aggressively than the historical facts of the decade. Sgt. Barry Sadler's patriotic "Ballad of the Green Berets" (which cast the American military in a popular light) was named *Billboard*'s number one single of 1966 rather than any of the often-cited protest songs from the period. The impression of a unified counterculture was challenged by the opening of the rock musical *Hair* in October of 1967, which revealed a number of fissures in the cultural ethos of the day. Despite its open rebellion against traditional sexual mores, American militarism, and middle-class values, the acclaimed play also revealed a deep and at times destructive divide between members of the Free Love movement, active draft dodgers, politicized antiwar protesters, and dedicated civil rights activists. It was a year and a decade of discontent and discovery more than a unified expression of resistance from a disenfranchised generation.

  Today: With occasional exceptions, American culture has settled into relative calm following the various configurations of rebelliousness and discontent that defined the mid-1960s. With media coverage of political events more pervasive than ever before in history, the average American citizen is inundated with details of almost every aspect of political and military strategizing, political decision making, and cultural trends that emerge in countries around the world. The politicization of resistance has been replaced in many cases by almost immediate globalization of challenges via social and traditional media.

---

to the history of American slavery. Ali was stripped of his heavyweight title and sentenced to five years in prison for draft evasion; he never went to prison, remaining a free man until the sentence was overturned on appeal to the US Supreme Court. As public resistance to

Sister Irene has a quiet life teaching Shakespeare *(©Di Studio | Shutterstock.com)*

Vietnam engagement continued to grow, Ali became a popular speaker at colleges and universities across the country.

More broadly, both the United States and Soviet Union escalated their race to land a person on the moon, and race riots continued to fray the fabric of community in cities across the United States. In a number of instances, violence erupted involving protesters and the National Guard troops deployed to bring order. Tensions were heightened in June, when noted civil rights activist James Meredith was shot while trying to march across Mississippi. In the same year, 1966, singer John Lennon, of the wildly popular rock group the Beatles, infamously said in a London newspaper, "We are more popular than Jesus." The statement sent ripples of indignation through older generations within Christian countries, including America. He would later apologize, but the controversy had already drawn attention to the fact that an entire generation of young people, reminiscent of Oates's Allen Weinstein, had started to question deeply the faith-based values that had shaped American culture for generations.

In short, 1966 was a year of tension and profound questioning, which is reflected in Oates's story. American culture, in particular, was pushing in this decade toward a new understanding of how faith, education, and art could be integrated more compellingly into the decision making of the country. A generation of engaged young people were increasingly feeling disenfranchised from positions of influence and, by extension, disempowered in their own lives. Allen's reaction to his parent's control of his life (ordering hospitalization and shock therapy, most obviously) is in many ways representative of his entire generation. Unable and unwilling to negotiate a sense of connectedness and fulfillment, he flees north to Canada only to end his own life in a tragically symbolic act of desperation.

CRITICAL OVERVIEW

As Cheuse observes, "from the beginning of her by now long career, Oates has always been a writer to conjure with, taking up the aesthetic legacy of Flannery O'Connor and embracing the

Dostoyevskian themes of crime and punishment, sin and redemption." More specifically, he continues, Oates's fascination is with "the constant presence of inevitable menace and mayhem in otherwise placid lives," which perfectly describes her focus on Sister Irene. An exemplar of a "placid life," she is forced to confront much about herself and her values when Allen Weinstein strides into her classroom.

Placing "In the Region of Ice" in the context of the acclaimed O. Henry Award, Henry Alley, writing in *Kenyon Review*, also aligns Oates with the powerful tradition of O'Connor, noting that "O'Connor's well-made plots, combined with a sense of menace, as applied to contemporary America, both during and after Vietnam, form for Oates a kind of tragedy of reduction." Speaking of Sister Irene specifically, Alley argues that she is a characteristic protagonist for Oates: a character "of limited vision who undergo[es] terrifying consequences in a narrative context stripped . . . of O'Connor's apocalypse."

In a similar vein, Schine observes that Oates's characters

> often question whether they have free will, and with good reason: they don't. The characters, the language and the stories all rush forward, but, like a herd of frightened animals, they are stampeding off the same high cliff. It is this fatalism combined with the suspenseful rhythm of her language that creates the odd, unsettling atmosphere of the stories.

An anonymous reviewer in *Publishers Weekly* notes that "Oates is never merely sensational, tracking hidden motives and emotions with a sharp eye for psychological detail—everything conveyed in lucid, rhythmic prose."

Often positioned as the foremost narrative stylist of her generation, Oates is, as Donna Seaman comments in *Booklist*, "an expert in the causes and effects of obsession, desolation, and annihilation." On the strength of stories like "In the Region of Ice," Seaman notes, her "daring oeuvre, immense in size, depth, and spirit, will stand as a pillar in American literature."

CRITICISM

Klay Dyer

Dyer is a freelance writer specializing in topics relating to literature, popular culture, and the

> **ALLEN SEEKS TO EVOKE IN SISTER IRENE A DEEPER UNDERSTANDING OF HIS VERY REAL DILEMMA IN THE WORLD AND, BY EXTENSION, OF THE POWER OF HER VERY PERSONAL FAITH TO MAKE A DIFFERENCE IN A LIFE FRAUGHT WITH THE 'RESTLESS VIOLENCE' OF 'LAWLESS AND INCERTAIN THOUGHT.'"**

relationship between creativity and technology. In the following essay, he explores the intertextual relationship between Oates's "In the Region of Ice" and Shakespeare's problematic play Measure for Measure.

In act 3, scene 1 of Shakespeare's *Measure for Measure* (1604), the character of Claudio, a young gentleman, speaks to his sister, Isabella, who is a novice to a great sisterhood of nuns:

> Ay, but to die, and go we know not where; To lie in cold obstruction and to rot; This sensible warm motion to become A kneaded clod; and the delighted spirit To bathe in fiery floods, or to reside In thrilling region of thick-ribbed ice; To be imprison'd in the viewless winds, And blown with restless violence round about The pendent world; or to be worse than worst Of those that lawless and incertain thought Imagine howling: 'tis too horrible! The weariest and most loathed worldly life That age, ache, penury and imprisonment Can lay on nature is a paradise To what we fear of death.

Given that Oates has long appreciated Shakespeare's plays for their explorations of "the momentum of lives, the accumulating fears, tensions, lies, and illusions that then erupt on stage within a two- or three-hour duration" (as she expressed in a 1982 interview with Leif Sjöberg), it is not surprising that she draws both her title and theme for "In the Region of Ice" from *Measure for Measure*, a play that underscores in powerful ways the classic difficulties associated with reconciling or balancing justice and mercy.

Set in Vienna, a Catholic city and the seat of the Roman Empire, the play has proved controversial for readers, who often find it an

WHAT DO I READ NEXT?

- Oates's *A Widow's Story: A Memoir* (2011) is powerful evidence of her skill as writer of nonfiction. Illuminating her struggle to adjust following the sudden and unexpected death of her husband Ray from a virulent hospital-acquired infection, this book is a deeply moving tale of life, death, love, and grief from one of the most private American writers of her generation.

- Similarly, Oates's *The Lost Landscape: A Writer's Coming of Age* (2015) is a vivid recounting of her early years growing up in rural western New York State. It is a compelling story of a another time and place that inspired one of the best story writers in contemporary America.

- Oates often cites Lewis Carroll's *Alice's Adventures in Wonderland* (1865) as the book that changed her view of the world and inspired her to look at life as an endless adventure. This is a particularly good selection for younger readers.

- Oates is often compared to fellow American story writer Flannery O'Connor (1925–1964), so a reading of O'Connor's *Complete Stories* (1977) will prove an interesting point of comparison into related but distinct views of the darkness that lingers below the surface of American society.

- *Dubliners* (1914), by Irish writer James Joyce, is an influential collection of short stories that explore middle-class struggles and values during times of great change and uncertainty. These stories were instrumental in establishing the Joycean epiphany—a sudden realization about the world—as a kind of standard of achievement against which other stories (and endings of stories in particular) would be measured.

- Canada has produced an abundance of internationally acclaimed short-story writers: Margaret Atwood, Margaret Laurence, and Mavis Gallant, to name but a few. The late Alistair MacLeod would be at or near the top of every list, and his *As Birds Bring Forth the Sun and Other Stories* (1992) is a masterful collection rich with stories that overlay character, setting, and theme as few other writers can.

- African Canadian storyteller M. G. Vassanji's *The Gunny Sack* (2005) takes many of the themes familiar to readers of Oates and transports them to Tanzania. Emotionally charged and impeccably executed, these stories are well worth reading.

---

overwhelmingly dark portrayal of human nature. The play opens in a society that has, under the rule of Duke Vincentio, become riddled with decay and corruption as laws are allowed to lapse and order slip into chaos. The duke names the immoral and merciless Lord Angelo his deputy and puts him in charge of reestablishing order across the city. Ostensibly removing himself under the pretense of taking care of business elsewhere, the duke returns to Vienna in disguise in order to observe what happens when an excess of liberty is suddenly replaced by an excess of restraint. As the scenes unfold, this play becomes an exploration of the tension between human nature and social rules, of the polarizing power dynamics of testing and tempting, and of the possibility of revelations both personal (through self-awareness) and communal.

But whereas Shakespeare plays this dilemma across a broad, densely populated canvas, Oates compresses the full range of Shakespearean experiences into a story about two characters: Allen, the deeply troubled young man who demands much of his teacher's attention and emotions, and Sister Irene, who suffers under his expectations only to discover that, despite her commitment to Christ's ethical teachings, she is unable to save him or herself in a world defined emotionally and intellectually by what can be best described as "a region of thick-ribbed ice"; that is, by a deep faith in reason and rationality at the expense of emotional openness.

A strongly intertextual story, Oates's narrative emphasizes a number of the key concerns that lie at the heart of *Measure for Measure*. By showing that Sister Irene cannot meet Allen's deepest, most personal needs, the story raises questions about the relevance of Christian doctrine when considered in the context of a life lived in a complex real world. A very capable and confident teacher who is most comfortable as "an instrument by which facts [are] communicated," Sister Irene struggles with "conflicts in her mind" when it comes to dealing with the cynicism and indifference of the world beyond the walls of her classroom. But when confronted with the passionate, questioning mind of Allen, she is immediately drawn into one of the central tensions informing Shakespeare's play: the longstanding and complex relationship between the life of a private individual and that person's role as a public servant. In Sister Irene, Oates combines the struggles of both the siblings Claudio and Isabella in *Measure for Measure* in order to reveal that mercy, however powerfully positioned in the Bible, cannot necessarily be converted into direct actions in either a private life (Irene as woman) or an institutional one (Irene as teacher). As Irene's struggles illuminate, there is something very personal about performing an act of mercy, and such an act is not always within reach of an individual at a given moment.

The relationship between public and private mercy was very much an issue in Oates's America of 1966. The Vietnam conflict was escalating dramatically under Lyndon B. Johnson's presidency, which was marked symbolically by congressional approval of the Gulf of Tonkin Resolution in August of 1964. Under this resolution, the president was free to conduct full-blown military actions in Southeast Asia without the formal declaration of war; in other words, the individual in the most powerful public office in the United States could unilaterally launch a full-scale war if he deemed it necessary. In this sense, Oates and Shakespeare wrote in very similar cultural times. Both were

writing in times during which the duties and power of a ruler, and in both cases a Christian ruler, were open to wide and public discussion.

In Shakespeare's England, King James I (like the fictional Duke Vincentio) reinforced the seventeenth-century belief that a ruler's authority came from God and that a good ruler was expected to attempt to be like God in his dispensation of justice and mercy. With his kingship, James ushered in a much greater bureaucracy and machinery of state intelligence gathering than England had ever seen previously. Importantly, James came to be associated with the idea of power in absentia ("in absence"), which turned out to be central to positioning himself as a kind of divine power, a delegation of the power to stand as the ultimate symbol of reason and ethical judgment.

What Allen seeks in Sister Irene is the kind of symbolic reassurance that King James and, in *Measure for Measure*, Duke Vincentio provided their followers: an all-powerful judge who can validate ideas and give followers the emotional and financial support to validate his intelligence, worldliness, and sanity. Such all-powerful judging was the ruler's (and teacher's or nun's) duty, and one that made him dangerously godlike in his influence.

Taken literally, this relationship reinforced the belief that a just ruler was exempt from the more common prohibition against vengeance and the measuring of punishment against those who sought to challenge or even overturn the social order. King James, like those before and after him, interpreted this as a responsibility to preserve order even if such a goal necessitated the use of extraordinary methods that could, for more common men in more common times, be seen as immoral. The link to 1960s America is clear: a president leveraged unusual destructive power in order to subdue a powerful enemy whose presence was perceived as a threat to the global good.

Thus, the common focal point of *Measure for Measure* and "In the Region of Ice" is in the inability of potential leaders to translate the Gospel into norms and practices for living in the real world. Put another way, both works explore the wide gap separating personal belief from public action. Oates's Allen is put into this world as a kind of test for Sister Irene, designed to reveal to her the limitations of her faith and the need for her to consider more fully the relationship between words (of mercy, of empathy, of caring) and actions based on those words. Tellingly, it is in this translation of words into action that Sister Irene reveals herself to be the victim of a debilitating stasis, unable to function effectively beyond the walls of her classroom and trapped perpetually in her own emotional ice field.

In a twist of appropriately Shakespearean proportions, Allen is converted from follower—a character in the world of the story whose catalytic presence provides a range of unexpected experiences for Sister Irene—to the powerful albeit flawed judge. It is Allen, in the end, who observes and evaluates Sister Irene's responses to his dilemma and action as a sort of advocate for his health. Moreover, he performs all of these functions, at times simultaneously, with a view to heighten Sister Irene's awareness of the moral complexities of her faith. Allen seeks to evoke in Sister Irene a deeper understanding of his very real dilemma in the world and, by extension, of the power of her very personal faith to make a difference in a life fraught with the "restless violence" of "lawless and incertain thought."

Mercy appears in both *Measure for Measure* and "In the Region of Ice" not as an abstract quality but as a practical awareness that can be counterbalanced, ideally, by a gradual healing that embraces an honesty of judgment. Both works also connect mercy to an aspect of the creative force itself, one that allows an individual to become the best self possible. Rather than suggesting that Christian doctrine should provide solutions to real-world problems, Oates's "In the Region of Ice" points to the limitations of any attempt to read human conduct through the pages of books or abstract ideas. The story prompts readers to look for something real and personal in order to embrace mercy in a way that can bring about a deep personal transformation.

Source: Klay Dyer, Critical Essay on "In the Region of Ice," in *Short Stories for Students*, Gale, Cengage Learning, 2017.

Greg Johnson

In the following excerpt, Johnson traces feminist themes in the collection "The Wheel of Love."

. . . Of all Oates's story collections, *The Wheel of Love* remains one of her finest and has been the subject of more critical discussion

At first, Sister Irene is angered by Allen, but she comes to look forward to seeing him in class *(©Aaron Amat | Shutterstock.com)*

than any other of her more than sixty books. Although much attention has deservedly been paid to Oates's relentless and virtuosic formal experimentation in these stories, *The Wheel of Love* is also notable for its complex, probing examination of gender issues and, in some cases, of explicitly feminist themes. The volume presents a broad spectrum of women whose thwarted attempts to achieve transcendence through romantic or family love ironically reveal their culture's delimiting view of female identity and feminine roles. The majority of the book's twenty stories have women protagonists: questing rebellious adolescents ("Where Are You Going?" and "How I Contemplated the World"), young women trapped in demeaning, anxiety-producing love affairs ("Unmailed, Unwritten Letters," and "I Was in Love"), and fearful, emotionally frigid women ("Bodies" and "In the Region of Ice").

Oates depicts these women's relationships as, again, versions of the Nietzschean will to power: because both family and romantic loves represent a battle of contending wills, women usually find themselves on the losing side because of their culturally enforced passive roles. If they

"ONE OF THE MAJOR THEMES OF *THE WHEEL OF LOVE*, IN FACT, IS THE EXTENT TO WHICH PEOPLE DELUDE THEMSELVES INTO CHERISHING ROMANTIC IDEALS OF LOVE, WHILE ACTUALLY SEEKING EITHER THE EGO-GRATIFICATION OF POWER OVER OTHERS OR A COWARDLY ESCAPE FROM INDIVIDUATION AND AUTONOMY."

sometimes appear victorious, as when a nun withdraws into the safety of emotional detachment after the suicide of a male student, it is because they have surrendered their autonomy to that of a male-prescribed institution. Male aggression and violence, whether through actual rape, psychological tyranny, or institutional domination, lie at the heart of all these women's torn and conflicted lives.

Ironically, Oates's feminist theme is perhaps even clearer in the five stories featuring male protagonists, since each of these characters is himself defeated by male-dominated, culturally approved systems of power. It is surely significant that none of these five is a sexually active male. In "Shame," Father Rollins is a Catholic priest whose submission to patriarchal orthodoxy has stifled his personal development. "Wild Saturday" portrays a young boy whose drug-saturated father and his friends—men compared to roosters and goats, natural symbols of male sexual rapacity—are clearly unable to provide the child any emotional nurture and security. In "Convalescing," a man recovering from a car accident has removed himself from sexual life, while "The Wheel of Love" features a widower who "ached to die." The fifth male protagonist, Alan in "An Interior Monologue," is a chaste, fearful chemist whose repressed homosexual desire for his best friend is displaced by an "acceptable" fascination with the man's wife. A sixth story, "Boy & Girl," is divided about equally between male and female viewpoints, and here the male is an acne-ridden, sexually insecure adolescent whose father sells germ-warfare technology to the American government. Like the medical tyrants in Oates's

novel *Wonderland* (1971), Dr. Pedersen and Dr. Perrault, the father deploys the biological destructiveness that in all Oates's fiction is a primarily male endeavor.

Oates's vulnerable young males, like the sons in "Boy & Girl" and "Wild Saturday," idolize their corrupt fathers, suggesting that as adults they will mimic their fathers' destructive behavior. Her young adult men, such as Father Rollins in "Shame" and Alan in "An Interior Monologue," are self-emasculated males attempting to avoid the pressures of their own sexuality. In the highly symbolic final scene of "Shame," for instance, Father Rollins has just paid a condolence visit to the wife of his deceased boyhood friend, and the woman has given him the parting gift of a small blue egg, the product of an "enslaved robin" (*WL*). Their meeting culminates when Father Rollins's repressed sexual energy causes him to "smash" the egg in his palm. The egg, a potential for life, "a miracle," becomes in Father Rollins's hand "just a mess, any kind of mess and not necessarily the mess of an egg" (*WL*). When the priest cleans himself with a tissue, Oates implies a symbolic masturbation which discharges the sexual tension that has developed between Father Rollins and the young widow. Instantly resuming his benign clerical persona and his habit of denial, the priest wads the tissue and puts it "neatly into his own pocket" (*WL*); but he is clearly enslaved by his repressions, which are figured by the black suit he wears (an outfit the widow says she envies, since she also would like "something I could hide in" [*WL*]). Cut off from male sexual power, both the widow and Father Rollins feel disabled and fearful, although like the other males in *The Wheel of Love* the priest cannot consciously acknowledge his own sense of inadequacy, but rather perceives himself (in rather hackneyed terms) as graced by a higher, spiritual power than transcends the imperatives of both nature and culture.

Such stories set Oates apart from polemical feminist writers, in that she does not view biological gender alone as a determining factor in human personality. Rather, the fate of Oates's characters is dictated by the success with which they arrogate to themselves the prerogatives— social, psychological, sexual—of masculine power. Thus the central issue, as in most of Oates's fiction, is that of personal will: her characters' struggles often suggest their will to power could be channeled constructively through an enlightened, moral restraint upon the raging needs of the ego. As she wrote in "New Heaven and Earth," an essay published shortly after *The Wheel of Love*, "in many of us the Renaissance ideal is still powerful. It declares: *I will, I want, I demand, I think, I am.* This voice tells us that we are not quite omnipotent but must act as if we were, pushing out into a world of other people or of nature that will necessarily resist us, that will try to destroy us, and that we must conquer." That such willful egocentricity is driven by biological factors, which are savagely reified in cultural, social, and family institutions, is a given in Oates's work. She dramatizes the nightmare of an acquisitive, youthful American culture whose energies are admirable but fatally misguided, serving not the goals of a "communal consciousness" predicted by Oates as a possible salvation for American culture, but rather by primitive drives toward power and domination.

. . . One of the major themes of *The Wheel of Love*, in fact, is the extent to which people delude themselves into cherishing romantic ideals of love, while actually seeking either the ego-gratification of power over others or a cowardly escape from individuation and autonomy. Although women, because of their lesser status within the culture, are more likely to become entangled in seeking either power or escape through love, Oates's male and child characters are likewise caught up in this violently misguided struggle for fulfillment, and are just as likely to be destroyed. Again, Oates's title is instructive: love is dramatized as a cycle, a torturous wheel, as is made clear by the lines from Stanley Kunitz's poem "Lovers Relentlessly," from which Oates's derives her title: "Some must break / Upon the wheel of love, but not the strange, / The secret lords, whom only death can change" (*WL*). Yet Oates's twist upon this theme is ironic, since those who seek death as an escape—Barbara Arber in "Accomplished Desires," Nadia Hutter of "The Wheel of Love"—can scarcely be viewed as lords of their fate. Rather, they are the most "broken" of all, and their suicides represent a bleak recognition of the cyclical, grasping hopelessness their lives have become.

Does Oates envision any possible transcendence of this arduous cycle? Are Oates's women doomed to a gender-determined imprisonment

that must end in either sexual violation, suicide, or tortuous exertions of will—such as Madeline Randall's in "You"—that result in grotesque mutations of female identity? One alternative, though a negative, life-denying one, is a retreat from emotional and sexual involvement altogether. Oates dramatizes this choice in two of her best stories, "In the Region of Ice" and "Bodies," which develop the same theme— the consequences of a cold withdrawal from passional life—in strikingly different ways.

Sister Irene chooses a religious life, encasing her body in a nun's habit and in the authoritative position of an English professor at a Catholic university, while Pauline Ressner chooses the way of art, becoming a sculptor whose white stone heads ("Her work has heads. She was interested only in the human head" [*WL*]) are emblems of her longing to escape the messy, imperfect world of "bodies." Both women are teachers, both keep themselves above the realm of human relationships, and both are described in terms of their personal coldness, Sister Irene with her "hard gray eyes" and a "face waxen with thought" (*WL*) and Pauline with her regal Nordic beauty, an "invulnerable" face covered with a "film of impersonality," her very skin "impregnable because it was so still and so cold" (*WL*). And both women are confronted by dynamic, passionate, deeply troubled men who commit suicide after being rebuffed. Thus Oates investigates not only the withdrawal of female sexuality into a safe but sterile region of ice, but also the moral consequences of refusing human compassion to another person.

Perhaps the finest of Oates's early, "traditional" stories—it is the earliest story in *The Wheel of Love* and is unusual in its lack of formal experimentation—"In the Region of Ice" is also the definitive example of Oates's frequent exploration of teacher-student relationships that move away from the typical, impersonal classroom encounter into an unpredictable and dangerous personal confrontation. Sister Irene's moment of terror comes when she realizes her Jewish student, Allen Weinstein, "was trying to force her into a human relationship" (*WL*). Although she later tries to help him, especially after receiving his letter from a mental institution hinting at suicide, she recognizes during a visit to his parents' home (during which she "could not stop shivering" [*WL*]) that her attempt at Christian love is only a feeble gesture compared to the rigid, icy self-containment her life represents. When Allen commits suicide, she cannot even feel surprise, and the final paragraph movingly summarizes her willfully chosen entrapment in a world safely devoid of feeling: "She was only one person, she thought, walking down the corridor in a dream. Was she safe in this single person, or was she trapped? She had only one identity. She could make only one choice. What she had done or hadn't done was the result of that choice, and how was she guilty? If she could have felt guilt, she thought, she might at least have been able to feel something" (*WL*).

By exerting her personal will, under the guise of a devotion to Christian principles, Sister Irene has actually lifted herself above the wheel of love altogether; her punishment will be to contemplate the moral ramifications of that choice for the rest of her life. In "Bodies," Pauline Ressner's rationalized life is similar, for she also believes she is avoiding life in devotion to the higher calling of her art. But as Pauline begins to be stalked by a troubled young man, Anthony Drayer, she has violent, chaotic dreams that signal the turbulence of the unconscious, "bodily" drives she has so firmly repressed. Just as Sister Irene is supported by the Church, Pauline is from a wealthy family, lives in a house that is like "a small museum" (*WL*), and patterns herself after "the mold of her father: tall, lean, composed, with a patient, cool kind of grace, never hurried" (*WL*).

Like Sister Irene, turning away from Allen Weinstein's urgent plea for friendship, Pauline has always "backed out of people's lives, turning aside from offers of friendship, from urgency, intensity, the admiration of men who did not know her" (*WL*). Her ultimate confrontation with passion is even more jarring than Sister Irene's, for Drayer slashes his own throat in her presence, splashing his blood onto her. This incident signals a reversal in Pauline's life, forcing her into the turbulent realm of passion in which she begins "listening intently to the workings of her body" (*WL*). Fantasizing that she is pregnant, finally succumbing to a catatonic state and psychiatric hospitalization, Pauline drifts permanently into a world of madness, in which the psychiatrist can do nothing but hold "her stone fingers" (*WL*). Becoming one of her own stone heads, she imagines herself as "an angel of death, a beautiful woman with outspread wings, though her body is shaped unnaturally from the waist down" (*WL*). Like "In the Region of Ice," "Bodies" powerfully conveys the extremes of personal will as it attempts to thwart the conditions of nature: both Sister Irene and Pauline lose not only their female identity, but their very humanity. . . .

Source: Greg Johnson, "Early Feminism," in *Joyce Carol Oates: A Study of the Short Fiction*, Twayne Publishers, 1994, pp. 41–44, 51–54.

Greg Johnson

In the following excerpt, Johnson looks at the loneliness of the characters in the story "In the Region of Ice."

Joyce Carol Oates has remained committed to the short story form throughout her career, having by 1987 published fourteen volumes of stories since her first collection, *By the North Gate*, appeared in 1963. As William Abrahams has remarked, Oates writes stories "not as a diversion or spin-off from the writing of novels, but as a central concern in her work—a fortunate recognition that the shorter form is peculiarly suited to her." Since the mid-1960s her stories have been ubiquitous in magazines like the *Atlantic* and *Esquire*, in scores of literary journals, and in the two major annual anthologies, *Prize Stories: The O. Henry Awards* and *The Best American Short Stories*. (In both of these series her work has appeared more often than that of any other author, and both have extended her a special award for continuing achievement.) By the mid-1980s Oates had published more than three hundred stories, some of which are among the finest examples of the form in American literature.

In *The Wheel of Love* (1970) Oates displays the impressive range of fictional technique and subject matter that characterizes all her short story volumes. This collection includes superb examples of the traditional, "well-made" story—most notably "In the Region of Ice"—along with highly experimental stories which share with much innovative writing of the late 1960s and early 1970s an interest in manipulating time, point-of-view, and certain formal conventions in order to revitalize the genre. "Radical experimentation," Oates has remarked, "which might be ill-advised in the novel, is well suited for the short story. I like the freedom and promise of the form." Thus "Unmailed, Unwritten Letters," which uses the

THIS TAUTLY DRAMATIC STORY UNFOLDS
WITH APPEALING GRACE AND SIMPLICITY."

epistolary mode to describe the inner life of an anxiety-ridden woman engaged in an adulterous love affair; "Matter and Energy," a story that moves freely back and forth in time, showing how a young woman's obsession with her mentally unstable mother has precluded her own emotional development; and the title story, moving relentlessly backward in time to describe a professor's doomed marriage to a neurotic, suicidal woman. In such stories Oates achieves powerful effects—in particular, an uncanny heightening of emotional intensity—that could not have been realized in a more traditional narrative.

In later collections the experiments continue. *Marriages and Infidelities* (1972), for instance, includes modern reworkings of classic stories, like Franz Kafka's "The Metamorphosis" and James Joyce's "The Dead." *The Hungry Ghosts* (1974), *Crossing the Border* (1976), and *All the Good People I've Left Behind* (1979) include groups of "linked" stories which form a longer, loosely connected narrative when the volume is read straight through. Oates has remarked, in fact, that all her collections are deliberately shaped artistic constructs: "Each of the story collections is organized around a central theme and is meant to be read as a whole—the arrangement of the stories being a rigorous one, not at all haphazard."

As its title implies, the central subject in *The Wheel of Love* is the "different forms of love, mainly in family relationships." Four of the stories, among the most often anthologized of Oates's works, may here serve as a representative sampling of her enduring themes. In "In the Region of Ice," Sister Irene is a woman who, under the guise of a Christian vocation, has cut herself off from the perils of human love. "Where Are You Going, Where Have You Been?" describes a young girl's initiation into the realm of male-dominated sexuality—one of the earliest of Oates's stories (it first appeared in 1966) to show explicitly feminist concerns. In "The Wheel of Love," describing Professor David Hutter's fatal attraction to

a glamorous but unbalanced woman, Oates reveals the emptiness and sterility of a life from which romance has fled. "How I Contemplated the World from the Detroit House of Correction and Began My Life Over Again," one of the most experimental stories in the volume, presents in the guise of a teen-age girl's notes for an English-class essay a biting satire on affluent suburban life and a portrait of family "love" as a form of spiritual imprisonment.

First-prize winner in *Prize Stories 1967: The O. Henry Awards*, "In the Region of Ice" remains one of Oates's most powerful and finely constructed stories. When Sister Irene, "young and brilliant," begins teaching at a Jesuit University, she accepts the self-effacing role expected of a nun, "a figure existing only for the benefit of others, an instrument by which facts were communicated." Oates subtly reveals the fear of other people and especially of human relationships that resides behind Sister Irene's competent teaching and her cool exterior, her "serious, hard gray eyes . . . a face waxen with thought." The story's major conflict arises when a student named Allen Weinstein enters her life, someone who is her opposite in every way: she is Catholic, female, reserved, and stable; Weinstein is Jewish, male, gregarious, and volatile. Though she admires his probing intellect, he quickly becomes a source of fear: "She was terrified at what he was trying to do—he was trying to force her into a human relationship."

This tautly dramatic story unfolds with appealing grace and simplicity. After challenging Sister Irene both intellectually and emotionally, Allen disappears and then sends her an anguished letter from a nearby mental institution. The letter includes a passage from Shakespeare's *Measure for Measure*, which Sister Irene correctly interprets as a veiled suicide threat and a cry for help. Her student's crisis propels Sister Irene into practicing her Christianity. When she goes impulsively to visit Allen's parents and plead on his behalf, the story conveys the excitement of authentic moral action. But when she witnesses the affluent but loveless home life of the Weinsteins, "Sister Irene felt [Allen's] sickness spread to her." Thus her brief, uncharacteristic moment of spontaneous charity and moral determination quickly ends: "The strange idea she had had on the way over, something about understanding Christ, came back to her now and sickened her. But the sickness was small. It could be contained." By the time Allen returns to visit her, Sister Irene has retreated back into her own "region of ice." When Allen cries out, "I want something real and not this phony Christian love garbage," she has nothing else to offer him. He curses her and flees her office, and thereafter Sister Irene lives "anonymous in her black winter cloak, quiet and stunned." Unsurprised by the news of Allen's suicide, Sister Irene is left to perceive only her own ice-bound consciousness, her continuing inability to feel love: "She had only one identity. She could make only one choice. What she had done or hadn't done was the result of that choice, and how was she guilty? If she could have felt guilt, she thought, she might at least have been able to feel something."

Bleak as this ending is, it is not really despairing; Sister Irene discovers the possibility of human love but decides that it simply isn't available to her. Allen Weinstein, after all, is uncontrolled and wildly demanding; he may be seen to represent the child-self in all of us, demanding love, undivided attention, immediate gratification. Possessing universal human needs, Allen lacks the necessary maturity and control that might allow him to negotiate those needs with another adult person. Thus he becomes, for Sister Irene, a "crystallization of her own loneliness." He not only suffered loneliness but "he embodied it, he acted it out, and that was perhaps why he fascinated her. It was as if he were doing a dance for her, a dance of shame and agony and delight, and so long as he did it, she was safe."

As the daughter of "whining, weak people," Sister Irene had developed in childhood a negative image of love, determined not to "compete" for it as her parents had competed for hers. Likewise when she visits the Weinstein home, she finds a cold, loveless environment in which she "could not stop shivering." Although she recognizes the emotional genuineness of Allen himself, he represents yet another negative facet of love, its naked craving and desperation. Her experience with Allen only confirms Sister Irene in her aloof isolation. Just as Allen had committed suicide in Quebec, which causes Sister Irene to daydream about "the plains of white snow to the north, the quiet, the emptiness, the sweep of the Great Lakes up to the silence of Canada," so is Sister Irene fated to live out a frigid life of emotional sterility and nonfeeling. . . .

Source: Greg Johnson, "The Short Stories (I): *The Wheel of Love*," in *Understanding Joyce Carol Oates*, University of South Carolina Press, 1987, pp. 92–98.

SOURCES

Alley, Henry, "The Well-Made World of the O. Henrys, 1961–2000," in *Kenyon Review*, Vol. 25, No. 2, Spring 2003, pp. 36–58.

Altman, Robert, *The Sixties*, Santa Monica Press, 2007.

Cheuse, Alan, Review of *High Lonesome*, in *World Literature Today*, Vol. 80, No. 5, pp. 33–34.

De Groot, Gerard J., *The Sixties Unplugged: A Kaleidoscopic History of a Disorderly Decade*, Harvard University Press, 2008.

Oates, Joyce Carol, "In the Region of Ice," in *High Lonesome: New and Selected Stories 1966–2006*, Harper-Collins, 2006, pp. 231–48.

Review of *High Lonesome*, in *Publishers Weekly*, Vol. 253, No. 6, February 6, 2006, pp. 41–42.

Schine, Cathleen, "People Who Hurt People," in *New York Times*, April 30, 2006, http://www.nytimes.com/2006/04/30/books/review/30schine.html?_r = 0&page wanted = print (accessed March 1, 2016).

Seaman, Donna, Review of *High Lonesome*, in *Booklist*, Vol. 102, No. 14, March 15, 2006, p. 29.

Sjöberg, Leif, "An Interview with Joyce Carol Oates," in *Contemporary Literature*, Vol. 23, No. 3, Summer 1982, pp. 267–84.

Young, Marilyn B., John J. Fitzgerald, and Tom A. Grunfeld, *The Vietnam War: A History of Documents*, Oxford University Press, 2002.

FURTHER READING

Johnson, Greg, *Invisible Writer: A Biography of Joyce Carol Oates*, Plume, 1999.

> In this astute exploration of how Oates's writing has been informed by the twists and turns of her life, Johnson reveals little-known facts about her personal history while tackling head-on many of the myths that have arisen about this brilliant woman.

Martin, Robert K., and Eric Savoy, *American Gothic: New Interventions in a National Narrative*, University of Iowa Press, 2009.

> This insightful collection of thirteen essays explores the persistence of the gothic in American culture by providing discussions of the various influences that have shaped this genre over time, from the histories of gender and race to the emerging cultures of cities. Special attention is paid to the issues of slavery and race in texts from both black and white authors, including

Ralph Ellison and William Faulkner. In the view of the editors and contributors, the gothic is not so much a historical category as a mode of thought haunted by history, a part of suburban life and American culture.

Oates, Joyce Carol, *In Rough Country: Essays and Reviews*, Ecco, 2010.

A collection of piercing essays on the works of such writers as Edgar Allan Poe, Emily Dickinson, Jean Stafford, Roald Dahl, Shirley Jackson, Flannery O'Connor, Cormac McCarthy, and Philip Roth. What is clear from this collection is how deeply Oates is drawn to writers and themes that inform her own work, such as the gothic, the satiric, feminist theory, and works with a strong humanist coloring. In the section titled "Nostalgias," Oates delves deeper into the influence of Lewis Carroll on her childhood and writing .

———, *On Boxing*, Doubleday, 1987.

A fight fan since her youth, Oates follows in the tradition of boxing-loving writers like Ernest Hemingway and Norman Mailer in this collection, which is expanded from an article she originally wrote for the *New York Times Magazine*. It is still considered a classic piece of sports writing.

SUGGESTED SEARCH TERMS

Joyce Carol Oates

"In the Region of Ice" AND Oates

Oates AND 1960s

Oates AND colleges OR universities

Oates AND guilt

Oates AND mental illness

Oates AND students

Oates AND teachers

Oates AND Jewish

The Jewbird

BERNARD MALAMUD

1963

Pulitzer Prize–winning Jewish American author Bernard Malamud's "The Jewbird," first published in the news magazine *Reporter* in 1963, takes the form of a classic animal fable. A talking crow that calls itself a Jewbird named Schwartz takes refuge from "anti-Semeets" (as he calls them in his Yiddish accent) in the apartment of Harry Cohen and his middle-class, highly assimilated family. Despite being a crow, the bird acts like an old immigrant Jew, with the disconnect between his persona and his body providing Malamud's characteristic humor. Malamud uses this fantastic inspiration to explore the nature of immigrant and Jewish identity in America and the depths of human psychology. For Malamud, the most profound meaning in literature is conveyed through symbols, and he purposefully creates this story out of the conventional symbolic language discovered by Austrian psychiatrist Sigmund Freud. The story is included in *A Malamud Reader*, published by Farrar, Straus and Giroux in 1967.

AUTHOR BIOGRAPHY

Malamud was born in Brooklyn, New York, on April 26, 1914. His father, Max, was a poor grocer. He and his wife, Bertha, were Russian Jewish immigrants. On Malamud's own account, he grew up in a household impoverished in terms

Bernard Malamud (©*Nancy R. Schiff / Getty Images*)

of art and literature; his parents owned no books or prints, nor was he exposed to the traditions of the Jewish life of his Eastern European ancestors. He became acculturated only through his education in high school and university. As he grew up, he was an eager film viewer and credited the films of Charlie Chaplin with teaching him narrative. While acknowledging his Jewishness, Malamud considered himself an American writer who happened sometimes to write on Jewish subjects. He felt he had little connection to Jewish tradition or to Jewish religious life, which was not especially important in his family. He knew Hasidic traditions only though writers like Sholem Asch, whose works he read in later life. Malamud attended City College for a BA and then Columbia University for an MA (1942) in English, partially on loans and partially working part time, sometimes for the Census Bureau but mostly teaching night school English classes to adults obtaining a GED. In 1945, he married Ann de Chiara, who came from an Italian Catholic immigrant background. Both families disapproved of what was then considered a

mixed marriage. Ann had a bachelor's degree from Cornell.

Despite their Ivy League educations, making a living proved a daunting task for the Malamud family, whether because of their immigrant status or for some other reason. Just at the time Malamud started to look for a college teaching job, the requirements to teach began to shift to include a PhD, while the requirements to teach high school were moving toward including a degree in education. Ann typed up nearly three hundred letters of application for university teaching jobs around the country, and in 1949 Malamud began work at the only job he was offered, at Oregon State University in Corvallis. Even there he was allowed to teach only composition, not literature. Malamud devoted himself to writing and soon became a regular voice in the leading magazines. He published his first novel, *The Natural*, in 1952. It is also his best-known work, thanks to the 1984 film adaptation by Barry Levinson starring Robert Redford. While the book is ostensibly about baseball, Malamud used a carefully crafted system of symbols to encode an allegorical moral meaning in the book. This was his standard technique of writing and is certainly apparent in his 1963 animal fable "The Jewbird." Malamud's next novel, *The Assistant* (1957), was based on the life of his father as a Jewish grocer in New York during the Great Depression. *The Fixer* (1967), about anti-Semitism in Czarist Russia, won the Pulitzer Prize. By 1961, Malamud's growing fame as a writer enabled him to move to a more prestigious position at Bennington College in Vermont. Malamud published three volumes of short stories: *The Magic Barrel* (1958); *Idiots First* (1963), which included a reprint of "The Jewbird"; and *Rembrandt's Hat* (1974). He also published five additional novels, of which the last, *God's Grace* (1982), is a fantasy in which the sole human survivor of a nuclear war and a second divine flood attempts to rebuild civilization, working with a population of chimpanzees. Malamud died of heart failure in his New York apartment on March 18, 1986.

PLOT SUMMARY

The story takes place in the Manhattan apartment of the Cohens, a middle-class Jewish family. A bird flies in through the open window one evening during dinner. It is summer, which

MEDIA ADAPTATIONS

- A dramatic adaptation of "The Jewbird" was staged by the Northwoods Ramah Theater Company (written and directed by Annie G. Levy). It was performed at the theater's home in Conover, Wisconsin, in 2006 and off-Broadway in 2009. Schwartz is represented by a puppet that is manipulated and voiced by a puppeteer dressed as a black-hat Hasid who appears fully onstage.

the family usually spends at a resort in the Catskills, but the father's mother is dying, so they had to return to the city. The bird appears to be a crow and hops around the table a little before flying off to perch on top of the open kitchen door, crying out, "Gevalt, a pogrom!" after Harry, the father of the family, swats at him.

The wife, Edie, is impressed that the bird can talk, and Harry engages it in conversation. It can talk with the same facility as a human being. The bird explains that he is hungry and wants to eat, preferably his own lamb chop. He merits charity, he claims, because he is running from anti-Semites. The family wonders which anti-Semites would attack a bird. He explains that they are eagles, vultures, hawks, and sometimes crows. Harry asks if he, the bird, is not a crow. The bird replies that he is a Jewbird and then proves it by going through the ritual of Jewish prayer.

Harry asks the bird if he is not a dybbuk (a wandering soul) or ghost. The bird denies being a dybbuk, though once, he claims, one of his female relatives was afflicted by one. The bird identifies himself as Schwartz. Edie suggests, "He might be an old Jew changed into a bird by somebody." Claiming not to know, the bird shrugs his shoulders like a human and Edie and Maurie, the son, offer him herring, which the bird politely accepts. (Although it is modern American, homogenized herring, not the ethnic delicacy the bird was expecting, he knows better

than to complain about charity.) Harry, however, orders Schwartz to leave once he has eaten, though the bird has no place to go. Maurie pleads on the bird's behalf, and Harry allows him to stay the night in the apartment.

The next morning, Edie asks if the bird can't stay, since he is no trouble. Harry again concedes, but he says it will not be for long and expresses a deep hostility and suspicion of Schwartz: "He's a foxy bastard. He thinks he's a Jew."

Edie buys Schwartz a birdhouse to live in on the apartment balcony; he would prefer to live inside, but Harry will not allow it. Harry also buys him some dried corn, but Schwartz's aged digestion cannot tolerate it, so he sticks with his herring. Harry tries to provoke him by treating him like a bird.

Maurie has real trouble with his schoolwork, so that autumn Schwartz begins to tutor him, bringing his marks up. For all that he is like "an old Jew," Schwartz is capable of some birdlike behavior, which amuses the boy. When Schwartz wanders into a discarded grocery bag on the floor, Maurie jokes that he is looking to build a nest. The boy's grades continue to improve, and Harry starts to think of an Ivy League school for his son. The bird is not that optimistic. This causes another altercation between Harry and Schwartz.

The bird tries to keep out of Harry's way. Schwartz is polite and deferential in the face of all Harry's verbal attacks, using the self-effacing nature of Yiddish idiom as a defense, with characteristic phrases like "Excuse me, I'm not complaining. . . . You're complaining" or "Snoring . . . isn't a crime, thanks God." Harry takes advantage of being left alone with Schwartz to verbally attack him, mocking him for smelling of herring and suggesting that he may be some sort of devil after all. Harry wonders aloud if the bird doesn't want to take his place sleeping next to his wife. Discussing the matter later with Edie, Schwartz admits he smells of the food he eats but suggests that others, meaning Harry, "smell because of their thoughts or because who they are."

Finally, in November, Harry, risking that Maurie can keep up with his schoolwork on his own, tells Schwartz to leave, "or it's open war." Not knowing how he could fend for himself, however, the bird stays. Harry buys a cat for Maurie, who had always wanted one for a pet, and the animal spends all of its time trying to kill the bird. Harry also takes to popping paper bags in the middle of the night outside the birdhouse, to keep Schwartz from sleeping and increase his anxiety.

Some weeks later, on the same day that Harry's mother dies, Maurie brings home a report card with a failing grade in math. This is too much for Harry. When Edie takes their son to his violin lesson, he chases Schwartz into his birdhouse with a broom and then physically pulls him out, intending to throw him off the balcony, whirling the bird around his head to give his throw greater force. Harry finally flings Schwartz into oblivion, but not before the bird gives him a terrible bite on the nose. The bird sinks to the pavement, and Harry throws his birdhouse after him. He reports to his wife and child that Schwartz attacked him (pointing out the wound on his nose) without provocation, so he threw him out, and the bird flew off.

In the spring, after the snow has melted, Maurie "found a dead black bird in a small lot near the river, his two wings broken, neck twisted, and both bird-eyes plucked clean." Assuming this is Schwartz, he asks his mother who could have done it, and she replies, lapsing into Schwartz's Yiddish accent, "Anti-Semeets."

CHARACTERS

Harry Cohen

Harry Cohen is the antagonist (villain) of "The Jewbird." He is implacably and irrationally opposed to Schwartz from the moment the bird enters the apartment. He swats at the bird, who recognizes the violence as a pogrom, or racist attack, against Jews. He persecutes the bird throughout the story and eventually attacks and (presumably) kills him. While Harry's antipathy to the bird drives forward the plot of the story, the reader must become more interested in trying to discover the reason for it. By far, the most popular explanation offered by critics is that Harry is a Jewish anti-Semite. Eileen H. Watts, in her 1996 *Melus* article, gives a standard articulation of this view and principally interprets "The Jewbird" through a study of Harry's character. She is somewhat off balance in her argument, beginning with the supposition that Harry is an unqualified success, describing him as "an established frozen foods salesman . . . living in a penthouse apartment." *Penthouse* has a resonance of wealth and

social prominence, suggesting the inhabitants of one of the skyscrapers south of Central Park in midtown Manhattan, able to pay an exorbitant price for the view from the upper stories. This is not Harry. According to Malamud, Harry lives in a "top-floor apartment on First Avenue near the lower East River." This is a working-class immigrant neighborhood with buildings of fewer than ten stories, built before World War I without elevators. The rents become cheaper as one goes up to the higher, more inaccessible stories. The height of his apartment marks Harry's middling status, not his success. Watts argues that in order to assimilate and become American, Harry has become an anti-Semite. She claims that "his anti-Semitism is really an American strain internalized" and that he "is the mouth-piece for Gentile anti-Semitism." This argument cannot be discounted, since Schwartz recognizes Harry's initial attack as a pogrom and, later, after Harry has evidently murdered Schwartz, his own wife blames the death on "anti-Semeets."

Watts's assessment of what Harry's anti-Semitism consists of is more problematic. She is right in pointing out that the first lines of the story refer to the quota system for allowing the immigration into America of Jewish refugees during the 1930s, but since World War I all immigration into the United States has been controlled by quota, not merely that of Jews (a point that is becoming an issue again now with reference to refugees from the civil war in Syria). So this could point to a more universalist theme. The same is true of Harry's attempts to make Schwartz eat dried corn as bird feed. According to Watts, this sends the message of anti-Semites to Jews: "You're lucky to be here; be happy with what little you have." This is the rhetorical stance of the political right to any recipients of government aid, not just immigrants and certainly not just Jews. Watts says that when Harry tries to articulate his hatred for Schwartz, he speaks only in generalities, saying that the bird is a troublemaker, the same kind of vague complaint anti-Semites make against Jews (unless they launch into detailed fantasies about the Jews' control of the banking industry). The same is true for all immigrants throughout US history, however, going back to the Irish immigration before the Civil War. Watts is certainly on the mark when she observes that Schwartz is representative of the Jews of the generation of Harry's father and that "he is probably ashamed of and looks down on the behavior and speech of low-class, eastern European Jews—in other words, we presume, the behavior of Cohen's own parents." It is not difficult to read Harry as embodying anti-Semitism, despite his being a Jew, but this can also be read as a type of American opposition to the immigrant "other," not just Jews. There is also an element of generational conflict. Watts supposes that Harry heartlessly embraces anti-Semitism because he longs to be assimilated and become an American. She overlooks a more sympathetic reading of his character. Perhaps Harry wishes to cast out his own Jewishness (as he ritually throws Schwartz into the oblivion of the night) because he is tired of being the victim of anti-Semitism and he knows no amount of assimilation will change that.

The fact that Harry makes his living selling frozen food is interesting and certainly is not something Malamud chose to repeatedly bring up in the story for no reason. Watts observes that Harry sells frozen food because he is cold-hearted, and this is undeniably true. Even so, the whole idea of mass-produced frozen food is antithetical to traditional Jewish cooking and hence Jewish culture. So it is another sign that Harry is desperately trying to leave his tradition (and this symbol could have the same significance if Harry had been Italian or Chinese or any other kind of immigrant).

Harry Cohen's Mother

Harry's mother is never named and never appears in person in the narrative. Her falling into illness sets the story in motion by recalling Harry and his family from Kingston to Manhattan so they can be nearer to her to help when she is sick. It is certainly no coincidence that Harry bides his time and turns to outright violence against Schwartz only after his mother is dead, though how her being alive restrained him is not apparent in the manifest content or surface narrative of the story.

Edie Cohen

Edie is Harry's wife and Maurie's mother. Like all the domestic tasks of the household in the prefeminist 1960s, the work of tending to Schwartz, feeding him his herring, falls to her. She is also the bird's confidant in hearing his complaints about her husband's mistreatment of him, but she is hardly in a position to side with Schwartz against her husband merely

because he is in the right. She counsels patience and endurance in the face of his adversity but cannot do much more than feed the bird for his assistance to her son. At the end of the story she must realize that, whatever anti-Semeets killed him, whether Harry himself or the hawks and ravens the bird originally fled from, her husband is ultimately responsible for his death, killing something her son loved.

Morris Cohen

Morris (named after his maternal grandfather), called Maurie, is the middle-school-aged child of Harry and Edie. Although he is not well developed as a character for the reader, he is the member of the Cohen family closest to Schwartz. The bird devotes his time to tutoring the boy in his school subjects, considerably improving his grades. Harry, who had neglected the task himself, is pleased with the improvement that might allow his son to attend an Ivy League school and gain more of the social advancement he craves for his family. His intellectual gifts are not superior, however, and Harry blames the messenger when Schwartz tells the father this truth about his son. Maurie seems to conceive of Schwartz as a pet or plaything, in many respects no different from the way he views the cat Harry buys to vex Schwartz and who soon begins to sleep in Maurie's bed. The boy shows real affection and real grief for the bird, however, when he finds what he presumes to be Schwartz's body revealed by the melting spring snow.

Schwartz, a Jewbird

Schwartz, who is a crow, or Jewbird, is the main character and protagonist (hero) of the "The Jewbird." The bird is originally referred to by the neuter pronoun *it*, as if it were an animal. After Schwartz identifies himself as a Jewbird, the narrative voice refers to the creature with the masculine *he*, as if he were a person. Schwartz obviously has the speech, personality, and mannerisms of an Eastern European immigrant Jew of the generation before Harry's. In other words, he could easily be a caricature of Maurie's grandfather. At the same time, he is a bird. Malamud uses this disconnect in an otherwise realistic story to kindle his own imagination and at the same time that of the reader. The fantasy element of the talking bird disposes the reader to dig into the story to find out what is actually going on.

Schwartz claims that the jewfish is his second cousin once removed, offering, as it were, some connection to the animal kingdom. There is a fish known as the jewfish, a large species of grouper that got its name because it was popular among early Jewish immigrants to Jamaica and other English colonies in the Caribbean, since it was the largest fish, clean according to Mosaic Law, that they could eat. Malamud has stated that one inspiration for "The Jewbird" was hearing of the jewfish for the first time. The term has only rarely been used in an anti-Semitic context, but the fish has nevertheless recently been renamed the goliath grouper. *Jewfish* is usually not capitalized in discussions of sport fishing, but Malamud capitalizes it. Finally, it should be noted that Internet searching makes it possible to turn up the kind of information that neither Malamud nor earlier scholars could reasonably have had access to. In a rather old article, the ornithologist Earle R. Greene, in a note in the *Auk*, mentions that there is a species of grackle (*Crotophaga ani*) native to southern Florida and Cuba that in Cuba is called the Jewbird, or rather he gives that translation of what must be a Spanish original.

THEMES

Jewish Culture

The folkloric character of "The Jewbird" has its roots in Jewish tradition. The Hebrew Bible, of course, contains animal fables in which beasts are granted the power of speech (for example, the serpent in the Garden of Eden and Balaam's ass). More particularly, when the Cohen family is presented with something that cannot exist in the modern Western world, a talking bird with fully human mental faculties, they try to understand it within the context of Jewish tradition. Harry asks the bird if he is a dybbuk or some other kind of ghost. A dybbuk is a prominent element of Jewish folklore. The 1937 Polish film *The Dybbuk* is probably the most important Yiddish film and tells the basic folktale. The dybbuk is the ghost of a young man who was passionately in love with a woman (whether his fiancée or someone socially unobtainable.) who meets an untimely death before his love can be consummated and whose ghost comes back to

possess the woman. The spirit must then be exorcised by the spiritual power of a rabbi. Although in modern American culture reincarnation is associated with Asian religions such as Buddhism, Edie suggests that the bird may be the reincarnation of an old Jew. In fact, belief in reincarnation is common in Hasidic Judaism. It is part of Hasidism's Kabbalistic theology, which ultimately derives from Greek Neoplatonism, and Platonic philosophy embraced the Pythagorean doctrine of reincarnation. Hasidism holds that, though he would not be revealed until the day of the Lord, the Messiah was reincarnated in each generation. The followers of each of the great rabbis wondered what exalted position their leader would be reincarnated into in the generation of the Messiah.

Social Class

One of Harry's chief concerns in "The Jewbird" is upward social mobility. We do not know the work his father did, but, given his class and time, it was probably relatively menial. (Malamud's own father's work as a grocer gives a good idea of the possibilities.) On the other hand, with the prosperity the United States experienced after World War II, Harry has been able to enter the rising middle class, selling frozen food; the reader may imagine he is an account executive for a frozen food firm, competing to sell his company's product wholesale to grocery store chains and restaurants around New York. He has ambitions for his family to rise higher. He wants his son to attend an Ivy League school, which would certainly secure him a much better job still. This is one thing that infuriates Harry about the Jewbird. Schwartz, reporting on Maurie's intellectual ability, casts this judgement: "A scholar he'll never be, if you know what I mean, although maybe a good mechanic. It's no disgrace in these times." Harry considers this an attack and an insult. For a start, Schwartz, who clearly represents an older generation of Jewish immigrant than Harry, is thinking in terms of the Depression era. *Mechanic* here probably has its old-fashioned meaning of someone who works with machines, that is, a factory worker. This indeed would have been a good job to aim at in 1933, but in 1963 Harry wants much more for his son. Schwartz's use of the term *scholar* is also probably archaic, meaning a rabbi. To a first-generation immigrant, born on the Polish shtetl,

TOPICS FOR FURTHER STUDY

- A bestiary is a traditional form of young-adult literature. *The Book of Imaginary Beings* is a bestiary by Jorge Luis Borges, illustrated by Peter Sis. Andrew Hurley's translation was published in 2006. The book is a collection of descriptions of imaginary creatures, including familiar ones such as the dragon (Western and Chinese) and more obscure animals such as Buraq, the beast on which Muhammad flew in one night from Mecca to Jerusalem. Write up (and, if you wish, illustrate) an entry for a bestiary on the heading *Jewbird*.

- Three geographical locations are mentioned in "The Jewbird:" the Lower East Side, where the Cohens live; the Bronx, where Harry's mother lives; and Kingston, New York, the resort town where the Cohens are staying prior to the grandmother's illness. Use the Internet to find photos of these areas in the 1950s or early 1960s and make a presentation of them to your class.

- In his 2007 biography of Malamud, Philip Davis suggests that "The Jewbird" was an inspired rewriting of Howard Nemerov's short story "Digressions around a Crow." There are certainly obvious similarities. The story concerns a crow that befriends a young boy one summer. His father is jealous not of the crow, but of the fact that it prefers his son, ignoring the father's own politically correct environmental concern for birds. At the end of the summer, the bird disappears; it is unclear whether it migrated or, as suggested by some black feathers near the dog house, it might have been killed and eaten by the family pet. Write a paper comparing the two stories and explore any deeper resonances between them. The Nemerov story is often reprinted, for instance, in the 1993 collection *A Howard Nemerov Reader*.

- Edgar Allan Poe's poem "The Raven" is often cited as an obvious source of inspiration for "The Jewbird." The connection is anything but obvious, since Poe's bird cannot properly talk but can recite only one human word (as many crows have learned to do); yet the raven seems to be a messenger from the world beyond death. Both birds can be understood more fully as symbolic of the two works' human main character's psychological anguish. Write a paper comparing the two works.

the position of rabbi would be as high as one could hope to rise, but Harry, assimilated into American culture, does not consider it for a moment. Harry's view has been so entirely changed that he wants the American dream for his son and his family.

STYLE

Magic Realism

Reading "The Jewbird" from a background in contemporary literary criticism will quickly suggest to the reader that he is dealing with a work of magic realism, a fictive work made in the image of reality but into which magic erupts, causing confusion and dislocation and thereby calling into question every assumption about the nature of reality. Malamud had a different idea about his stories like "The Jewbird." He simply called them fantasy, which he defines as "fairy tales, stories of gods wandering the earth, miraculous Bible stories and morality tales, stories of knightly adventure, fables of various sorts, ghost stories—the world of the presently unreal." Malamud's reason for writing fantasy and for suggesting that others read it is equally simple, because it kindles the imagination and leads to fresh ways of thinking. Malamud

The protagonist of the story is a crow named Schwartz (©redpip1984 | Shutterstock.com)

also observes the hostility of the literary establishment to fantasy:

> Every so often I write a short fantasy and am later surprised to hear that an editor who had read the story had asked my agent why I was still on that kick; or after it is published I am surprised by a remark of a reviewer who happens to mention the story, that he sees no good in my going on with fantasy at this stage of my career.

Malamud surveys the reviews for Saul Bellow's novel *Henderson the Rain King* and observes that even reviewers who praised the book went out of their way to note that they personally did not approve of fantasy or that it was impossible to develop modern literature in any useful way through fantasy. One may add that the same prejudice accounts for the critical rejection J. R. R. Tolkien experienced. Perhaps one may learn from Malamud that critics invented the category of magic realism to praise works of fantasy by Latin American authors they did not find it culturally expedient to denigrate. In any case, Malamud considers that the effective part of literature, or at least of his literature, is the use of symbolic

expression, and in "Jewbird" the fantastic elements are symbols narrating the dissolution of Jewish identity in the assimilationist waters of the American dream.

Yiddish

The Jewbird of Malamud's story's title is most likely a native Yiddish speaker and fills his English with Yiddish words and Yiddish phrases. Perhaps the most common, or stereotypical, is the exclamation *Gevalt*. The word means "violence" and is a cry for help by mentioning what one is being threatened with: compare the English exclamation *Murder!*, often seen in literature but probably not used that frequently in speech. In practice, *Gevalt* has a usage similar to the English "Oh my god!" There is some resonance in the story, since who but God could help a Jew from the kind of anti-Semitic violence the Jewbird is fleeing? The Jewbird's name is Schwartz, a common enough Jewish (as well as German) name. It means "black," in keeping with the bird's appearance as a crow. When the Jewbird is called upon to prove he is a Jew by praying, Malamud makes a pun, calling the action "dovening" (more often spelled *davening*). The root is the Hebrew word for "prayer" (itself a loan word in Yiddish), with the English *–ing* ending tacked on. It refers to highly formalized recitation of prayer accompanied by rocking, almost dancelike movements. To pray in the traditional fashion, a Jew must wear a shawl and amulets called *tallith* in Hebrew and Yiddish and the almost equally incomprehensible *phylacteries* in English. The Jewbird uses several other Yiddish words, including *spitz* (the heel end of a loaf of bread), *grubber yung* (an insolent youth), and *shicker* (alcoholic). Many of the bird's odd-sounding expressions, such as "Where there's charity I'll go" or "a scholar he'll never be," follow Yiddish word order. The habit of answering with a question and the use of an aphoristic style meant to raise ordinary discourse to the level of theological debate—seen in a phrase like "Does God tell us everything?"—are also characteristic of Yiddish.

HISTORICAL CONTEXT

Ashkenazi Culture and Assimilation in America

In the late nineteenth and early twentieth centuries, many Ashkenazi Jews from Poland and Russia immigrated to the United States, settling in enclaves in the large eastern cities, especially New York. Their ancestors had originally lived in Germany but had been forced to flee to Eastern Europe by pogroms (massacres of Jews by anti-Semites) at the time of the Black Death in 1348–1350. The Ashkenazi population in Eastern Europe was largely wiped out in the Holocaust, an event that lurks behind Malamud's story with its repeated references to anti-Semites. The translation of Ashkenazi culture to America and its assimilation into the broader American culture form the background from which "The Jewbird" emerges. Malamud is clearly conscious of the erosion of unique Jewish culture as Jews melt into the mass American culture. This is shown, almost incidentally, in language. Yiddish is a Germanic language that Ashkenazi Jews preserved to communicate among themselves in Eastern Europe and brought to America, where it has proved less resilient because assimilation to American culture has been relatively easy—something that was impossible in Poland or Russia. The Jewbird is the most Jewish character in the story. He seems to be a native Yiddish speaker and sprinkles his English with many expressions from Yiddish, such as "Gevalt." His Yiddish accent is evident in his pronunciation of "anti-Semeets." The father, Harry Cohen, understands the bird's Yiddishisms but probably does not speak Yiddish himself (or not well). To his son, Morris, they are simply foreign; he does not understand them and does not even properly know what Yiddish is. He observes that the bird talks "in Jewish." Schwartz seems to represent the generation of Harry's father, and the knowledge of Yiddish declines throughout the generations. The reader is meant to ask if each generation also becomes less Jewish and what preserving Jewish identity means after the Holocaust.

In America, food as a carrier of culture has proved particularly resistant to the forces of assimilation, whereas the Ashkenazi populations more easily absorbed Polish dishes. The Cohens naturally keep kosher, dining in the opening scene on lamb chops rather than pork chops. The particular Jewish cuisine, however, is herring. The Jewbird asks for herring and explains, "If you haven't got matjes, I'll take schmaltz." Herring was a common food in the Hanseatic towns around the North and Baltic Seas. When the Ashkenazi Jews fled into these areas, they took up herring in their own cuisine, and now, in America, it seems typically Jewish. Matjes is herring caught early in the fish's life cycle and hence is particularly soft and usually soused in brine. Schmalz (literally, "fatty") herring is caught just before breeding, when the fish have large fat reserves. Because all herring today must be frozen when caught (to kill parasites), these seasonal distinctions have been largely lost in the commercial product mixed from the catch of the whole season. The Jewbird is a connoisseur of these epicene traditions, whereas the Cohens are lucky to have in the house a jar of marinated herring, something that would have been unknown in the fish markets of Danzig or Riga. Here, too, Jewish culture is shown to be ebbing away. Harry sells frozen food, a homogenized, mass-produced commodity quite antithetical to the traditional Jewish kitchen.

Anti-Semitism

Political anti-Semitism was not dead in America by 1963. Groups like the Liberty Lobby, second only to the John Birch Society in its influence on right-wing politics, were openly anti-Semitic. Its leader, Willis Carto, insisted that Jewish lies (meaning the

COMPARE & CONTRAST

- **1960s:** Any father with a middle-class income could pay tuition for a son, even at an Ivy League school, whose annual cost would amount to only a few weeks' salary.

  Today: Tuition at Harvard, for example, is over $60,000 per year (probably equivalent in modern dollars to Harry's annual income) and, except in the case of a wealthy family, generally has to be financed through scholarships or student loans.

- **1960s:** Even in the wake of the Holocaust, anti-Semitism is still a serious problem for American Jews, especially in terms of social mobility (institutions like the New York Athletic Club were de facto closed to Jews) and attacks against property (petty vandalism).

  Today: The number of reported anti-Semitic incidents in recent years has risen, but at least part of this rise is due to the redefining of anti-Semitic attacks to include criticism of Israeli political and military policies and actions, even when made by Jews and Israeli citizens. In one incident, for instance, an Israeli-born teen from New Jersey made statements on Twitter calling Israel a terrorist force and was accused of bullying by her school principal. However, attacks against Muslim Americans, while fewer in number, have recently become a serious problem, apparently resulting in several murders and assaults in 2015 and 2016.

- **1960s:** Because it was the ancestral language of most American Jews, Yiddish is widely known in the Jewish community and a general interest newspaper focused on mainstream American issues and culture like the *Daily Forward* is still published in Yiddish.

  Today: Knowledge of Yiddish is diminishing because of assimilation, and it is used as an everyday language mostly by Jews who purposefully wish to guard their communities against assimilation, such as the Chabad Hasidim.

Holocaust) had prevented the West from seeing the true significance of the Russo-German war, leading the United States to actually support its enemy, Communist Russia. Although one thinks of enlightenment finally bringing anti-Semitism to an end with the defeat of the Nazis, even in America, this was not immediately the case; an anti-Semitic political constituency was not without influence on the right (as with anti-Catholicism), and social anti-Semitism also persisted.

CRITICAL OVERVIEW

Malamud's reputation has grown considerably since his death, and he is now one of the most studied American authors of his generation, resulting in many substantial treatments of "The Jewbird." Samuel Irving Bellman, in his article "Women, Children, and Idiots First: Transformation Psychology," which included one of the first scholarly treatments of "The Jewbird," calls attention to the fact that Malamud "is bringing the riches of classic Yiddish literature, modernized somewhat, to our present day 'lonely crowd' society in which Jews are indistinguishable from Gentiles." He feels, however, that Malamud is the victim of a *Jewish mystique* (a phrase he coins after Betty Friedan's *feminine mystique*) by which reviewers attempt to limit and control Malamud's identity as a writer. Accordingly, Bellman relates "The Jewbird" to Edgar Allan Poe's poem *The Raven*, a point that later critics frequently repeat, though without much elaboration.

Philip Davis, in his 2007 biography of Malamud, suggests that "The Jewbird" was an inspired rewriting of Howard Nemerov's short story "Digressions around a Crow." Sidney

Cohen, enraged, chases Schwartz out of the apartment (©Ollyy | Shutterstock.com)

Richman, in his survey of Malamud's short stories collected by Harold Bloom, analyzes "The Jewbird" in terms of Malamud's larger body of work. He concludes that

> if Schwartz is a bird, he is also an exemplary image of the Malamudian victim. . . . Schwartz is constantly pursued by anti-Semites and by fate. Moreover, and most importantly, Schwartz is also the compound image of opportunist and saint who tests to the extreme the humanity and the compassion of others.

The chief subject of this testing Richman finds to be Harry Cohen, whose jealousy of the bird he attributes to Schwartz's usurpation of Harry's role as father. When Harry throws Schwartz out into the night, he "in the process flings redemption, wisdom, and fatherhood with it." Although he praises the story's humor, Richman thinks "The Jewbird" is not as successful as some of Malamud's earlier fantastic stories. He finds that "the naturalistic end is simply too flat: the inevitable fall is too traditional to overcome the weight of the fantasy."

Eileen H. Watts's article in *Melus* is one of the most frequently cited analyses of "The Jewbird." She sees the story as an exploration of Jewish self-hatred, in which Harry has internalized the anti-Semitism of American culture and acts it out against Schwartz. For Watts, Jewish assimilation must entail wanting to become American and realizing that means hating Jews, though she judges the strategy is ultimately doomed to fail: as anti-Semites become aware that a Jew is becoming more like them, they recognize in his transformation only the triumph of their own position and marginalize him as an outsider all the more. Watts insightfully points out that the narrative comments in Schwartz's initial swooping in through the open kitchen window—"It's open, you're in. Closed, you're out and that's your fate"—refers to quotas on accepting Jewish refugees from Germany. She also provides a key interpretation of Harry's final attack against Schwartz, when he whirls the bird overhead to gain momentum to fling him away from the balcony. Watts observes that this is a sort of scapegoat ritual, "a parody of *shlogen kappores*, a ritual performed just before Yom Kippur in which a chicken symbolically receives one's sins, is flung around one's head and then discarded." Harry may then be taken to be flinging out the sin of being a Jew.

CRITICISM

Bradley A. Skeen

Skeen is a classicist. In the following essay, he applies Malamud's own preferred Freudian form of criticism to "The Jewbird."

The story of "The Jewbird" is fantastic. Malamud inserts into the real world an element that is quite impossible and could be explained only by a miracle: a talking bird, and one with a fully human personality and command of language. Even the characters in the story wonder if they aren't in some kind of magical Hasidic folktale with a dybbuk or a ghost or a devil. Someone who was part of that traditional world might accept the story for itself, but a contemporary reader, disconnected from tradition by the Enlightenment and postmodernism, wants to know what the story means; today's reader has been trained to reflexively think that any narrative is covering over some other meaning that can therefore be discovered. Malamud is perfectly aware of the tendency, as he admitted in an interview in the *Paris Review*:

> I don't like questions of explication: What did I mean by this or that? I want the books to speak for themselves. You can read? All right, tell me what my books mean. Astonish me.

He seems not to want the reader to find out from him what the story means, but instead for the reader to tell him what the story means. Although Malamud reads like a very traditional writer, it is the essence of postmodernism for the reader, not the author, to create the meaning of the text. As an author, Malamud is reflecting perfectly the views of the postmodernist critic Roland Barthes, expressed in his essay "The Death of the Author." He views the meaning of the text as something completely created by the reader.

How could the reader go about creating meaning in "The Jewbird?" Each reader will be in a position to read his own meaning into the story, based on his own background, his own experiences, his own opinions. A traditionally minded reader, however, might not be entirely through with Malamud simply on reading the

WHAT DO I READ NEXT?

- *Collected Fictions* (translated by Andrew Hurley in 1998) is a comprehensive collection of the Argentinian writer Jorge Luis Borges's short stories. One of Borges's main techniques is magic realism, the sudden breaking in of fantastic elements into a realistic world, similar in style and effect to "The Jewbird."

- *The Natural* (1952) is Malamud's first novel. While it ostensibly concerns a baseball team in the National League pennant race, Malamud consciously set out to give the work deeper meaning by infusing into it symbols drawn from Arthurian myth.

- Malamud acknowledges the influence of Sholem Asch on his own writing, as a conduit of Jewish tradition. Asch's 1946 novel *East River* is set in the same New York neighborhood as "The Jewbird" and deals with the same Jewish experience of immigration, anti-Semitism, and assimilation.

- Edward A. Abramson's *Bernard Malamud Revisited* (2004), in the Twayne United States Authors Series, is an introductory level and comprehensive analysis of Malamud's work, intended for students.

- *Between Heaven and Earth: Bird Tales from around the World* (2004) is a collection of animal fables about birds by folklorist and young-adult novelist Howard Norman. He compiled the book in conjunction with students from one of his graduate seminars, each of whom developed a folktale from his own culture in Australia, China, Norway, Sri Lanka, and Zimbabwe.

- Robert Alter's *After the Tradition* (1969) examines the position of Judaism and a specifically Jewish literature in America, using Malamud together with Elie Wiesel and Saul Bellow as representatives of modern Jewish writing.

story; he might first want to coax out a little more of the meaning Malamud put there.

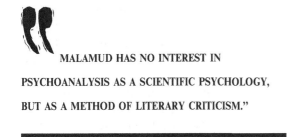

Malamud, in his own critical work, has identified himself as a Freudian, at least in some sense. In a chapter of his *Talking Horse* that began as an address to a group of New York psychoanalysts, he refers to psychoanalysis as "that body of psychological lore which is derived from Freud." Malamud has no interest in psychoanalysis as a scientific psychology, but as a method of literary criticism. He says, "The whole science of psychoanalysis is set up to interpret these meanings [in a work of literature] as it does dream symbols, just as it is set up to arrange and interpret biographical data, especially the writer's relation and attitude to his mother and father, in terms of unconscious psychic patterns which are evident in neurosis." For Malamud, literature is essentially a set of symbols by which the author communicates more meaning to the reader, or at least from which the reader receives more meaning, than is directly set down on the page. He finds psychoanalysis an ideal form of criticism because with

> symbolism, where the author encloses the meaning within objects, or signs, which when juxtaposed with other objects or signs, may sometimes alter the original meanings, as they are altered in dreams, the reader is compelled to translate the meanings out of these objects and juxtapositions, and he may, because such is intended by the writer, come up with more than one meaning of equal validity.

Above all, psychoanalysis allows for the possibility that the reader will legitimately ("legitimate" in the sense of coming from the author) understand meaning that the author did not intentionally—consciously—set down, a possibility that fascinated Malamud.

Talking about his novel *The Natural*, again in the *Paris Review*, Malamud says,

> I love metaphor. It provides two loaves where there seems to be one. Sometimes it throws in a load of fish. The mythological analogy is a system of metaphor. It enriches the vision without resorting to montage.

This is a remarkable statement. It illustrates, through metaphor, the very point Malamud is making through his surface discourse. The reader can understand simply what he says, but the text can be fully understood only by a reader who is familiar with the Gospel miracle of the loaves and the fishes to which it metaphorically refers, symbolizing its own meaning. Malamud does not explain it; he leaves it to the reader to create his own meaning, and a reader who does not know the story will create his own meaning for the text, so that metaphor will always result in meaning.

It is certainly possible to give a thoroughly Freudian reading of "The Jewbird," one that provides meaning to the story and one that might have astonished Malamud (without necessarily exhausting all interpretative possibilities for the story). Whether or in what sense that reading is *true* seems to be a question that would not have interested the author. An important point of the story that the reader may miss the first time he looks at it (the kind of detail Malamud gave great attention to) is that it is set in motion by the onset of Harry's mother's terminal illness (otherwise the Cohen family would have stayed in the Catskills and never encountered Schwartz) and reaches its climax at the same time she dies (which provokes Harry's final attack on the bird). Malamud is especially concerned with the meaning of the overlooked, as he says in the critical studies in his *Talking Horse*: "It can readily be seen—life and art being as complex as they are—that not all meanings, particularly in the hidden and symbolic levels, will necessarily yield to a first or second reading." Thus something that is never mentioned in the story, Harry's relationship with his mother, seems to take on importance. It is remarkable that as far as the story is concerned, Harry completely ignores her. In popular culture, the Jewish mother is an important bearer of Jewish identity. In rejecting her, Harry is rejecting his own Jewishness as he tries to assimilate into American society. Assimilation is often pointed to as the main theme of the story; Harry wants his son to go to an Ivy League school and become an American, not, as an outsider, the victim of anti-Semitism. To the degree that he is to become American, he must cease to be Jewish. Harry is a Jewish anti-Semite, in that he wants to stop being a Jew and be something else, something that bears the same relationship to being a Jew that bulk frozen food bears to Schwartz's beloved matjes and schmaltz. Harry is often seen as the source of the anti-Semitism that persecutes and kills Schwartz.

How would Harry have experienced anti-Semitism in 1963 in New York? Harry would feel it most acutely in limits on his pretensions to social advancement. Social connections that could lead to business advancement at the time were often made in exclusive men's clubs. The New York Athletic Club was perhaps the most prestigious and was the subject of much agitation in the 1960s, because it turned away Jewish members. It did nothing so crude as putting a sign saying *restricted* in the front window, as many businesses and apartment buildings in America did. Nevertheless, membership in the club began with nomination by an existing member. Moreover, any nomination could be stopped by any single member. So an outsider, such as a Jew, would have little chance of gaining access to the contacts enjoyed by its insiders. Other clubs, such as the Yale Club and others whose memberships were limited to graduates of a particular Ivy League school, automatically excluded Jews, who were rarely admitted to those schools. This is why Harry is so intent on getting Maurie into an Ivy League school, because it is the only way to break through the prevalent anti-Semitism. Harry could also expect that many of the men he did business with made jokes against Jews and used anti-Semitic slurs behind his back. At the same time Harry perceived the limits and discrimination he faced, he had to swallow the abuse because complaining might have meant loss of business. Keenly aware of the anti-Semitism he experiences in his business life, Harry conjures up a spirit persecuted and eventually murdered by anti-Semites; he feeds into it all of the aggression and hostility he feels toward clients and suppliers who make no secret of looking down on him as a Jew, but which he dare not express to them. He is taking out revenge in kind against Schwartz.

"The Jewbird" is fantastic rather than naturalistic for a reason. Fantasy allows Malamud to deal with psychological truths that cannot be directly expressed. No one wants to commit the crimes of the Greek king Oedipus, murdering his father and sleeping with his own mother. According to Freud, however, every man wants to do precisely that and hides the truth from himself in his unconscious dreams and fantasies. In that primal fabrication lies the beginning of art and civilization. In killing his Jewish identity, is Harry not killing his own patrimony? His own father? Is Schwartz not Harry's father? Certainly, he is an old Jewish man of the right generation. Reacting to the strangeness of a talking bird, Harry calls up three possibilities known to him from Jewish legend that would allow such a thing. Was Schwartz a dybbuk, a ghost, or a devil? The bird denies the first and the last possibilities, but, although he claims not to know what he is, he never denies that he is a ghost. The conversation shifts in another direction, so once again the reader may not notice this the first time through the story. Given Malamud's interest in finding meaning that is overlooked, it must be concluded therefore that a ghost is exactly what Schwartz is—and, indeed, the ghost of Harry's father reincarnated, as Edie (a name that surely suggests Oedipus) figures out. The Oedipal desire to kill the father then explains Harry's otherwise inexplicable hostility to the sympathetic Schwartz. Schwartz is the spirit of all Harry's insecurities, and Harry must kill him to exorcise his own Jewishness.

Another vital fact of the story that is easy to miss is the single statement Harry makes to justify his hatred of the bird: "Next thing you'll want to sleep in bed next to my wife." The implications of the statement are almost too unpleasant to think about, so the reader might well unconsciously skip over the line. This kind of dreamlike fantasy can be understood only in Freudian terms. Projection is a psychological mechanism by which a person is intensely ashamed of something about himself and pretends (to himself and others) that the offending quality really belongs to someone he hates. Harry unconsciously wants to violate every law of human decency and seduce Schwartz's wife, so he puts on a show of supposedly hating Schwartz because he insists the bird unnaturally desires to seduce his own wife, Edie. If Schwartz is the ghost of Harry's father, then any armchair analyst can see here the middle-class Oedipus lusting after his own mother, a literary commonplace of the 1960s. If, like Oedipus, he could marry his mother after killing his father, Harry waits until his mother dead and safely out of the way before his act of murder, because he is equally drawn to and repelled by the act.

Maurie is heartbroken when he finds Schwartz's broken body (©Gladskikh Tatiana | Shutterstock.com)

This Freudian reading of "The Jewbird" allows the reader to fuse together Harry's self-hatred of his own Jewish identity (best understood as a wish to be free from anti-Semitism), the drive of American Jews to assimilate to the general culture, and deep psychological truths of Freud's theory of the Oedipus complex, all working together to shape a fictional world that is all too naturalistic in its blend of hatred and ambition but which can be fully expressed only through the fantastic.

Source: Bradley A. Skeen, Critical Essay on "The Jewbird," in *Short Stories for Students*, Gale, Cengage Learning, 2017.

Robert Solotaroff
In the following excerpt, Solotaroff highlights the theme of assimilation in "The Jewbird."

By the late 1950s Malamud likely felt that the characteristic strategies of the fiction of the folk ghetto would serve more to imprison his imagination than release it, and it was time to move on. On the whole he moved into more realistic modes. Unlike his first two novels, *A New Life*, which he wrote between 1958 and late 1960 or early 1961, is set in a particular time, and in a particular political climate. When the novel's protagonist, S. Levin, steps off a

"

MALAMUD'S USUAL POSITION IS THAT THE
DEGREE TO WHICH A JEW IS ASSIMILATED
CORRESPONDS TO THE DEGREE THAT HE HAS BEEN
CORRUPTED BY CONTEMPORARY AMERICAN
SOCIETY, AND HE DOES NOT DEVIATE FROM THIS
STANCE IN THE STORY."

train on the last Sunday in August 1950, he has to add to his own "backlog of personal insecurity his portion of the fear that presently overwhelmed America. The country was frightened silly of Alger Hiss and Whittaker Chambers, Communist spies and Congressional committees, flying saucers and fellow travelers, their friends and associates, and those who asked them for a match or the time of day." The setting is neither the surreal product of the collision between the contemporary mythology of baseball and past mythologies (as in *The Natural*) or the folk ghetto of *The Assistant*. Even if we did not know from Malamud's life or the geographic and academic details that Eastchester, Cascadia, *is* Corvallis, Oregon, we can recognize the setting easily enough: a mediocre English department of the state agricultural college, in an attractive small town, in beautiful natural surroundings. In short, Malamud tried for the first time to dramatize his abiding moral concerns against the manners and relative affluence of a representative slice of post–World War II America.

. . . Although hesitant to discuss the sources of his stories, Malamud did offer some background for "The Jewbird." Upon reading Howard Nemerov's "Digressions Upon a Crow," a sketch the poet published in the spring 1962 *Carleton Miscellany*, Malamud "said to myself, thinking of a jewfish, suppose the bird had been Jewish. At that point the story came to life." Schwartz, the Jewbird of Malamud's story, would have fared well had he flown into the home of the narrator of Nemerov's sketch. But instead of finding a haven in the suburban or rural house of Nemerov's bookish, witty man—so kindly that he has fed the area's grosbeak population for years and is

horrified by a gamekeeper's suggestion that he wring the neck or run his car over a sick gull that he has been nursing—Schwartz flies into Harry Cohen's apartment, on the east side of Manhattan. There he lands "if not smack on Cohen's thick lamb chop, at least on the table, close by" (*IF*). The thickness of his chop, like the thickness of his hairy-chested body and his up-to-date job selling food frozen in hardened masses, complement Cohen's gross, obdurate sensibility; "Grubber yung [slob, lout]" (*IF*), Schwartz later caws at the frozen food salesman. When Schwartz responds to Cohen's first gestures—a curse and a missed blow—with "Gevalt [heaven], a pogrom!," Cohen's wife, Edie, and Maurie, his ten-year-old son, are appropriately astonished. But Cohen has little time for the improbabilities of either the physical or moral world and can only demand to know what the bird wants. Correspondingly, when Schwartz proves he's a Jew by fervently dovening (or praying in Hebrew), Cohn wants to know why the bird wears no hat and no phylacteries, as the ritual requires, and if he's not "some kind of ghost or dybbuk" (*IF*).

Schwartz is neither, just somebody's cranky, sly, Old World Jewish uncle who moves into crowded quarters for a while and who, at his advanced age, likes "the warm, the windows, the smell of cooking . . . to see once in while the *Jewish Morning Journal* and have now and then a schnapps because it helps my breathing, thanks God." He is also a bird with dusky, bedraggled feathers and, like Susskind, that other skinny-legged fugitive from anti-Semitism, an opportunist, though he uses wheedling instead of Susskind's arrogant onslaughts. On the surface Schwartz is one of those "just boil me a potato" visitors: "whatever you give me, you won't hear complaints." But when Cohen brings home a bird feeder full of dried corn, Schwartz rejects the food with a haughty "Impossible" (*IF*). Still, the old bird is physically and emotionally vulnerable in many ways that Susskind is not, and it is the combination of the bird's fragility, decency, and opportunism that tests the humanness of each member of the Cohen family.

If the story mixes modes in a new way, with the Jewish uncle/talking bird dropped into a realistic setting, the ethical framework is familiar: each character is defined in terms of his or her Jewishness. For once, Malamud associates morality with response to ritual: Cohen is unmoved by the bird's praying, but Edie bows her head and Maurie rocks back and forth; mother and son want to offer the weary traveler the traditional sanctuary the father would deny. Edie and Maurie are able to house Schwartz for four months for two reasons. First, Cohen's relationship to his mother preserves a vestigial tie to his Jewish past. On the August night that Schwartz first flies through their open window, the Cohens have returned early from vacation only because Harry's mother is ill. Second, "though nobody had asked him, Schwartz took on full responsibility for Maurie's performance in school," and the good-hearted but unintelligent boy's grades improve enough for Cohen to boast "If he keeps up like this. . . . I'll get him into an Ivy League college for sure" (*IF*).

To an unusual degree for a Malamud story, "The Jewbird" deals with that great theme of twentieth-century Jewish-American fiction, assimilation. Malamud's usual position is that the degree to which a Jew is assimilated corresponds to the degree that he has been corrupted by contemporary American society, and he does not deviate from this stance in the story. Racism in large part follows from the projection onto others of qualities that secretly frighten or shame the racist, and Schwartz does embody to Cohen the Jewish origins that he would like to expunge. The bird also represents difference—in the workings of the story a comically uncanny sort—that excites the racist's characteristic xenophobia: "whoever heard of a Jewbird?" (*IF*) is one of Cohen's many objections to the bird's presence. Malamud interestingly complicates things by making the Jewbird seem to Cohen able to help complete his flight from his Jewishness. To have a son in an Ivy league school would extend his, Harry Cohen's, rise in WASP society and for this he needs the more patient, erudite Schwartz—though the bird tries to puncture his grand design for Maurie's academic future.

Of course the qualities that make Schwartz a fine companion for Maurie and Edie also threaten Cohen's sense of himself as the dominant male in the house. In a characteristically comic but telling moment, he accuses Schwartz of wanting to sleep next to his wife. The bird's reply typifies the way in which the comic possibilities of his characterization usually work to lessen the seriousness with which we respond

to the conflict between him and the frozen food salesman: "Mr. Cohen, . . . on this rest assured. A bird is a bird" (*IF*).

Though Cohen's solution is similar to that of a good many anti-Semitic countries, who permitted the Jews to stay but subjected them to increasing torments, the comic slipperiness generated by Schwartz's dual identity as bird and Jewish uncle lessens the pain of the parable. Malamud finally explodes the strange blend of the antic and the upsetting by having Cohen's mother die on the same day Maurie receives a zero on an arithmetic test. Cohen's restraints are loosed as surely as were those of the Cossacks or a gentile mob before they descended upon a shtetl; he either kills "the broken hearted bird" or badly damages Schwartz and leaves him for the other predators of the world to finish off. When Maurie finds, with the melting of the snow in the spring, "a dead black bird in a small lot near the river, his two wings broken, neck twisted, and both bird-eyes plucked clean," the reader suddenly falls through the comic afterglow to the painful remembrance of what many humans have done and what many humans (and perhaps animals) have suffered. Edie tells her son that Schwartz was killed by "Anti-Semeets" (*IF*), but the implicit accusation of her husband does not at all suggest that "Edie, in skinny yellow shorts" will now be able to stand up to her husband "with . . . beefy shorts" (*IF*). Beneath all of the story's wonderful comedy is the sense that the brutes still run things. . . .

Source: Robert Solotaroff, *"Idiots First,"* in *Bernard Malamud: A Study of the Short Fiction,* Twayne Publishers, 1989, pp. 67, 77–80.

Joel Salzberg

In the following excerpt, Salzberg compares "The Jewbird" to Edgar Allan Poe's "The Raven."

Unlike other literary modes, parody describes not an intrinsic structure or quality in a work but rather a condition of relationship to another text or set of texts. Parody creates a theoretical juxtaposition in which the more recent work ironically re-presents selected elements of its antecedent, usually through mocking exaggeration. As Jonathan Culler has noted, parody typically places in tension two authorial perspectives: "the order of the original and the point of view which undermines it." This subversive process resists easy explanation, however, since it resides in the play of differences and similarities between texts. In order for parody to occur, there must be a patent resemblance—usually in style or theme—between the second text and the first. Yet the element of parody emerges only when we perceive the disparities lodged in this network of correspondences: the verbal deviations, contextual changes, and transformations of familiar narrative patterns. Though parody typically employs overt distortion (and can be said to fail when its target is not immediately recognizable), it may, like other forms of irony, possess a complexity of purpose and implication. In a single work, the parodist may undertake to satirize the content of an earlier text, the affectations of its author, the formal conventions he utilized, or the cultural values projected in his writing. The parodist may (like Jane Austen in *Northanger Abbey*) aim to lampoon a specific genre or aesthetic tradition. Or he may be engaged in a more private enterprise: to exorcise a secret demon and thus rid himself of an earlier writer's perplexing and undesired influence.

Among the multiple uses of parody, this last strategy seems both more interesting and, because it involves an esoteric intention, less susceptible to analysis. An initial clarification comes, however, from Proust, who in acknowledging the entrancing effect of Flaubert's writing declared:

> Concerning Flaubertian intoxication, I wouldn't know how to recommend too highly to writers the purgative, exorcising force of parody. When one has just finished a book, he not only wishes to continue to live with its characters, . . . but also our inner voice, which has been conditioned during the entire reading to follow the rhythm of a Balzac or a Flaubert, wants to continue to speak like them. One must let it have its way a moment, let the pedal prolong the sound; that is, create a deliberate parody, so that afterward one can again recover his originality and not create involuntary parody all of his life.

Proust suggests that this method of regaining one's authorial voice entails a willful, temporary surrender to the language of the earlier text. By sustaining the sound of this "rhythme obsesseur," the writer frees himself from the repetition mechanism which produces inadvertent parody. Proust's formulation describes a purgative impulse present to some extent, perhaps, in all parody, since mockery tacitly expresses (as Harold Bloom might say) an anxiety about the influence of an earlier work and a

> THUS THE LITERAL EVENTS MIRROR THE KEY STAGES IN MALAMUD'S PRESUMED ORDEAL WITH THE POEM; THE NARRATIVE BECOMES A METATEXT ON ITS OWN COMPOSITION."

desire to break its hold. Yet it seems equally apparent that self-conscious exorcism must produce a form of parody unlike the transparent derision of Fielding's *Shamela* or Hemingway's *The Torrents of Spring*. The difference will be one of kind rather than degree, inasmuch as the Proustian "pastiche volontaire" develops not from a sense of the foolishness of the earlier work but rather from an awareness of its haunting insistence. Since in this scheme ironic emulation reflects both the avowal and displacement of an influence, we should anticipate in literary exorcism a quality antithetical to conventional parody: ambivalence.

This is precisely the condition which obscures the filiation between Bernard Malamud's story "The Jewbird" (From *The Magic Barrel*) and Poe's famous poem, "The Raven." To gain further insight into the phenomenon Proust has adumbrated, I wish to treat these works as a provisional model of the complex linkage produced by exorcism. I assume at the outset that a parodic relationship exists; that the purpose of this ironic representation is unclear; and that this ambiguity signals the unfolding of an exorcistic project. To explain: it seems almost self-evident that Malamud's tale consciously exploits the dramatic situation of "The Raven," for in both works a black bird of mysterious origin and seemingly magical intelligence flies in an open window and takes up residence in the protagonist's apartment. We see both birds perched above a doorway, uttering words that torment the human listener; gradually we realize that the bird objectifies some aspect of the protagonist's experience with which he has failed to come to terms. The man is oppressed by the bird's presence and tries to learn its ultimate purpose, but failing to do so, he implores the bird to leave. Presented so starkly, these parallels seem obvious, and it is a matter of some astonishment that critics have barely mentioned the connection. Yet this neglect illustrates one of the odd features of exorcistic parody: it is simultaneously overt and discreet, unmistakably present yet playfully elusive.

Of course thematic parallels do not in themselves constitute parody; the effect of sly imitation emerges rather through the comic variations worked upon "The Raven." Such disparities lend ironic resonance to verbal echoes: Poe's persona commands the bird, "Tell me what thy lordly name is on the Night's Plutonian shore!" But Malamud's Harry Cohen, a frozen food salesman, snarls less poetically: "So what's your name, if you don't mind saying?" Poe's speaker expresses his fears about the raven's hellish origins: "'Prophet!' said I, 'thing of evil!— prophet still if bird or devil!—'" The same uncertainty afflicts Cohen, who asks the Jewbird, "You sure you're not some kind of ghost or dybbuk?" Later he repeats the question, using the exact contraries of Poe's speaker: "But how do I know you're a bird and not some kind of a goddamn devil?" The vulgarity epitomizes Malamud's transformation of the Poe material; Cohen's modern slang and the banal details of his world create an indirect contrast to the formal elegance of "The Raven."

Closer attention to dramatic parallels further sharpens our sense of potential parody in "The Jewbird." The initiatory event in each work is the appearance of a mysterious bird, and in "The Raven" this moment suggests the advent of nobility: "In there stepped a stately Raven of the saintly days of yore; / Not the least obeisance made he; not a minute stopped or stayed he; / But, with mien of lord or lady, perched above my chamber door." When the Jewbird arrives, however, there is a conspicuous lack of decorum: "The bird wearily flapped through the open kitchen window of Harry Cohen's top-floor apartment on First Avenue near the lower East River. . . . This black-type longbeaked bird—its ruffled head and dull eyes, crossed a little, making it look like a dissipated crow—landed if not smack on Cohen's thick lamb chop, at least on the table, close by." After Cohen takes a swat at him, the Jewbird shifts to a more familiar position: "The bird cawed hoarsely and with a flap of its bedraggled wings—feathers tufted this way and that—rose heavily to the top of the open kitchen door, where it perched staring down." Malamud's caricature of Poe's raven possesses some critical justification: we recall that the bird initially

provokes a smile from Poe's narrator; that its crest is "shorn and shaven"; that its appearance is laughably described as "grim, ungainly, ghastly, gaunt." Malamud further distorts these qualities to make the Jewbird "bedraggled," "scrawny," and malodorous; at one point Cohen explodes, "For Christ sake, why don't you wash yourself sometimes? Why must you always stink like a dead fish?"

Whether ominous or merely offensive, the bird's presence at last becomes so aggravating that the protagonist commands his visitor to leave. Poe's persona beseeches the raven: "Get the back into the tempest and the Night's Plutonian shore!" Less grandiosely Cohen warns the Jewbird, "Time to hit flyways. . . . Now scat or it's open war." Here, however, Malamud's story departs from its analogical relationship to the poem. Whereas Poe's character ultimately realizes that he will never escape from the raven's influence, Cohen indeed declares war on Schwartz the Jewbird; reversing the nemesis relationship, he buys a cat and permits it to stalk the feathered intruder. Hence near the end of the tale we see Schwartz perching "terror-stricken closer to the ceiling than the floor, as the cat, his tale flicking, endlessly watched him."

But despite these entertaining parallels, made to seem all the more glaringly by selective emphasis, Malamud's evocation of "The Raven" does not produce the effect of conventional parody— mockery through distortion. Indeed, although he appropriates Poe's central concept (a visitation by a mysterious talking bird), reduces it to comic terms, and develops a set of verbal and dramatic similarities laced with ironic disparities, Malamud refrains from anything like overt ridicule of Poe's poem. Instead, he submerges the parody and directs his satire at an aspect of the Americanized Jew personified by Cohen: a contempt for the customs and manners of Old-World Jews. As Robert Alter has pointed out, these traditional ways are embodied in Schwartz, the wandering Jewbird, whose chutzpah and fondness for herring and schnapps disgust the "assimilated" Cohen. As Alter explains, the bird represents for Cohen "the stigmatized stereotype of a kind of Jew that he emphatically wants to leave behind. Cohen is really attacking part of himself in his hostility toward Schwartz." The essential truth about the frozen-food salesman emerges at the story's end when Cohen's son finds the remains of Schwartz's body and asks who killed him; his mother answers, "Anti-Semeets." In this sense, the tale dramatizes a familiar theme in recent Jewish fiction: the Jew's complicated and sometimes scornful attitude about his own cultural roots.

Understandably, critical attention to "The Jewbird" has dealt almost exclusively with this issue; in satirizing Jewish anti-Semitism, Malamud attacks a problem of social, ethnic, and political significance. His decision not to lampoon "The Raven" seems therefore understandable, since blatant parody would have compromised the satirical assault and diminished its effect. Yet the verbal echoes and dramatic parallels remain; the poem lingers as an ironic, ghostly presence in "The Jewbird," seemingly unrelated to the surface narrative and its satirical objectives. What do these traces then signify? It would be possible to argue that Malamud conjures up elements of the poem to remind us of Poe's notorious anti-Semitism; however, this reading depends more upon external information about Poe than upon textual evidence. One could also argue that the bluntness of Cohen's language and the banality of his ordeal are designed to mock through parodic inversion the ornate rhetoric and Romantic melancholy upon which the effect of "The Raven" depends; but this analysis seems tenuous at best, since "The Jewbird" displays neither explicit scorn for the poem nor visible hostility toward the Romantic sensibility.

And so we return to the original paradox: the poem obtrudes as a palpable yet phantasmic influence, which dominates the foreground of "The Jewbird" while remaining nearly invisible—a kind of purloined letter. And the more intently we seek the function of this allusion/illusion along the plane of satirical meaning (in relation to the attack on Jewish anti-Semitism), the less certain we become of its instrumentality. Aside from the curious fact that, as in "The Raven," the appearance of the Jewbird coincides with the death of a woman (here, Cohen's mother), the overlapping between the two texts seems almost gratuitous. But it does not occur by chance: at the very least, these parallels imply a sustained imaginative engagement with the poem. And if we are willing to move from the level of overt satire to consider Cohen's struggle with Schwartz figuratively, as the reflection of Malamud's reflection on "The Raven"—that is, as metaphor—quite a different understanding of the action emerges. From this perspective, the relationship between Cohen and the bird seems analogically to represent the author's effort to free himself from the persistent, improbable influence of "The Raven." Ludicrous but inescapable, the bird (poem) torments Cohen (Malamud) by insinuating itself into his private world. For a time, Cohen accepts its presence and allows it to have its way, but to reassert his authority, he finally attacks the bird and flings it out the window. Thus the literal events mirror the key stages in Malamud's presumed ordeal with the poem; the narrative becomes a metatext on its own composition. This oblique view of "The Jewbird" also reveals an absolute disjunction— perhaps symptomatic of literary exorcism— between public and private implication. Cohen's final gesture (the destruction of Schwartz) clarifies the incommensurability of satirical and parodic meaning: while on one level this pogrom illustrates the shameful anti-Semitism that Malamud obviously disparages, on another it conversely represents a necessary, purgative process—the writer's effort to cast out a literary bête noire, the influence of "The Raven."

Such a theory of composition enables us to come to terms with the ambiguous evocation of Poe which informs "The Jewbird." Apparently "The Raven" epitomized those aspects of Poe's writing which constituted for Malamud its imaginative contagion; to break its hold, Malamud indulged in authorial play, allowing the idea of the poem to express itself in idiomatic Yiddish humor, in a comic form possessing its own integrity and purpose. While Ham Cohen is said to receive a "permanent scar" from his bout with the Jewbird, the evidence of Malamud's fiction seems to indicate that through this ironic transformation of "The Raven," he effectually liberated his work from Poe's influence. Despite his fascination with magic and the supernatural, for example, Malamud appears not to have drawn upon the Gothic fantasies of his predecessor; as Professor Alter has shown, he derives this occult interest principally from the motifs of Jewish folklore. Yet critical emphasis on ethnic, Jewish elements in his fiction has perhaps obscured Malamud's response to goyish American literature. That this dimension will assume greater interpretive importance seems inevitable in the wake of *Dubin's Lives*, a 1979 novel depicting the troubled love life of a Jewish biographer whose literary obsessions include Thoreau, Emerson, and Twain. A passing reference to "the miserable youth of Edgar Allen

Poe" reminds us of the obsession Malamud had already displaced in writing "The Jewbird."

Although the foregoing discussion offers only a preliminary inquiry into the exorcistic process described by Proust, it nevertheless suggests some of its characteristic features. Further study in this direction will, I think, reveal the surprising extent to which this mechanism underlies significant contemporary fiction. Its wide currency seems, upon consideration, predictable enough; Emerson's remark that genius is "the enemy of genius by over-influence" gets at the crux of a pervasive authorial problem which exorcism seeks to resolve. Precisely because great writing weighs upon subsequent writers, exacting the tribute of conscious or unconscious emulation, any author who wishes to establish his own voice must come to terms with the "enemy"—the genius of his predecessors. The purposeful strategies of exorcism (not to be confused with Professor Bloom's subliminal conflicts) can be discerned in a number of familiar modern texts: Alter has observed, for instance, that *Henderson the Rain King* involves a "composite parody" of the twentieth-century "personal or mythic quest into dark regions." Noting a doubleness of ambiguity similar to the effect for exorcism, Alter calls Bellow's novel almost a "perfect parody, catching the outlandishness of its literary models and at the same time putting them to serious new uses that make it an independent imaginative entity." A comparable ironic mimesis occurs in the fiction of Nabokov, where Tony Tanner has recently uncovered the very tactics described by Proust: "This game, like many games, is also a form of defense; it is a way of distancing an influence and reducing its potency. Proust said that a writer might parody another writer to become free of his spell and thus able to write his own novels. Just so we could see Nabokov keeping at bay, for example, Poe and Dostoievsky in *Lolita*."

Insofar as the "over-influence" of genius upon genius implies that imaginative tension at the heart of parody, it seems probable that the most revealing cases of exorcism will prove to be those in which an important writer simultaneously acknowledges and subverts the influence of an earlier master: Bellow overthrowing Conrad; Nabokov confronting Poe; Thomas Wolfe in *Look Homeward, Angel* fending off Joyce's *Portrait of the Artist*; William Styron in *Lie Down in Darkness* grappling with *The Sound and the Fury*; or Hemingway in *The Old Man and the Sea*

reducing *Moby-Dick* to a mutilated fragment. Moreover, highly influential works should be expected to generate more exorcistic parody than other works; it seems entirely possible to construct a history of ambiguously parodic response to certain classic texts. Thus a novel like *The Scarlet Letter* might be examined in terms of its ironic evocation in works like Faulkner's *As I Lay Dying* and Updike's *A Month of Sundays*. Comparative studies of this kind would shed light not only upon the distinctive imaginative order created by each writer but also upon the psychology of literary influence, raising such questions as why certain prominent features induce parodic response. Such approaches are made possible by the recognition central to this discussion—that the desire to break the spell of an earlier writer produces a peculiar form of parody indicative of the parodist's uneasy relationship to the predecessor and his work.

By its nature, all parody involves a systematic play of similarity and difference; but in literary exorcism this process functions as a kind of therapeutic game, a conscious and controlled manipulation of those elements in another author's writing which have exerted a persistent and perhaps inexplicable effect. By appropriating and transforming these materials, by marking them as his own and subordinating them to his own imaginative ends, the parodist effects a psychological release and completes the demystification (or detoxification) of the prior text. Restraint governs the procedure; while the transposition of borrowed elements to a new environment provides ironic overtones and implications, the earlier text never becomes the explicit object of ridicule: the name of the demon cannot be spoken. Indeed, as we discover in "The Jewbird," these transposed elements are sometimes so fully subsumed by the narrative in which they occur that they acquire a phantasmic quality. This paradoxical phenomenon of visibility/invisibility can thus be understood finally as a function of the contradictory process described by Proust as exorcism. One regains his authorial voice by losing it: the obsessive material assumes a tangible form as the parodist allows it to have its way for a while; yet the whole enterprise depends upon his ability to reassert control, to subordinate this material to his own creative purposes, and at last to slide it beneath the surface of the liberating text. Only through this arcane ritual, it would seem, can he free himself from the literary influence which haunts him like an ominous bird of yore.

Source: Joel Salzberg, "Parody as Exorcism: 'The Raven' and 'The Jewbird,'" in *Critical Essays on Bernard Malamud*, G. K. Hall, 1987, pp. 108–15.

SOURCES

Barthes, Roland, "The Death of the Author," in *Image, Music, Text*, translated by Stephen Heath, Hill and Wang, 1977, pp. 142–48.

Bellman, Samuel Irving, "Women, Children, and Idiots First: Transformation Psychology," in *Bernard Malamud and the Critics*, edited by Leslie A. Field and Joyce W. Field, New York University Press, 1970, pp. 11–28.

Chomsky, Noam, *Necessary Illusions: Thought Control in Democratic Societies*, South End, 1999, pp. 317–18.

Davis, Philip, *Bernard Malamud: A Writer's Life*, Oxford University Press, 2007, pp. 238, 274, 324.

Dinnerstein, Leonard, *Anti-Semitism in America*, Oxford University Press, 1994, p. 162.

Greene, Earle R., "Notes on Certain Birds of the Lower Florida Keys," in *Auk*, Vol. 61, No. 2, April 1944, pp. 302–304.

Levy, Richard, *Antisemitism: A Historical Encyclopedia of Prejudice and Persecution*, ABC-CLIO, Vol. 1, p. 107–108, 420–21.

Malamud, Bernard, "The Jewbird," in *A Malamud Reader*, Farrar, Straus and Giroux, 1967, pp. 460–69.

———, *Talking Horse*, edited by Alan Cheuse and Nicholas Delbanco, Columbia University Press, 1996, pp. 43–52, 124–25, 130–35.

"Numerous Sport Clubs in New York Are Closed to Jews and Negros," Jewish Telegraphic Agency, July 14, 1959, http://www.jta.org/1959/07/14/archive/numerous-sport-clubs-in-new-york-are-closed-to-jews-and-negroes (accessed January 16, 2016).

Richman, Sidney, "The Stories," in *Modern Critical Views: Bernard Malamud*, edited by Harold Bloom, Chelsea House, 1986, pp. 71–100.

Schroeder, Shannin, *Rediscovering Magical Realism in the Americas*, Praeger, 2004, pp. 78–79.

Stern, Daniel, "Bernard Malamud, The Art of Fiction No. 52," in *Paris Review*, No. 61, Spring 1975, http://www.theparisreview.org/interviews/3869/the-art-of-fiction-no-52-bernard-malamud (accessed January 13, 2016).

Wang, Yanan. "A N.J. Teen Who Tweeted 'Israel Is a Terrorist Force' Was Called to the Principal's Office for 'Bullying,'" in *Washington Post*, January 8, 2016, https://www.washingtonpost.com/news/morning-mix/wp/2016/01/08/a-n-j-teen-who-tweeted-israel-is-a-terrorist-force-was-called-to-the-principals-office-for-bullying/ (accessed March 25, 2016).

Watts, Eileen H., "Jewish Self-Hatred in Malamud's 'The Jewbird'," in *Melus*, Vol. 21, No. 2, Summer 1996, pp. 157–63.

FURTHER READING

Bellow, Saul, *Henderson the Rain King*, Viking, 1959.
Bellow's fantastic novel concerns a wealthy young protagonist who sets out for Africa to find meaning in life. Through a series of adventures and philosophical discussions that verge on the miraculous, he more or less fails in his purpose. For Malamud, Bellow's novel demonstrates how the fantastic could be fruitfully used in modern realist literature as well as the intolerance of the literary establishment to fantasy.

Malamud, Bernard, *The Assistant*, Farrar, Straus and Giroux, 1957.
In this novel Malamud tells the story of an immigrant Jewish grocer during the Depression, a tale based on the life of his own father, Max.

Reitter, Paul, *On the Origins of Jewish Self-Hatred*, Princeton University Press, 2012.
Reitter gives a historical survey of the surprising and changing use of the term *Jewish self-hatred*. Before World War I the term was employed by both Zionists and anti-Zionists to attack each other. Anti-Zionists were said to hate themselves and therefore did not wish to found their own state, while Zionists were said to be doing the dirty work of the anti-Semites by getting the Jews out of Europe. Between the wars, Viennese Jewish intellectuals attempted to rehabilitate the term, using it to mean a criticism and rejection of tradition that could become a sort of messianic model for the reform of all cultures by removing the stumbling blocks that tradition set in the way of achieving social reform based on equality (feminism, gay rights, etc.). Today the term is mostly used to denote Jews who are in any way critical of the state of Israel.

Smith, Janna Malamud, *My Father Is a Book: A Memoir of Bernard Malamud*, Houghton Mifflin, 2006.
In this memoir, Malamud's daughter presents a general biography of her father as well as personal recollections, such as the description of the anti-Semitism Malamud experienced from his in-laws.

Solotaroff, Robert, *Bernard Malamud: A Study of the Short Fiction*, Twayne, 1989.
Solotaroff offers an introductory level assessment of Malamud, together with detailed discussion of each of the stories, including "The Jewbird."

SUGGESTED SEARCH TERMS

Bernard Malamud

"The Jewbird" AND Malamud

Jewish American literature

Hasidism

animal fable

anti-Semitism

symbol

Yiddish

psychoanalysis

Like a Winding Sheet

ANN PETRY

1945

First published in 1945 in the NAACP publication *Crisis* Ann Petry's "Like a Winding Sheet" was met with instant acclaim and named the best American short story of the following year. This single success earned Petry a Houghton Mifflin Literary Fellowship Award, which launched her career as a novelist and facilitated the completion of her next major achievement. *The Street*, Petry's harrowing best seller published only a few months later, explores many of the same topics of discrimination, urban poverty, and domestic deterioration prefigured by "Like a Winding Sheet." By portraying the story's main character as both oppressed and oppressor, pitiable and despicable, Petry masterfully resists a clear-cut model of victimization. She aligns the abuses of personal and professional life to allow readers insight into the complex system by which societal and domestic injustices inform and perpetuate each other.

"Like a Winding Sheet" (which is collected in *The Norton Anthology of African American Literature*, 2003) relates the actions and emotions of an exhausted laborer, Johnson, over the course of a single, twenty-four-hour period. In a way that is both accessible and intimate, the story immerses readers in Johnson's mounting sense of frustration as he struggles through the workday and experiences a subsequent skewing of good judgment. The cyclical pattern of the narrative paired with the repetition of powerful images results in a mesmerizing effect that mirrors the crippling fatigue of its central character. In the space of

Ann Petry (©*Richard Meek / Getty Images*)

only a few pages, "Like a Winding Sheet" manages to evoke not only the plight of a single man but also that of an entire society, passing over individual blame for collective culpability.

AUTHOR BIOGRAPHY

Petry was born Ann Lane in Old Saybrook, Connecticut, on October 12 to a pharmacist father and chiropodist mother. The exact year of Petry's birth remains a matter of some speculation, and available biographies vacillate between 1908 and 1911 as the most likely dates. The youngest of three girls, Petry demonstrated a talent for writing while still in high school and gained local renown among her peers after creating a slogan for a popular brand of perfume. This small success prompted her to continue honing her writing skills while also pursuing an apprenticeship as a pharmacist under her father. By the 1930s, Petry had discarded her medical aspirations entirely and traded in her quiet hometown for the hustle and bustle

of New York City, seeking employment as a contributing journalist to the Harlem newspapers the *Amsterdam News* and the *People's Voice.*

This firsthand experience of the then-impoverished Harlem neighborhood constituted Petry's first exposure to the urban squalor and misfortune that would later populate her best-loved novels and short stories. Informed by her employment as a street journalist, Petry's creative endeavors soon took flight, and by the 1940s, her compelling fictional vignettes began to appear in various literary publications. One of these early stories, "Like a Winding Sheet," published by the NAACP's *Crisis* magazine in 1945, catapulted Petry to national acclaim and won her a Houghton Mifflin Literary Fellowship Award. With her newfound financial support and literary connections, Petry was able to complete and publish her best-known work, *The Street*, only a few months later.

Her initial foray into the world of the novel proved a tremendous success, and soon Petry became the first African American woman to sell more than a million copies of a novel. She would later publish two more novels set in New England and New York, respectively, and several historical biographies aimed at instructing and inspiring African American children along the path to greatness. Her numerous short stories were later anthologized for the benefit of future generations of readers in the single collection *Miss Muriel and Other Stories* (1971).

Petry married fellow writer George D. Petry in 1938, and the couple lived in New York City for a decade before returning to Connecticut in 1948 to raise their only daughter, Elisabeth Ann. Petry remained here for the rest of her life and, in 1997, died after a brief illness only a few miles from the town of her birth.

Remembered as a philanthropist and social activist as well as a best-selling novelist, Petry never faltered in her dedication to inner-city youth and was actively engaged in both the NAACP and the New York Foundation. She also worked closely with Harlem neighborhood schools and lectured widely on issues of segregation, discrimination, and African American empowerment.

PLOT SUMMARY

Although intending to rise early and surprise his wife, Mae, with breakfast, Johnson awakes to an empty bed and the sound of running water in the bathroom. He is almost immediately aware of the persistent aches in his limbs and remains in bed evaluating the state of his muscles. Mae finishes up in the bathroom and greets her husband warmly, likening the covers tangled around his body to a "winding sheet" used in funerary preparation. Johnson resists this comparison out of superstition and learns, to his horror, that the afternoon is already well advanced. He is in danger of being late for his shift at work.

After considerable difficulty, Johnson rises and devours his breakfast without any enjoyment. Mae thumbs through the household calendar while her husband is eating and discovers it is Friday the thirteenth. Johnson spends a few extra minutes arguing with Mae and persuading her to go to work despite the day of ill omen, only to find, when he finally succeeds, that his shift has already begun. In his frustration, Johnson considers verbally berating or hitting his wife as he believes other men in his position might. He finds himself unable to follow through with either of these options, however, and hurries off to work to face the inevitable abuses of the overseer.

Upon his arrival, Johnson finds the plant choked with lines of workers trying to leave after their shift, further delaying his ability to punch in and start on his nightly duties. Johnson begins his shift in misery and begins to lament the amount of time he is forced to spend on his feet. He fantasizes about being in a position of authority rather than a lowly laborer so that he could institute changes to increase production and worker comfort.

Disrupting his meditations, the shift supervisor, Mrs. Scott, calls out over the rumble of machinery and catches up to Johnson pushing his cart. She begins to upbraid him for being late to arrive to work, and when Johnson attempts to explain his exhaustion and the mounting ache in his legs, she counters with a racial slur and an unjust generalization regarding his performance. Without taking time to consider his actions, Johnson confronts Mrs. Scott about her use of language. Although his words are soft at first, Johnson's reprimand of his superior slowly builds in conviction and intensity, prompting him to ball up his fists and advance on her. Taken aback and terrified, Mrs. Scott hastily apologizes and retreats, maintaining a wary distance from Johnson for

the remainder of the shift. He continues to perform his duties, willing himself to calm down and let go of his anger over the incident. He begins to lament his softness of temperament and takes to fantasizing about physically battering the overseer, a course of action he believes would be both just and therapeutic.

Still shaken up from the workday, Johnson is released from his shift amidst a flood of fellow workers and stops on the way out to collect his week's pay. Rather than brave the long subway ride back to his Harlem tenement, he decides to linger at an all-night diner near the plant and collect himself. The warm lights, the buzz of camaraderie, and the aroma of coffee begin to lull Johnson into a temporary state of detached relaxation as his aching muscles gradually loosen. When he reaches the front of the line and requests a cup of coffee, the girl behind the serving counter explains he will have to wait while another urn is being brewed. Johnson interprets this refusal, and the unconscious tendency of the girl to lift her blonde hair from her neck, as sure signs of her discrimination against him. For the second time that day, Johnson experiences the almost uncontrollable urge to lash out and strike a woman. He leaves the diner overcome with indignant fury and boards the subway with many of his fellow workers. Each rumble and roar of the train along the track seems to intensify the throbbing in his head and the agony in his legs.

At long last, Johnson returns to his humble abode to find his wife singing along merrily to the radio. He has little energy left to do anything but collapse against a door jamb and watch as she fixes her hair in the mirror and models different outfits from her wardrobe. Mae immediately senses her husband's dark humor and inquires about his day at work. Johnson is dismissive of his spouse's attempt at caring conversation but cannot stop himself from criticizing her vanity. Immediately, he begins to regret his peevishness and sinks down in a chair on top of his wife's carefully folded work overalls, resulting in further bickering between the couple.

Mae attempts to defuse the situation through humor, teasingly referring to her husband with the same racial slur used by Mrs. Scott earlier in the night. Before Johnson can stop himself, he experiences a tightness along his arm and lashes out, hitting her squarely in the mouth. The sound and sensation of hard knuckles against soft flesh at once exhilarates and horrifies Johnson, and he is unable to curb his outpouring of pent-up fury. In his reverie of violence, Johnson struggles for a word to describe the force that seems to animate his limbs against his will. His last thought as he strikes his wife again and again is of a tightly wrapped winding sheet, closing in and constricting the last vestiges of his humanity.

CHARACTERS

The Girl

The nameless blonde girl behind the serving counter informs Johnson that the diner has temporarily run out of coffee. Johnson interprets her every word and gesture as signaling contempt for his racial heritage, a belief that incites him to a murderous fury. The girl seems unaware of the effect she is having on Johnson, however, and takes her time cleaning and refilling the coffee urn.

Johnson

The central character of the story, Johnson, is a struggling laborer who finds himself gradually seduced by the prospect of violence as a means of easing his daily frustrations. Johnson enjoys a loving, supportive marriage with Mae, who also works late-night hours to help shoulder living expenses in the city. Despite his blessings at home, however, Johnson is increasingly plagued by muscle spasms and pains in his legs that make long shifts of standing nearly unbearable. This constant discomfort and resultant sense of inadequacy make Johnson forget his gentle nature and look to lash out, at anyone or anything, in retaliation.

Mae Johnson

Johnson's devoted wife, Mae, is vivacious and quick to laugh, qualities that allow her to resist the stress of her own job. Her bubbly personality is at once endearing and infuriating to her husband who, though he loves her dearly, comes to see her perpetual good humor as his personal failure to assert domestic control. Before the end of the story, Mae has no reason at all to fear Johnson's dark moods and enjoys an equal and open relationship with her husband.

Mrs. Scott

Johnson finds it strange that the foreman assigned to his shift is not a man but a disgruntled, red-faced woman known to him as Mrs. Scott. Responding to Johnson's difficulty being punctual and his proffered excuse, Mrs. Scott launches a fierce verbal attack, stooping to the use of racial slurs and stereotypes in an ill-advised attempt to vent her frustration. Despite Mrs. Scott's bluster, she seems entirely taken aback when Johnson refuses to suffer her abuses, and she quickly retreats when faced with his tangible fury. Although the incident does not come to blows, this initial interaction between Johnson and his superior acts as the catalyst for further instances of confrontation and violence as the story progresses.

THEMES

Racism

Although Petry intentionally blurs the line between actual and imagined racism in "Like a Winding Sheet," feelings of perceived inadequacy and discrimination consume Johnson and contribute to his mounting fury throughout the workday. When Mrs. Scott berates Johnson at the plant, he does not object to her anger, which he considers entirely justified, but rather her use of a racial slur and stereotyping. This initial proud stand against prejudice, however, soon takes on the trappings of resentment rather than righteousness, becoming increasingly inseparable from Johnson's personal frustrations. By the time Johnson is released from his shift and is denied a cup of coffee by the girl behind the serving counter, his view of the exchange is itself tinged with unreliability and prejudice. The small detail that nearly prompts Johnson to violence, the girl's habit of fondling her blonde hair, suggests that his extreme distaste for her extends beyond the content of her character into racial considerations.

The final exchange between Johnson and Mae that culminates in the story's violent conclusion is ambiguous. In a spirit of teasing jest rather than hateful bigotry, Mae repeats the racial slur used earlier in the night by Mrs. Scott, causing her to become the instant victim of her husband's pent-up fury and frustration. Mae's innocent intent, coupled with her husband's horrified loss of control, reflects Petry's understanding of internalized discrimination and the cycle of violence it promotes.

Domestic Violence

Throughout the story, Johnson grapples with his insecurities as a husband and attempts to reconcile his own views on marriage with conflicting societal conventions he observes around him. His

TOPICS FOR FURTHER STUDY

- The apology of Mrs. Scott to Johnson in the story seems particularly inadequate, more panicked retreat than sincere act of contrition, and fuels Johnson's anger rather than affording him peace. His newfound sense of the power of physical intimidation and force seems to contribute to his confrontation with Mae later that same day. Craft a letter of apology for Johnson on behalf of Mrs. Scott, doing your best to right the wrong done by her words and proposing constructive, nonviolent alternatives for coping with daily frustrations and injustices.

- In crafting her compelling short story, Petry makes ample use of popular symbols of ill omen and superstition to foreshadow and encourage shared associations between reader and character. Upon first waking, Johnson feels acutely uncomfortable, a state compared to that of a corpse in a winding sheet, whereas Mae, heedful of the unwholesome connotations of Friday the thirteenth, is hesitant to leave her home even to go to work. Collaborating with a partner, brainstorm comparable superstitions from your own cultural upbringing, discussing some triggers of supernatural foreboding you might hold in common. Then, using a poster board and some drawing supplies, create a visual montage of these symbols to reflect your personalized understanding of the significance of the winding sheet in the story.

- Like Johnson, we are all subjected to labels and generalizations by others, some complementary and others antagonistic to our personal sense of identity. Take a few minutes to catalogue as many of these labels and descriptors as you can think of. Then, using the online program Wordle, construct your own word cloud. Lastly, admire your finished product and reflect on the tangled interplay between elements of perception and character, sharing your thoughts with your peers if you feel comfortable.

- Filtered through Johnson's exhausted consciousness, "Like a Winding Sheet" takes on an unsettlingly episodic quality, falling prey to occasional narrative lapses and distortions of perception. As a consequence, the reader is left to wonder to what extent sleep deprivation and physical discomfort contribute to Johnson's breach of judgment at the end of the story. To gauge the effect of fatigue on your own feelings and thought processes, compose two short journal entries on the same day, one immediately upon waking and the other at what you feel is the height of your productivity and intellectual clarity. Compare these two accounts of your mental state, and make note of any discernible differences between them. Consider whether any of your observations run parallel or counter to the feelings and behaviors of Johnson as related in the narrative.

- Addressing emotional rather than physical domestic abuse, Junot Díaz's short story "Fiesta, 1980" paints a disturbing portrait of a chronically unfaithful father from the perspective of his youngest son, Yunior. Forced to accompany his namesake on adulterous excursions, the boy is pulled apart by his conflicting desire to keep his father's secret while safeguarding the dignity of his mother. The resulting emotional confusion manifests itself physically in bouts of motion sickness and nausea and, as evidenced by other stories of Yunior's adult life, establishes a lifelong pattern of disastrous romance. After reading "Fiesta, 1980" compose a brief epilogue to Petry's story informed by your new understanding of the self-perpetuating cycle of abuse.

Johnson lingers in bed before getting up for work *(©Stacey Newman / Shutterstock.com)*

predisposition towards tender, equitable treatment of his wife, for instance, clashes with his understanding of masculinity as the embodiment of unquestionable authority. When he takes the time to gently persuade Mae to go to work rather than raising his voice or threatening to strike her, Johnson feels confused and somewhat unmanned in his role as husband. He bases his perceived domestic shortcomings on the example set by other men in his small circle of association.

Although neither Mrs. Scott nor the unnamed diner worker are members of Johnson's family, both kindle in him the same feelings of impotence and inadequacy, as does Mae. If anything, these emotions are heightened by the untouchable racial status of the two women and the disdain, whether real or imagined, with which they treat Johnson. By undermining his sense of his own social standing outside of the home, both characters strengthen Johnson's resolve to assert his authority over Mae, the one woman he feels he can control, and thereby become master under his own roof.

Even driven by crippling frustration and insecurity, Johnson is at first unable to relinquish his love and respect of Mae and quarrels needlessly with her. Only when provided with convenient provocation, in this case Mae's utterance of the same hateful word used by Mrs. Scott, does Johnson's gentle nature give way to brutality. Even in the mindless intensity of his assault on Mae, some small part of Johnson's rationality rails helplessly against this act of violence. Ironically, it is through the very pursuit of masculine authority and dignity that Johnson reaches his most powerless and pathetic state.

Employment

An unrelenting sense of fatigue permeates "Like a Winding Sheet" and imbues the narrative with a nightmarish quality of unreality. From the moment he wakes up, Johnson realizes that he is still suffering the physical and emotional side effects of the previous shift and dreads his imminent return to the plant. Forced to sleep during the day and toil at night, Johnson struggles to recalibrate his internal clock and, as a consequence, becomes irritable and confused. This sometimes results in Johnson's being late for his shift and suffering the abuses of overseers like Mrs. Scott.

Once at work, Johnson is forced to be on his feet all night without any respite, the incessant clamor of the machinery deafening his ears and accentuating the ache of his muscles. He spends much of his time internally cataloguing the inefficiencies of production and fantasizing about instituting worker-friendly changes. Johnson realizes he is not alone in his hatred of the work and laments how irritable and antagonistic his fellow laborers become towards one another as the night progresses. Later, in the diner, Johnson is struck by the warmth and camaraderie engendered by animal comforts like a simple cup of coffee, working to ease the fatigue and misery of the workers and remind them of their common cause.

While the exact nature of her work remains unspecified by the story, Mae works long and irregular hours just like her husband. With her unshakable good humor and optimism, she provides a compelling counterbalance to the aching, exhausted Johnson.

STYLE

Conflict

The hostility existing between Johnson and his environment—whether in the workplace with Mrs. Scott, in the diner with the unnamed serving girl, or at home with Mae—fuels the evolution of the plot and informs Johnson's state of mind. As his sense of antagonism grows, so too does his tendency to become defensive and edgy, causing him to misinterpret simple interactions with potentially disastrous consequences. Conflict is so pronounced and pervasive in "Like a Winding Sheet" that the line between friend and foe is often obscured, as evidenced by the bickering factory workers or the fatal outburst of Johnson towards his undeserving wife.

Foil

Through her unflagging optimism and pleasant demeanor, Mae helps to accentuate the less desirable qualities of her fellow characters, serving as a foil not only to Mrs. Scott but also to Johnson himself. Although struggling with the exact same poverty, relentless cycle of labor, and inadequate rest as her husband, Mae poses a striking alternative to his internalized resentment and insecurity. She does not allow the antagonisms of the outside world to define her sense of self-worth or poison her relationship with Johnson, clinging stubbornly to happiness and her sense of humor despite the difficulties of daily existence.

Foreshadowing

Foreshadowing, the suggestion of future plot developments by the author, appears throughout "Like a Winding Sheet." Although the recurring image of the shroud and the inauspicious setting of the story on Friday the thirteenth all contribute to a sense of vague foreboding, more telling is Johnson's mental reenactment of violence on both Mrs. Scott and the serving girl before his confrontation with Mae. By the time Johnson returns home after his trying shift, the line between imagination and action has already begun to dissolve, leaving readers with a sense of anxious inevitability.

Induction

Although it is a comparatively brief incident, the interaction between Johnson and the oblivious server at the diner is a crucial instance of induction, the forming of a generalized opinion, whether right or wrong, on a basis of specific observations. In this case, Johnson becomes convinced of the disdain and bigotry of the serving girl through little more than his observation of her unconscious mannerisms. Ironically, this induction mirrors the central source of tension in the story, the racial generalizations made by Mrs. Scott in response to Johnson's late arrival at work. Through this striking juxtaposition, Petry suggests not only the immense risks associated with inductive reasoning but also the easy susceptibility of all segments of society to generalizations.

HISTORICAL CONTEXT

Having emerged from the Second World War victorious and fired by the promise of a brighter future, the America of the second half of the 1940s was a nation in which newfound idealism struggles against the injustices of the past. This struggle was especially pronounced in the gradual loosening of institutionalized discrimination, prefiguring the civil rights movement of the 1960s, and a pronounced surge of organized labor strikes across the nation.

Although institutionalized American slavery was abolished in 1865 following the end of the Civil War, widespread legalized discrimination

COMPARE
&
CONTRAST

- **1940s:** The years 1945 and 1946 mark the largest labor strikes in American history, reflecting the very climate of discontent Johnson experiences at his own job. Fueled by legitimate grievances and shows of solidarity referred to as "sympathy strikes," workers from the oil, auto, engineering, meatpacking, film, coal, and steel industries protest in unison for the advancement of labor rights.

  Today: Opposition to the Labor Management Relations Act, better known as the Taft-Hartley Act, continues to rage seventy years after its 1947 inception. Initially designed to cripple the inordinate power of unions over American industry, the legislation results in a marked decline in union membership in the decades following the Second World War, culminating in an all-time low in 2015.

- **1940s:** The state of California breaks national precedent by declaring wife beating and child abuse jailable felonies, sparking widespread contempt for the statute on the declared basis of sexual discrimination against men.

  Today: The landmark Violence Against Women Act, first passed in 1994, is reauthorized in 2013 in gender-neutral language in an attempt to extend equal accommodation to male victims of domestic abuse.

- **1940s:** In 1948, three years after the end of the Second World War, President Harry Truman orders full racial integration of the US Armed Forces. This well-intentioned, if somewhat belated legislation aims to provide all American soldiers, regardless of the color of their skin, equal access to training, weapons, and medical supplies.

  Today: Even half a century after the civil rights movement and the full legal integration of American society, periodic racial tensions continue to plague the nation. Following the police shooting of African American teenager Michael Brown, racially motivated riots erupt in the streets of Ferguson, Missouri, and rage from early August to late November of 2014.

---

persisted in every corner of the nation until the signing of the Civil Rights Act of 1964. Published in 1945, Petry's "Like a Winding Sheet" was the product of an era in which segregation was still commonplace, whether practiced on an individual basis in the North or integrated into law by Jim Crow statutes in the South, and African Americans were denied basic civil liberties next to their white counterparts.

On the labor front, workers across the nation rebelled against perceived injustices in the workplace, starting a wave of dissatisfaction and reform that, by the end of 1946, touched the lives of over two million workers across unrelated industries. In response to this disastrous domino effect, the highly controversial Labor Management Relations Act was passed the following year in an attempt to limit the tremendous power of American unions.

CRITICAL OVERVIEW

Although the bulk of criticism on the work of Petry focuses on her 1946 best seller *The Street*, the same scholarship is equally applicable to her short story of that previous year, "Like a Winding Sheet," which garnered Petry national acclaim. As evidenced by the title and content of a contemporary review by Lucy Lee Clemmons, "Grime, Garbage, and Ugliness," the initial reception of Petry's work in 1946 vacillated between grudging admiration and subtle, albeit unmistakable condescension. In particular, the grotesque realism, intentionally fragmented narrative, and subversive gender messages embodied by her stories presented cause for aversion and even concern, according to the standards of contemporary American taste. Clemmons's review of Petry's work is marked not only by a narrowness of vision

Mae teases Johnson affectionately, telling him he looks like a huckleberry in a winding sheet (©And-One | Shutterstock.com)

but also by intolerance for the author's depiction of alternative domestic models that she deems corrosive to societal well-being:

> Mrs. Petry has chosen a small canvas on which to paint the characters she creates; for the book contains only a few, and of these only five are essential in the development of the story. . . . *The Street* is good reading. It is not a pleasant story; for it depicts the sordid side of life among Negroes, showing the struggle and heartbreak which so many Negro women and children must bear because of broken homes, so often the result of women being forced to work in order to support the family.

Petry's preoccupation with urban deterioration and the plight of the African American community in her fiction immediately, and perhaps unfairly, linked her to fellow author Richard Wright in the critical imagination. To combat this early generalization, modern Petry scholarship focuses on qualifying the relationship between the two landmark writers and crediting each with their distinct contribution to the genre. Although the literary creations of both are forced to grapple with the difficulties of advancement in society, exhausting themselves in pursuit of the fabled and elusive American dream, Petry brings a uniquely feminine spin to the genre. In his scholarly examination "A Distaff Dream Deferred? Ann Petry and the Art of Subversion," Keith Clark elaborates how Petry pioneers dynamics of gender within race and gives voice to long-marginalized black women. "While Richard Wright is considered the 'father' of the genre, and *Native Son* (1940) its quintessential document," Clark explains, "Ann Petry emerged as another strident voice—a progenitor or native daughter."

Clark further asserts that far from disparaging the American dream in her writing, Petry appropriates the vision and redefines its terms in a uniquely feminine, African American context. Faced with hostility on every front, Petry's female characters are often forced to seek emotional and monetary security through any means necessary, offending the pronounced, prudish moral sensibilities of the American 1940s and 1950s. In keeping with Petry's vision of the American dream as American nightmare, other scholars like Evie Shockley emphasize the gothic distortions of her unforgiving urban landscapes. This pervasive touch of unreality in Petry's novels and short stories, Shockley maintains, is too often obscured by the more striking and less subtle instances of gritty realism that were first recognized as the hallmarks of her work.

In a recent collection of Petry scholarship assembled by Alex Lubin, *Revising the Blueprint: Ann Petry and the Literary Left*, special emphasis is given to the political ideologies and peculiarities of style that render Petry's fiction so memorable and unique. According to a review of *Revising the Blueprint* by Larry R. Andrews, the contributing scholar Paula Rabinowitz examines Petry's singular blending of "tabloid journalism, pulp fiction, and *film noir* mixed interestingly with high modernism's multiplicity of narrative voices," which makes her work haunting, bizarre, and viscerally gripping.

CRITICISM

Jeffrey Eugene Palmer

Palmer is a freelance writer, scholar, and high school English teacher. In the following essay, he

WHAT DO I READ NEXT?

- Published in 1946, only months after "Like a Winding Sheet," *The Street* is Petry's best-known success and the first novel by an African American woman to sell more than a million copies.

- Richard Wright's acknowledged masterpiece, *Native Son*, was published in 1940. The novel documents the struggles of an African American youth to scratch out a living on Chicago's South Side. Stylistically and thematically, it is the work most frequently compared by critics to the novels and short stories of Petry.

- Published in 1982, Alice Walker's modern classic *The Color Purple* provides a stirring account of domestic violence, poverty, and female empowerment within the African American community in the Deep South.

- *This is How You Lose Her* is a 2013 collection of short stories by Dominican American author Junot Diaz that documents the perpetuation of machismo, infidelity, and unhealthy attitudes towards women within the family of the narrator, Yunior.

- Arthur Miller's iconic 1949 play *Death of a Salesman* follows the tragic trajectory of an aging and broken salesman, Willie Loman, and his growing estrangement from those he most loves.

- Author and former victim of domestic abuse Susan Koppelman assembles over thirty stories documenting violence against women in her celebrated 1996 story collection *Women in the Trees*.

- Published by best-selling poet Sylvia Plath in 1963, the semiautobiographical novel *The Bell Jar* is a stirring, darkly humorous account of one woman's descent into depression and mental illness.

- Charlotte Perkins Gilman first published "The Yellow Wallpaper" in 1892. The short story is a harrowing examination of the effects of isolation and intellectual stagnation on emotional and mental stability.

- *In Dubious Battle* is a 1936 novella by John Steinbeck that highlights the complexities and ambiguities of a fruit-picking strike during the Dust Bowl era in American history.

- Walter Dean Myers's gritty and thought-provoking piece of young-adult fiction *Monster* was published in 2004 and details the trial of African American teen Steve Harmon, who is accused of murder. Like Petry in her short story, Myers masterfully blurs the lines between perception and truth.

- In her 2014 critical study *Domestic Abuse in the Novels of African American Women*, scholar Heather Duerre Humann draws upon the work of many of Petry's most celebrated contemporaries and successors to further explore this difficult topic.

---

traces the theme of isolation in "Like a Winding Sheet" and its effect upon the central character, the struggling laborer Johnson.

Nightmarish details of Johnson's exhausted, aching limbs, shameless bigotry in the workplace, and the graphic horror of unchecked domestic violence take center stage in Petry's "Like a Winding Sheet." Taken together, these unsettling particulars obscure a more subtle but no less important detail of Johnson's descent into violence and misery. Although he attributes his gradual slipping of emotional control to racially motivated injustices suffered throughout the day, it is the loneliness rather than the indignation caused by this discrimination that most upsets his delicate emotional balance.

A persistent sense of not belonging plagues Johnson throughout the story, not only when he is laboring at the plant or lost among the swarming multitudes of the city, but at home in

> CAUGHT BETWEEN THE LABORIOUS AGONIES
> OF WORK AND HIS DOMESTIC INSECURITIES,
> JOHNSON FEELS HIS LAST CHANCE AT TRULY
> BELONGING FADE WITH THE STEAM OF THE
> DWINDLING COFFEE."

his own bed and in the company of his loving wife. From the moment he begins his day—groggy, pained, and unaccustomed to rising at so late an hour—Johnson feels excluded from the domestic routine enjoyed by other, more fortunate individuals. The story opens with the suggestion of loneliness, as symbolized by an empty bed, and under the subtle but unmistakable pall of failed intention:

> He had planned to get up before Mae did and surprise her by fixing breakfast. Instead he went back to sleep and she got out of bed so quietly he didn't know she wasn't there beside him until he woke up and heard the queer, soft gurgle of water running out of the sink in the bathroom.

As insignificant as this incident might appear to the casual reader, it anticipates the entire trajectory of Johnson's stress-filled day and lays the groundwork for his emotional isolation even from the one he holds most dear. Furthermore, when Mae comments laughingly on the shape of her husband on the bed and likens him to a corpse in a "winding sheet," Johnson is especially resistant to this comparison because it confirms his already-present conviction of exclusion from the world of the living. The surreal quality afforded by this gothic symbol is evoked later in the narrative as well and contributes to critic Evie Shockley's understanding of how elements of the unreal anticipate and even shape the concrete perceptions of Petry's characters. Shockley points out that *The Street*" teems with metaphorical figures of vampires, monsters, and ghosts—creatures whose status as 'the living dead' reinforces the novel's central gothic convention: the trope of 'live burial.'" The symbols of living death that Shockley identifies in *The Street* are also pronounced in "Like a Winding Sheet" and affirm Johnson's detachment from any of the joys of life.

The significance of the empty bed and the shroud to Johnson's fraying equilibrium is matched by the sense of alienation he experiences towards his wife's consistent good humor in the face of their mutual hardship. Her cheerfulness is a quality he finds at once charming, infuriating, and utterly unfathomable. The resentment this breeds in Johnson is heightened by his growing suspicion of personal inadequacy, of diminished, careworn masculinity in the face of Mae's inexhaustible vitality and happiness. In his already established pattern, Johnson expresses this worry in terms of his estrangement from his own gender and exclusion from the domestic norms upheld by other men in his small social circle. Rather than laying down the law at home, he speaks to Mae "persuasively, urging her gently. . . . He couldn't bring himself to talk to her roughly or threaten to strike her like a lot of men might have done. He wasn't made that way." He feels his difference from a "lot of men"—his perceived deficiency—very acutely.

Ironically, the very incident that sums up Johnson's plight in the mind of most readers, his furious confrontation with Mrs. Scott, has comparatively little effect on his sense of isolation. The laborer's distaste for his job, the aching monotony of being on his feet all night, and the tyranny of the foreman indicate that Johnson has no expectation of anything but discomfort and hostility within the environment of the plant. Although he experiences deep anger and indignation at being branded with so cruel a racial stereotype, the incident does little more than affirm the already well-established antagonism between overseer and employee.

Tellingly, Johnson expends far more complex consideration on the fraying camaraderie of his fellow workers at the plant, noting the strain of exhaustion and unhappiness on their interactions with one another. He notes that as "the hours dragged by . . . the woman workers had started to snap and snarl at each other." Though he cannot hear their exact words over the noise of the plant's machinery, he observes how they "gestured irritably with their hands and scowled as their mouths moved." Although he still resists integrating himself into the herd, Johnson finds the deterioration of the atmosphere of fellowship singularly striking and upsetting. His insightful description of this phenomenon as the shift winds to a close demonstrates not only his regard for harmony but also his heightened sensitivity to the social signals given off by others. It is this same sensitivity, in combination with distortions of mounting anger and insecurity, that later contributes to his disastrous misinterpretation of Mae's intent at the close of the story.

Initially upon being released from the shift and collecting his Friday paycheck, Johnson feels an inexplicable disgust at the prospect of joining the closing-time exodus of his fellow workers toward the subway. He decides to avoid the "rush of workers" by lingering at an all-night café, a seemingly incidental decision that leads to an important development in the story. As Johnson approaches the café, he is encouraged by its "brilliant, enticing" lighted windows and the "life and motion" he sees inside. He watches his fellow workers

> walk to the porcelain topped tables carrying steaming cups of coffee and he saw that just the smell of the coffee lessened the fatigue lines in their faces. After the first sip, their faces softened, they smiled, they began to talk and laugh.

Johnson is seduced, somewhat against his initial instinct, by the collective goodwill and camaraderie emanating from the small diner and decides "on a sudden impulse" to join the ranks of his fellow laborers. When he ventures into the café, the "sound of the laughter and of the voices, helped dull the sharp ache in his legs." A sudden wave of well-being and belonging washes over him for the first time since his reluctant waking earlier that afternoon. Under the influence of this newfound sense of fellowship, he even begins to forget the frustrations of his own day and the persistent agony in his limbs. At long last, Johnson finally begins to feel at home.

The nightmarish, isolating symbol of the winding sheet that begins and ends the story is here replaced by the no less striking but infinitely more cheerful symbol of the black and frothy brew. For the first and only time in his day, Johnson surrenders to utter happiness and allows himself to feel the warmth of uninhibited companionship, which he resists even with Mae. When he joins the line and prepares to partake in this sacrament of goodwill, however, the magical beverage runs out, as if to reaffirm Johnson's perpetual status as an outsider.

Although he attributes his resulting fury entirely to the mannerisms of the offending waitress, which, at least to Johnson's mind, suggest discrimination, this refusal is devastating on another, unacknowledged level. Caught between the laborious agonies of work and his

domestic insecurities, Johnson feels his last chance at truly belonging fade with the steam of the dwindling coffee. This symbolic confirmation of Johnson's homelessness, of being excluded from the comforts afforded by both family and friends, echoes Shockley's analysis of another distinguishing feature of Petry's work, which Shockley calls "gothic homelessness." Shockley defines this concept as "the frightening uncertainty of the domestic boundaries that are supposed to safeguard those within its walls—or to evoke the horrifying exclusion (or potential for exclusion) from membership in one's would-be 'family.'" Johnson feels that he does not belong, and every event in the story reinforces this feeling.

While it is tempting to interpret Johnson's plight in "Like a Winding Sheet" entirely as a gradual buildup of frustration and racially motivated indignation, the signs of Johnson's emotional isolation are equally compelling. The entombment suggested by his cramped Harlem apartment and heightened by the imagery of the winding sheet are representative of the desolate loneliness felt so deeply by the story's central character. It is this emotional hollowness, as much as fury, which drives Johnson to his terrible, desperate act of violence. In keeping with Petry's established literary pattern, the symbolic absence of home in "Like a Winding Sheet" is actualized, ultimately, by the very real destruction of domestic peace.

Source: Jeffrey Eugene Palmer, Critical Essay on "Like a Winding Sheet," in *Short Stories for Students*, Gale, Cengage Learning, 2017.

Calvin C. Hernton

In the following excerpt, Hernton examines "The Street" by Ann Petry.

In 1946, with the publication of *The Street*, Ann Petry made a very special contribution to the tradition of black literature. Her novel includes all of the themes of protest historically associated with black writing. But the novel goes beyond these themes and is a milestone in the development of black writing because of its import for the specific tradition of black women writers. In one sweep, *The Street* captures the essence of the literature written by black women in the past while it brings to light the issues of the literature proliferated by today's black women. Moreover, in 1946, Retry made the boldest stroke that a black woman author has ever dared. *The Street* was the first writing in

When he gets to work, Johnson thinks about the changes he would make at the factory if he were in charge (©*michaeljung | Shutterstock.com*)

which a black man is killed by a black woman for being an unmitigated villain in the oppression of that woman.

It should be repeatedly emphasized that black women have always criedout against injustice. The first American-born woman to speak in public was black. In the early 1800s in Boston, Marie Stewart rallied in defense of her black sisters. "Oh, Ye Daughters of Africa!" she called to them. Although Stewart spoke and wrote for the uplifting of both women andmen, she was jeered by the men because she was a female. Pleadingly she cried out to the men, "What If I Am a Woman!" Again, in 1827, inthe first newspaper owned by black men (*Freedom's Journal*), Stewart sent in a letter under a pseudonym,"Matilda," pleading with the men to include specifically black women in the uplifting of the race. During the heyday of the anti-slavery and women's rights struggles, another voice, Sojourner Truth, cried out to the world, "Ain't I a Woman!" Then when the men were pursuing their newly won freedom, another black woman, Anna Julia Cooper, pleaded the question of "When and Where" would black women enter. All during the

1800s and well into the twentieth century black women writers, poets, and novelists, continued to plea for the humanity of black women. It should be noted also that Frank J. Webb, W. E. B. DuBois, Benjamin Brawley, Wallace Thurman, and especially Jean Toomer and Langston Hughes, along with other early black men writers, had also written of the hardships and virtues of black women. But no one until Petry, male or female, had so thoroughly portrayed black women as victims of Multiple Oppression, and no one had so boldly portrayed black men as the levelers of a significant measure of that oppression.

The Street marked the juncture between the restraining colorations of nineteenth-century Victorian "colored lady's" writings (as in Frances Harper's *Iola LeRoy*, 1892, and even later in Gwendolyn Brooks's *Maude Martha*, 1953) and the forging of a proletarian black woman's fiction. Since the first wave of black migration out of the South shortly after the demise of Reconstruction, black women had been coming to the northern cities. But there had simply been no serious treatment of black underclass women, neither in the narratives and early novels, nor in the "primitivist" and "tragic mulatto" portrayals of Harlem Renaissance writers, such as Claude McKay and Nella Larsen or Jessie Fauset. Although Janie in Hurston's *Their Eyes Were Watching God* (1937) was a breakaway from the restraining Victorian portrayal of black women, and despite Dorothy West's Cleo Judson in *The Living Is Easy* (1946), until Petry there had been no such women as Lutie Johnson, Min, and Mrs. Hedges in the entire history of black fiction. No one had made a thesis of the debilitating mores of economic, racial and sexual violence let loose against black women in their new urban ghetto environment. In both texture and substance, *The Street* is the first work of social realism and naturalism written from an all but complete Womanist Perspective.

. . . That *The Street* is a pioneer work of womanist/feminist protest is unmistakable. But it does not go beyond protest. What Alice Walker's novel *The Color Purple* does for rural blacks in the South, *The Street* achieves for black people in the urban North. However, unlike in *The Color Purple*, Ann Petry's novel does not offer any positive process of affirmation and overcoming. Lutie revolts but she revolts alone; it is an emotional, unplanned revolt—she explodes.

In 1968, twenty years after Lutie Johnson explodes, two black psychiatrists, William Grier and Price Cobbs, published a best-selling study entitled *Black Rage*. They devoted fifteen pages to black women in a chapter entitled "Acquiring Womanhood," in which they made glaring Freudian endorsements about the value of "feminine beauty and narcissism" for black women, and discussed how hard it is for black women to feel beautiful and narcissistic in white racist America.

Nothing is mentioned in the entire book about the *rage* black women might feel from the political, economic, and sexist oppression that they suffer. The only concern black men have for black women is that the women feel beautiful, be good mothers, and provide and experience good sex.

The explosion of Lutie Johnson foreshadowed the necessities for the more positive processes of black women's liberation. The modern successors of Ann Petry are busy depicting and mapping out these processes: the coming together of all women in sisterhood; the organizing and raising of consciousness; acclaiming the value of womanist ways and women-identified women; the naming of women's oppression as *sexism*; the affirmation of nurturing women; blues women, such as Shug in *The Color Purple*, Mattie in *The Women of Brewster Place*, and the women in *The Salt Eaters*, to mention but a few. This is not to take away from Petry's novel. The issues are all there, precisely and painstakingly detailed. What is needed are the solutions and the tactics. One of the women in the beauty parlor sees Lute near the end of her rope, burdened and filled with the blues, and the woman remarks, "Somep't must have walked over your grave."

The explosion of Lutie Johnson marked her own death as a Negro Lady Heroine and initiated a new life as a Black Woman Hero. The explosion of Lutie Johnson, the murder she committed, is being transformed by today's women writers into a positive act of love and liberation. Bigger Thomas killed Mary Dalton and Bessie Mears with only thoughts of fear and trembling. Lutie Johnson killed Boots Smith in an explosion of pent-up rage against the oppression of herself, against the oppression of Min, against the oppression of all black women and all black people.

Source: Calvin C. Hernton, "The Significance of Ann Petry," in *The Critical Response to Ann Petry*, edited by Hazel Arnett Ervin, Praeger, 2005, pp. 95–96, 115–16.

SOURCES

Andrews, Larry R., Review of *Revising the Blueprint: Ann Petry and the Literary Left*, in *African American Review*, Vol. 42, Nos. 3–4, 2008, pp. 72–73.

Brecher, Jeremy, "The World War II and Post-war Strike Wave," Libcom website, December 17, 2009, https://libcom.org/history/world-war-ii-post-war-strike-wave (accessed March 20, 2016).

Callahan, Cynthia A., "Petry, Ann," Hutchins Center for African American Research, http://hutchinscenter.fas.harvard.edu/petry-ann-12-oct-1908-30-apr-1997-author-and-pharmacist-was (accessed March 30, 2016).

Clark, Keith, "A Distaff Dream Deferred? Ann Petry and the Art of Subversion," in *African American Review*, Vol. 26, No. 3, 1992, pp. 495–505.

Clemmons, Lucy Lee, and Ann Petry, "Grime, Garbage and Ugliness," in *Phylon (1940–1956)*, Vol. 7, No. 1, 1946, pp. 98–99.

"Freedom from Discrimination Timeline," Annenberg Classroom website, http://www.annenbergclassroom.org/Files/Documents/Timelines/FreedomFromDiscrimination.pdf (accessed March 20, 2016).

"History of Battered Women's Movement," Indiana Coalition Against Domestic Violence website, 2016, http://www.icadvinc.org/what-is-domestic-violence/history-of-battered-womens-movement/ (accessed March 20, 2016).

Horsley, Sarah K., "Ann Petry," FemBio website, 2008, http://www.fembio.org/english/biography.php/woman/biography/ann-petry/ (accessed March 20, 2016).

Lattin, Vernon E., "Ann Petry and the American Dream," in *Black American Literature Forum*, Vol. 12, No. 2, 1978, pp. 69–72.

Petry, Ann, "Like a Winding Sheet," in *The Norton Anthology of African American Literature*, edited by Henry Louis Gates, Nellie Y. McKay, William L. Andrews, and Houston A. Baker Jr., 2nd ed., W.W. Norton, 2003, pp. 1496–504.

Shockley, Evie, "Buried Alive: Gothic Homelessness, Black Women's Sexuality, and (Living) Death in Ann Petry's 'The Street,' in *African American Review*, Vol. 40, No. 3, 2006, pp. 439–60.

Thomas, Robert McG., Jr., "Ann Petry, 88, First to Write a Literary Portrait of Harlem," in *New York Times*, April 30, 1997, http://www.nytimes.com/1997/04/30/arts/ann-petry-88-first-to-write-a-literary-portrait-of-harlem.html (accessed March 20, 2016).

"VAWA Inclusion Mandate," SAVE: Stop Abusive and Violent Environments website, http://www.saveservices.org/inclusive-vawa/inclusive-vawa/ (accessed March 20, 2016).

FURTHER READING

Clark, Keith, *The Radical Fiction of Ann Petry*, LSU Press, 2013.
> Published in 2013, *The Radical Fiction of Ann Petry*, by Keith Clark, represents the attempt by modern criticism to distinguish the unique literary contributions of Petry from those of her African American contemporaries, like Richard Wright.

Petry, Elisabeth, *At Home Inside: A Daughter's Tribute to Ann Petry*, University Press of Mississippi, 2009.
> Written by Elisabeth Petry, *At Home Inside: A Daughter's Tribute to Ann Petry* provides an intimate, honest account of one of the twentieth century's most influential African American novelists.

Wald, Alan M., *Trinity of Passion: The Literary Left and the Antifascist Crusade*, University of North Carolina Press, 2007.
> This volume gives insight into the exact nature and degree of Petry's political involvement in the movement from which many critics consider her inseparable.

Wilson, Sondra K., *The "Crisis" Reader: Stories, Poetry, and Essays from the N.A.A.C.P.'s "Crisis" Magazine*, Modern Library, 1999.
> *The Crisis Reader* contains the best-loved stories, poems, and essays of the magazine in which Petry first published many of her most famous works.

SUGGESTED SEARCH TERMS

Ann Petry

"Like a Winding Sheet"

Ann Petry AND The Street

Ann Petry AND short stories

Ann Petry AND literary left

Ann Petry AND naturalism

Ann Petry AND prejudice

Ann Petry AND Richard Wright

Looking for a Rain God

BESSIE HEAD

1966

Although Bessie Head's "Looking for a Rain God" was first published in the magazine the *New African* in 1966, it was not until the 1977 publication of her short-story collection *The Collector of Treasures and Other Botswana Village Tales* that the story reached a wide, transcontinental audience. Most of the stories in the collection are, as the title suggests, reworkings of oral tales that Head heard in Serowe, a town in what would become the nation of Botswana. But Huma Ibrahim reports in *Bessie Head: Subversive Identities in Exile* that "Looking for a Rain God" was based on an actual newspaper account of two men facing trial for killing children in an attempt to bring rain during the early 1960s, one of the region's periods of prolonged drought.

Head's fictional version of these events raises themes and images that appear generally through her work: the tasks of daily life in rural Botswana; the hardships of that life, especially in the face of a harsh climate; and the conflict between traditional culture and modern European-derived culture. The story is brief—just over fifteen hundred words—and narrated in a dispassionate third-person voice that neither comments on nor judges the characters' actions and motives.

AUTHOR BIOGRAPHY

Bessie Amelia Emery was born July 6, 1937, in Pietermaritzburg, a large city in South Africa.

The story takes place in a large village in southern Africa (©*Sam DCruz / Shutterstock.com*)

She never knew the identity of her father, a black South African who may have been a stable hand. Her mother, a white woman named Bessie Birch Emery, had been placed in a mental institution by her family, who felt strongly that pregnancy outside of marriage—and with a man of another race—was clear evidence of mental illness. At the time, South Africa followed apartheid, a system of strict segregation laws that stripped black residents of most civil rights and made it illegal for the races to mix. The baby Bessie was born in the mental hospital and was immediately placed in foster care with a family of "colored," or mixed-race, people. She was not told until she was fourteen that her foster family, the Heathcotes, were not her birth family. By this time, she had been sent away from the Heathcotes, who were so poor they could barely feed themselves, and placed in an Anglican mission school for colored girls, St. Monica's. Her birth mother had died in the hospital, and young Bessie never had the chance to know her.

Bessie loved reading and writing, and she decided to become a teacher. At the age of twenty, she began a short-lived career as an elementary school teacher. As she grew older and learned more about race relations and gender relations in her country, she became more political. She moved to Cape Town and joined the staff of the *Golden City Post*, a newspaper with a large black readership. As the paper's only female reporter, she was poorly paid. Her financial difficulties combined with mental illness that would follow her all her life, and she did not remain a journalist for long, though she never stopped writing. In 1960, she married journalist Harold Head, and their son, Howard, was born in 1962. That same year, she published a poem, her first professional publication, under the name Bessie Head. But life was still difficult. Head continued to battle mental illness, she found apartheid and politics to be soul-crushing, and when her marriage broke up she found that she could not make enough as a writer to support herself and her son. Looking for a fresh start, in 1964 she took Howard and moved to Serowe, a small village in the British protectorate of Bechuanaland, which in 1966 became the independent nation of Botswana.

Head had chosen Serowe because she had lined up a teaching job there, but the job lasted only a short time. She turned again to writing to try to earn her living, and this time found some success. In 1966, the year Botswana became an independent nation, she sold some stories and essays, including "Looking for a Rain God," to the *New African*, a magazine that became influential and that celebrated its fiftieth anniversary in 2016. In 1969, she published her first novel, *When Rain Clouds Gather*, and became something of a sensation. She published more novels, short stories, and essays and traveled the world as a writer and speaker. Head continued to suffer from mental illness and, finally, alcoholism. On April 17, 1986, when she was only forty-nine, she died of hepatitis.

PLOT SUMMARY

The setting of "Looking for a Rain God" is made clear by the subtitle that accompanied the story when it was originally published in *New African* magazine: "A Story of Botswana." The characters in the story are poor farmers living in a rural village in Botswana, a country in southern Africa. As is the custom, they live in the village most of the year but grow their crops on land a few days' walk away. As the story begins, the region is in the seventh year of a terrible drought that began in 1958. In a normal year, the narrator explains, the people could find water and shade, flowers and fruit, as they traveled to their fields. But this year, after such a prolonged drought, the ground is hard and dry; no one has been able to grow any crops for at least two years. Despair has led many men to commit suicide, hanging themselves from trees. Hunger and desperation are everywhere—except, the narrator notes, among the "charlatans, incanters, and witch-doctors" who make money selling fake spells and magical objects promising to bring rain.

In early November—the beginning of summer in this part of the world—rain finally does fall. The rainfall is not heavy, but it is enough to make seedlings sprout in the soil and to make the ground soft enough to work. At a village *kgotla*, or community meeting, it is decided that plowing season has begun, and families move toward their croplands. Among them is a family headed by the old man Mokgobja, two granddaughters, their parents, and the mother's unmarried sister. With some goats for milk and two oxen for plowing, they arrive at their land and begin the annual tasks of clearing away the wild thornbush and deepening the well. For a week or two, all is well. The rain continues to fall every day, and the father, Ramadi,

plows the soft earth so it will be ready for planting. But by mid-November, the rains stop.

Now, after they had been so optimistic, the family becomes discouraged. The sky is clear blue, with no hint of more rain to come, and without more rain there is no point in planting the seeds they have brought with them. With no more growing things to eat, the goats have stopped producing milk. The women reach the breaking point with their worry, and they wail and moan and stamp their feet. The men feel just as desperate, but they maintain an outward calm because that is what men are supposed to do. Only the two little girls, Neo and Boseyong, do not seem to realize how bad things are; they spend their days happily playing with sticks and rags that they have made into dolls.

Then Mokgobja remembers an old custom from before the time that Botswana was ruled by the British, when the old traditions still held. It is a faint memory, almost buried by the Christian beliefs and teachings that have been pressed upon the people for many years. To bring rain, he convinces the others, they must sacrifice the bodies of the two girls to appease the rain god. Only then will rain fall again. Desperate with hunger and fear and worn out by the wailing and the heat, the adults agree. The narrator does not explain how the children are killed or how their bodies are "spread across the land," only reporting that it has been done. But still the rain does not come, and the family has no choice but to pack up and return to the village.

Of course, the girls are missed. Neighbors ask where the children are, and the family tries to convince the other villagers that the girls died naturally while the family was away. But when the police investigate, the mother breaks down and confesses, and the two men are sentenced to death. The laws do not endorse ritual murder, no matter how dire the reasons for it, but the whole village is saddened by the events. They all know that they have been just as desperate for relief from famine and drought and that they themselves could easily have been pushed to do something terrible if it would only bring rain.

CHARACTERS

Boseyong

Boseyong is one of the two little daughters of Tiro and Ramadi. Like most children, Boseyong and her sister, Neo, are largely unaware of the difficulties their parents face in the drought. While the adults become more and more discouraged by the lack of rain and what it means for their food supply, the girls stick to themselves, playing house with their dolls—merely sticks with rags tied around them—in an imaginary world. The narrator observes that the girls' "funny" comments to the dolls echo what they hear their own mother, Tiro, saying; their play consists of a barrage of scolding followed by spankings. (In fact, Tiro is never seen addressing the girls at all, much less scolding or spanking them.) When their hunger and desperation grow beyond what they can bear, the adults remember an old tradition that calls for the sacrifice of children to appease the rain god. With nothing left to try, they kill the girls. The killing of the children is not described; the narration jumps to "after it was all over." But the sacrifice does not work, and the family returns to the village without the children and without having brought rain.

Mokgobja

Mokgobja, more than seventy years old, is the patriarch of the family, the father of Ramadi. Mokgobja is too old to help with the work of clearing and plowing, but he retains an important role in the family. He is the only one of the family old enough to remember a time before the British missionaries and colonialists influenced every part of life in Botswana; when he was a child his people still practiced traditional faiths instead of the Christianity that the British brought. When he was a young child, he remembers, he witnessed a ceremony in which children were sacrificed to "a certain rain god" who gave rain in exchange for the sacrifice. As he begins to remember details of the ritual, he becomes more and more convinced that it is their only chance. He persuades his son, and the children are killed. When the family returns to the village without the girls, they try unsuccessfully to hide the truth about what happened to the girls. Mokgobja and Ramadi are put on trial and given death sentences.

Neo

Neo is the sister of Boseyong and the daughter of Tiro and Ramadi. Like her sister, she is unaware of the terrible situation the family is in, lost in her world of make-believe. With Boseyong, she is killed by her family, sacrificed to the rain god, and her body is spread across the fields.

Nesta

Nesta is the unmarried sister of either Tiro or Ramadi, and so is the aunt of Neo and Boseyong. Nesta has no independent action in the story. She and Tiro together work hard on the farmland, clearing brush, building a rough fence, and digging out the well. As the rain refuses to fall and the family's situation grows more dire, the two women wail and cry, loud and long, every night. The narrator claims that their wailing is what actually leads to the killing of the girls, because the noise adds to the tension surrounding the family.

Ramadi

Ramadi is the father of the children, Neo and Boseyong, the husband of Tiro, and the youngest son of Mokgobja. As the only male of the family who is still strong enough to work the land, he is responsible for plowing the fields himself after the women have cleared them. When the rain does not come, Ramadi is as worried as any of the others, and the wailing of the women increases his stress, but as a man he knows that he may not show any concern. As Mokgobja begins to remember the old ritual of sacrifice, he whispers his idea to Ramadi first. Only as the worrying and the wailing get worse do the men share their plans with the women. In the end, it is the two men, Ramadi and Mokgobja, who are held accountable for the killing, either because they actually carried it out or because in that culture, men are considered more responsible for the actions of a family. Ramadi and his father are both sentenced to death.

Tiro

Tiro is the mother of Boseyong and Neo, and the wife of Ramadi. With Nesta, she works to clear the land and dig the well. Although her interactions with the girls are never shown in the story, it appears she must be a stern mother, based on the scoldings and the spankings that the girls give to their dolls. When the rain stops and it becomes harder to provide food for the family, Tiro and Nesta begin a nightly ritual of crying and stamping their feet, and this, according to the narrator, is what pushes Ramadi to agree to the plan to sacrifice the children. When the girls have been killed and rain still does not fall, Tiro and the others return to the village and try to avoid questions about how the missing girls died. It is Tiro who finally breaks down and confesses what has happened.

THEMES

Survival

One intriguing aspect of the narrative structure of "Looking for a Rain God" is how long it takes the narrator to introduce the main characters. The entire story is only nine paragraphs long, and the first two paragraphs—more than a quarter of the story—are spent in setting the scene. The story opens with a description of the Botswana bush at its most pastoral: although the lands are "lonely," in a typical year there is water just below the surface so the people traveling to their farmlands can "quench their thirst," and they can "rest at shady watering places" full of trees and flowers, moss and wild-growing fruit. It is lovely and peaceful. But soon the language changes, and what was "lush" and "soft" becomes "dismal" and "hard" with the arrival of a long drought. This drought changes everything. As it continues, life gets harder and harder for the farming people, and by the seventh year, the summer has "become an anguish to live through." Before Mokgobja and his family are named in the story, it is clear that they are struggling for their very survival. Many have not survived, as the first paragraph reveals: in their "desperation" many men have already committed suicide by hanging.

Mokgobja and the family travel to their lands at the first rains, as they have always done, but they are tricked into optimism; the rains stay only long enough for Ramadi and the women to begin the work of clearing and plowing, and then the rain stops again. It has been hard before, but this year the drought is especially serious. The family has already sold most of the cattle that would have traditionally marked and ensured their wealth. All they have left are two goats for milk, a donkey to pull their cart, and two oxen for plowing—and the goats have stopped giving milk. Planting is impossible. All the adults are stretched to the breaking point by the fear of what they know is ahead: "the starvation of the coming year." This starvation is not a metaphor. Without sufficient rain and clean water, thousands of people in Africa literally starve to death each year. True hunger can easily affect a person's ability to think clearly and make long-range plans. It is not difficult to believe, therefore, that fearful, desperate people would try anything to assure their survival. Of course, the ritual killing of the children does not work. The rain still does not fall, and the family still faces a "deathly silence" and "devouring heat." But it is certainly not difficult for the other villagers to understand what happened; they agree "in their hearts" that they might have done the same.

Cultural Conflict

Written shortly before Botswana became independent from Great Britain, "Looking for a Rain God" presents a time when the old traditional African cultures were being pushed aside in favor of European ways of thinking. This transition has taken over a long period of time, starting in the late 1800s, when what is now called Botswana was first overwhelmed by the British, continuing through 1966, when Botswana became an independent country, and on to the present, as the people of Botswana today attempt to be both modern enough to claim a place among the world's industrialized nations and traditional enough to hold on to their heritage. This tension between old and new, African and European, traditional and Christian is represented in the story by the family patriarch, Mokgobja, a man in his seventies. Mokgobja is old enough to remember life before the Europeans came, when "the customs of the ancestors still ruled the land." He has memories of a ritual the ancestors used to bring rain during drought, but the memories have become faint after "years and years of prayer in a Christian church." He is the only one in the family familiar with this ritual; presumably the younger generations know only Christianity. Yet Ramadi, and then the women, are close enough to tradition that they respect their elder and his wisdom, and they inhabit a cultural place that does not immediately disregard what must seem a strange plan: to sacrifice their children to appease a rain god.

When the family returns to the village, the new ways show their dominance. Instead of the *kgotla*, or community meeting, that established the time for heading to the croplands, the family is investigated by the police and the men are punished by death according to "statute books" (with the written laws implying the new ways). In this culture that straddles a line between old and new, the villagers follow the new laws and go along with the idea that ritual murder must be "stamped out," but they are still close enough to the old ways that they understand how the murders were committed.

TOPICS FOR FURTHER STUDY

- Find a brief crime report in a local or national newspaper (many newspapers include a log of police activity and small articles along these lines). Turn the article into a short story in which you give a fictional background and motive for the crime. Try, as Head did, to make your criminal sympathetic, or at least understandable. You may wish to give the same news article to a group of student writers and compare the different stories you create.

- Find stories and tales about drought from a variety of cultures. You might consider stories easily found on the Internet, including the Nebraskan tale of Febold Feboldson or the story of "The Boy Who Could Speak with Birds" from India. Libraries and bookstores are likely to have some of the many picture books that tell stories about drought: *Coyote and the Grasshoppers: A Pomo Legend* (1998), by Gloria Dominic; *The Princess Who Lost Her Hair: An Akamba Legend* (1993), by Tololwa M. Mollel; or *The Name of the Tree: A Bantu Tale Retold* (2002), by Celia Barker Lottridge. In an essay, compare two or three of the stories with "Looking for a Rain God" and explain how Head's style of narration is or is not like the styles of these traditional tales.

- Research how modern farming practices, including irrigation and the use of chemical fertilizers and pesticides, have changed agriculture in Botswana and other dry regions of Africa. Prepare a PowerPoint presentation that shows the benefits and the pitfalls of these practices.

- Write a play or screenplay in which you imagine the trial of Mokgobja and Ramadi, accused of the ritual killing of the two girls.

You may wish to consider the following questions: Will the mother of the children testify? Will Mokgobja (or another elder with a long memory) speak up for traditional ways? What attitude will the prosecutors display toward the old rituals? Will friends and neighbors show any sympathy for the family's suffering? Present your version of events as a play or a video.

- How does the United States draw lines between traditional or religious practices and civil laws and protections? Research a legal case that involves parents refusing medical care for their children on religious grounds (for example, *Prince v. Massachusetts*), employees refusing to work on their day of worship (for example, *Sherbert v. Verner*), or business owners refusing to provide services to people whose lifestyles they do not approve of (for example, a case involving the Masterpiece Cakeshop). Write an essay in which you explain the conflicting claims and the tension between them.

- Prepare a presentation about the Bamangwato tribe, the ethnic group that has lived for centuries in the land where "Looking for a Rain God" takes place. Include what you can learn about their traditional religious, political, and farming practices, as well as information about family structure and daily life.

- Authors often use fiction to explore harsh times in history. Read *Nory Ryan's Song* (2002), a novel about the potato famine that occurred in Ireland in the nineteenth century. Write a dramatic recitation piece in which characters from Botswana and from Ireland tell about their common struggles with hunger.

The villagers face starvation after a seven-year drought (©*Przemyslaw Skibinski | Shutterstock.com*)

Gender Roles

In most cultures, certain roles are traditionally assigned to men and to women. In "Looking for a Rain God," Head shows these roles in the Botswanan village she depicts. The first details come when the family is introduced. First is the patriarch Mokgobja, and the group is identified as "the family of the old man." He is the most important member of the family and gets the primary position. The two girls and women are mentioned, and then "the father and supporter of the family, Ramadi." As the story continues, it may not be clear why Ramadi is labeled "the supporter." He and the two women work together to clear the land, build a hedge, and dig a well. The main distinction is that Ramadi works with animals, driving the donkey cart and the oxen. It appears from the games the children play that the women are responsible for cooking and for carrying water. Farming is hard work, and everyone pitches in, but some chores are assigned according to gender.

When the family's desperation grows, the men and women behave differently. After the rain refuses to fall, it is "the women of the family who finally [break] down under the strain" and begin wailing and stamping their feet. The men, the narrator says, are just as worried and stressed, but "it was important for men to maintain their self-control at all times." It falls to Mokgobja to figure out a plan, and when he seizes on one he tells Ramadi about it first before they try to persuade the women. Ramadi, says the narrator, was brought to the breaking point not by the drought and fear of starvation but by the "nightly wailing of the women."

In the end, it is the children's mother who breaks the silence first and confesses what has happened to the girls, but it is the two men who are sentenced to death for the killing. In this society, each gender has distinctive roles, distinctive responsibilities, and distinctive shares in the blame.

STYLE

Setting

"Looking for a Rain God" is set in a small village in Bechuanaland (now Botswana), probably not far from the city of Serowe. As the narrator explains in the beginning of the first paragraph, the land where the story takes place is usually well watered and fertile. However, the story begins in a period of severe drought. The drought began in 1958, and the story takes place "towards the beginning of the seventh year," so the events occur in 1964, two years before independence. In the story, "the people" of the village still retain many traditional and rural practices: most live on what they grow themselves; they farm their land with little technology except for an ox-pulled plow; they hold a community meeting called a *kgotla* to decide when to begin the farming season; they use "skin blankets" instead of manufactured textiles; and they are led in their desperation to purchase "talismans" from "charlatans, incanters, and witch-doctors." Although they practice Christianity, at least one member of the family, Mokgobja, faintly remembers rituals from before Christianity came to the village.

As the drought has continued, the trees and other plants have withered, the land has become dry and hard, and the air itself is "so dry and moisture-free that it burned the skin." It is November, which is summer in the Southern Hemisphere and the beginning of the wet season in Botswana. In the story, the first rains that lure the family out to their lands fall in early November, and it is mid-November when the rains stop falling again and everything dries up again. The setting drives everything that happens in the story. If the climate were not so harsh—or if the drought occurred today, when technology has made survival less mysterious and less impossible—Mokgobja and his family might feel desperate and might spare the children's lives.

Point of View

For most of the story, the narrator of "Looking for a Rain God" tells the story in the third person, using pronouns like "he" or "they," and cannot see into the mind of any of the characters. The narrator is able to observe and relate only what a person actually watching the events unfolding could have seen and heard—not any motivations or thoughts that happen internally. This kind of narrator is said to be speaking from a third-person objective point of view. This creates a distinctively detached feeling from the narrator, who makes comments about men who "just went out of their homes and hung themselves to death" or how "the summer had become an anguish to live through" without really demonstrating any emotion. The narrator mentions "anguish" and "hope" without lingering to examine or display these feelings. Furthering this sense of distance, the only characters whose speech is quoted are the girls playing with their dolls; there are no quotations from the important and dramatic conversations that must have occurred among the adults as they agreed to sacrifice the children to appease the rain god. The narrator simply reports in a calm, cool way that these conversations have taken place in whispers.

The one exception to the objectivity of the narrator—the only thing that the narrator reports that could not be observed by an outsider—is the "ancient memory [that] stirred in the old man." His memory of the ritual from "the customs of the ancestors" is mentioned but not described. Mokgobja describes it in whispers to the rest of the family, and the narrator and readers cannot hear what he says. It should be said that the narrator does not seem interested in the details, preferring to remain uninvolved in the details.

This detachment carries through even when something horrible happens—when the two children are killed. The narrator reports that nothing changed "after it was all over and the bodies of the two little girls had been spread across the land." There is no pity shown for the girls or for the parents who were pushed to such a terrible decision. Back in the village, the family is said to wear "ashen, terror-stricken faces," but the narrator still refuses to explore their feelings or reactions to the death of the girls or the additional deaths of the father and grandfather. Although the narrator claims that "the story of the children hung like a dark cloud of sorrow over the village," the narration never focuses on any sad person, and there is no sorrow in the narrative voice.

HISTORICAL CONTEXT

Botswana: From Protection to Independence

The 1950s and 1960s were turbulent years across the African continent. Since the latter part of the

COMPARE
&
CONTRAST

- **1960s:** Botswana, which receives rainfall in small quantities and on an unreliable schedule, suffers one of its periodical cycles of drought lasting many years, leading to hunger and political tension.

  Today: The early 2010s mark one of Botswana's most severe droughts in decades. In November 2015, the nation's president, Ian Khama, asks citizens of Botswana to come together to pray for rain.

- **1960s:** After a successful independence movement in the protectorate called Bechuanaland, which has been under British control since the 1880s, the British allow a constitution and democratic elections, which finally leads to the establishment of the new nation of Botswana on September 30, 1966. Its first elected president is independence leader Seretse Khama.

- **Today:** Botswana is a democracy with two main political parties, three branches of government (executive, legislative, and judicial), and regularly scheduled elections. Its fifth president, Ian Khama, is the son of the country's first president. He was elected to office in 2009 and again in 2014.

- **1960s:** Botswana is one of the poorest countries in the world.

  Today: Botswana has many people living middle-class lives. According to the World Bank, it has one of the highest gross national incomes per person of all the African nations.

- **1960s:** Botswana has only about five miles of paved roads, making travel difficult.

  Today: Botswana has more than five thousand miles of paved roads and another ten thousand miles of improved but unpaved roads.

---

nineteenth century, the so-called "scramble for Africa" meant that the continent was being explored, settled, colonized, and fought over by Europeans looking for raw materials, markets for manufactured goods, and other economic advantages. Although the African societies attempted to keep the Europeans out, they were unable to resist the Europeans' superior weapons and economic power. Much of southern Africa, including the lands that are now in the nations of the Republic of South Africa, Zimbabwe, and Botswana, came to be controlled by the British.

Head was born in South Africa, a colony of the United Kingdom from the early nineteenth century until 1961. (One lingering effect of the influence of the British is evident in Head's British-style spellings of "ploughing" and "amongst," which she would have learned in British-sponsored schools.) She came to adulthood during a period of intense political and militant opposition to the white British minority who had created apartheid, a system of laws that kept the black majority poor,

separate from the whites, and unable to participate in elections or other means to improve their lives. South Africa became an independent country, no longer a British colony, in 1961, but the laws keeping black South Africans separate and unequal only increased, as black people demanded equality. Head participated in protests against apartheid and used her writing to speak out for justice, but she, like many others, felt beaten down by the unfairness of life in South Africa. When she finally left the country of her birth for a teaching job in neighboring Bechuanaland, she knew that under the terms of her leaving she would never be able to return.

Bechuanaland was never technically called a colony of the British. Instead, it was known as a protectorate. The British used their military and diplomatic influence to keep other countries out, but they allowed the tribal chiefs to rule their own people. The British government did not try to wipe out the people or their ways of life, but Christian missionaries did influence

When a storm finally comes, the rain–and the villagers' joy–is short-lived (©*pinkomelet | Shutterstock.com*)

many people to give up their traditional religions and ways of life. The Bechuanaland Protectorate was among the poorest parts of Africa, and the British were not much interested in it. This was both good and bad for the Africans: the British did not take control of the limited natural resources, but neither did they invest in making the land and the people more prosperous. In exchange for protection, though, at the end of the nineteenth century the British began charging each family a "hut tax," which many families could not afford. Resentment toward the British grew.

Through the first half of the twentieth century, many people in Bechuanaland became more aware of what was happening in other parts of the world. Some, including the man who would become Botswana's first president, even traveled to Europe to study law, economics, and other disciplines to help prepare their homeland to become a modern nation. The calls for independence grew, especially among people from the cities. In small rural villages, many people were focused on their families, their villages, and their tribal identities and less concerned with national politics. The British had

said from the beginning that they wanted Bechuanaland to one day rule itself, and when independence leaders gave the British an official proposal for self-rule, the British accepted. The Republic of Botswana, with Seretse Khama as its president, became an independent nation on September 30, 1966. Independence did not solve all of the people's problems. There was still not enough rain, not enough land that could be used for crops, not enough other ways to feed a family. And Botswana and its people had been changed forever by its long period under British influence; there was no going back to traditional legal, religious, or other cultural practices. When Head submitted "Looking for a Rain God" to the South African magazine *New African*, her adopted home was well on its way to independence but not yet free.

CRITICAL OVERVIEW

Head is undeniably one of the most highly regarded African writers of the twentieth century. As is the case with many writers, her short stories are often taught in schools, but her reputation rests mostly on her novels. *The Collector of Treasures and Other Botswana Village Tales* (1977), the book in which most readers first encountered "Looking for a Rain God," was Head's fourth book published in Europe, following three novels. Part of Heinemann's African Writers Series, it was published in England as an inexpensive paperback suitable for use in colleges and schools, and it was nominated for an award by the *New Statesman*, a London magazine of politics and culture.

"Looking for a Rain God" has not been studied in depth, although *The Collector of Treasures* as a collection has received some notice from scholars. It is common for a writer's novels to draw more attention than his or her short stories, although short stories are more frequently studied in academic settings. As Greta D. Little explains in her entry on Head in the *Dictionary of Literary Biography*, "Short stories are not likely to draw significant critical attention, and Head's are no exception." Little admires the shorter works, and considers the thirteen "dramatic, poignant stories" in the book to be "finely constructed," but she observes that their primary importance is that they "represent Head's deepening commitment to her new home in Botswana and to its cultural heritage." Previously, Michael Thorpe had offered another explanation for the lack of scholarship concerning Head's stories in an article in *World Literature Today*. He wrote, "Hers are rooted, folkloristic tales woven from the fabric of village life and intended to entertain and enlighten, not to engage the modern close critic." In other words, Head was attempting through her stories to give the Western world a taste of the lively and educational traditional oral culture of her adopted home. Thorpe notes that the collection as a whole calls readers to "learn again to choose between good and evil," and he calls "Looking for a Rain God" the "most terrible yet most compassionate of her stories."

Other critics have agreed with Thorpe that Head's concern in her stories is to help readers learn, but they have focused on her desire to teach a new way of thinking about the roles of women. Loretta Stec, for example, in an essay titled "The Didactic Judgment of a Woman Writer: Bessie Head's *The Collector of Treasures*," describes Head's attempt through her tales "to examine the position and power of women in Botswana society and the clashes

and continuities in gender roles between traditional ways of life and those of modernity initiated by imperialism." Kenneth W. Harrow also examines Head's stories in this light in an essay in *Callaloo*, observing that in *The Collector of Treasures* "the very boundaries between men and women, between past and present roles . . . are called into question."

CRITICISM

Cynthia A. Bily

Bily is a professor at Macomb Community College. In the following essay, she examines forces of instability in "Looking for a Rain God."

From the beginning of her life, Bessie Head was a person adrift, with no clear sense of belonging. Her parents were a white mother and an unknown black father whose relationship was illegal in South Africa under apartheid. Maxine Sample sums up Head's first months after her mentally ill mother proved unable to care for her: "The biracial child, whose birth certificate designated her as white, was given to [a white] Afrikaans family who, upon discovery of Head's dark features, returned the child." This began years of being shuttled from foster family to Anglican mission school until "Head was declared a ward of the state and remained so until discharged at age eighteen." As a young adult, Head lived in seven cities in eight years, finally leaving the oppression of South Africa on a one-way visa for Serowe, Bechuanaland (which would later become Botswana). But Serowe did not become the home Head hoped for; she bounced from job to job (often because her own mental illness made her an unstable employee) and felt unwelcome, as many refugees in Botswana did. By the time she was writing "Looking for a Rain God" and other stories for the *New African* magazine, she found herself, as Craig MacKenzie puts it in the biography *Bessie Head*, "with no money, no friends, no family, no home, no job, and no country that wanted to claim her."

The idea of not belonging—of finding oneself somewhere between two homes, two cultures, but belonging to neither—is a strong underlying current in "Looking for a Rain God." The people of the unnamed village, particularly Mokgobja and his family, live in a time and place without the cultural roots that give

WHAT DO I READ NEXT?

- Head's most famous novel is *When Rain Clouds Gather* (1968), a story about an exile from South Africa who, like Head herself did, makes a new home in Botswana before its independence. As he struggles to establish himself in a new country, Makhaya Maseko must learn to balance the traditional ways of the village with newer ideas and ways of life presented by British colonialists. Although Head later came to feel that the prose in this novel showed her immaturity and lack of experience, the book is widely read and admired.

- "Looking for a Rain God" is one of thirteen stories in Head's collection *The Collector of Treasures and Other Botswana Village Tales* (1977). Many of the stories focus on rural village life and are based on stories from Botswana's oral tradition. The most well known include "Jacob: The Story of a Faith-Healing Priest" and "Life."

- A much sunnier view of life in Botswana than Head's is presented in a series of novels by Alexander McCall Smith, whose main character, Precious Ramotswe, often speaks of her love for Botswana and its people. In *The No. 1 Ladies' Detective Agency* (1998) and more than a dozen subsequent books, Precious solves mysteries and guards human decency. Though she lives and works in Botswana's capital city of Gaborone, she still owns her late father's herd of cattle and practices traditional manners.

- *A Long Walk to Water* (2010) is a young-adult novel of historical fiction by Linda Sue Park. It tells the stories of two eleven-year-old children in Sudan: Nya, a girl who walks eight hours every day to fetch water for her family in 2008, and Salva, a boy who must walk from Sudan to a refugee camp in Ethiopia in 1985. As the novel progresses, the two stories intersect, and offer a powerful look at life in a country where water is scarce and precious.

- *Botswana and Its National Heritage* (2012) is a well-illustrated introduction to the history, culture, and politics of Botswana by a British-born teacher and community organizer, Sandy Grant, who first arrived in the country in 1963. Grant established an important museum and craft center in Botswana and has documented the daily life of people there. The book includes many black-and-white photographs from the period before independence and a clearly written history of that period and beyond.

- In *Hold Tight, Don't Let Go* (2015), by Laura Rose Wagner, two teenage cousins struggle to survive in the aftermath of the devastating earthquake that hit Haiti in 2010. The story demonstrates the strength of the two girls in the face of tremendous adversity, but it also shows what desperate people can be driven to do.

---

stability to individuals and their societies, and when disaster in the form of a severe drought strikes, they do not know where to turn for direction. The narrator is being literal with the statement "no one knew what to do."

The story takes place in Botswana in 1964 or 1965. More accurately, it takes place in the Bechuanaland Protectorate, a protectorate of the United Kingdom; at the time in which the story is set, Bechuanaland was neither a colony nor an independent nation but a land caught in between. A proposal for independence had been submitted and accepted, but the Republic of Botswana was not officially established until 1966. Governance was in a state of flux during this period, as customary tribal practices were overlaid with bureaucracy introduced by the British and the emerging country worked

> **ALL ARE CAUGHT IN A CHANGING WORLD THAT CANNOT GIVE THEM DIRECTION WHEN PLANS GO OFF COURSE OR SUPPORT THEM WHEN THINGS FALL APART."**

through how it would balance elements of the two at the national and local levels. In a society with little transportation and communication technology—Mokgobja and his family walk to their croplands with their goods piled up on a donkey cart—people in a small rural village would have heard some of the political rumblings from the cities, but they would not be major participants in the coming changes. Their lives, in other words, would have remnants of the old ways and customs and hints of modernism but would fall squarely in neither culture.

At the beginning of the wet season (and the beginning of the story), the lives of "the people" seem thoroughly traditional and rural. The narrator describes the "lonely" lands and the "wild bush" in the first two sentences, not naming the people or the village. These lands could be in any isolated rural place in a dry climate; the time could be any time in the past few hundred years. By the end of the second paragraph, however, the time frame comes into focus ("towards the beginning of the seventh year" after the drought began in 1958) and the location is established as one in which thornbushes are the dominant plants, November is a summer month, and "witch-doctors" offer advice.

Details in the story show how the daily lives of "the people" are unlike what city dwellers in the 1950s and 1960s would have experienced. It is not simply a matter of their not having cars or telephones or newspapers. Their lives are shaped by poverty and by tradition. For one thing, most of them "had lived off crops" until the drought became serious, and when they travel from the village to their lands they carry with them "skin blankets" and cookware. Ramadi plows his land with a hand plow pulled by two oxen. The two girls, Neo and Boseyong, have only "sticks around which they tied rags" for dolls. Through the first two paragraphs of

the story, no character is named and no character takes an individual action; it is always "the people," or "the majority" or "a number of men." Although the people have clearly been farming the same lands for a long time, no one takes it upon himself to use experience or expertise to decide when the planting season should begin. Instead, "people [are] called to the village *kgotla* to hear the proclamation of the beginning of the ploughing season."

In *Culture and Customs of Botswana*, James Raymond Denbow and Phenyo C. Thebe explain that the *kgotla*, which can refer either to the place where the gathering is held or to the gathering itself, began in the nineteenth century as an opportunity for the men in a community to come together to discuss important matters. Denbow and Thebe mention that every *kgotla* ends with the cry "*Pula, Pula*": "meaning 'let there be rain,' the cry of *Pula* resonates significantly with the inhabitants of such a dry country." No one from this village would consider leaving the village for the lands until this important step is completed; in matters of reading the skies and working the land, the community provides direction.

But traditional practices cannot save a farmer who is living through a severe drought. Even today, with farming techniques including machines, irrigation, and chemicals, it is extremely difficult to raise crops in Botswana. Mokgobja's family has done everything they know how to do, but they cannot make it rain. Although "their hopes had run so high," they are faced only with "despair." Ramadi and the women are clearly hard workers, but they are caught in a time and place that offers nothing to help them; they are not aware of modern farming methods, and they have no memory of whatever wisdom their ancestors gained from living through centuries of cyclical weather patterns. Only the seventy-year-old patriarch, Mokgobja, feels the stirring of "an ancient memory." (As the twentieth century has progressed, memories of the old ways have not, apparently, been retained or passed down to the next generations.) Mokgobja's memory will highlight another way in which the family is caught in the middle—between the "customs of the ancestors" and modernity.

Ironically, it is Mokgobja's memory of "a certain rain god" that introduces the idea of Christianity in the story. Until the old man starts to remember, there has been almost no mention of faith or of any kind of god. In good

Two girls are sacrificed in an effort to bring the rain, and their mother reveals the truth when the police arrive *(©Laurin Rinder / Shutterstock.com)*

times, the people enjoy the water and the shade, but if they give thanks to any deity the narrator does not mention it. Similarly, when times are bad—when men are filled with despair and commit suicide, or when Tiro and Nesta "finally [break] down under the strain of waiting for rain"—there is no indication that the village or the family pray for assistance. In the first sidelong glance at religious or spiritual matters, the narrator appears to mock the very idea of looking to higher powers for help in a drought; he lumps "incanters, and witch-doctors" in with the "charlatans" who are making money from the foolish hopes of people who think "little talismans and herbs to rub on the plough" will help them. However, when Mokgobja starts to remember the time "when he was very young and the customs of the ancestors still ruled the land," the narrator explains for the first time that these customs have been pushed aside by "years and years of prayer in a Christian church." In matters of religion, these people seem to be caught between two worlds or, more accurately, to be situated between two worlds but not really inhabitants of either. Mokgobja and his family are not familiar with the "customs of the ancestors," but they seem to derive no comfort or guidance from the newer Christian church,

either. They have no body of knowledge or faith beyond their own experience once they are away from the community, out in the "lonely" lands, and with nothing bigger than themselves to draw on they are overwhelmed by the catastrophic drought.

When the "terror, extreme and deep," of the child sacrifice has fallen and the family returns home, the narrator emphasizes the changing nature of governance in the village. The family had set out for the fields because the *kgotla* said that it was time for them to go. But after they have tried and failed to grow their crops, they return to a village ruled under the British legal system. It is not a tribal council but the police who investigate the deaths. Mokgobja and Ramadi are sentenced to death by the words in "the statute books," which say that "ritual murder [is] against the law and must be stamped out with the death penalty." Under this system, laws are laws. The fact that a family could be driven to such despair is "inadmissible evidence." However, the last lines of the story highlight the conflict the villagers face. Even though they have in some way agreed to this system of supposed justice, they know that there is no justice in this case. The community has not been healed by the sentencing, and "the sorrow was not assuaged."

Mokgobja, Ramadi, and the rest of the villagers are as adrift in "Looking for a Rain God" as Head was for most of her life. Head's sense of loss was compounded by mental illness. In their worry over looming starvation, Tiro and Nesta "stamp their feet and shout as though they [have] lost their heads." All are caught in a changing world that cannot give them direction when plans go off course or support them when things fall apart. Changing political, religious, and cultural practices are shifting the ground under their feet, leaving all of them "only a hair's breadth" from disaster.

Source: Cynthia A. Bily, Critical Essay on "Looking for a Rain God," in *Short Stories for Students*, Gale, Cengage Learning, 2017.

Joyce Johnson

In the following excerpt, Johnson discusses the irony of the story's ending.

The thirteen short stories that are included in *The Collector of Treasures* provide a composite picture of Botswana village life. Highlighting personal emotional and psychological experiences of individuals, they explore hidden connections and correspondences among seemingly unrelated incidents. Although the stories were written at different times and were not conceived of, to begin with, as a collection, in their present arrangement they constitute a cycle, employing both internal linking and external framing devices. While they do not share characters in common, they are all set in the same locality. As a group, they are connected by the overarching theme of the conflict between values associated with the African past and ideas introduced by the contact with Europeans. This theme, as examination of individual stories shows, attracts subthemes related to the exercise of power and the nature of evil.

The stories are, moreover, linked by the underlying trope of treasure rescued from the refuse dump, which is familiar from *The Cardinals*. The organizing principle is thus that of an assemblage—in this instance, a literary composite of heterogeneous elements in terms of story type and subject matter. Odds and ends of material that might be discarded, but for the storyteller's skill, are collected in an artistically pleasing composition in which a high level of patterning can be discerned. Each story has a

> WHEREAS IN THE NOVELS HEAD FOUND IDEAS FOR HER PLOTS IN HER OWN EXPERIENCES, IN THE SHORT STORIES, HER FICTIONALIZED REPRESENTATIONS OF LIFE DRAW ON HER OBSERVATIONS OF OTHER PEOPLE."

distinctive quality or focus that establishes its individuality, while fitting into a broader thematic unit. Finally, the opening and closing stories are linked by their reference to the art of storytelling and the different contexts that they highlight. The first refers specifically to a traditional form and setting—the clan history recounted by old men of the tribe. The final story describes a woman storyteller who focuses on details of individual lives in a domestic setting. These two stories thus provide a frame for the intervening ones.

Individual stories are also linked by the recurrence or reversal of plot elements. Nine stories, for example, mention or describe a marriage. The story "Heaven Is Not Closed" depicts an ideal marriage in which a woman manages to maintain an equable relationship with her husband, despite an initial obstacle to their marriage. This contrasts with the marriage described in the next story, "The Village Saint," in which a wife, attempting to dominate her husband, destroys the relationship. In a later story, "Life," the incompatibility of a husband and wife has tragic consequences. The situation depicted, that of a husband who murders his wife, is reversed in a later story with an equally tragic outcome. Such stories, taken together, present variations on the same theme, while the individuality of each is established by its specific focus.

Stories may also be grouped together according to the particular vices or social evils that they highlight. In general, they explore instances of prejudice, exclusivity, hypocrisy, greed, intolerance, pride, malice, and arrogance. Two or more stories excoriating the same vice may, however, utilize different modes or reflect different perspectives. "The Village Saint" and "The Special One," for example, both satirize hypocrisy and maliciousness, among other things. The first relies largely on caricature, parody, and verbal irony, emphasizing the comic aspects of the situation described, while the second contemplates more covert and amorphous expressions of evil. In the latter story, it becomes more difficult to specify what is evil or to distinguish between innocence and guile.

Stories blend elements from different narrative types associated with the short story (for example, legend, fable, sketch, exemplum, and parable). Local folk elements are also integrated through construction of setting, thematic concerns that involve reference to folklore and folk beliefs, and the use of devices associated with traditional oral narrative. Head's reliance on folk/oral traditions is evident in her projection of the narrator who dramatizes the story and establishes the context in which it is produced. Stories convey an impression of improvised narratives composed in response to the immediate stimulus of events within the local environment. The collection thus includes local clan history that has been handed down over time, the anecdote centering on a village personality or peculiar circumstance, and the "nine days wonder" kept in circulation by gossip and surmise.

Whereas in the novels Head found ideas for her plots in her own experiences, in the short stories, her fictionalized representations of life draw on her observations of other people. In these stories, as in the novels, she is concerned with the relationship between art and life, taking further the idea behind Mouse's attempt in *The Cardinals* to transform a news report into a short story. As Ranko does in *Maru*, her narrator seems to "sit on the edge of any situation and take pictures, including the minutest detail," but she also possesses the insight that distinguishes Maru from Ranko. Recognizing homologies among personal, social, and historical circumstances, she uses the individual case to "verify" her intuitions and certain general ideas that she has about life. The situations that Head chooses for her stories are thus paradigmatic, allowing for reflection on broad themes as well as issues relevant to the immediate sociopolitical context. An examination of individual stories reveals qualities similar to those informing the novels: blending of narrative modes, layering of meaning, concision, and a concern with narrative technique.

. . . The events described in this story are set against the background of immediate preindependence Botswana. The year is 1965, the seventh year of the seven-year drought that started in 1958. The old custom of summoning the people to the *kgotla* or tribal assembly to hear "the proclamation of the beginning of the ploughing season" continues, although after six years of drought people are dying from the famine. It is a climate in which "only the charlatans, incanters and witch doctors" prosper. Whereas the previous story suggests the emergence of an enlightened socioeconomic outlook, this depicts a reversal or setback as characters give way to atavistic impulses and "revert to primitive states of animalistic behaviour" that favor the survival of the fittest.

The tracks and shady watering places that are nostalgically recalled in the first paragraph emphasize the changes that have taken place in the landscape. As the opening sentence suggests, it is as if the "wild bush" would reclaim that land cleared by the farmers: "It is lonely at the lands where the people go to plough. These lands are vast clearings in the bush, and the wild bush is lonely too." The "lonely" bush representing the land in its original state and the clearings testifying to humans' encroachment on the land suggest a contrast between the old and the new, which are again shown in conflict in this story. The wild bush held in check by the vast clearings also concretizes the idea of ancient customs held in check by new ideas.

The story, which focuses on the fortunes of a single family in the seventh year of the drought, conveys a strong impression of reality. The family includes an old man, Mokgobja; his two granddaughters; their parents; and the children's aunt. Mokgobja's family have ploughed their farm at the bush in readiness for the planting season, when the rains again fail to appear. The breakdown in the family begins with the women, but it is Mokgobja, the old man, who persuades the other adults that the rain god can be bribed to fulfill their expectations of rain. An "ancient memory" stirs in him, and he eventually recalls the details of a rainmaking ceremony that "had been buried by years and years of prayer in a Christian church." The family, at his instigation, sacrifice the two little girls to the rain god, but the rain does not fall.

This realistically told story, giving a vivid description of a specific locale, has strong symbolic import. The idea of the conflict between the old and the new and between past and present conveyed in the opposition of "wild bush" and "vast clearings" has a parallel in the opposition between the "ancient memories" that stir Mokgobja's mind and the "years and years of prayer in a Christian church." A "subtle story of strain and starvation and breakdown" leading to ritual murder and human sacrifice, it draws attention both to the characters' desperate circumstances and to the brutal murder of the two children. Mokgobja and his family act out of fear to ensure survival in the ensuing year, for persistent drought, so far, has conditioned them to anticipate further drought. Ironically, it is the final year of the drought. The cruelty of the elders is matched by the cruelty of events.

This cosmic irony is also reflected in the symbolism of drought, an image of both a catastrophe in the peasant community and a force that tests the people's capacity for endurance. Moreover, Mokgobja and his accomplice in the ritual murder, the girls' father, Ramadi, who are sentenced to death for their crime, need no longer fear starving to death in the next year. . . .

Source: Joyce Johnson, "Dredging the River: *The Collector of Treasures*," in *Bessie Head: The Road of Peace of Mind: A Critical Appreciation*, University of Delaware Press, 2008, pp. 133–35, 148–49.

SOURCES

Bopa, "Botswana: Batshu Puts Nation before God," in *Botswana Daily News*, November 10, 2015, http://all africa.com/stories/201511110950.html (accessed February 10, 2016).

Denbow, James Raymond, and Phenyo C. Thebe, *Culture and Customs of Botswana*, Greenwood, 2006, p. 23.

"GNI per Capita, Atlas Method (Current US$)," World Bank, 2016, http://data.worldbank.org/indicator/NY.GNP.PCAP.CD (accessed February 26, 2016).

Harrow, Kenneth W., "Bessie Head's *The Collector of Treasures*: Change on the Margins," in *Callaloo*, Vol. 16, No. 1, Winter 1993, pp. 169–79.

Head, Bessie, "Looking for a Rain God," in *The Collector of Treasures and Other Botswana Village Tales*, Heinemann, 1977, pp. 57–60.

Ibrahim, Huma, *Bessie Head: Subversive Identities in Exile*, University Press of Virginia, 1996, p. 45.

Kras, Sara Louise, *Botswana: Enchantment of the World*, Scholastic, 2008.

Little, Greta D., "Bessie Head," in *Dictionary of Literary Biography*, Vol. 117, *Twentieth-Century Caribbean and Black African Writers, First Series*, edited by Bernth Lindors and Reinhard Sander, Gale Research, 1992, pp. 179–93.

MacKenzie, Craig, *Bessie Head*, Twayne's World Authors Series, No. 882, Twayne Publishers, 1999, pp. 23–30.

Morton, Fred, Jeff Ramsay, and Part Themba Mgadia, "Drought," in *Historical Dictionary of Botswana*, Scarecrow Press, 2008, pp. 97–98.

Sample, Maxine, "Artist in Exile: The Life of Bessie Head," in *Critical Essays on Bessie Head*, edited by Maxine Sample, Praeger, 2003, pp. 1–9.

Stec, Loretta, "The Didactic Judgment of a Woman Writer: Bessie Head's *The Collector of Treasures*," in *Critical Essays on Bessie Head*, edited by Maxine Sample, Praeger, 2003, pp. 121–30.

Thorpe, Michael, "Treasures of the Heart: The Short Stories of Bessie Head," in *World Literature Today*, Vol. 57, No. 3, Summer 1983, pp. 414–16.

Wallerstein, Immanuel, "Africa for the Africans," in *The Horizon History of Africa*, edited by Alvin M. Josephy Jr., American Heritage Publishing, 1971, pp. 496–528.

FURTHER READING

Abrahams, Cecil, ed., *The Tragic Life: Bessie Head and Literature in Southern Africa*, Africa World Press, 1990.

> This collection of ten critical essays also includes a short biography by the editor and an essay by Head herself on "social and political pressures." Although the essays mention "Looking for a Rain God" only briefly, several of them shed light on the story indirectly, including Nigel Thomas's essay on narrative strategies, Horace I. Goddard's on imagery, and Femi Ojo-Ade's on the *The Collector of Treasures*.

Brown, Lloyd W., *Women Writers in Black Africa*, Greenwood, 1981.

> Although it is no longer up to date, this book is still important because it was the first full-length critical study of women writers from Africa and because it is written in an accessible style that makes the volume interesting and helpful for readers who are not experts. Brown's study addresses Head alongside other notable African women such as Ama Ata Aidoo, Buchi Emecheta, and Flora Nwapa.

Eilersen, Gillian Stead, *Bessie Head: Thunder behind Her Ears*, David Philip Publishers, 1995.

> This analysis of Head's life was the first book-length study of the author, and it is still considered the definitive biography. Eilersen gained access to Head's unpublished letters and other papers. She also learned a great deal about Head's mother and the mother's family, enabling her to write a thorough, insightful, and compassionate biography. Eilersen provides

helpful information about the historical and political climate of South Africa and Botswana and describes the complicated connections between Head and her publishers.

Head, Bessie, *A Woman Alone: Autobiographical Writings*, edited by Craig MacKenzie, Heinemann, 1990.

After Head died, MacKenzie assembled these bits of memoir, sketches of life in South African and Botswana, and critical essays about cultural, political, and social issues. The pieces vary in quality and polish, but they reveal a thoughtful and sensitive mind at work.

————, *A Gesture of Belonging: Letters from Bessie Head, 1965–1979*, edited by Randolph Vigne, Heinemann, 1991.

For this volume, Vigne has selected 107 letters that Head wrote to him during her early years in Botswana. Vigne was editor of the *New African* magazine and a strong supporter of Head and her work. In these letters, Head discusses her literary ambitions, her fluctuating mental stability, and her doubts about having chosen to live as an exile from her South African birthplace. She also writes about her early life and gives sketches of life in Botswana.

Warger, William H., Nancy L. Clark, and Edward A. Alpers, eds., *Africa and the West: A Documentary History*, Vol. 2, *From Colonialism to Independence, 1875 to the Present*, Oxford University Press, 2010.

In gathering primary sources for this project, the editors aimed to present documents that would interest students from middle school through college. This book collects letters, journals, reports, legal documents, book excerpts, and even a test from a German school, to show what the people who witnessed and participated in the intersections between African and European cultures were thinking and doing. Chapters 4, 5, and 6, on decolonization, independence, and the legacies of authoritarianism, are especially helpful for understanding Head's writing.

SUGGESTED SEARCH TERMS

Bessie Head

"Looking for a Rain God"

The Collector of Treasures

African writers

African women writers

Africa AND gender roles

Africa AND drought

Botswana AND independence

The Man Without a Country

"The Man without a Country" is a short story by American writer Edward Everett Hale. It was first published in the *Atlantic Monthly* in December 1863 and then reprinted in Hale's book *If, Yes, and Perhaps*, in 1868. A modern edition is available: *The Man without a Country and Other Tales* (Wildside Press, 2008). The story begins in the early years of the nineteenth century. It tells of Philip Nolan, a young army officer who, as a result of his association with Aaron Burr—a real-life US politician who was tried and acquitted of treason in 1807—is charged with treason. During Nolan's testimony he exclaims that he hopes he never hears of the United States again. Shocked at his outburst, the judge grants him his wish, and from then until his death in 1863 Nolan spends his entire life on US navy ships with everyone onboard under strict orders never to mention to Nolan his country or anything about it. All his reading material is censored to ensure that he knows nothing of what has happened in the United States. He repents of his words and over the years acquires a deep love of his country. The story, written during the US Civil War, was extremely popular in its own day and for decades afterward. When Hale wrote it, his intention was to arouse patriotic feelings about the United States that would aid the Union cause.

EDWARD EVERETT HALE

1863

AUTHOR BIOGRAPHY

The author of many nonfiction books as well as novels and short stories, Edward Everett Hale was

The protagonist of the story is American army lieutenant Philip Nolan (©n4 PhotoVideo / Shutterstock.com)

born on April 3, 1822, in Boston, Massachusetts. His father, Nathan Hale, was the owner and editor of a newspaper. Hale had some illustrious forebears. He was the grandnephew of Captain Nathan Hale, a hero of the Revolutionary War, and his uncle, Edward Everett, was a senior politician and admired orator.

Hale showed precocious abilities as a young boy and enrolled at Harvard College at the age of thirteen. He graduated in 1839 and then taught at Boston Latin School while studying for the ministry. He became a Unitarian minister in 1842 and pastor of a church in Worcester, Massachusetts, in 1846. In 1852, he married Emily Baldwin Perkins, the niece of Harriet Beecher Stowe. They had eight children. In 1856, Hale became the minister of the South Congregational Church in Boston, a position he held until 1899. He was known for expounding a liberal theology and promoting education, and he also participated in the antislavery movement.

By the 1850s Hale was also a writer of fiction, an editor, and a journalist. His first short story had been published in the *Boston Miscellany* in 1842. Beginning in 1859, Hale published short stories in the *Atlantic Monthly*. "The Man without a Country" was published in that magazine in 1863, and it became his best-known story and is today the work for which he is chiefly remembered. However, in his own day, he was quite well known for stories such as "My Double and How He Undid Me," "Ten Times One Is Ten," "The Rag-Man and the Rag-Woman," and "The Skeleton in the Closet."

From 1857 to 1861, Hale was coeditor of the *Christian Examiner*. In 1863, he was associate editor of the *Army and Navy Journal*, and he became a fellow of the American Academy of Arts and Sciences in 1865. In 1870, he founded the magazine *Old and New*, and he continued to edit it until 1875, using it to publish many of his own pieces. During the 1880s and 1890s, Hale edited *Lend a Hand Record*, *Mrs. Merriam's Scholars*, and *New England Magazine*. The subject of his published books included biography, travel, and reminiscences, as well as fiction. His novels include a sequel to "The Man without a Country," titled *Philip Nolan's Friends*, published in 1876. Hale was chaplain of the US Senate from December 1903 until his death, in Roxbury, Boston, on June 10, 1909.

PLOT SUMMARY

The story begins like a factual narrative. A first-person narrator refers to a death notice, in the *New York Herald* on August 13, 1863, of a man named Philip Nolan. Nolan is reported to have died on board the US corvette *Levant* in May. The narrator says he happened to notice this item because he was stranded at Mackinac (in Michigan), waiting for a steamer and was reading the news. He notes further that the notice refers to a man who has been known as "The Man without a Country" for many decades. The narrator then says he will tell Philip Nolan's story. Up to this point, Nolan's life has been shrouded in secrecy.

The narrator proceeds to tell Nolan's story. Nolan was a young army lieutenant who excelled at his duties. He had met Aaron Burr in 1805, while Nolan was stationed at Fort

MEDIA ADAPTATIONS

- "The Man without a Country" has been adapted for film several times, in 1917, 1918, 1925, and 1937. Most recently, in 1973, it was an ABC made-for-television film, directed by Delbert Mann and written by Sidney Carroll. Cliff Robertson starred as Philip Nolan. In 1974, the film was nominated for a Primetime Emmy Award for Best Cinematography for Entertainment Programming for a Special or Feature Length Program Made for Television.

- In Benjamen Walker's *Theory of Everything* podcast, the story is updated, with the host himself having cursed his own country and been sentenced to spend his life in a hot-air balloon. The podcast is available in three parts at http://toe.prx.org/2014/08/man-without-a-country-1-of-3/.

- An audio recording of "The Man without a Country" is available from LibriVox at https://librivox.org/the-man-without-a-country-and-other-tales-by-edward-everett-hale/, read by David Wales. Running time is seventy-eight minutes.

Massac in New Orleans. Burr was a politician who in that year was vice president of the United States. (The previous year he had attained notoriety when he killed his political rival, Alexander Hamilton, in a duel.) After that, Nolan would write to Burr, although Burr never replied to his letters.

Burr returned to the fort some time later, and he and Nolan went sailing together, during which time Burr enlisted his support for his political ambitions. (The story goes on to explain in detail what those were. In fact, Burr had ambitions to conquer some of Louisiana, and he hatched a plot with James Wilkinson, the commander in chief of the US Army, to accomplish this goal.) Burr was arrested, charged with treason, and acquitted on September 1. Other officers, including Nolan, were also tried for

treason. Nolan was found guilty in a court-martial, during which he exclaimed "D——n the United States! I wish I may never hear of the United States again!" These words shocked Colonel Morgan, who was in charge of the court.

The narrator explains that the United States meant little to Nolan. He had been raised in areas that were then known as the West and kept company with Spanish officers and French traders; he made commercial expeditions to Vera Cruz (in Mexico) and hunted horses with his brother in Texas (which was then part of Mexico). The narrator points out, however, that Nolan had also sworn to be faithful to the United States and wore the uniform of a US officer. As a punishment for his statement, the navy granted him his wish. From that moment, in September 1807, until his death, he was never to hear the name of United States again. This was why he was a man without a country.

After Morgan told him what his punishment was to be, he was taken into the custody of the navy, and Morgan ordered that no one was to mention the United States as long as Nolan was aboard ship. President Thomas Jefferson approved the sentence, the narrator says. Nolan was taken from New Orleans to the North Atlantic coast by sea and then sent on a long cruise. Part of the instruction to the crew was "you will provide him with such quarters, rations, and clothing as would be proper for an officer of his late rank, as if he were a passenger on your vessel on the business of his Government." He was to be treated well and not even reminded that he was a prisoner, but he was never to hear the name of United States or be given any information about it.

On this and on subsequent cruises, Nolan was not allowed to talk to the men, unless an officer was present. He could mix freely with the officers, of whom the narrator was at one point one. The captain always asked him to dinner on Mondays. Other than that, Nolan ate alone.

The narrator remembers an incident that happened onshore soon after he joined the navy. He was with some of the older officers in Alexandria, on their way to Cairo. They talked about Nolan. It came out that he was allowed to read books, as long as they were not published in the United States and made no mention of it. He was permitted to read foreign newspapers too, as long as someone had studied them first and cut out any paragraph or advertisement that mentioned the United States.

In a long cruise up the Indian Ocean on Nolan's first voyage, a man named Phillips had borrowed a lot of English books from an officer. One of the books was *The Lay of the Last Minstrel*, by Sir Walter Scott, which was very popular at the time. None of the officers thought the poem would present any problems regarding Nolan, so he was allowed to take part as they read it aloud to one another. However, during Nolan's turn to read, he came upon a passage about how terrible it must be for a man who, traveling in foreign lands, had no home country to return to. Nolan choked up and was unable to continue.

After that, Nolan seemed changed and interacted with people less frequently. He was transferred to a ship in the Mediterranean, for his second cruise. It seemed then to dawn on him that he would never be going home. All told, he made about twenty of these transfers and at one time or another was onboard half of the navy's vessels, but he never came closer than one hundred miles to his homeland.

On that second cruise, on the *Warren*, a southern lady named Mrs. Graff danced with him at a ball on the ship, anchored in the Bay of Naples. Nolan had known her in Philadelphia. After they had talked for a while, he asked her what she had heard from home. She responded that she thought he was the man who never wanted to hear about home again and went off to join her husband. Nolan never danced again.

The narrator then goes on to a happier story about Nolan, dating back to the War of 1812 against the British. The ship Nolan was on was engaged in a battle with an English ship. After an enemy shot hit the gun crew, killing and injuring many, Nolan took over operations as if he were the officer in charge. Oblivious to the danger he was putting himself in, Nolan ensured that the gun was loaded and fired repeatedly.

After the battle was over, the Commodore asked Nolan to attend a ceremony on the quarter-deck. At the ceremony, the Commodore told Nolan he would be named in dispatches (accounts of the battle sent by the commanding officer to the Navy Department, in which individuals who gave noteworthy service were mentioned by name). He was also given a dress sword, which was an old French sword, to wear on such ceremonial occasions. Nolan was overcome with emotion. The Commodore

also wrote to the War Office asking that Nolan be pardoned, but he received nothing in reply.

The narrator then says that Nolan was with Captain Porter when the Nukahiwa Islands were taken. (These are islands in the South Pacific, now known as some of the Marquesas Islands. In 1813, they were taken by Captain Porter, commanding the USS *Essex*. The United States did not retain control of them, however.) Nolan played an important role in that action, too, and the narrator wishes that he had been left in joint charge of the islands.

Continuing his story, the narrator says that Nolan, who must have been about eighty years old when he died, must have been on every sea in the world but rarely on land. He developed a daily routine. He would read for five hours and then for two hours write in his notebooks and scrapbooks, recording what he had been reading. His subjects included history and natural sciences. He also illustrated his notebooks with his own drawings. For another two hours he would study natural history; the men would bring him birds and fish, and he would also study centipedes, cockroaches, and the like. The remainder of his time he would spend walking and talking.

The narrator first met Nolan about six or eight years after the War of 1812, when he was a midshipman. One day in the South Atlantic they intercepted a schooner that had slaves aboard. (This was after the slave trade was made illegal.) The officer sent to take charge of the ship returned and asked if there was anyone aboard who spoke Portuguese. Nolan stepped forward and said he would be happy to act as interpreter. The narrator went with him. The scene on the boat was chaotic. The slaves had had their handcuffs and ankle cuffs removed, and these were now being placed on the slave traders. The slaves did not understand what was happening. They were talking excitedly in many dialects. Nolan was able to explain to two of the slaves that they were free, and those men informed as many of the others as could understand them. The newly freed slaves danced with delight, and some kissed Nolan's feet.

The officer in charge, whose name was Vaughan, planned to take them to Cape Palmas, but that was far from their homes, and they protested. Nolan had to translate their desperate requests to be allowed to return to their own country and see their own families again. Naturally enough, this was very hard on Nolan. Eventually Vaughan agreed that he would take the freed slaves wherever it was that they called home. They rejoiced once again.

Back in their boat, Nolan said to the young narrator, "Youngster, let that show you what it is to be without a family, without a home, and without a country." He told the young man that he must always think of family and home and to serve his country's flag, no matter what happened. The narrator was frightened by the passionate but calm way Nolan spoke. After that, Nolan befriended the narrator, teaching him mathematics and lending him books. The narrator met him again in 1830 and later did his best to get him freed from his ordeal in exile. But in Washington, DC, government officials pretended that no such man existed. The narrator then comments on how great Nolan's repentance was and how he gently accepted his fate.

In 1845, after Texas was annexed by the United States, there was some discussion among the officers about whether Texas should be cut out of the map in Nolan's atlas, as the United States had been when the atlas had been bought for him. They decided not to do so, since that would be like telling him that Texas was now part of the United States. The truth almost slipped out in an incident that took place when the narrator was commander of the *George Washington* corvette in South American waters. Nolan was at the dinner table and after hearing a story told about riding half-wild horses in Buenos Aires, told a story of how he and his brothers had hunted horses in Texas. Then he asked what had become of Texas, thinking that it was probably independent by now. There were two officers from Texas at the table, but none of the officers was willing to answer Nolan's question. The narrator, however, needing to break the awkward silence, ventured the remark, "Texas is out of the map, Mr. Nolan," which might have given Nolan a clue as to what had happened.

That was the last time the narrator ever saw Nolan. He now remarks that since writing Nolan's story he has received a letter from Danforth about Nolan's last hours. Nolan, who was known to be not well, said he would like to see Danforth. He had made his small berth into a shrine to the United States, with the US flag, a picture of George Washington, and a drawing of an eagle. At the foot of his bed was a map of the United States he had drawn from memory.

Nolan appealed to Danforth to tell him everything about the history of his country before he died. Danforth agreed to do so. At Nolan's request, he told him the names of the thirty-four states. Nolan knew that there were thirty-four because of the number of stars on the flag. After that, Danforth tried to relate fifty years of US history in an hour, and he emphasized the positive aspects of it, such as the coming of steamboats, railroads, and telegraphs and the Smithsonian. But he said nothing of what he calls the "infernal Rebellion," a reference to the Civil War. Then Nolan read prayers from the Presbyterian *Book of Public Prayer* that thanked God for taking care of the United States and asked God to bless the president of the United States. Nolan said he had read those prayers for fifty-five years. Danforth then left him, and Nolan died within an hour. He left a note asking to be buried at sea but also that a monument be erected in his name at Fort Adams or Orleans with the inscription "He loved his country as no other man has loved her; but no man deserved less at her hands."

CHARACTERS

Aaron Burr

Aaron Burr was a prominent US politician in the early nineteenth century. In the story, he befriended Nolan and drew him into his treasonous scheme to conquer part of Louisiana and set himself up as some kind of emperor. He was tried for treason but acquitted in early September 1807.

The Commodore

The Commodore was the captain of a US frigate during the War of 1812 against the British. Nolan was also on the ship and performed valiantly during the battle, which earned him praise from the Commodore, who presented him with a ceremonial sword and mentioned him in dispatches.

Danforth

Danforth is an acquaintance of the narrator's. He was onboard the *Levant* when Nolan died, and it is he who writes the letter to the narrator describing Nolan's last hours. Danforth explains that Nolan knew he was dying and begged Danforth to tell him about the United States. Danforth knew all about Nolan's punishment and that he would be breaking the law if he granted his request. Nonetheless, he felt pity for Nolan and talked to him for an hour about US history.

Mrs. Graff

Mrs. Graff is a southern lady who danced with Nolan at a ball on a ship in the Bay of Naples.

Nolan had known her in the United States, and he tried to get information from her about the country. She, knowing his story, refused to tell him anything and walked away from him.

Lady Emma Hamilton

Lady Emma Hamilton was the wife of the English ambassador to Naples, Italy, in 1798, when the British were in that city. She was famously beautiful and was a well-recognized figure in Naples. The narrator believes she may have been at the same on-ship ball that Mrs. Graff and Nolan attended in the Bay of Naples.

Frederic Ingham

Frederic Ingham is the narrator of the story. He is a navy officer, and as the story unfolds he gives various clues as to the development of his career and his relations with Nolan. He was a young midshipman when he first met Nolan in about 1820. He found him shy and not very talkative, but he soon saw another side of Nolan when their ship intercepted a schooner that was carrying slaves, and he witnessed firsthand Nolan's important role in that episode. After that, Nolan befriended him. He would walk the deck with Ingham when it was Ingham's watch. He lent him books and taught him mathematics, and Ingham was sorry when his cruise came to an end. Ingham says that he met Nolan again in 1830 and on several occasions after that and lobbied the War Department, trying to get Nolan released. By this time, it seems, Ingham was fairly well known in Washington, DC, and thought he had some influence on lawmakers. The last time the narrator saw Nolan was when he was commander of the *George Washington* corvette in South American waters, sometime in the mid- to late 1840s. He wrote to Nolan twice a year after that, but Nolan never replied. As he tells Nolan's story, Ingham pieces together bits of the story from various accounts told to him by others. He tries to sort out what is true from the many myths that have grown up around Nolan's life.

Colonel Morgan

Colonel Morgan was an old man who was in charge of the court-martial of Philip Nolan. He was shocked by Nolan's outburst, and after a fifteen-minute private conference with the court, decided Nolan's punishment.

Philip Nolan

Philip Nolan is the central character in the story. He was a young lieutenant in the US Army who seemed to have a great career ahead of him. He is described as a "dashing, bright young fellow" and served in what was known as the "Legion of the West,"—the western division of the army. However, his career took a downward path when he met and was befriended by Aaron Burr, a prominent politician who had ambitions to take control of part of Louisiana. Burr enlisted Nolan's support in his enterprise, and Nolan ended up being charged with treason, as Burr also was. Nolan's unfortunate remark at his court-martial, that he never wanted to hear of the United States again, led to his long exile from the country, which lasted for over fifty years until his death in 1863. Deprived of any knowledge of his country, Nolan quickly repented his hasty words, and over the years he developed to a marked degree the patriotic feelings that he had formerly lacked. Nolan quietly accepted his fate, and he worked on improving his mind by private study. He also showed courage in battle during the War of 1812 when the ship he was on was in a battle with a British frigate. Everyone who knew Nolan had a high opinion of him.

Phillips

Phillips is a naval officer who told the narrator the story of how Nolan came to read aloud some verses from *The Lay of the Last Minstrel* that speak of love of country and of home. Phillips had borrowed the book from an English officer. Phillips told the narrator that Nolan was never the same after this incident.

Captain David Porter

Captain David Porter was the captain of the frigate *Essex*, responsible for the taking of the Nukahiwa Islands in the South Pacific in 1813. Nolan was also on that expedition. Porter claimed the islands for the United States, but the US Congress never ratified the claim.

Vaughan

Vaughan was the officer in charge of the US Navy ship in the South Atlantic that intercepted a schooner and freed the slaves onboard.

THEMES

Patriotism

Patriotism is the love of one's own country. It seems to be a natural emotion that people feel without being told to do so, and it is reinforced by many elements in a society and culture—in

TOPICS FOR FURTHER STUDY

- Imagine that you were to encounter a modern-day Philip Nolan, who had heard nothing of the United States for the previous twenty years. You have just ten to fifteen minutes with him, and you decide to tell him what you believe to be the most important events and developments in the United States over that period. Give a class presentation, with the premise that all the class students are modern Philip Nolans. Then take a few minutes to explain your reasoning about how you selected the things you decided to tell, and answer any questions your classmates might have.

- "The Man without a Country" is famous for its celebration of patriotism. Write an essay in which you describe the differences between patriotism, nationalism, jingoism, and cosmopolitanism. In today's interconnected global economy, is cosmopolitanism more desirable than patriotism? Can nationalism be a force for good, or is it dangerous?

- Research the career of Aaron Burr and give a class presentation about what his intentions were when he traveled to what was then the western frontier of the United States around 1805. Two years later he was charged with treason, and Burr's actions around that time are alluded to in "The Man without a Country." What actually happened?

- What link, if any, is there between the actions of Danforth and Ingham in telling Nolan's story and the actions of whistle-blowers such as Edward Snowden in the 2010s? Is Snowden, as of 2016 living in exile in Russia, also a man without a country because, like Danforth and Ingham, he followed his conscience and released information the US government would have preferred to keep secret? Or should Snowden be considered, as some do, a traitor to his country? Give a class presentation on the topic and then lead the ensuing discussion.

- Using the Internet, research American patriotism as it manifests today, according to opinion surveys. Is patriotism on the rise in the mid-2010s, is it diminishing, or is it about the same as it has always been? Does the research show that young people are more or less patriotic than older people? If there is a difference, what might be the reason for it? Conduct a survey among your classmates about the level of patriotism they feel and why. Create an entry in your blog in which you summarize your findings and invite your classmates to comment.

- Read *Nothing but the Truth*, a 2010 young-adult novel by Avi, in which Philip Malloy, a ninth-grader, gets into trouble at school for humming during the national anthem instead of listening with respectful attention. The novel explores the issue of patriotism. Write an essay in which you discuss the similarities and differences between the issues involving Philip Nolan in "The Man without a Country" and those involving Philip Malloy.

---

the United States, for example, by flying the flag from public buildings and many private residences, the playing of the national anthem before major sporting events, and suchlike. Patriotism is also eternally invoked and exploited by politicians of every stripe.

When Philip Nolan, the fictional character in "The Man without a Country," was growing up, around the last decade of the eighteenth century, the United States was a very young country and much smaller than it is today. However, it seems from the story that people still had strong patriotic feelings and expected others to share them or at least not insult them. The shocked reaction of Colonel Morgan who presides over Nolan's court-martial, shows that Nolan's contempt for the United States was not a common or acceptable view. Without trying to excuse Nolan, the narrator points out that Nolan had lived in places in the South that at the time were colonies of Spain or France (before the Louisiana Purchase of 1803); he had also spent time in Mexico and just did not have the deep feeling for the United States that was expected of him as a US army lieutenant.

As the story unfolds, however, it becomes one long lesson about the desirability and even the necessity of patriotism, as one of the most natural and abiding feelings a man or woman might possess. Nolan, condemned to spend his life on the seas in US Navy vessels, learns soon enough that when he hears nothing at all about the United States, his home country, he feels the lack acutely. Over the years, he develops in full measure the patriotic feelings he formerly lacked. All the episodes in the story are designed to show his growing awareness of patriotic feelings. This development begins on his very first voyage, which takes him to the Cape of Good Hope. He finds himself reading aloud a passage from *The Lay of the Last Minstrel* about the miserable fate of those who have no country to call home. He is so affected by the passage that he cannot go on reading. On his second cruise, when he meets and dances with Mrs. Graff at the ball onboard the *Warren*, he tries to elicit from her some news of home, but she refuses to tell him anything. The disappointment he feels is emphasized by the narrator's plain comment, "He did not dance again." The fact that within five years or so of his sentence Nolan had acquired the kind of unshakable patriotism required to be of service to his country is emphasized by his brave feats on deck during the battle with the British frigate in the War of 1812. The fact that he cherishes the ceremonial sword given to him by the captain to honor his contribution is another sign that Nolan is no longer the same man who renounced his country at the court-martial. The incident in which he acts as translator for the freed slaves on the schooner who are desperate to return to their own countries also affects him deeply. Immediately afterward, he takes the narrator, then a young midshipman, aside and gives him a lecture about patriotism:

> No matter what happens to you, no matter who flatters you or who abuses you, never look at another flag, never let a night pass but you pray God to bless that flag. Remember, boy, that behind all these men you have to do with, behind officers, and government, and people even, there is the Country Herself, your Country, and that you belong to Her as you belong to your own mother.

He also decorates his berth on the ship with patriotic symbols and wants nothing more than to hear in his dying days about all the events he had missed. Part of his own epitaph, which he writes himself, reads: "He loved his country as no other man has loved her."

US History

Nolan was at sea for over fifty years, and during that time the United States grew tremendously. Near the end of the story, that period in US history is given prominence, since Nolan is desperate to hear about it, and Danforth's account of it augments the patriotic theme of the story by emphasizing the great and good deeds the United States has accomplished. For his contemporary readers, Hale no doubt hoped that his extolling of the achievements of the United States would help to rally support to the Union cause during the Civil War.

In his letter to the narrator, Danforth gives few details, since obviously his correspondent would understand the references, although today's reader might need some background information. Danforth's account emphasizes the military success, geographic expansion, and technological and educational achievements of the United States. He tells Nolan of the War of 1812, which he calls the "English war," and alludes to Andrew Jackson (1767–1845), seventh president of the United States, who was famous for winning a battle against the invading British force at New Orleans. Danforth mentions "old Scott," which is a reference to Winfield Scott (1786–1866), one of the great generals in US history, who commanded forces in several major conflicts, from the War of 1812 to the Civil War. (Danforth calls him "old Scott" because was still alive in 1863, when the fictional letter was written, at the age of seventy-seven.) Danforth also mentions Robert Fulton (1765–1812), a technologist who was a pioneer of commercial steamboat travel, and he makes a generalized reference to "railroads, and telegraphs . . . inventions, and books, and literature" and colleges. Specifically, he mentions West Point, the US Military Academy, which was actually founded in 1802, before Nolan's exile, but underwent considerable modernization in the 1850s. Danforth also mentions the Smithsonian Institution, founded in 1846, and what he calls the Naval School, which is the US Naval Academy, founded in 1845. He mentions "Crawford's Liberty," a reference to the Statue of Freedom, created by sculptor Thomas Crawford, which was installed

When Nolan is put on trial for treason, he renounces his country and is sentenced to spend the rest of his life at sea (©*Alvov | Shutterstock.com*)

atop the Dome of the US Capitol in Washington, DC, in 1863. "Greenough's Washington" is a reference to a sculpture by Horatio Greenough of George Washington, erected in 1832 to mark the centennial of Washington's birth. Danforth also tells Nolan about the states that have been added to the United States since 1807, including Texas (1845), California (1850), and Oregon (1859). (A total of eighteen states joined the Union between 1807 and June 1863.)

STYLE

Verisimilitude

The story is written to give the impression that it is, in fact, a true story, faithfully told by a navy officer who pieces together the details from various sources available to him, including a newspaper obituary, naval archives and other official documents, letters, personal memories, incidents he has been told about, and even a letter he has

purportedly received from a friend. Right at the beginning, the narrator refers to a death notice about Philip Nolan that appeared in a specific publication (the *New York Herald*) on a specific date (August 13, 1863). He says he wants to tell Nolan's story, which up to this point has remained unknown. He claims that all official records of Nolan were likely destroyed when Washington, DC, was burned during the War of 1812. The overwhelming impression given is that this is a nonfiction account of an interesting and highly unusual case. The little trick employed by the narrator of saying on and off that he does not know or recall all the details of a particular incident or exactly where or when it took place adds to the feeling that the narrator is doing his best to assemble this true story. For example, he states, referring to Nolan:

> I do not know certainly what his first cruise was. But the Commander to whom he was intrusted,—perhaps it was Tingey or Shaw, though I think it was one of the younger men,—we are all old enough now—regulated the etiquette and the precautions of the affair.

This is a mingling of fact and fiction, since Thomas Tingey and John Shaw were historical characters (navy officers, both).

These kinds of storytelling techniques are employed throughout, giving the effect of verisimilitude, although Hale well knew (and others were slow to realize) that there were also some historical inaccuracies that rather gave the game away as far as fact or fiction was concerned. For example, the death notice states that Nolan died on board the corvette *Levant* in 1863, but the *Levant* had been lost at sea in 1861.

Episodic Structure

The story has an episodic structure in that it relates a series of discrete incidents rather than providing a narrative with a developing, sustained plot. Although each episode may show the theme of Nolan's discovery of patriotism, the episodes are only loosely connected by a narrative thread and are not told in chronological order. This manner of telling the tale is necessitated by the nature of the material the narrator has to work with, and it is quite in keeping with the need for verisimilitude. As the narrator writes:

> I cannot give any history of him in order: nobody can now: and, indeed, I am not trying to. These are the traditions, which I sort out as I believe them, from the myths which have been told about this man for forty years.

COMPARE
&
CONTRAST

- **1807:** The Abolition of the Slave Trade Act is passed by the US Congress.

  1863: The Emancipation Proclamation, which frees all the slaves in the states of the Confederacy, goes into effect on January 1.

  Today: African Americans are still involved in efforts to assert their civil rights. The group Black Lives Matter is formed to bring attention to and end police violence against African Americans.

- **1807:** Thomas Jefferson is president of the United States, which consists of seventeen states, the most recent being Ohio, added in 1803.

  1863: Immediately before the Civil War begins, the United States consists of thirty-four states, the most recent being Kansas, added in January 1863. (The figure includes South Carolina, even though it seceded from the Union in 1860.) The US president is Abraham Lincoln.

  Today: The United States comprises fifty states. As of 2016, Barack Obama is in the last year of his second term as US president.

- **1807:** Although American literature has yet to distinguish itself from its colonial origins, in 1808 one of the most prominent American writers of the nineteenth century, William Cullen Bryant (1794–1878), publishes a poem, *The Embargo*, as a pamphlet of twelve pages. Bryant is thirteen years old at the time.

  1863: American writers active during the 1860s include Nathaniel Hawthorne, Walt Whitman, Ralph Waldo Emerson, Henry Wadsworth Longfellow, and Henry David Thoreau. In 1863, Longfellow publishes *Tales of a Wayside Inn*.

  Today: Among the greatest living American writers are Philip Roth, Toni Morrison, Thomas Pynchon, Don DeLillo, Tom Wolfe, and Joyce Carol Oates.

HISTORICAL CONTEXT

A Warning to Others

When Hale sat down to write "The Man without a Country," he had in mind an actual contemporary example of what he considered a lack of patriotism. He even explains this in the course of the story, when the narrator says that after having written the story, he had to decide whether to publish it "as a warning to the young Nolans and Vallandighams and Tatnalls of to-day of what it is to throw away a country." The first reference is to Clement L. Vallandigham, an antiwar Democratic candidate for governor of Ohio in the elections of 1863. (The antiwar Democrats were also known as Copperheads.) Vallandigham was a southern sympathizer, and in August 1863, according to Jean Holloway in *Edward Everett Hale: A Biography*, he declared that "he did not want to belong to a nation which would compel by arms the loyalty of any of its citizens; he did not want to belong to the United States." Hale wrote his patriotic story soon after, as a response to Vallandigham and hoping thereby to influence the November election. Publication was delayed until December, however; in practice, this made little difference, since Vallandigham lost the election in a landslide. (In May 1863, Vallandigham had been banished to the South by President Lincoln for his antiwar activity, after which Vallandigham had made his way to Canada, and he was still in Canada at the time of the election.)

The second reference is to Josiah Tattnall, a name that would have been known to Hale's readers in 1863 but will be less familiar to twenty-first-century readers. Tattnall (1795–1871) was an American naval officer with a long record of service. In the late 1850s Tattnall was commander of

Nolan decorates his room in the ship with patriotic symbols (©*Patrick Rolands | Shutterstock.com*)

the East India Squadron in Hong Kong. In 1859, in defiance of US neutrality, Tattnall ordered the chartered steamer he commanded to assist British ships that were attacking Chinese forts. He defended his actions, as noted in the *New Georgia Encyclopedia*, by citing the proverb "blood is thicker than water." His comment became famous, and Hale obviously considered Tattnall's actions disloyal to the United States. Tattnall, who was from Georgia, later served in the Confederate navy.

The American Civil War

In 1863, the American Civil War was at its height, and the outcome remained uncertain. In May, Confederate forces under General Robert Lee won the Battle of Chancellorsville, Virginia, and Lee made plans for the invasion of the North.

In July, about the time that Hale, a firm believer in the Unionist cause, was writing his story, one of the most momentous battles of the entire war, and also the bloodiest, took place. This was the Battle of Gettysburg, Pennsylvania. In a three-day struggle, the Confederate forces were turned back from their invasion of the North. On November 19, 1863, in the same week that "The Man without a Country" was published in the *Atlantic Monthly* (the actual date on the magazine was December), President Abraham Lincoln returned to the site of the battlefield to give the Gettysburg Address, a short speech that was to become one of the most famous speeches in human history. In his speech, Lincoln laid out the principles behind the Unionist cause.

CRITICAL OVERVIEW

When "The Man without a Country" was first published, many readers took it to be a true, factual story, and this misperception persisted for some time. One resident of Boston even wrote to Hale saying that he distinctly recalled Philip Nolan's court-martial in 1807. Hale was later at pains to point out that the story was a work of fiction.

When it was reprinted in Hale's book *If, Yes, and Perhaps*, it received praise from William Dean Howells, who would go on to become one of the most prominent literary critics of the nineteenth century. Reviewing the book in the *Atlantic Monthly* in 1868, Howells applauds the verisimilitude of the tale, writing (as quoted by Jean Holloway in *Edward Everett Hale: A Biography*) "Philip Nolan, amidst all the sad impossibilities of his fate, was so veritable a man, that many have claimed to know his history apart from Mr. Hale's narrative."

The story has continued to fascinate readers since, being reprinted often. Holloway notes that forty years after the end of the Civil War, an American magazine editor asked his readers to list their favorite stories. Almost every list included "The Man without a Country."

In his introduction to a deluxe illustrated edition of the story in 1936, Carl van Doren comments, as so many others have done, on how convincing the story is and how it seems to be a factual account of something that actually happened. Van Doren comments further:

> Once the central situation is accepted, the incidents that follow in what looks like artless veracity serve to confirm the tale. Even though the imaginary narrator . . . slips at times into the idiom of a sermon, he writes for the most part like a sailor, plainly, with the desire to get at the truth and tell nothing else.

More recently, Samuel I. Bellman, in *Dictionary of Literary Biography*, describes the story as "Hale's classic of American patriotism" and as an "excellent" example "of what would later be called the 'well-made short story'" that flourished in the 1880s, written by writers such as Thomas Bailey Aldrich and H. C. Bunner. "Some of Hale's short fiction may be seen as prototypical for these stories of ingenious situations reaching unexpected conclusions," according to Bellman.

CRITICISM

Bryan Aubrey

Aubrey holds a PhD in English. In the following essay, he discusses the questions "The Man without a Country" raises about the nature and extent of patriotism and the behavior of the US government in the case of Philip Nolan.

When Edward Everett Hale died in 1909, his contemporaries considered that a very great man had passed away. Hale was revered as a moral leader, and the *Review of Reviews*, as quoted by Jean Holloway in *Edward Everett Hale: A Biography*, wrote that some would regard him as "the greatest of living Americans." Holloway also notes that "in chorus the reviewers bestowed the accolade of immortality upon his best-known story," which was, of course, "The Man without a Country."

Over one hundred years after his death, Hale's fame is much diminished, and of the more than sixty books he wrote, very few are read today. "The Man without a Country," however, remains in print in a number of different editions, a testament to the continuing appeal of this ingenious and didactic tale about the necessity of patriotism.

The story cannot be properly understood, however, outside its historical context. In 1863,

THE PRESENTATION OF NOLAN IN SUCH A FAVORABLE LIGHT, HOWEVER, DOES RAISE QUESTIONS REGARDING THE JUSTIFICATION FOR HIS LONG AND NEVER-ENDING PUNISHMENT. WAS JUSTICE SERVED IN THIS CASE?"

when it was first published, the United States was facing a grave threat to the continuance of the indissoluble Union that the Founders had envisioned. The story makes only one direct reference to the Civil War, when Danforth, in his letter to Ingham, the narrator, explains that he could not bring himself to say a word to Philip Nolan about "this infernal Rebellion!" The parallel between Nolan's act and the rebellion of the Confederacy is clear, though; the latter is Nolan's individual act ("D——n the United States!") writ large, with huge and terrible consequences.

Hale wanted to tap into and nourish patriotic feelings about the United States and impress upon his readers what a great and majestic nation it had become. In service of this end, he has his main character, Nolan, repent and suffer much for his rejection of his own country. Nolan finds out very quickly that not having a country to return to or call home is a distressing, soul-destroying experience. The story, however, is not quite that simple and raises questions about the nature and extent of patriotism and also the behavior of the US government. Readers will notice that apart from Nolan's one outburst at the court-martial (for which the narrator offers mitigating circumstances without actually excusing Nolan), he is presented in an entirely positive manner. The reader quickly sympathizes with him and his plight. Nolan is a gentle, considerate, sensitive, intelligent man who uses his endless time onboard US naval ships to read, write, and study. At moments of crisis he performs extremely well—showing great bravery and lack of regard for his own safety, he takes over from the incapacitated gun crew when the frigate he is on is engaged in battle during the War of

WHAT DO I READ NEXT?

- *The Man without a Country and Other Tales* (2016) is a collection of Hale's stories issued by the Leopold Classic Library.

- *The Man without a Country: And Other Naval Writings* (Naval Institute Press, 2002) is a collection of Hale's fiction and nonfiction naval writings, with an introduction by Robert D. Madison.

- *The Pocket Book of Patriotism*, by Jonathan Foreman (2005), is laid out as a time line of the key events in US history. It also includes quotations and speeches from well-known historical figures, excerpts from patriotic songs, and interesting facts. The book covers the period from the Revolutionary War to the terrorist attacks on the United States of September 11, 2001.

- *Vicksburg, 1863*, by Winston Groom (2010), received high praise from reviewers. It is a gripping account of the campaign of US general Ulysses S. Grant against the Confederacy, beginning in 1861 and culminating in a victory at Vicksburg in July 1863, when the city surrendered following a long siege. Both Vicksburg and Grant are mentioned in "The Man without a Country," when Danforth tells Nolan about US

history, although Danforth offers no details and does not even mention the Civil War.

- *A Young People's History of the United States: Columbus to the War on Terror* (2009), by Howard Zinn, is a highly acclaimed history for young readers.

- In *Seeking Palestine: New Palestinian Writing on Exile and Home* (2012), edited by Penny Johnson and Raja Shehadeh, fifteen Palestinians write about their experience of being exiled from the place they regard as home.

- Born just seven years before Hale, Thomas Bangs Thorpe (1815–1878) was a popular writer in his day. His story "The Big Bear of Arkansas," first published in 1841, is a humorous tale about hunting bears in what was then the frontier wilderness. The story is often compared to the stories of Mark Twain and was greatly admired by no less a literary figure than William Faulkner. The story can be found in an anthology compiled by Willam T. Porter, *The Big Bear of Arkansas: And Other Sketches, Illustrative of Characters and Incidents in the South and South-West* (2015).

1812, and he also performs a very useful function as translator from the Portuguese during the incident when the slaves aboard the pirate schooner are freed. He is also kind to Ingham, the narrator. When Ingham was a young midshipman, he recalls, Nolan befriended him, teaching him mathematics and lending him books. Nolan is also an exemplary prisoner in the sense that he learns from his offense and over the years quietly cultivates a love of the country he is no longer allowed to set foot in. Accepting of his fate, he becomes a true patriot in exile, and the epitaph he writes for himself ("He loved his country as no other man

has loved her; but no man deserved less at her hands") shows not only patriotism but also humility.

The presentation of Nolan in such a favorable light, however, does raise questions regarding the justification for his long and never-ending punishment. Was justice served in this case? In this story, which extols patriotism and presents the United States as a country worthy of admiration and devotion, does the US government behave toward Nolan in a way that commands respect? The answer must surely be no. Ingham thinks so, too. As a man of some influence, he obviously felt that Nolan had suffered enough for his youthful mistake and tried hard to get him released. The passage in which Ingham reveals the efforts he made over the years to deal with the government in Washington, DC, on Nolan's behalf is highly revealing:

> I moved heaven and earth to have him discharged. But it was like getting a ghost out of prison. They pretended there was no such man, and never was such a man. They will say so at the Department now!

Nolan is thus caught in a kind of Kafkaesque nightmare in which the government bureaucracy denies he even exists. He has, in effect, been "disappeared," as modern parlance has it. Denying that the man even exists means that his case can never come up for reconsideration; nor can it can ever be the subject of public discussion. Nolan's crime, it seems, was to be inconvenient; he said something he was not supposed to say, and for that the US government disappeared him, imposing on him an extremely unusual, and many might say cruel, punishment. No advocate of his can ever penetrate the bureaucratic stonewalling and deceit that continues over decades regarding his case. Why, the reader may wonder, does the US government deny the existence of Philip Nolan? Is it in some way ashamed of its behavior, that it does not want it to come to light? The entire matter reveals a curious irony about this story that is supposed to reveal, in Danforth's words "the grandeur of his [Nolan's] country and its prosperity."

Moreover, both Ingham, the narrator who publishes the story, and Danforth, who breaks the law by telling Nolan the history of the United States, are aware that in doing so they may face prosecution. Ingham argues at the beginning of the story that there may have been a good reason for the secrecy surrounding Nolan, but telling his story now that he is dead can do no harm. Nevertheless, he realizes he is putting himself in legal jeopardy: "I do not know but I expose myself to a criminal prosecution on the evidence of the very revelation that I am making," he says, and it is only when he receives Danforth's letter that he puts his doubts aside and decides to publish. As for Danforth, he writes in his letter to Ingham:

> Danger or no danger, . . . who was I, that I should have been acting the tyrant all this time over this dear, sainted old man, who had years ago expiated, in his whole manhood's life, the madness of a boy's treason?

One might ask, if Danforth thinks himself to have been a tyrant in continuing, in effect, to punish Nolan, what does that say about the role of the US government, the official representative of the very country that "The Man without a Country" purports to praise to the skies? In the case of Philip Nolan, it is hard to avoid the conclusion that with its long-running bureaucratic intransigence and opaqueness, not to mention its cruelty, the US government does not exactly cover itself with glory. The irony of the situation is most apparent, since the callousness of the collective entity that is held up for admiration is only corrected and alleviated by the actions of two decent men acting not as government officials but as individuals: Danforth, who acts out of compassion, and Ingham, who acts on the belief that it is time for the truth to be told. One might say that they are implicitly making a distinction between patriotism—love of country—and the actions of a particular government in a particular case. Patriotism, in such a view, must not be blind but must make a sober assessment of the extent to which any action taken by the government of the day embodies the ideals and moral principles of the nation and then, if necessary, take action accordingly, based on individual conscience. It is a lesson that is perhaps not quite the one Hale had in mind when he wrote the story, but it is important nonetheless.

Source: Bryan Aubrey, Critical Essay on "The Man without a Country," in *Short Stories for Students*, Gale, Cengage Learning, 2017.

SOURCES

Bellman, Samuel I., "Edward Everett Hale," in *Dictionary of Literary Biography*, Vol. 74, *American Short-Story Writers before 1880*, edited by Bobby Ellen Kimbel and William E. Grant, Gale Research, 1988.

Hale, Edward Everett, *The Man without a Country*, with an introduction by Carl Van Doren, Heritage Press, 1936.

Holloway, Jean, *Edward Everett Hale: A Biography*, University of Texas Press, 1956, pp. 133, 157, 261.

"Josiah Tattnall (1795–1871)," in *New Georgia Encyclopedia*, http://www.georgiaencyclopedia.org/articles/history-archaeology/josiah-tattnall-1795-1871 (accessed February 7, 2016).

"Robert Fulton," in *Who Made America?*, PBS website, http://www.pbs.org/wgbh/theymadeamerica/whomade/fulton_hi.html (accessed February 6, 2016).

Van Doren, Carl, Introduction to *The Man without a Country*, Heritage Press, 1936, p. x.

"Winfield Scott," History.com, http://www.history.com/topics/winfield-scott (accessed February 6, 2016).

FURTHER READING

Adams, John R., *Edward Everett Hale*, Twayne Publishers, 1977.

This is the only book that offers a concise survey of Hale's work in all genres.

Bar-Tel, Daniel, and Ervin Staub, eds., *Patriotism* (Nelson-Hall Series in Psychology), Wadsworth Publishing, 1999.

This is a collection of essays in which psychologists, sociologists, philosophers, a political scientist, and a historian discuss patriotism. The authors examine the origin and history of patriotism and the role it plays for individuals and groups.

Cohen, Joshua, ed., *For Love of Country?*, Beacon Press, 2002.

This is a debate, sparked by the first essay in the book, "Patriotism and Cosmopolitanism," by Martha C. Nussbaum. Nussbaum argues for the superiority of cosmopolitanism over patriotism, but many of the fifteen authors whose essays make up the remainder of the book disagree with her.

Isenberg, Nancy, *Fallen Founder: The Life of Aaron Burr*, Viking Penguin, 2007.

This is a sympathetic biography of Burr, the politician and adventurer who gets the fictional Philip Nolan in trouble in "The Man without a Country." The book includes an account of Burr's trial for treason in 1807, the same year in which Nolan faces a similar charge.

SUGGESTED SEARCH TERMS

Edward Everett Hale

"The Man without a Country" AND Hale

Aaron Burr

Burr AND treason trial

War of 1812

patriotism

patriotism AND nationalism

Clement L. Vallandigham

Josiah Tattnall

Tale of the Unknown Island

JOSÉ SARAMAGO

1997

The 1998 Nobel laureate in literature, José de Sousa Saramago, in his *Tale of the Unknown Island* (1997 in Portuguese; 1999 in English), creates a fairy tale for the modern world. In this story an unnamed man must battle against a world under the control of an entrenched bureaucracy. He can find himself only by leaving the control of that world, voyaging to the last unknown island. Surprisingly, the meaning that Saramago, an anarcho-communist whose writings have been censored by the Portuguese government for showing insufficient respect for religion, finds is the old answer provided by Christianity—that love is the beginning of wisdom and that an individual's first responsibility is to his fellow human beings. The difference is, in Saramago's view, that he, as a communist, wants people to actually live according to love rather than to pay lip service to love as an empty ideal in a world filled with oppression and exploitation. Although *The Tale of the Unknown Island* is not especially long for a short story, it was printed as a separate volume in the original Portuguese as well as in its English translation. The English version was translated by Margaret Jull Costa and published by Harcourt Brace.

AUTHOR BIOGRAPHY

Saramago was born into a peasant family in the Portuguese village of Azinhaga on November 16, 1922. The family nickname Saramago (Portuguese

Jose Saramago (©*Sueddeutsche Zeitung Photo / Alamy*)

for "radish") was accidentally written on his birth certificate. His father, José de Sousa, served in the French army during World War I and, based on this experience, obtained a job as a policeman in Lisbon, where he moved his family. Saramago's mother, Maria, worked as a maid. His family sent Saramago to a grammar school in the hope of improving his station in life, but they could not afford the tuition for a high school, so Saramago studied briefly at a technical college and began work as an auto mechanic. He eventually was able to find work as a translator and a reporter. He married Ilda Reis in 1944, with whom he had a daughter. The couple divorced in 1970. Throughout this period Portugal underwent dramatic political change. The country was ruled by the fascist dictator António Salazar from 1933 until his death in 1968. Although the fascist regime continued until 1974, the political situation became fragmentary. Saramago was able to openly join the Communist Party in 1969. He was an anarcho-communist, a faction opposed to the Soviet Union and which took its inspiration from the Russian philosopher and anarchist Pyotr Kropotkin. The movement stressed the original communist ideal of

local control and personal freedom and rejected the rigid state control of the economy in Soviet communism. In 1974–1975, Portugal became a democracy, and Saramago was promoted to an assistant editorship at his newspaper, the *Diário de Notícias*. Then a military coup made it impossible for Saramago, as a communist, to work at a newspaper or anywhere else. He decided therefore that the time had come for him to make his living as a writer.

By 1977 he had published his first novel, *Manual of Painting and Calligraphy*. This was quickly followed by collections of short stories (*The Lives of Things*), drama (*A noite*), poetry (*The Year of 1993*), and more novels, Saramago's preferred form. In 1986 Saramago met the journalist Pilar del Río, whom he married in 1988. She served as the English translator of many of his works, though Margaret Jull Costa would translate *The Tale of the Unknown Island*. Perhaps Saramago's two most important works are his novels the 1982 *Memorial do convento* (which literally means "memoir of the convent" but which was translated as *Baltasar and Blimunda*) and his 1991 *The Gospel*

According to Jesus Christ. By that time, Portugal was a neoliberal democracy with a government similar to those of most other European countries and was a member of the European Union. Nevertheless, the Portuguese government intervened to prevent the book from being considered for the prestigious Aresteion literary prize on the ground that its depiction of God and Jesus as possessing realistic human personalities was offensive to Portugal's largely Catholic population.

After this, Saramago moved to Lanzerote in the Canary Islands, a Spanish territory. Saramago published the allegorical story *The Tale of the Unknown Island* in 1997, a year before he was awarded the Nobel Prize in Literature. Like that of any contemporary writer, a good deal of Saramago's work consisted of going on long tours of speaking engagements, where he was more likely to speak about the principles of anarcho-communism than about his writing. After the government attack on *The Gospel According to Jesus Christ*, Saramago also began to work toward founding what would become the European Writers Parliament, envisioned as a union of writers meant to guarantee authors' freedom of speech. Before Saramago could attend the inaugural meeting of the institution in Istanbul, he died at his home on Lanzerote of leukemia on June 18, 2010.

PLOT SUMMARY

Like a fairy tale that begins "once upon a time," *The Tale of the Unknown Island* does not take place at any specific time or in any exact place. A man goes to the palace of the king to ask him for a boat. He uses the special door for petitioners. Usually such a petition is passed up and down a rigidly hierarchical bureaucracy, but the man derails all that by telling the cleaning woman who actually answers the door only that he wants to see the king. Moreover, he refuses to leave the doorway until the king comes, which will interfere with the smooth operation of the government, because other petitioners cannot make their requests while he is blocking the doorway. The problem appears to be quite serious, since he has brought a blanket with him and seems to intend to sleep in the doorway until the king comes to see him. This actually suits the king,

who has no interest in hearing petitions. On the other hand, it would cause dissatisfaction if people realized the king's indifference.

After three days, the king finally comes, answering the door himself for the first time in history. The man tells the king that he wants a boat, to search for an unknown island. The king tells him that all islands are known; they are on the maps. Those are the known islands, the man counters; he wants to find the unknown one. He has no particular information about any such islands, but it seems to him that an unknown island must exist. The king has no intention of giving a boat to a person who seems to him a madman. When the man insists that the king give him one anyway, as if he and not the king were the one in charge, the king is on the verge of sending for his guard. But the crowd waiting in line at the door for favors calls on the king to give him the boat; they want him out of the way so that they can have their turn with the king, and the crowd of spectators in the street agrees. So the king decides to give the man a boat; he will provide a boat but no crew.

The man takes the king's card bearing instructions for the harbormaster to give him a boat, and the cleaning lady follows him, leaving no one to open the door to other petitioners. The harbormaster questions the man and finds out that he is not a mariner but that he talks as if he knows what he is doing as a sailor. The harbormaster, too, doubts there are any unknown islands left, but the man insists there must be. The harbormaster agrees to give the man an old but seaworthy boat, a caravel from the Age of Exploration that was used, probably, to find many islands then unknown. The cleaning woman, who has followed the man secretly, reveals herself and says that the caravel is the boat she wanted for him. The man does not remember her from the palace, but he is happy to take her along. The man leaves her to inspect the boat while he goes off to look for a crew.

When the cleaning woman boards the ship, she is attacked by seagulls guarding the nests they have made on it and then cleans the deck and repairs the sails. The man returns. He brings dinner for the two of them, but no crew. Every sailor he has talked to wants to go on doing the profitable work he is engaged in, not go off looking for an unknown island in whose existence he does not believe. The man reveals to the cleaning woman that his interest in the unknown island is related to the search for understanding his own identity.

The cleaning woman leads the man on an inspection of the ship. She seems to have picked up nautical terminology and expertise in the same way as the man, absorbing it from the ship, the sea, and the sky. The woman suggests that if they cannot find a crew, they will have to sail the caravel themselves. Even the man balks at the impossibility of this, but they go to their dinner. They discuss the long and laborious preparations they would have to make to sail, even if everything goes well. The woman affirms that whether they sail or not, her life has been changed forever. After dinner they go below deck to sleep, and the cleaning woman misinterprets the longing for her in the man's eyes as longing for the unknown island.

The man dreams that the ship is setting out to look for the unknown island with a crew and all necessary provisions, including livestock. The ship also carries as many women as it does sailors, an unrealistic motif that reminds the man he is only dreaming. The cleaning woman is not there; she has jumped out of the ship at the last moment, jealous of the man's obsession with the unknown island. Then he finds that the sailors are not sailors; they had merely come along hoping to seize the unknown island (which they do not believe in) for themselves. They taunt the man, telling him that the sea and the ship cannot teach him how to sail. When the man sees a known island, he tries to sail past it, pretending it is a mirage. The men who are not sailors demand the man take them there, and the caravel sails there by itself. There they disembark, taking all the livestock and accompanied by the seagulls that are living on the boat together with their chicks. In the rush to leave, the men who are not sailors tear open bags of topsoil in which seeds have sprouted, turning the deck into a plowed field. In the dream, the man sails on alone as trees grow from the ship's timber. Finally, he takes a scythe to harvest the wheat growing in the field on the deck.

The man awakes, finding himself in the cleaning woman's arms. Their bunks, once on the port and starboard sides of the boat, respectively, have fused together. At dawn, they paint the name of the ship on its prow. "Around midday, with the tide, The Unknown Island finally sets to sea, in search of itself."

CHARACTERS

Cleaning Woman

Like all characters in *The Tale of The Unknown Island*, the cleaning woman is never referred to by a name. She is indeed, at the beginning of the story, a cleaning woman in the king's castle. Besides her duties cleaning and sewing, she also has the unofficial task of answering the door for petitions. The cleaning woman is the last link in the chain of the bureaucratic hierarchy between the king and the people. Arguably, she is one of the most important, since she actually connects the chain to the people. Nonetheless, she completely lacks the status and, from a practical viewpoint, the salary of any of the bureaucrats. Her vital labor, without which the government could not function, is completely devalued, with the result that she is exploited by the hierarchy above her and in no way rewarded for her true value to them. This stands for the unjust character of modern Western culture. It also indicates that the ruling hierarchy is entirely unconcerned with the people and their genuine needs. How else could their petitions be left to be heard by a cleaning woman?

Interestingly, one can associate the cleaning woman's two functions through a pun. Her role as a cleaner would associate her with the ordinary English meaning of *janitor* (presenting, however, a problem with the masculine ending of that noun), whereas the Latin for *janitor* suggests her role as "doorkeeper." Although *janitor* is far more rare in Portuguese than in English, the same wordplay is possible. However, once she meets the man who comes to petition the king, she leaves her position in the castle to follow him as a sort of disciple. It is eventually made apparent that she falls in love with the man. Naturally, once she is in love, she experiences emotional excitements she had previously never known and finally enters into union with the man in a profound way, which makes it possible for them to set out on the allegorical quest for the island. Both the man and the cleaning woman fall in love with the other individually. The man is oblivious to the woman's feelings, while the woman thinks his evident signs of love are for the quest to find the island.

The cleaning woman is used as a vehicle for satire by Saramago, more in his capacity as a writer than as a communist ideologue. When the cleaning woman hears the king's philosopher say that "each man is an Island," she recalls to the man, "being a woman, I paid no attention to him." This is perhaps a complaint against the feminist insistence that the masculine not be used as the default gender in cases where both genders are meant together or neither gender in particular is meant. This would seem to arise from a confusion over the concept of grammatical gender and biological gender identity. This usage is common to all the Indo-European languages, however, and Saramago seems to be saying that there is no precedent for suddenly and arbitrarily changing such a deep structure of language.

Harbormaster

The harbormaster is the one who actually gives the man his caravel. He taught the king everything he knows about the sea, including that there are no more unknown islands.

King

The king is not, as might be the case in a fairy tale, a symbolic figure of justice (or, indeed, of injustice). Rather he is the head of a bureaucracy that sees its task as managing the populace of the country so that they give the king as much as possible while asking him for as little as possible. Every petition for a favor from the king has to be passed up through layer after layer of bureaucracy:

> The first secretary would call the second secretary, who would call the third secretary, who would give orders to the first assistant who would, in turn, give orders to the second assistant, and so on all the way down the line to the cleaning woman.

This was simply to give notice of the petition. The actual petition and any discussion about it would have to be passed up and down the chain again, each item in turn. At each step the king would introduce delay, because he was really occupied in dealing with matters that concerned gifts made by the people to the government. Finally, a written report on the matter would have to be composed and circulated, and then the decision about the petition would be made arbitrarily. The cleaning woman "would give a yes or a no depending on what kind of mood she was in." This procedure, all too familiar to anyone who has ever dealt with a bureaucracy, is eerily similar to the recommendation made in an Office of Strategic Services manual during World War II, which has only recently been declassified. The manual was for the use of industrial managers and bureaucrats in Nazi-occupied Europe, suggesting ways that they could sabotage the Nazi war effort whenever they were forced to cooperate with the German authorities. Among other strategies for slowing down and stopping work, the manual recommends:

> Insist on doing everything through "channels." Never permit short-cuts to be taken in order to expedite decisions. . . .
>
> When possible, refer all matters to committees, for "further study and consideration." . . .
>
> Demand written orders. . . .
>
> Do everything possible to delay the delivery of orders.

The king has established the very same procedures, not to thwart an occupying army but to thwart the legitimate concerns of the nation's people.

King's Philosopher

The king's philosopher appears briefly and indirectly, when the cleaning woman recalls her past conversations with him. The only thing she quotes, in fact, is the single statement "each man is an island." Still, this is a key passage for understanding Saramago's meaning. Saramago intends for the reader to be reminded of the famous line from John Donne's *Devotions upon Emergent Occasions* (1624): "No man is an island." That is a statement of the Christian doctrine of subsidiarity. One can explain this doctrine technically by saying that it means that authority and responsibility ought to be distributed as locally as possible. For instance, it is the responsibility of the parents to make sure their child does not starve. If the parents cannot find food for their child because of an economic crash caused by financial speculation, then the responsibility for and authority over whether the child starves must be passed upward to the people who can reform society in such a way that the parents *can* obtain food for their child.

Far easier to understand is the classic statement of the doctrine by Martin Luther King Jr., in his "Letter from a Birmingham Jail," written while he was, in fact, in jail for protesting the injustice of African Americans' being denied the civil rights that all American citizens are due: "Injustice anywhere is a threat to justice everywhere. We are caught in an inescapable network of mutuality, tied in a single garment of destiny. Whatever affects one directly, affects all indirectly." King clarifies Donne's metaphor: no man is an island, cut off from others by the sea, but everyone is directly connected to as well as responsible for everyone else. The philosopher's statement looks like a direct negation of subsidiarity. Given that he works for the king, probably that is the way he meant it. A common bureaucratic response to subsidiarity is to claim instead that everyone has particular duties and responsibilities and cannot be called upon outside that narrow scope. If an individual is suffering, it must be one's own fault, and the whole world cannot be changed to help.

Man

The man is the main character of the story. He wants to obtain a boat from the king, on which he will sail in search of the unknown island. He is opposed to the beliefs of the civilization depicted in the story, which hold that there are no more unknown islands. This is far from representing a disagreement about geography; the man sees the voyage as an act of self-discovery, which will help him understand himself and integrate himself into society (not the one he is leaving) once he has found the island. So it is really the possibility of self-understanding that the king and the world he represents more than anything about geography that the king and his agents deny. When he requests the boat, the man stymies all the usual bureaucratic measures meant to forestall such requests by acting in a direct way that the bureaucracy cannot understand, and it yields to him simply to be rid of him.

In a key scene for understanding the man's character and thereby the larger meaning of Saramago's story, the cleaning woman tells him that the king's philosopher once told her, "each man is an island." In line with the inhuman bureaucratic spirit of the king's government, this probably means that people are not responsible for helping each other. The man characteristically wants to understand the statement quite differently, as a reflection of his own ideas. In that case, he makes it mean that "you have to leave the island in order to see the island, that we can't see ourselves unless we become free of ourselves." This, in itself, is not easy to comprehend. Trying to restate the man's pronouncement in a way she can understand better, the cleaning woman says, "unless we escape from ourselves." The man disagrees that this accurately summarizes his meaning. What he seems to mean is that each individual must come to understand himself objectively, as if he were studying a different person. While a person may not be able to free himself of his own experiences and particular desires, he can understand the things that make him an individual and take them into

account. That could be what it means to become "free of ourselves." This is not an "escape from ourselves," because the individual's nature is not changed but instead understood and, to the extent necessary, tamed. There is no escape, because our own natures cannot be left behind. The man ends the discussion of philosophical matters so he can hear what the cleaning woman has learned about the ship, but this clearly is not the end of his philosophy. For him (unlike, most probably, the king's philosopher), the goal of understanding oneself as an individual is not to stand in isolation from others but to prepare to join in union with others. This he eventually does by falling in love with the cleaning woman, expressing the individual (anarchic) and communal (communistic) elements of Saramago's own philosophy.

Much of the later part of the story is the man's dream, in which he is isolated from the society he has created on the boat. Once he awakens, he finds the very nature of reality transformed (seen in the shape of the boat) and is able to join in common with the cleaning woman and begin the voyage of self-discovery on the ship that they already recognize as their goal, having named it *The Unknown Island*.

Men Who Are Not Sailors

In the man's dream he sets off in his caravel without the cleaning woman (meaning that there can be no completion), but with the crew of sailors who refused, in real life, to sail with him. The men (accompanied by an equal number of women) tell the man that they are only looking for a better place to live. "You're not sailors," he accuses them, and they reply, "We never were." They do not believe in the unknown island, and they want only to take advantage of the man to be transported to some port where they will have a better place to live—a seemingly innocuous request until they threaten to murder the man if he does not obey them. They also tell him that it is impossible for the sea to teach him how to sail. The man and the ship itself are anxious to have them disembark, which they do with a vast amount of livestock, evidently beginning a colony on one of the known islands.

THEMES

Fairy Tale

Saramago purposefully constructs *The Tale of The Unknown Island* in such a way as to put the reader in mind of fairy tales. He has two

TOPICS FOR FURTHER STUDY

- Like *The Tale of the Unknown Island*, Oscar Wilde's "The Selfish Giant" (originally published in 1881) is a literary fairy tale. Unlike Saramago's story, Wilde's has a surface narrative meant to entertain children while it tells a more profound story through allegory. Both stories criticize the societies in which they were written, but "The Selfish Giant" does so by invoking traditional social criticism derived from the Gospels. Write a paper comparing the two stories.

- Its fairy-tale nature makes *The Tale of The Unknown Island* highly suitable for adaptation as a cartoon. Using a simple but effective style of animation, like the shadow puppet technique of the German film director Lotte Reiniger, would enable such a film to be made in a single semester or even a quarter. Prepare such a cartoon for your class.

- Saramago was an anarcho-communist, espousing a set of political beliefs that owed its origins to Pyotr Kropotkin as much as to the Prussian philosopher Karl Marx. Adherents of anarcho-communism managed to establish government by its principles both in Russia during the revolution and in Spain during the civil war, although both experiments were brutally wiped out through military force by Leninist-Stalinist communists. Gain familiarity with anarcho-communism through reading representative works of Kropotkin, such as *The Conquest of Bread* (http://dwardmac.pitzer. edu/Anarchist_Archives/kropotkin/conquest/ toc.html) or *Fields, Factories and Workshops* (http://dwardmac.pitzer.edu/anarchist _archives/kropotkin/fields.html), or historical monographs like the German anarchist

and historian Max Nettlau's *A Short History of Anarchism* (1996), and write an essay examining *The Tale of the Unknown Island* in the context of anarcho-communist ideas.

- The early fifteenth century was a time of exploration in China. The admiral Zheng He led a fleet of gigantic vessels called treasure ships on voyages around the Indian Ocean, reaching as far as Mecca and Kenya. The purpose of the voyages was to collect tribute (hence the term *treasure*) that the Chinese imperial system believed was owed to it by all other earthly rulers, who were viewed as tributary to China. Although Chinese merchants certainly continued to trade in the Indian Ocean, the program was halted because of infighting among Chinese bureaucrats after Zheng's death in about 1433, preventing the voyages from having any larger historical consequences. Make a PowerPoint presentation to your class on the voyages of the treasure fleet, emphasizing parallels with *The Tale of the Unknown Island*. Although there are many sources available on the Internet on this subject, they generally derive from the popularizing historical studies of Louise Levathes (*When China Ruled the Seas*, 1994) and Edward L. Dreyer (*Zheng He: China and the Oceans in the Early Ming Dynasty, 1405–1433*, 2006). An account of the voyages by Zheng's Arabic translator, Ma Huan, was written in 1433 and translated into English in 1970 (reprinted 1996) by Feng Ch'eng-Chün under the title *Ying-Yai Sheng-Lang: Overall Survey of the Ocean's Shores*. Be wary of sources that make the unfounded claim that Zheng explored the Americas.

---

objectives in this. First, he wants the reader to accept the story as simple and childlike in its innocence, as fairy tales are often perceived to be. Second, Saramago also has the subversive

and contradictory intention to suggest to the reader that his story is highly complex and that its true meaning has to be sought under its surface, reflecting another popular belief about

The king believes that the world has all been mapped but grants the explorer a boat (©*Anneka* / *Shutterstock.com*)

fairy tales, that they have deeper allegorical meanings. Like a fairy tale, Saramago's story takes place in no definite time or place (though he does mention steamships a few times to make clear that the time is after the Age of Discovery). One of the characters is a king who is simply the king, without a name or further title; another main character is a servant, as is often the case in fairy tales. The fairy tale theme of adventure and travel, often to unspecified locations like the end of the earth or where the sun sets, is recalled in the quest for the unknown island. Saramago calls the story a *tale*, rather than simply giving it a title like *The Unknown Island* in the modern manner. While future events or other important pieces of information are often revealed to characters in fairy tales through dreams, in Saramago's story, the text itself becomes a dream.

The connection between dreams and fairy tales—the idea that they are generated through analogous processes in the unconscious—has often been observed by psychoanalysts like Erich Fromm in his *The Forgotten Language* (1951), as well as by folklorists, as in *The Oxford*

Companion to Fairy Tales (2000). At the same time, there is something very unlike a fairy tale in *The Tale of The Unknown Island*. Besides the story of exploration, there is an entirely different narrative thread in the story—one that is not so much presented through symbols and allegories as insinuated sarcastically throughout the text, namely, a criticism against bureaucracy, capitalism, and every aspect of the state and society that Saramago, as a communist and anarchist, found oppressive. The reader is meant to take the viewpoint of the man who wants a boat and slyly rejoice in the exposure of the dishonesty, pettiness, and hypocrisy of characters like the king and the men who are not sailors. In this way Saramago uses the fairy tale genre, with its supposed presentation of simple truths, to persuade the reader to take his side in his social criticism. *The Tale of the Unknown Island* is a literary fairy tale—an entirely original work that imitates or refers to the style and content of traditional folktales that existed for centuries in oral form before being collected and written down, but which does not itself use any traditional material.

Dreams

The original impulse to study and record fairy tales as they were told among the illiterate classes of Europe came out of nationalism. The fairy tales were thought to be a pure and authentic expression of the national soul, as if they were an expression of the unconscious dreamworld of a people. While this is better understood as a metaphor than a scientific interpretative strategy, it is true that psychologists have observed a certain similarity between the narrative of fairy tales and the narrative reports of dreams. Saramago does not exploit this connection in the way that many other authors have done, creating a literary fairy tale with an elaborate encoded allegorical message composed in the language of Freudian or Jungian psychology. Rather, in *The Tale of the Unknown Island*, Saramago uses the act of dreaming itself in a symbolic or metaphorical way. Before their first dinner on the ship, the man suggests to the cleaning woman that he is not so much interested in a voyage of discovery as in a voyage of self-discovery. Then, when they retire for the night, the story shifts to telling the man's dream:

> He had wished her sweet dreams, but he was the one who spent all night dreaming. He dreamed that his caravel was on the high seas, with the three lateen sails gloriously full, cutting a path through the waves, while he controlled the ship's wheel and the crew rested in the shade.

The entire rest of the story recounts his dream, except for the last few lines. He suddenly has a crew, and they mutiny. The ship transforms itself into an image of the world, complete with plowed fields and a forest. Even when he supposedly wakes up from his dream, the narrative is no less fantastic, with the entire shape of the ship changing and the man and the cleaning woman sailing it by themselves. The ship, which they christen *The Unknown Island*, then goes in search of itself. The ship becomes a symbol for the world as well as for individual identity in the world.

STYLE

Punctuation

Many modern authors, from James Joyce to Anthony Burgess, abandoned traditional punctuation, such as quotation marks, in the same way that poets abandoned the formal constraints of meter. The accepted conventions must have seemed a way of controlling and therefore limiting literature, which they hoped could have an unlimited growth in new directions. Saramago is famous for his long sentences, which can often go on for a page or more. His sentences, however, are not large syntactic units as in the Ciceronian style (named for the Roman statesman Marcus Tullius Cicero, who perfected it), which uses so-called periodic sentences, or sentences that do not make complete sense until the end. (This style, imitated in English by many authors, including Samuel Johnson and Thomas Jefferson, uses a complicated but related set of ideas set down in a single grammatical unity.) Rather, Saramago's text could generally be repunctuated in a more conventional manner as a series of short sentences if an editor were bold enough to do so. In particular, Saramago punctuates a long conversation between two characters as a single sentence, separating the speech of the two only by commas and signaling the change of speaker with a capital letter (more confusing in English, with its capitalized pronoun, than in Portuguese). Perhaps Saramago's intention is to destabilize the reader by defeating his complacent expectations.

Intertextuality

Quotation is a straightforward matter when an author reproduces the exact words of any other author, marking them with quotation marks and naming their source. In the case of very well-known quotations (e.g., "To be or not to be" or "A thing of beauty is a joy forever"), however, the author may reproduce the exact words without attributing them, confident that the reader will recognize them from his own knowledge. In an intertextual reference, however, the author neither quotes nor attributes the work of the other author but just discusses it, again relying on the knowledge of the reader to engage with the referenced text. Saramago engages the reader in several intertextual conversations in *The Tale of the Unknown Island*. In one case, the cleaning woman recalls that the king's philosopher used to tell her that "each man is an island." Saramago expects the reader, on the basis of his own knowledge, to compare the statement to John Donne's famous line "No man is an island," from his *Devotions upon Emergent Occasions*.

A more extended discussion is had about the ancient Greek poet Homer, who also goes unmentioned. The author of the *Iliad* and the

Odyssey repeats descriptive epithets throughout the works. For example, the goddess Athena is always owl-eyed, and the city of Pylos is always sandy. Perhaps the most famous of these epithets has been rendered in English, since the time of Andrew Lang's Edwardian translation of Homer, as the "wine-dark sea." This is what lies behind the discussion between the cleaning woman and the man about whether the sea is dark or not. The woman initially says that the man speaks "as if we were still living in the days when the sea was dark." She is suggesting that the man means "dark" as a metaphor for "unexplored," allowing for the possibility of an unknown island. He responds, however, that he is speaking more literally and that "the sea is always dark." When asked if he is sure the island exists, he says that he is: "As sure as I am that the sea is dark." The woman leaves the island aside and takes up her objection to the description of the sea as dark, saying, "Right now, seen from up here [on the deck], with the water the color of jade and the sky ablaze, is doesn't seem at all dark to me." The man insists this is an illusion.

Later, "The blaze in the sky was dying down, the waters grew suddenly purple, now not even the cleaning woman could doubt that the sea really is dark, at least at certain times of the day." Saramago is engaged throughout this passage not only with the text of Homer but also with the history of modern Homeric scholarship. Briefly put, the problem is that no one has any idea what Homer might mean by the "wine-dark sea." What the Greek text actually says is *epi oinopa ponton*. There is no problem understanding the Greek. It means "on the wine-faced sea" or "on the wine-eyed sea." What does that actually mean? How is the sea wine-faced? The idea that it means that it is dark does not originate with Lang's famous translation (which Saramago, who never learned English well, is unlikely to have been aware of). A medieval Greek dictionary, authored by Hesychius, glosses the phrase as "black," and standard dictionaries of ancient Greek today usually offer that as at least a possible meaning of the term. That is perhaps explained by the fact that the Greek word used for "black" (*melas*) can mean a range of colors from black to dark red, that is, the color of wine, as suggested by Saramago's description of the sea as "purple" at sunset. This, too, seems to be no more than a guess, albeit a medieval one, and not a solution to what Homer had in mind, since the sea is generally no more black than it is

the color of red wine. Saramago, in his tale, tries to solve the problem by suggesting that the word is meant to describe the sea at a certain time of day, in a certain light; since that is its most proper aspect, if it is dark, then it is always dark. It is perhaps no coincidence that a few years before Saramago wrote his story, the same suggestion was made in a scholarly article on the subject by R. Rutherford-Dyer in the journal *Greece & Rome*. Saramago must have found the hypothesis appealing and decided to use it in the playful fashion he does in his own story; if the hypothesis is not an island (i.e., the thing the man is searching for), it is at least a new discovery about the sea. The idea has not had much traction in the following decades, because Homer provides no context that would limit his expression just to sunset or dawn, so the solution to the problem of the wine-dark sea remains undiscovered.

HISTORICAL CONTEXT

The Age of Exploration

Traditionally the name Age of Exploration, or Age of Discovery, has been given to the period beginning in the fifteenth century when new developments in naval architecture allowed Europeans to sail freely in deep Atlantic waters, exploring the coast of Africa and the American continents and eventually circumnavigating the globe. Today a term like *age of reconnaissance* would seem more appropriate. After all, the areas then being reached by Portuguese and Spanish caravels, while they were unknown to Europeans, were perfectly well known to the people living there. Another factor in using a more accurate term is that the voyages were not made for the purpose of the disinterested increase of scientific knowledge but for economic and political exploitation—the foundation of colonial empires. Saramago is most interested in this distinction. As a postmodernist, Saramago is drawn to the disjunction between historical facts and their representation in mass culture. He stresses the dichotomy when he says, "There is no law, at least not to the knowledge of a cleaning woman, that going in search of an unknown island must necessarily be a warlike enterprise." This is as good as to say that exploration was inherently militaristic, even if it is generally pretended otherwise.

The man who wants a ship, in contrast, genuinely wants to find the unknown island as a means

COMPARE & CONTRAST

- **1990s:** The idea of discovering new islands is purposefully chosen by Saramago as something that is fantastic and impossible, since it was not generally believed that any undiscovered islands could still exist.

  Today: In the last few years, since 2011, hundreds of new barrier islands (sandbars that form along certain coastal regions) have been found on satellite imagery, and at least one island has been found in the Arctic, revealed by the loss of sea ice due to climate change.

- **1990s:** Feminists object to the use of the masculine as the default gender, a tendency Saramago perhaps satirizes through the cleaning woman, not realizing that a generic proposition in the form *each man* is equivalent to *each human being* and therefore could also apply to her.

  Today: Harvard and several American schools are allowing students to identify themselves by whichever gender pronoun they like, without reference to their biological gender, and are giving students the choice to invent their own pronouns (such as *ze* or *hir*) without any etymological foundation or precedent in the history of language.

- **1990s:** Particularly as seen in public protests in 1992 at commemorations of Columbus's discovery of the New World, there is a nascent skepticism, especially in the academic community, about the traditional narrative that the Age of Discovery was an unalloyed good and part of the general progress of civilization, a spirit that Saramago engages in *The Tale of the Unknown Island.*

  Today: A critical stance emphasizing the damage done by Europeans to the Americas (through the introduction of industrial and plantation slavery, the smallpox virus, and other ills), though it is far from the mainstream narrative, has a higher public profile.

---

of personal intellectual or even spiritual growth, and he eventually finds what he is looking for inside himself (or together with the cleaning woman), whereas the crew of men who are not sailors want to possess the island (or an island) and take it for themselves. In the historical course of exploration, Portuguese merchant ships, supported by the regime of Prince Henry the Navigator, followed the coast of Africa south, searching for gold and slaves and eventually establishing stations along the way that became centers of colonial administration. (Many of these were later seized, in turn, by Britain and France as they became dominant naval powers in the seventeenth and eighteenth centuries.) No doubt, Portugal's leading role in this history attracted Saramago's attention to the subject matter. The Portuguese eventually realized that if they could get around the African continent, they could enter the Indian Ocean. This was attractive because, at the time, there was a tremendous demand in Europe for spices (pepper and nutmeg, e.g.) that were grown in East Asia (a region hardly known to Europeans), and the trade in these luxury items was monopolized by Arab merchants. The Arabs were able to make the voyage between the Red Sea and India thanks to the natural weather system of the Indian Ocean (the monsoon), which promoted a single annual round trip. In one voyage between 1497 and 1499, the Portuguese captain Vasco da Gama finally made it around the Horn of Africa and, with the help of an Arab navigator, reached India.

About the same time, the Genoese merchant Christopher Columbus persuaded the Spanish monarchy to invest in a voyage meant to cross the Atlantic and reach Asia by sailing around the world. Contrary to the myth promulgated by Washing Irving in the biography of Columbus he wrote at the four hundredth anniversary of

The explorer sets out in search of the unknown island (©*Algol / Shutterstock.com*)

his voyage in 1892, in Columbus's day no educated person had thought the earth was anything except a sphere for the preceding two thousand years. The existence of the Americas intervening in the middle of the ocean had been completely unexpected. It was a fortunate accident for Columbus, however, since he had badly miscalculated the size of the globe and lacked sufficient supplies for a voyage all the way to Japan. Columbus's immediate response on finding the Americas, however, was to scour the Caribbean islands for gold and slaves, just as was the case in Africa. Ferdinand Magellan (or at least his crew, since he himself was killed in the Philippines) completed the first circumnavigation of the globe in 1518–1522, sailing around the southern tip of South America on the way out and around Africa on the return. In the seventeenth century Dutch ships (since by that time the Netherlands was the predominate naval power) discovered Australia and surrounding regions. On one of his voyages (1642), Abel Tasman sailed from the Dutch colonies in Indonesia due south; he then turned east and skirted the southern tip of Tasmania (named after him), traveled along the coast of New Zealand (named after a region in Holland), and returned to Indonesia, circumnavigating Australia without ever suspecting its existence, though in 1644 he did find it. Eighteenth-century voyages,

mostly by English ships, such as the expeditions of James Cook, mapped most of the Pacific in detail. Only Antarctica was left unknown to European (or, in this case, any human) culture, until 1820, reaching the situation where there was little possibility of a new unknown island.

CRITICAL OVERVIEW

Saramago was scarcely known in the English-speaking world before winning the Nobel Prize in 1998, and his works only then began to be translated systematically. Moreover, there was little literature in English devoted to Portuguese writing in general that might have supported the evaluation of his work. As a consequence, there is still little critical work available in English on Saramago. Surprisingly enough for so esoteric an author, a number of his works have been filmed and released in the United States, including *The Stone Raft*, *Blindness*, "The Embargo," and *The Double* (as *The Enemy*), building his reputation among a wider American audience. Fernanda Eberstadt's profile in the *New York Times Magazine* from 2007 is perhaps the best general introduction and assessment of Saramago in English. Besides giving a biographical study of Saramago (based on direct interviews of her subject and his close associates), Eberstadt solicited the literary opinion of the leading critic Harold Bloom. He considered Saramago as the second-greatest living author after Philip Roth but noted that his political views hampered his acceptance among American intellectuals. He referred not to Saramago's communism, but to his criticism of the state of Israel for its treatment of the Palestinians.

The Tale of the Unknown Island, fortuitously translated just a year after its publication, virtually coincided with the Nobel Prize, so it garnered a small number of reviews, not accidently by native Portuguese speakers. Moacyr Scliar, a Brazilian novelist, in his review in *Hopscotch: A Cultural Review*, praises *The Tale of the Unknown Island* as "a wonderful introduction to the oeuvre of José Saramago." He contrasts the old-fashioned fairy tale style supported by the story's "almost baroque style" with Saramago's characteristic Leftist message. He also observes the allegorical character of the story: "His island is a metaphor, and his protagonist is a discoverer not of land but of love." George Monteiro, writing in *World Literature Today*, similarly finds *The Tale of the Unknown Island* useful as an introduction of Saramago's work. He says of the story: "If I am not mistaken, there are in this fantastic quest meanings that shift more specifically among the spiritual and psychological meanings that work both individually and historically." Saramago's story has also been used in work done on islands as a literary or philosophical symbol. David Lowenthal's "Tragic Traces on the Rhodian Shore," a history of the island as a literary symbol, uses it to contextualize fictitious islands in literature and deals also with Saramago's novel *The Stone Raft* (1986), in which the Iberian Peninsula detaches itself from Europe and sails around the Atlantic. Mark S. Jackson and Veronica della Dora, in their article "Spectacular Enclosures of Hope," reference the hope for the future they see in Saramago's unnamed man's quest for the unknown island and his eventual discovery instead of love—seeing it as a symbolic expression of the ideology behind the construction of artificial islands (invariably covered with fantastically expensive high-rise apartments and shopping malls) being built in the Persian Gulf by the elite classes of the oil-rich countries of the region.

CRITICISM

Rita M. Brown

Brown is an English professor. In the following essay, she examines Saramago's postmodernist analysis of Western culture and the role of the individual in it in "The Tale of the Unknown Island."

The metaphor of a voyage on a ship for the story of a person's life is deeply embedded in the English language. We speak of the course of life, but life does not have a course; a ship at sea follows a course. Under the same expression, a new experience is heading into uncharted waters. To experience a disaster is to be shipwrecked, while meeting with a fortuitous turn of events is coming into a safe harbor. This metaphor did not enter English from its Indo-European roots (the Indo-European homeland being somewhere in central Asia, far from the sea). Rather, it entered English from the Greek and Latin literature that formed a vital element of the English-speaking world's intellectual heritage. This metaphor was even more firmly embedded in Saramago's native Portuguese, a romance descendant of Latin. His use of the "life as voyage" metaphor, though it is based on the most ancient traditions of Western literature, is nevertheless postmodern in character.

One of the earliest and most important works of Greek literature is the *Odyssey* of Homer. In this epic poem, the hero Odysseus spends ten years trying to sail back to his home in Ithaca after he engineered the capture of the city of Troy. He and his men offended Poseidon by slaughtering and eating a herd of cattle sacred to him, so the god sends a storm to blow Odysseus's fleet off course. He and his men encounter one trial after another—for example, the giant Polyphemus, who kills and eats many sailors until Odysseus blinds him in his sleep and tricks him out of the chance of taking revenge; the witch Circe, who turns Odysseus's men into swine until he is able to free them; and the sea monsters Scylla and Charybdis living on either sides of a strait through which Odysseus safely navigates, but with the loss of six men. When his life is not in danger, Odysseus is cast away on various islands. Finally, he alone of all his soldiers and sailors return home, having sailed to the literal end of the earth, where he had to summon up the ghost of the seer Tiresias to guide his return, and having traveled to countless islands of which he had never even

WHAT DO I READ NEXT?

- *The Cloak of Dreams: Chinese Fairy Tales*, by Béla Balázs (translated in 2010 by Jack Zipes), is a collection of literary fairy tales inspired by the author's knowledge of Chinese culture and literature.

- Saramago's *The Gospel According to Jesus Christ* (1991; translation 1994) is probably his most important work and one that drew the condemnation of the Portuguese government as offensive to religion. The novel tells a life of Jesus generally based on the canonical Gospels but in which God is motivated by an all-too-human jealousy of the other religions in the Roman Empire and in which Jesus is reluctant to become responsible for all the human suffering that will become entailed in the history of Christianity (through the Inquisition, the Crusades, etc.).

- *Vermeer's Hat* (2007), by Timothy Brook, is a study of what has traditionally been called the Age of Exploration or the Age of Discovery. Its approach is unusual. Brook examines a half dozen paintings by the seventeenth-century painter Jan Vermeer, all showing middle-class Dutch homes, and traces the connection between various objects shown in the paintings to their colonial origins in the world beyond Europe.

- *The Island of the Day Before* (1994; translation 1995), by Umberto Eco, is a novel about the Age of Exploration and the transition from magic to science as the basis of European thought. The title refers to the sight of a shipwreck in the Pacific thought by its sole survivor to be on the international dateline.

The novel is a fantasy, treating certain metaphysical beliefs, like the idea of the doppelganger (or evil twin), as a physical reality.

- Fairy tales are generally regarded as children's literature (the original title of Grimm's *Fairy Tales*, for instance, could be translated as *Children's Household Tales*), although they have been preserved precisely to the degree that they have been of interest to an adult audience. With its illustrations and fairy tale surface, *The Tale of the Unknown Island* might seem to be aimed at children too, though they are not at all its audience. The famous fairy tales of Hans Christian Andersen (which began to be published in 1835), which for the most part share with Saramago's tale the property of being literary fairy tales and not traditional stories, are, however, principally aimed at children. Through allegory and other techniques, however, the texts often appeal to adult readers in a way that the child audience will probably miss. Anderson's fairy tales also share with *The Tale of the Unknown Island* the characteristic of being instruments of social criticism of the author's contemporary world.

- Saramago's novel *The Stone Raft* (1986; translated 1994) is thematically similar to *The Tale of the Unknown Island.* It is a fantasy in which the Iberian Peninsula breaks off from Europe and drifts into the Atlantic while characters from Spain and Portugal find themselves drawn to each other. It was filmed (in Spanish) in 2002 by George Sluizer. It was also the inspiration for the 1993 short story "England Underway," by Terry Brisson.

---

heard. In Homer, Odysseus's wanderings are events that take up a decade of his life, and they are merely adventures, not the hero's whole life. Things changed in the reception of the *Odyssey*, as it was read by later Greeks.

Greek literature was full of texts telling stories about gods (myths), such as Hesiod's *Theogony* and the work of the tragedians Aeschylus, Sophocles, and Euripides, but it had little in the way of a religious text. When

"

> SARAMAGO DOES NOT USE THE METAPHOR
> OF A SEA VOYAGE TO DESCRIBE LIFE; RATHER, HE
> PRESENTS A DESCRIPTION OF A SEA VOYAGE AND
> EXPECTS THE READER TO DECIPHER IT AS A
> METAPHOR FOR LIFE."

the first philosophers wanted to have a text that would tell them how human beings ought to live, they found themselves at a loss in their tradition. One response was to look at a classic work like the *Odyssey* and read it in a different way. If the work was metaphorical, then its symbols could be interpreted to produce an entirely different meaning from what is apparent through a simple reading. The plot of the *Odyssey* was taken to be a symbolic representation of the course of life not only from birth but also from reincarnation (a belief of many Greeks) through the stages of a life, death, and the afterlife. The same is true of any sea voyage, which has a beginning, a number of stages (ports of call, for instance), and an end, often back at the same place as the beginning. All of this can be made to stand for a life; in fact, that phrase is unclear without saying, *made to stand for the course of a life.*

Once the sea voyage is established as a metaphor for a life, it can be and has been extended quite widely. The political history of a city, for instance, becomes a ship facing the vicissitudes of fortune on its voyage. Plato is one of the earliest authors to use the metaphor (as in his dialogue "Statesman"):

> However, we see many instances of cities going down like sinking ships to their destruction. There have been such wrecks in the past and there will surely be others in the future, caused by the wickedness of captains and crews alike. For these are guilty men, whose sin is supreme ignorance of what matters most.

One can perhaps see an echo of this famous passage in Saramago with his man as the good captain and his men who are not sailors as the wicked crew. In a communist, one might expect the opposite—that the collective would be virtuous in the face of an oppressive overlord. The

anarchic strain in Saramago's beliefs, however, privileges the individual over the collective. Perhaps another way to look at it is to take the man, indeed, as a virtuous captain and the king and his bureaucrats as a wicked crew.

A well-known further extension of the metaphor is the ship of the church. Far back into the second century, as soon as there were bishops and theologians, they described the church and its journey toward salvation as a voyage with themselves as the helmsmen, guiding their crew (ordinary Christians) to the safe harbor of salvation. The metaphor is still current. Pope Benedict XVI, quoted by the Vatican News Service in 2012, for instance, stated that "the documents of Vatican Council II are, even in our own time, a compass guiding the ship of the Church as she sails on the opens seas, amidst tempests or peaceful waves, to reach her destination."

Saramago does not use the metaphor of a sea voyage to describe life; rather, he presents a description of a sea voyage and expects the reader to decipher it as a metaphor for life. This reversal is a postmodern approach to symbolism. Unexpectedly, perhaps, *modern* as a term of literary history means the writing of the nineteenth and early twentieth centuries. It was marked by an irrepressible optimism in the progress of Western civilization: industrial, scientific, moral, and in every other way. Postmodernism is not so confident, having seen Western civilization produce two world wars, the Great Depression, the Cold War and with it the possible destruction of the entire human race, and the industrial degradation of the environment. An important attitude of postmodernist literature to literature itself is to consider that all discourse, whether a novel or a poem or, indeed, a painting or a political speech, is a narrative that attempts to create an image of reality. An image is never going to correspond exactly to what it describes, so the content is not determined by reality but rather by other factors, of which one of the most important is the political.

Many postmodernists, and certainly the anarcho-communist Saramago among them, see society represented in a set of master narratives as progressive, just, equal, and peace loving, based on altruism and high-minded principles and values, but they consider this a distraction meant to cover the real nature of Western culture as oppressive and exploitative. This skepticism suggests a response in the form of irony, which can often introduce playful, comedic overtones into postmodern literature, despite the serious subject matter. The central irony is that postmodernism looks for the truth by tearing down what is accepted as the truth. It is correspondingly interested in finding and dismantling other aspects of cognitive dissonance between the image and the reality of society (e.g., that blacks were separate but equal in the Jim Crow South or that under capitalism workers have a level playing field with billionaire industrialists). Master narratives are devalued because they are seen as deceptive rhetorical devices meant to justify the oppressive structures of traditional culture. Postmodernism seeks to expose the entire organization of society as a deception. Supposed ideals like freedom and equality are privileged precisely to draw attention away from the actually prevailing racism, sexism, and exploitation that serve the elite class.

The Tale of the Unknown Island embraces the inherent playfulness of postmodernism. Much of the matter of the story is a social satire against the modern world but couched in the outward trappings of a fairy tale, a typical form for the presentation of a master narrative of the traditional world. (The fairy tale has a moral: virtue is rewarded, good triumphs in the end, and so on.) Even so, the satirical figure of the king, for instance, is not a character from a fairy tale, representing the virtuous or, indeed, the corrupt and villainous ruler. Instead, he has created an impenetrable bureaucracy actually meant to paralyze the function of government, the typical theme of a late-modern author like Franz Kafka. The voyage to the unknown island is precisely a voyage to the last place where the dominant oppressive culture does not exist, a place that is not under the colonial control of Portugal or Great Britain or any other power. Saramago draws on another tradition, ancient philosophy, to find that the only place free of tyranny is inside the individual. The man explains that he wants to find the unknown island because "I want to find out who I am when I'm there on that island. . . . If you don't step outside yourself, you'll never discover who you are." It is only in isolation from the oppressive West and its creation of culture through its narratives that an individual can freely flourish. This need not be on a physical island (to which one may compare the popularity of countercultural communes in the 1960s) but must come from recognizing oneself as free from social control. One can explore the self if one is free from the impulse to obey and let others control.

The triumph of Saramago's anarchic individualism comes with the true union of individuals between the man and the cleaning woman. Their union of equals is the true communist ideal, not a relationship of exploitation. Saramago is at pains throughout the story to suggest that one learns by acting, that the sea will somehow teach the man how to sail. In fact, such knowledge can be transferred only by a master to a pupil, but he makes it stand for another kind of learning, which Saramago never mentions explicitly but only demonstrates in action. The man and the cleaning woman learn to love by loving, because it is something that cannot be done by an individual alone. This union of individuals is a symbol for the way that society ought to be organized. Saramago paradoxically returns to old master narratives, a love story and the Christian ideal that society should be founded on love. From a postmodernist perspective, Christianity betrays that idea when Paul says, "Slaves, obey your earthly masters" (Colossians 3:22 NIV). In practice, the promise of Christian love has been used to draw attention away from the exploitative hierarchies of Western culture. Saramago is in quest of a society where love is not a rhetorical distraction from prevailing inequality and exploitation but is truly the basis of human relationships, personal, economic, and of every other kind, an unknown island indeed.

Source: Rita Brown, Critical Essay on "Tale of the Unknown Island," in *Short Stories for Students*, Gale, Cengage Learning, 2017.

John Schulze

In the following review, Schulze describes Saramago's writing as "precise and elegant."

Originally released in 1978 as *Objecto Quase*, the recently re-released *The Lives of Things* is an intriguing collection of short stories written by Nobel Laureate Jose Saramago, perhaps Portugal's most famous, if not most rebellious, author. While best known for his relatively recent novels *The Gospel According to Jesus Christ* (1991), *Blindness* (1995), and *Death with Interruptions* (2005), this collection offers an insight into the beginnings of his unique prose style and his philosophical aesthetic.

It's often been said that every story has already been told and that each new story is nothing more than an iteration, a reiteration, a reinterpretation, or simply a retelling. Saramago's stories

The end of the story is ambiguous, leaving the reader uncertain about whether the explorer actually finds the island (©*Africa Studio | Shutterstock.com*)

are evidence that this assertion is not true. This is primarily because Saramago's writings explore permutations. Mathematically, permutations are a way of arranging a given set of variables. Saramago imagines the variables one might encounter in a particular situation and explores the infinite in their possibilities by masterfully offering his readers multiple narrative avenues. This complex approach speaks to his capacity to remain familiar and refreshingly "new" in his stories. The tales challenge the common notion of order and embrace the chaos that ensues in its pursuit but are rewarding as they continue to unfold in your mind long after the text has been read.

In "The Chair," the opening story from his collection, the reader is invited to explore a piece of furniture, a chair. Not just any chair, but the deck chair that supposedly collapsed under Portugal's longtime dictator António Salazar, which (allegedly) resulted in a cerebral hemorrhage and the man's eventual demise. Saramago, instead of examining the man, chooses to focus his readers' attention on the chair. For instance, we meet the termites that have burrowed into the wooden

legs and weakened the structural integrity of the chair. These creatures have a rich life as Saramago anthropomorphizes them as western gunslingers fighting over a woman. It's this hidden world—and the events that occur there—that influences the known world. This theme recurs throughout many of Saramago's stories.

Rarely do Saramago's characters have names. His perspective encompasses the human condition, and although he does address the individual, it's often in terms of archetypes: the king, the reporter, the groundskeeper. From this vantage point, his stories take on both the political and the situational. In "Embargo," Saramago depicts one man's unwilling escapade in a car that travels from one fueling station to another under its own volition during the Arab oil embargo of the 1970s. His embarrassment over purchasing a mere liter of fuel after waiting hours in a fuel line is meant to evoke a larger message about consumerism and the hunger—as awkward as it is—that it demands.

"Reflux," another story in the collection, is an allegorical tale that explores the absurdity of a society that believes in the infallibility of its "royal personage," which, of course, could easily be read as any political leader, politician, or bureaucrat who rules with absolute authority. In a distinctly Kafkaesque style, Saramago delineates the herculean task of the exhumation of all the deceased of the entire country and the relocation of these corpses into a single expansive and walled graveyard. The undertaking (pun intended), meant to remove the specter of death from the monarch's purview of perception, inevitably results in unintended consequences that reveal the ruler's limitations and also comments on the larger aspect of humanity's futile attempts to regulate things beyond their control.

Saramago's precise and eloquent prose can be halting at times as be sets out to clearly define and describe situations and thoughts while simultaneously acknowledging and qualifying alternative narrative possibilities, but it is his wit and verve that give his meanderings a smart playfulness. To enjoy this collection, one must not only be accepting of Saramago's circuitous storytelling but one must embrace the notion that the journey is the destination, and that order is not the aim.

Source: John Schulze, Review of *The Lives of Things*, in *Prairie Schooner*, Vol. 87, No. 23, Summer 2013, p. 166.

George Monteiro

In the following review, Monteiro characterizes "The Tale of the Unknown Island" as typical of Saramago's work.

Were it not for its hefty listed price, this little book might well be taken for the kind of keepsake that publishers sometimes produce for an author's friends or their own favored customers. As it is, the book seems destined for the remainder tables at Borders or Barnes & Noble. Once there, it might well begin to serve its purpose, which is, as I see it, to bring the curious reader in a very modest way to an acquaintance with the fiction of the 1998 Nobel laureate in literature (see *WLT* 73:1, pp. 5–18).

The *Tale of the Unknown Island* is characteristic of Saramago's work in several ways. It is presented as an unmediated tale that is both fantastic and allegorical, both playful and disarmingly serious. It mixes a king, a chain of command and communication, a cleaning woman who doubles as keeper of the door for petitions to the king, and a would-be sailor who asks for a ship which he does not yet know how to sail. The sailor reveals that he intends to search for the unknown island, which, according to the king and everyone else, does not exist since it does not appear on maps. Of course it doesn't appear on maps, argues the sailor; otherwise it would not be unknown. When the king issues the order to give the sailor his ship, the cleaning woman, tired of her menial and unsatisfactory duties, accompanies the sailor. Sleeping aboard ship while it is still in port, the sailor dreams of sailing, sailing right through sightings of land, for he will consider as his goal only the unknown island. When he awakens, he discovers the woman at his side. The two of them then paint on the side of the ship, a caravel the name of the hitherto unchristened vessel: it is to be called The Unknown Island. The last sentence of the tale reads: "Around midday, with the tide, The Unknown Island finally set to sea, in search of itself."

If I am not mistaken, there are in this fantastic quest meanings that shift more specifically among the spiritual and psychological meanings that work both individually and historically. The ship, after all, is a caravel. The tale is not without its instances of Saramago's characteristic play. If the sailor is not yet a sailor when he sets out and the cleaning woman/doorkeeper is really a lover and working companion, neither of them knows either where he or she is going or what he or she is actually seeking. Only by sailing out, perhaps, can they find the island within. There are other avenues to Saramago's imagination—through the more complexly nuanced fables of, say, *Memorial do convento* (Eng. *Baltasar and Blimunda*), *O ano da morte de Ricardo Reis* (Eng. *The Year of the Death of Ricardo Reis*), and *O Evangelho Segundo Jesus Cristo* (Eng. *The Gospel According to Jesus Christ*)—but the deftly translated *Tale of the Unknown Island* will do the trick for the curious reader making his first visit to the imaginary world of this now much-honored writer.

Source: George Monteiro, "Review of 'The Tale of the Unknown Island,'" in *World Literature Today*, Vol. 74, No. 3, Summer 2000, p. 686.

SOURCES

"Concilar Documents: A Compass to Guide the Ship of the Church," Vatican Information Service, October 10, 2012, http://visnews-en.blogspot.com/2012/10/conciliar-documents-compass-to-guide.html (accessed February 14, 2016).

Eberstadt, Fernanda, "José Saramago, the Unexpected Fantasist," in *New York Times Magazine*, August 26, 2007, http://www.nytimes.com/2007/08/26/magazine/26saramago-t.html?_r = 2&oref = slogin (accessed February 14, 2016).

Fromm, Erich, *The Forgotten Language: An Introduction to the Understanding of Dreams, Fairy Tales, and Myths*, Rinehart, 1951, pp. 7–8, 155–56.

Haase, Donald, "Psychology and Fairy Tales," in *The Oxford Companion to Fairy Tales*, edited by Jack Zipes, Oxford University Press, 2000, pp. 404–408.

Jackson, Mark S., and Veronica della Dora, "Spectacular Enclosures of Hope: Artificial Islands in the Gulf and the Present," in *Ecologies of Affect: Place Nostalgia, Desire, and Hope*, edited by Tonya K. Davidson and Rob Shields, Wilfrid Laurier University Press, 2011, pp. 293–313.

King, Martin Luther, Jr., "Letter from a Birmingham Jail," Martin Luther King Jr., Research and Education Institute, http://okra.stanford.edu/transcription/document_images/undecided/630416-019.pdf (accessed February 14, 2016).

Lowenthal, David, "Tragic Traces on the Rhodian Shore," in *Historic Environment*, Vol. 17, No. 1, 2003, pp. 3–7.

Plato, "Statesman," in *The Collected Dialogues of Plato, Including the Letters*, edited by Edith Hamilton and Huntington Cairns, Bollingen Series 71, Princeton University Press, 1961, p. 1072.

Rutherford-Dyer, R., "Homer's Wine-dark Sea," in *Greece & Rome*, Vol. 30, No. 2, 1983, pp. 125–128.

Saramago, José, "Nobel Lecture," http://www.nobelprize.org/nobel_prizes/literature/laureates/1998/saramago-lecture.html (accessed February 14, 2016).

———, "The Nobel Prize in Literature 1998—Biographical," http://www.nobelprize.org/nobel_prizes/literature/laureates/1998/saramago-bio.html (accessed February 14, 2016).

———, *The Tale of the Unknown Island*, translated by Margaret Jull Costa, Harcourt Brace, 1999.

Scliar, Moacyr, Review of "The Tale of the Unknown Island," in *Hopscotch: A Cultural Review*, Vol. 2, No. 2, 2000, p. 174.

Simple Sabotage Field Manual, Office of Strategic Services, 1944, https://www.cia.gov/news-information/featured-story-archive/2012-featured-story-archive/CleanedUOSSSimpleSabotage_sm.pdf (accessed February 14, 2016).

Thurston, H., "Symbolism," in *Catholic Encyclopedia*, 1912, http://www.newadvent.org/cathen/14373b.htm (accessed February 14, 2016).

FURTHER READING

Arnold, David, *The Age of Discovery, 1400–1600*, Routledge, 2013.

> This second edition surveys recent scholarship on the subject and presents a history of European exploration and the technological advances that supported it. It also covers subjects of emerging interest such as the economics of exploration and biological exchange between Europe and the newly encountered areas.

Homer, *The Odyssey*, translated by Robert Fitzgerald, Farrar, Straus and Giroux, 1961.

> The frequently reprinted translation is only one of dozens available in English. Homer's *Odyssey* and his *Iliad* are the earliest surviving examples of Western literature. *The Odyssey* describes the voyage of its unwilling hero through a variety of fantastic islands spread across an imaginary world created in a Greek civilization that knew little of the world outside its coastal waters.

Saramago, José, *Baltasar and Blimunda*, translated by Giovanni Pontiero, Marvill Panther, 1987.

> One of Saramago's best-known novels, *Baltasar and Blimunda* is set in the seventeenth century and uses a surrealistic style to tell the story of a soldier and his love affair with a servant from the convent of Mafra and their interaction with Bartolomeu de Gusmão, a priest and a leading figure in the Enlightenment in Portugal and an early figure in the development of hot air balloons.

———, *The Lives of Things*, translated by Giovanni Pontiero, Verso, 2012.

> This is Saramago's first collection of short stories, originally published in Portuguese in 1978.

SUGGESTED SEARCH TERMS

José Saramago

"The Tale of the Unknown Island" AND Saramago

fairy tale

anarcho-communism

Age of Exploration

wine-dark sea

Portuguese literature

postmodernism

This Morning, This Evening, So Soon

JAMES BALDWIN

1960

James Baldwin's short story "This Morning, This Evening, So Soon" was first published in the *Atlantic Monthly* magazine in September 1960 and included in his 1965 short-story collection, *Going to Meet the Man*. The unnamed narrator is an African American man who has spent twelve years in France, during which he has become a famous actor and singer, married a Swedish woman, and had a son. The story is an extended meditation on the narrator's voluntary exile from the United States as he prepares to return to America with his family. During a last night of revelry in Paris, his success as an African American in France is juxtaposed with the misfortunes of Boona, an acquaintance from North Africa. Boona suffers discrimination by the French in a way that the narrator does not.

"This Morning, This Evening, So Soon" tackles several themes Baldwin examined throughout his career, including cultural alienation, racial prejudice, and the importance of family. Like the narrator, Baldwin spent many years in France in order to escape entrenched racial discrimination in the United States. Ultimately, the story ends on a hopeful note as the protagonist takes solace in the love of his family. The story is widely taught in schools and has been reprinted in several anthologies, including *The Best Short Stories by Black Writers: The Classic Anthology from 1899 to 1967* (Little, Brown, 1967), edited by Langston Hughes.

James Baldwin (©*Glasshouse Images / Alamy*)

AUTHOR BIOGRAPHY

James Baldwin was born on August 2, 1924, in the Harlem neighborhood of New York City, to Emma Berdis Jones. Baldwin's biological father was never part of his life. His mother married a minister, David Baldwin, when James was young and eventually had eight more children. The family was quite poor. Baldwin recalled his childhood as being filled with violence, not only from his stepfather but also from the largely white police force, which beat black people with little or no provocation. His stepfather died on James's nineteenth birthday, the same day that Harlem, an impoverished black community, erupted in a riot over the shooting of a black soldier by police officers. This riot later inspired Baldwin's essay "Notes of a Native Son."

After several years spent as a Pentecostal preacher when he was a teenager, Baldwin turned his back on religion. He gravitated toward Greenwich Village, an enclave of poets, artists, and musicians a couple of miles south of Harlem. He

formed mentorships with the poet Countee Cullen (1903–1946) and the artist Beauford Delaney (1901–1979). He also came to realize he was gay. Baldwin began to feel that to become the writer he wanted to be, he needed to free himself from the limitations of racist America. He moved to France in the late 1940s, following other African Americans who had found it to be a relatively open and tolerant society.

For a while he lived in Paris, and around 1970 he moved to the south of France, where his home became a frequent stop for African American celebrities of the day. Harry Belafonte, Sidney Poitier, Miles Davis, Ray Charles, Nina Simone, and Josephine Baker, all celebrities in the entertainment world, visited him. It was during Baldwin's years in self-imposed exile that he created the works for which he is known today.

Baldwin's semiautobiographical first novel, *Go Tell It on the Mountain*, was published in 1953 and focused on the role of religion in the life of an African American teenager in 1930s Harlem. *Notes from a Native Son*, a collection of ten essays about racism in America, was published two years later. Both works are considered classics of twentieth-century American literature.

Though he is known best for his essays, novels, and short stories, Baldwin also published poetry, drama, and experimental fiction throughout his career. *Going to Meet the Man* (1965) includes some of Baldwin's most famous short stories, including "This Morning, This Evening, So Soon" and "Sonny's Blues" (1957), another story with an unnamed narrator and a plot about the violence and opportunity-starved lives of Sonny and his brother in post–World War II America.

Baldwin was an important figure in the civil rights movement in the United States. He returned to the United States in 1957 to report on the bus boycott in Montgomery, Alabama, and the march to Selma, Alabama, both historical events that galvanized the movement. In Charlotte, North Carolina, Baldwin met with Martin Luther King Jr. (1929–1968), who welcomed his insightful writing on civil rights. Many of the essays Baldwin wrote during this visit were published in influential magazines, such as the *New Yorker* and *Harper's*. During another civil rights trip in 1963, Baldwin made the cover of *Time* magazine for his activism and met twice with Attorney General Robert Kennedy, who was the major force behind the passage of the Civil Rights Act of 1964. That same year, he appeared at the civil rights March on Washington, DC, where Martin Luther King Jr. gave his "I Have a Dream" speech. Although he was associated with many civil rights leaders and organizations of the day, Baldwin believed the best way to achieve racial integration was to meld the tactics of Nation of Islam leader Malcolm X (1925–1965) with those of Martin Luther King Jr. He also hoped that socialism would take hold in the United States.

One of Baldwin's brightest legacies was the number of other writers he inspired. Maya Angelou (1928–2014) was spurred by Baldwin to write *I Know Why the Caged Bird Sings*, and Nobel Prize–winning author Toni Morrison (b. 1931) was influenced by him and wrote his obituary in the *New York Times*. Baldwin died of stomach cancer on December 1, 1987, in Saint-Paul-de-Vence, France, and is buried at Ferncliff Cemetery in Westchester County, New York.

MEDIA ADAPTATIONS

- "This Morning, This Evening, So Soon" is available on audio CD as part of the 2011 AudioGO edition of *Going to Meet the Man*, narrated by Dion Graham. The run time is seven hours and forty-eight minutes.

PLOT SUMMARY

The unnamed narrator watches as his good-natured wife, Harriet, and his older sister, Louisa, get ready to spend their last evening out in Paris before the whole family moves to the United States. Harriet is from Sweden; Louisa and the narrator are from Alabama. The narrator has lived in Paris for the past twelve years. As an African American, he found it impossible to follow his dreams in his native country. In Paris, he has become a famous film actor and singer, thanks to his friend, Vidal, a respected and aging director.

He admires how Harriet's kindness makes up for his crankiness and how she has created a stable and happy home life for their seven-year-old son, Paul. The narrator has been having nightmares about returning to New York, even though his many fans eagerly await him. Harriet says that "nothing ever turns out as badly as you think it will." He is inclined to agree, although he worries that his son may suffer persecution owing to his mixed racial heritage. Paul is very excited to see America for the first time; to him it seems exotic.

The narrator is thankful that he met Harriet in Europe, where their interracial relationship was allowed to flourish. In the United States, their love would have been forbidden, and Paul would never have been born. "If I had never left America, I would never have met her and would never have established a life of my own, would never have entered my own life," he thinks.

The narrator takes Paul down to Madame Dumont's apartment to spend the night. Harriet and Louisa are going to do touristy things, like go to the Folies Bergère and drink at Harry's Bar. The narrator is going out to dinner with Vidal. As he waits for Vidal, he contemplates how many of the North Africans he used to know in Paris have departed. Many of those who settled in France after the Tunisian war of independence are disabled and do not receive enough government support to survive. "I once thought of the North Africans as my brothers and that is why I went to their cafés," the narrator says. He acknowledges his difficult relationship with them. The North Africans resent the French and want to destroy them, but the narrator loves the French because, he says, they "left me alone." He loves Paris, too, which "is the city which saved my life . . . by allowing me to find out who I am." He is troubled by his affection for a people who discriminate against other black people; he recognizes the hypocrisy of the situation.

In an extended flashback, the narrator recalls his only visit to America after having moved to France. It was eight years earlier, when his mother died. On the ship over, one of the things he noticed was how Americans' friendliness is based on a fake interest in others, which makes developing a real friendship difficult. It was "as though they were all members of the same team and were acting on orders from some invincibly cheerful and tirelessly inventive coach." He is asked to sing a few songs for the passengers, but singing in front of white people makes him uneasy. They cannot possibly understand what the songs mean to him. "Nothing was more familiar to them than the sight of a dark boy, singing, and there were few things on earth more necessary," he thinks. He sings several jazz and gospel classics, such as "Take This Hammer" and "Precious Lord." His set is a great success, and everyone is friendly to him for the rest of the night.

The next morning, people are distant toward him. When the Statue of Liberty comes into view, the other passengers are excited, but he says that "she had always been an ugly joke for me." He desperately wishes he could return to France, where Harriet, his newfound love, awaits. Now he must remember how to "pitch my voice precisely between curtness and servility" and all the other techniques he learned to survive as a black man in America. As he disembarks the ship, a dockworker calls him "boy," a racist term, given that he is a man. The cacophony of the city deafens him.

Back in present-day Paris, Vidal arrives at the narrator's apartment. They share a drink

and talk about the narrator's impending departure. Vidal believes that Paul will appreciate America and want to know the land where his father was born. The narrator disagrees, saying that "America never gave him anything." Vidal replies, "It gave him his father." The narrator says only that he escaped America. Vidal reminds him how difficult it was to get a decent performance out of him as the character Chico, a biracial man who hates both his parents, during the film they made together. "How you hated me, you sometimes looked as though you wanted to shoot me!" Vidal reminds him.

The narrator flashes back to this event, when he and Vidal are discussing Chico's motivation for his actions. The narrator's acting is dismal. He has been basing Chico on the North African boys he knows in Paris, but what he really needs to do is explore his deep-seated anger from his own upbringing. When Vidal explains this, the narrator is livid. He does not like it when others are right about his behavior, and he resists exploring his painful past. Their conversation goes further. Vidal states that he himself has never done anything against the narrator, except in a historical sense of his being French. The narrator responds angrily, "I've never understood why, if *I* have to pay for the history written in the color of my skin, *you* should get off scot-free!" After he releases this anger, Vidal sends him back to the set. His subsequent performance makes him a star.

Back in the present, the narrator admits that his worst fear is what might happen to Paul. "I did not want my son ever to feel toward me as I had felt toward my own father," he claims. He felt pity and contempt for his father, a man who suffered many humiliations and died when the narrator was just a boy. His father had had no way to protect his son from the anger and hatred of white people. He tells Vidal about a job he got as an elevator boy in New York, because of the charity of a white man who was an old friend of his father's. He hated the city and the white man, who believed the narrator was not grateful enough to him. He tells Vidal how the police make a habit of beating up black men, either for sport or to prove their power over them. "They'll do anything, anything at all, to prove that you're no better than a dog and to make you feel like one."

The narrator tells Vidal why his sister Louisa never married. She was on a double date with the boy she loved and another couple, and they were stopped by the police. The police sexually assaulted the other girl, and the boys were unable to help her. To do so would have resulted in great bodily harm. Though Louisa loved her boyfriend, she could not face him again after the incident. He would never be able to protect her. The narrator still feels a similar fear, that he will be powerless to protect Harriet and Paul in America. Vidal tells him that he can always return to Paris, but the narrator knows that is beside the point.

Vidal and the narrator have dinner at a trendy nightclub. The place is full of young tourists, artists, and those who are impressed by the famous director and actor. Vidal loves the attention he receives from the young women. A group of African American students, two men and two women, one with a guitar, recognize him. Vidal is entranced with one of the girls; the DJ plays one of the narrator's songs. The beautiful girl approaches; her name is Ada Holmes, and she is surprised to see them. She knows the narrator is sailing for America in just a couple days; she tells him how much his movie and records mean to her and her friends. She offers to buy the men a drink, and the two gladly get up and join the students.

The other students' names are Ruth, Talley, and Pete. They met while sailing to Europe for the summer. Pete tells the narrator the he is in for a surprise; America has changed since he was last there. He talks of Black Monday—May 17, 1954—the day the Supreme Court decided in *Brown v. Board of Education* that separate schools for white and black students were unconstitutional. Vidal says that he does not understand Americans' infantile behavior. "There is something very nice about them, something very winning, but they seem so ignorant—so ignorant of life."

The narrator suggests that they all find an outdoor café where they can enjoy more conversation. During their stroll, the narrator is sad that these beautiful streets will soon be just a memory. They end up at the Deux Magots, a café famous for its literary patrons, and Pete plays his guitar, strumming and singing an old negro gospel tune. They all join in, and they attract a crowd of passersby. One of the passersby is the narrator's old acquaintance, a retired Tunisian prizefighter named Boona.

Immediately, the narrator regrets calling out to him. He realizes that the North African man may not fit in with the African Americans, not to mention Vidal. Boona is entranced with the young black women because they are

beautiful and polite. Women in Paris refuse to give him the time of day because he is an Arab. The narrator introduces him to the group and invites him to have a drink. Ada, discovering that Boona is from Tunis, mentions how much she would like to visit Africa, now that so many of its countries are gaining their freedom. Boona assures her that freedom is less than the victory it appears to be.

Vidal suggests leaving the café and moving on to a Spanish club. It is obvious he wants to get rid of Boona, who is spoiling the mood. But Ada, in her politeness, invites Boona along. Boona accepts. "He is very moved, people are not often nice to him," the narrator notes.

At the Spanish club, Talley and Ruth join the racially and culturally diverse crowd on the dance floor. Boona invites Ada to dance, which irritates Vidal. Pete calls the narrator outside and tells him that "your boy"—meaning Boona—"has goofed" and stolen ten dollars from Ada's purse; Talley has witnessed the act. This puts the narrator in an awkward position; he does not know what to do. He knows that if Boona committed the crime, it was only because he truly needed some money owing to his miserable predicament as an immigrant in Paris. The narrator thinks the solution is to replace the money himself. Ada joins them outside and apologizes for causing trouble. She wants to forget the incident.

Talley and Boona appear; Boona proclaims his innocence and urges the narrator to defend him and even search him for the missing money. The narrator does not know whom to believe; either Talley or Boona could be lying. For Boona it is crucial that the narrator believe he is innocent. "You believe me? My brother?" he asks, looking at the narrator "with a terrible intensity." The narrator says yes.

Ada approaches Boona and apologizes. She says she must have lost the money somewhere else and that she is sure he is a very nice person. The whole situation is not worth hurting his feelings. Boona still insists he is innocent. They both say goodbye to him. Boona kisses the narrator on both cheeks.

The magic spell of the evening has been broken. It is almost morning. Vidal wants to continue their festivities, but Ada knows that it is time to say goodbye. She thanks both men for a wonderful evening. Vidal wants to share a cab with the young people, but he is going in the opposite direction. Vidal bids a heartfelt farewell to the narrator, calling him Chico, and hopes that he returns to France some day. When Vidal's cab leaves, the narrator makes his way back home. Back at the apartment building, the narrator is cheerful. He retrieves Paul from Madame Dumont's apartment. The sleepy boy is not yet sure if he is excited about their upcoming journey "all the way to the new world," as the narrator optimistically deems it.

CHARACTERS

Ada

Ada is an attractive African American student vacationing in Paris. She is the first in the group of four students to introduce herself to the narrator and Vidal. Both Boona and Vidal are deeply attracted to her. She is witty and self-assured. She eagerly engages in conversation with Boona upon learning that he is from Tunis. When her money is stolen from her purse, she tries to smooth over the awkwardness of the situation. She lets Boona save face by assuring him that she must have lost it somewhere else and stating that she is sure he is a nice person.

Boona

Boona is an acquaintance of the narrator's; he is a former boxer from Tunis, the capital of Tunisia. As an immigrant in France, he occupies a social status on par with black people in the United States. He runs into the narrator, Vidal, and the American students while they are out for the evening and tags along with the group. He and Vidal compete for the attention of Ada. He is accused of stealing money from one of the women and vehemently denies it. He serves as a flash point of racial prejudice, forcing the narrator to confront the issue that makes him uncomfortable.

Madame Dumont

Madame Dumont is the concierge of the narrator's apartment building. She watches Paul for the evening while his parents are out. She is excited for Paul's upcoming journey.

Harriet

Harriet is the narrator's wife. She is from Sweden. In France, her relationship with a black man is not particularly scandalous. Harriet is good-natured and loves her husband and son very much. She is trying to learn as much about America from Louisa as possible so that she can protect them to the best of her abilities when they get there. She assures her husband that his nightmares about returning to the United States are an overreaction.

Louisa

Louisa, the narrator's sister, is a schoolteacher from Alabama. She represents his family ties and is proof that he has not rejected everything about his past. Louisa is proud of her southern heritage and loves the expressiveness of black language, because "language is experience and language is power." She is teaching Harriet various southern sayings in return for Harriet's teaching her Swedish and French; it is the first time in her life that she has been able to openly express her opinions to a white woman. Louisa is irritated by African Americans who try to act white and dismisses important figures in black culture, such as the singer Mahalia Jackson. In Paris, Louisa is finally free to express her feelings in a way that is not possible in the American South.

Narrator

The unnamed narrator is an African American man who left the United States for France twelve years earlier in order to find his true identity in a culture that is less fixated on racial discrimination and oppression. He has become a famous actor and singer, thanks to Vidal, and is now returning to the United States with his wife and son. His homecoming is symbolic of his long journey of self-discovery and self-acceptance. He is thankful to France for allowing him to live up to his potential and for allowing him to fall in love with Harriet and be a good father.

He is having nightmares about returning home and having to change how he interacts with white people owing to the entrenched racism of the country. His pessimism seems well-founded based on his past experiences. He is afraid he will not be able to protect his family, just as his father was not able to protect him as a child. Ultimately, he exhibits a cautious optimism when he tells his son they are going to a "new world." He recognizes that things in America may be getting better, or at least will not be as bad as they had been before. Even if America has not changed completely, he himself is a different person, perhaps more equipped to deal with adversity.

Paul

Paul is the narrator's seven-year-old son; he has never been to America. To him, the country seems exotic. His first language is French; he does not know much English and is confused by many idioms and by his southern aunt's unusual accent. Though he is half black, he has no frame of reference for the racism that his father has suffered and protected him from. He does not even seem to realize that he is biracial.

Pete

Pete is an African American student who is visiting Paris on vacation. He plays guitar and impresses the narrator with his impression of Chico.

Ruth

Ruth is one of the African American students.

Talley

Talley is one of the African American students. He believes he saw Boona take the money from Ada's purse.

Jean-Luc Vidal

Jean-Luc Vidal is a French movie director who made the narrator famous by eliciting his stunning performance as Chico by inciting his buried racial hatred. He is taking the narrator out for a last night in Paris. Vidal adores beautiful young women and tries to woo Ada. He is also jealous of Boona and the attention he garners, which is evidence of his racism. Vidal absolves himself of all racial sins, telling the narrator, "I have never done you any harm, except, perhaps, historically—I mean, because I am white—but I cannot be blamed for that." He is an older man, lonely, with no family left.

THEMES

Race Relations

As an African American writer of the 1950s and 1960s, Baldwin was naturally drawn to writing about race. "This Morning, This Evening, So Soon" examines race relations from a number of different viewpoints. The most obvious is that of an American expatriate. The narrator left the United States, the American South in particular, because systemic racism and discrimination prohibited him from reaching his potential as a human being. At that time African American men very often could not provide for or protect their families and suffered humiliation and violence at the hands of the white establishment, especially the police. This is shown in the narrator's discussion of his early life, the flashback to his visit for his mother's funeral, and the story of why his sister never married.

"This Morning, This Evening, So Soon" also examines race relations in France, which for African Americans was enormously better than in the United States. Most obviously, the narrator has been free to fall in love with a white woman, marry her, and raise a family. This was illegal in most of the United States at the time under antimiscegenation laws that forbade interracial marriages. The narrator is extremely grateful that his adopted country has allowed him to pursue his career and his personal life on his own terms. He dreads returning to America because of the judgment he will face in presenting his mixed-race family to society. He fears not being able to keep them safe, although his wife, Harriet, believes these fears are exaggerated. Nevertheless, Harriet is soaking up knowledge from Louisa to learn "how best to protect her husband and her son."

The character of Louisa, the narrator's sister who is visiting from Alabama, provides additional insight into race relations from the perspective of a black woman. Louisa is a schoolteacher who never married, having witnessed the brutal rape of a friend in front of her boyfriend in their youth. A black woman cannot rely on a black man to protect her. Such emasculation, which the narrator also mentions was the case with his father, is a major factor in the fragile nature of the African American family.

Vidal calls the racist laws in America "infantile behavior," without acknowledging his own racist behavior toward Boona. The narrator "understands that in the France of the period of the Algerian War, North Africans are the 'niggers' of that society," writes David Wright in the *CLA Journal*, and "as such, he feels an empathetic pull towards them." Yet when Boona, a North African, is accused of stealing from an African American, the narrator's allegiance is torn. He recognizes the racism of his beloved adopted country and feels caught in the middle.

Family Life

The theme of family life is evident from the first scene, in which the narrator is observing the

TOPICS FOR FURTHER STUDY

- Rewrite the scene outside the Spanish nightclub from Boona's point of view. Keep his dialogue but replace the narrator's thoughts with those of Boona. Describe his mental state. Why is it so important for him to have the narrator believe his innocence? Include at least two hundred words of interior monologue in addition to the existing dialogue. Include in his thoughts whether or not he actually stole the money.

- Create a time line from 1945 to 1965 that outlines the political situation between France and the North African countries of Tunisia, Morocco, and Algeria. Cite at least ten events that take place either in Africa or in France; do not forget to list the dates that all three countries gained their independence from France, the first independent rulers of the countries, and the Battle of Algiers. Write in complete sentences and provide the facts regarding who, what, when, where, and why. Present your time line on a poster board, and add at least five pictures representing important people or places of the time.

- Read Julia Alvarez's 1991 young-adult novel *How the García Girls Lost Their Accents*, which takes place in 1960, around the same time as "This Morning, This Evening, So Soon." The García family escapes a brutal dictatorship in the Dominican Republic and immigrates to New York City. The four García sisters are safer in New York than they were in the Dominican Republic, but they are caught between two cultures. Prepare an oral presentation for your class that briefly summarizes the events of the book and compares the García family's reasons for coming to the United States with the narrator's reasons for leaving the United States in "This Morning, This Evening, So Soon." How are they alike, and how are they different? Conclude your presentation by stating how you think the narrator's son, Paul, will adapt to life in the United States. Will he have the same hurdles to face as the García sisters? Do you think he will come to love America? Why or why not?

- Jazz, blues, and gospel music is important in many of Baldwin's stories, including "This Morning, This Evening, So Soon." In the flashback aboard the ship sailing to New York, the narrator sings five songs: "I'm Coming Home, Virginia," "Take This Hammer," "Take My Hand, Precious Lord," "Swanee River," and "Great Getting-Up Morning." However, he wishes he could sing "Strange Fruit." Find the lyrics to all these songs online, and write a blog post explaining (1) why the narrator chose those songs to sing; (2) why he does not sing "Strange Fruit"; and (3) what the narrator means when he says, "Nothing was more familiar to them than the sight of a dark boy, singing, and there were few things on earth more necessary." Post your answers to these questions and allow your classmates to comment.

---

daily interactions between himself, his wife, and his son and thinking how much they mean to him. The narrator's fear about returning to the United States is linked to his primary goal: keeping his family safe and happy. He loves his son, his wife, and his sister dearly but is having nightmares over their fate. Harriet assures him that "nothing ever turns out as badly as you think it will" and that "whatever is coming, we will manage it all very well." They proclaim their admiration for each other. While the narrator is comforted by her words, he also knows that she has no experience with the type of American racism they will face.

The narrator fears his son will come to resent him as he resented his own father for his powerlessness as the head of the household while he was growing up. "Paul has never been called any

The story centers around an African American man living in Paris (©*S.Borisov* / *Shutterstock.com*)

names, so far," he says, meaning that as a biracial child in America he is in for some serious harassment, given that marriage between blacks and whites is illegal in most places. Vidal believes that Paul deserves to know the country that formed his father, but the narrator disagrees. He does not credit the United States for who he is today; he credits France. Vidal also says that the family can return to France if it does not work out. But the narrator knows that to return to France would mean the damage would have already been done.

Ambivalence

Ambivalence describes the state of having conflicting feelings about something. "This Morning, This Evening, So Soon" explores the narrator's ambivalence about his adopted country, France, by contrasting his success in life and love with Boona's desperation. The narrator has become a famous actor and singer, while Boona is forced to steal to survive. The narrator is married to a beautiful Swedish woman, while French women will not even look at Boona.

Why is France so welcoming to African Americans but hostile to North Africans? The answer lies mostly in historical events, but the narrator is not concerned with this, only with how it plays out in daily life. Boona is from Tunis, the capital of Tunisia, on the northern coast of Africa, a country that has only recently gained its independence from France. He is considered Arab, not black, and this fact demonstrates that France indeed is a racist country—it just discriminates against Arabs instead of blacks. Similarly, North Africans from Algeria and Morocco, countries also ruled for many years by the French, also suffer discrimination, because they, too, are considered Arabs. This discrimination takes the form of not being able to get good jobs, being forced to live in ghetto areas, and being ineligible for enough welfare to survive.

While the narrator is sympathetic to Boona, knowing firsthand what it is like to be oppressed, he finds his sympathy tested after Boona is accused of stealing Ada's money at the club. (Even before then, he realizes that Vidal wants

Boona to disappear.) As David Farnell, writing in the *Bulletin of Central Research Institute Fukuoka University*, notes, Boona "is the negative reflection of the narrator, a reminder that the narrator is fortunate in being able to experience dislocation in a positive way."

Robert Tomlinson delves into this ambivalence in his essay about Baldwin's expatriation in the *African American Review*:

> The voyage toward self-discovery which the Parisian experience freed one to make was only granted at the price of physical deprivation and spiritual pain, and at its heart lay the existential knowledge that everything must be paid for.

That is, even though the narrator's exile in Paris has given him a family he loves and success beyond his wildest dreams, he remains tortured by his past and the life he was forced to leave behind. In a 1977 interview with Robert Coles for the *New York Times Book Review*, Baldwin stated that France was far from perfect, even if it allowed him to write in peace. It contains "plenty of arrogance, smugness among its intellectuals and upper bourgeoisie," which Baldwin encapsulated in the character of Vidal.

STYLE

Flashback

A flashback is a literary device that shows the reader something that happened before the time in which the story takes place. "This Morning, This Evening, So Soon" has two important flashbacks illustrating crucial events in the narrator's life that affect his current situation. The first is the lengthy scene in which the narrator returns to the United States to attend his mother's funeral. During the ocean voyage from France to New York, he dreads returning to his racist homeland and longs to get back to France, a country where he is free to love his Swedish girlfriend and pursue his dreams. He sings a few songs onboard, delighting the passengers, who are temporarily enamored of him. As they dock in New York, the mood changes; the passengers avoid eye contact, and his manhood is belittled by the first person he sees when he disembarks, a ship steward who dismissively calls him "boy." This flashback informs the reader how painful everyday experiences in a racist society can be.

The second, shorter flashback concerns the narrator's initial lackluster performance as Chico in the movie that Vidal is directing. Chico "is the son of a Martinique woman and a French *colon*," that is, a black mother and white father, who feels alienated from both cultures. The narrator explains that he is basing his performance on the North African men he has met in France. Vidal knows that to get a better performance from him, he must persuade the narrator to tap into his deep-seated rage, fomented during his youth in the American South, where he and other blacks were routinely harassed by white policemen and were denied their basic humanity through legal segregation. After this conversation, which does indeed make the narrator furious, the narrator delivers a performance that turns him into a celebrity.

These two flashbacks are effective because they *show* the reader specific examples from the narrator's past that explain his deep distrust of and ambivalence for his native country. Taking the reader out of the current action of the story to illustrate something is slightly jarring, but in a way that adds interest to the narrative. It provides a sense of immediacy to see the events firsthand, rather than hearing about them from the narrator secondhand.

Conflict

All works of literature have a conflict, though some are more obvious than others. "This Morning, This Evening, So Soon" is a story in which the conflict is largely internal—how will the narrator resolve his conflicting feelings about returning to his native country? Because this conflict is internal, it may appear to readers that not much happens in the course of the story. The narrator thinks about his family, converses with the director Vidal before their night on the town, and then encounters a group of students at a nightclub. At the end, he retrieves his son from the neighbor's apartment and prepares to leave for the United States. These events are far from thrilling, but the conflict is resolved in such a manner that the narrator's moody disposition at the start of the story, evidenced by his yelling at his son, is replaced by a feeling of hopefulness, related symbolically by the upward motion of the elevator and his declaration that they are on a journey to a "new world."

Note that the conflict is not about who stole the money from Ada's purse. That conflict is never truly resolved, and the incident does not take place until near the end of the story. That incident merely serves to illustrate that issues of race transcend national boundaries. Boona's precarious social position allows the narrator to see France's own racial discrimination clearly. Knowing that no culture is perfect gives him the perspective he needs to feel better about returning to the United States.

Interior Monologue

An interior monologue is a dramatic device in which the author reveals a character's unspoken thoughts. "This Morning, This Evening, So Soon" takes place entirely from the viewpoint of the unnamed narrator, and his unspoken thoughts reveal the conflict and resolution of the story. Outwardly, there is little action in the story, but inwardly the story is about the narrator's conflicting thoughts about returning to the United States. He wants to protect his wife and son, both of whom he loves dearly. But she is white, and his son is biracial, and he knows from experience that deep-seated racism will present formidable challenges. He left the United States in order to find out who he was. Now he is worried that he will not be able to continue being who he is. Vidal assures him that he can return to France. Madame Dumont tells him it will be a grand adventure for Paul. Harriet reassures him that everything will be fine, that he is always worried about his nightmares.

The interior monologue creates a story out of the events of a somewhat typical day. An important aspect of Baldwin's writing was to illustrate how the mind of the African American man was every bit as cerebral as anyone else's. An interior monologue that conveyed complex emotions and ambivalence, love, fear, and compassion helped humanize the black male in an era when he was still quite often demonized.

HISTORICAL CONTEXT

Jim Crow Laws and Brown v. Board of Education

"Jim Crow" is the informal name given to the laws passed after the Civil War in the American South to ensure racial segregation in all facets of life. (The name came from the 1828 song "Jim Crow" by Thomas Dartmouth "Daddy" Rice, one of the first white minstrel performers

to appear in blackface.) These laws remained in effect until the passage of the Civil Rights Act of 1964. Jim Crow laws established the concept of "separate but equal" for African Americans, meaning that blacks could not eat at the same restaurants, go to the same schools, or even use the same bathrooms and drinking fountains as white people. They did not get hired for good jobs or live in decent neighborhoods and were ineligible for loans from most banks. As the law of the land, particularly in Alabama, the narrator's home state, Jim Crow meant not only lack of freedom but also danger from the white power structure. Police and other figures of authority were able to commit crimes against black people with little fear of legal retribution. For the narrator, this is unbearable, and his solution is to move to a country that will respect his humanity.

The first US Supreme Court ruling to seriously challenge the Jim Crow laws was *Brown v. Board of Education* in 1954, which is decided while the narrator of "This Morning, This Evening, So Soon" is living in France. In this landmark decision, the court ruled that separate schools for black and white students are unconstitutional because they are inherently unequal. This was the first major victory of the civil rights movement and was the first step toward integrating public schools, especially in the South, although the process still took many years. In the story, Talley refers to this decision as "Black Monday," the derogatory term assigned to the event by racist southerners who were incensed that their status quo was beginning to crumble. Nevertheless, while this change seemed like a good thing, the African American students in the story recognize that this upheaval could have negative consequences for them by causing white people to become more violent. "Are you afraid?" Pete asks the narrator. "A little," he replies. "We all are," Ada adds.

Tunisia and France

While France seems to welcome African Americans and has rewarded the narrator with fame and wealth, the French are not immune to racism. This is established by the character of Boona, who is from Tunis, the capital of Tunisia. Tunisia is a small country on the coast of North Africa directly across the Mediterranean Sea from France. The French invaded and conquered the country in 1881. In 1957, very close to the time period in which the story takes place,

COMPARE
&
CONTRAST

- **1960s:** During the Paris massacre of October 17, 1961, French police attack a crowd of thirty thousand Algerian Muslims who are peacefully protesting France's war against Algeria. Up to two hundred protestors die after being beaten or forced to jump into the River Seine, but the French government refuses to acknowledge the tragedy, and no officers are charged with any crime.

   Today: On January 7, 2015, Algerian brothers Cherif and Said Koauchi, members of the Islamic terrorist group al-Qaeda, storm the Paris office of satirical magazine *Charlie Hebdo*, kill twelve people, and injure eleven more. The gunmen are incensed at the publication's depiction of the Prophet Muhammad.

- **1960s:** Corporal Roman Ducksworth Jr., an African American military police officer, is on leave and visiting his wife in Taylorsville, Mississippi, in April of 1962 when a white police officer orders him off a bus and shoots him dead. It is believed that the officer thought Ducksworth was a freedom rider testing recent bus desegregation laws. His killing is ruled a justifiable homicide.

   Today: The Black Lives Matter campaign is founded to protest continuing violence against African Americans by mostly white police personnel. The movement is launched following the acquittal of George Zimmerman in the shooting death of unarmed African American teenager Trayvon Martin in 2012. The movement gains many followers after a white officer shoots eighteen-year-old Michael Brown in the town of Ferguson, Missouri, in 2014, sparking several nights of protest and further police violence.

- **1960s:** Les Deux Magots is a café on the Boulevard Saint-Germain that has been open since 1884 and is renowned for its clientele of artists and writers. Famous patrons have included Simone de Beauvoir and Jean-Paul Sartre, Ernest Hemingway, Pablo Picasso, and James Joyce.

   Today: Les Deux Magots remains a popular tourist attraction in Paris's Latin Quarter, and a prime destination for students and intellectuals. It continues to be featured in many novels and films.

- **1960s:** Mahalia Jackson is widely regarded as the world's greatest gospel singer and performs to sold-out crowds throughout France and the rest of Europe. In 1961 she sings at President John F. Kennedy's inaugural ball.

   Today: Jackson continues to garner new fans, decades after her death. Her signature song, "Take My Hand, Precious Lord," is one of the most-remembered songs of the civil rights era, sung by Aretha Franklin at Jackson's funeral and by Beyoncé at the Grammy Awards in 2015. Jazz vocalist Ledisi sings it in the 2014 film *Selma*, about the 1965 voting rights march from Selma to Montgomery, Alabama, led by Martin Luther King Jr.

Tunisia gained its independence from France. Tunisia is a primarily Muslim country, and Muslims do not enjoy protection under French law in the same way Christians do. Though workplace discrimination against Muslims and Africans is technically illegal, it has been widely practiced for generations. Many North Africans immigrated to France throughout the twentieth century in search of jobs and economic opportunities, when their French-ruled homelands became mired in war and economic decline. This is what puts Boona in a tough situation. As he says, there is nothing back home for him; his family is suffering. He, too, suffers in Paris, and the narrator does not blame him for stealing to survive.

The North Africans fought alongside the French in World War II, helping to liberate the country from the Nazis. This encouraged many

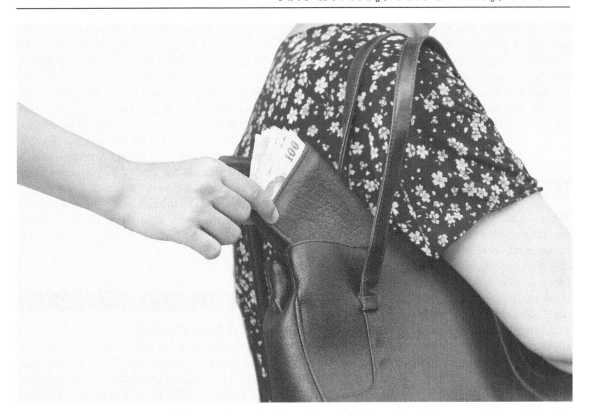

During an evening out, one friend claims to have seen another stealing money, and the accusation goes unresolved (©Toa55 | Shutterstock.com)

Africans to fight for their own independence after the war. During these conflicts in the 1950s, many North Africans, primarily Tunisians and Algerians, immigrated to France, Paris in particular. The French military created specialized Muslim zones, where these immigrants were required to live. They were hired for only the lowest-paying and most menial jobs. The Constitution of France, adopted in 1958, states that "France shall be an indivisible, secular, democratic and social Republic. It shall ensure the equality of all citizens before the law, without distinction of origin, race or religion." Part of Baldwin's reason for writing "This Morning, This Evening, So Soon" seems to be to prove otherwise.

African Americans in France

During the twentieth century, many African Americans, including many artists, writers, and musicians, moved to France because they believed the country allowed them freedoms that were not available to them at home. Baldwin himself moved to France when he was a young man and remained there largely for the

rest of his life. African Americans were indeed welcomed in France as a "model minority" and because of the country's fascination with both black and American culture. After World War I, many black US soldiers from the American South who had fought in France decided to stay, because they were welcomed and because they enjoyed equal rights.

During the 1920s, jazz music, a distinctly American form, became wildly popular, and France welcomed America's jazz musicians. Sidney Bechet, Arthur Briggs, and many others performed at Chez Bricktop, a jazz club owned by African American Ada Smith and frequented by many expatriates. Josephine Baker, an erotic dancer, singer, and actress, was one of the most famous Americans to become a French citizen in the 1930s. Many writers and artists associated with the Harlem Renaissance followed. During World War II, France was occupied by the Nazis, and most Americans returned home. After the war, many returned. African American writers who lived in Paris in the 1950s and 1960s included Richard Wright, author of *Native Son*, and

William Gardner Smith, two of the most influential writers of their time, along with Baldwin. Jazz musicians continued to perform to wide acclaim in these years, including Miles Davis, Kenny Clarke, and singer Nina Simone. Many of these authors and musicians stayed with Baldwin during the years he lived in the south of France.

CRITICAL OVERVIEW

When "This Morning, This Evening, So Soon" was published in *Going to Meet the Man* in 1965, Baldwin was best known as an essayist, and some critics dismissed his fiction as inferior. Noted literary critic Stanley Kauffmann, reviewing the book in the *New York Times Book Review*, writes that "it is crusted with cliché" and that "very little of this writing shows the incisiveness of prose, the rhythmic control, the attractively serpentine and dramatic structure, the simple care, that mark his other writing." Conversely, Denis Donoghue, writing in the *New York Review of Books*, states that both "This Morning, This Evening, So Soon" and "Sonny's Blues" "are far better than anything else Mr. Baldwin has done in fiction."

In just a little over a decade, however, the story became a highly regarded part of Baldwin's body of work. In *James Baldwin*, Louis H. Pratt characterizes the story as an exploration of "the estrangement of the black intellectual" and "alienation from one's country," which has its roots in the narrator's miserable childhood that stands in contrast to his current international success, a semiautobiographical situation for Baldwin. Writing in *CLA Journal*, David Wright notes that the unnamed narrator is Baldwin's homage to Ralph Ellison's unnamed narrator in *Invisible Man* and that the story explores many of the same themes as Ellison's classic. Instead of a literal underground, where Ellison's character lives, Baldwin's "'underground' [is] a positive space in which characters can come to terms with their past and, consequently, negotiate their identities in the present."

In the decades since its first publication, "This Morning, This Evening, So Soon" has become one of Baldwin's most popular stories, along with "Sonny's Blues." Writing in the *Bulletin of Central Research Institute Fukuoka University*, David Farnell examines the narrator's comfortable exile in France as an American expatriate: "As a member of a far tinier minority than he was in America, a minority that is no threat to France's social order, he is largely and blessedly ignored." In a review of the audiobook version of *Going to Meet the Man* in *Library Journal*, Valerie Piechocki writes that "This Morning, This Evening, So Soon" is part of a "familiar world with elements of frustration, anger, loneliness, and the desire for love." In an essay for *Journal of the Short Story in English*, Adrienne Akins comments that in the story "Baldwin reveals a deep awareness of the way in which the America that he loves and criticizes more than any other country in the world shapes the identity of her black sons and daughters."

CRITICISM

Kathy Wilson Peacock

Wilson Peacock is a freelance writer specializing in literature criticism. In the following essay, she analyzes the jazz, blues, and spiritual songs mentioned in "This Morning, This Evening, So Soon," explaining how they add nuance to Baldwin's themes.

James Baldwin's short story "This Morning, This Evening, So Soon," from his 1965 collection *Going to Meet the Man*, recounts a day in the life of an unnamed narrator, an American expatriate living in Paris, as he prepares to end his twelve-year exile and return to his native country. Like much of Baldwin's writing, the story is a semi-autobiographical meditation on race, ambivalence, and self-exile. The narrator of the story differs from Baldwin in a couple of meaningful ways—he is a successful singer and actor, and he is happily married to a white woman and has a seven-year-old-son—but they have in common a clear-eyed understanding that no society is perfect. Another thing the narrator and Baldwin have in common is a love of African American music, especially gospel, blues, and jazz. Baldwin imbues "This Morning, This Evening, So Soon" with musical references that, when analyzed, add texture and cultural weight to the story's themes.

The musical analysis begins with the story's title, which is not mentioned in the narrative at all. "Dis Mornin' An' Dis Evenin' So Soon" is the title of a nineteenth-century African American song from the South. It is the tale of a man named Old Bill who is shot to death in town and whose body is brought back home to his wife "wid his toes a-draggin'." Its origins are lost to history, but it was first collected by the renowned

WHAT DO I READ NEXT?

- *Invisible Man* (1952), by Ralph Ellison, is a novel about an African American man who considers himself metaphorically invisible owing to the inability of those around him to see him for who he is. Thus, he lives underground, listening to jazz music and writing the story of his life. The novel won the National Book Award for fiction in 1953 and is considered a modern classic.

- "The Man Who Lived Underground" (1942) is a short story by Richard Wright, an African American writer who lived in Paris at the same time Baldwin did. The story recounts how Fred Daniels, a black man, is falsely accused of murdering a white woman and escapes to the underground sewers. His story is a meditation on the sense of guilt and isolation that all people share.

- *Notes of a Native Son* (1955), by James Baldwin, is a collection of ten essays about race that were previously published in leading magazines, including *Harper's* and the *Partisan Review*. Topics include growing up with an abusive stepfather, suffering racism and discrimination as a young man in New York, and experiencing difficulties in adjusting to Parisian life. The title essay is one of his most famous and is his attempt to deal with his anger toward his father.

The book is regarded as a masterpiece of twentieth-century nonfiction.

- *Paris Noir: African Americans in the City of Light* (2012), by Tyler Stovall, explores how African Americans first settled in large numbers in Paris after World War I, where racism was not as entrenched as it was at home. They were soon followed by writers and performers, eager to pursue their art in a more tolerant society. The jazz musicians followed; except for during World War II, the climate remained inviting and tolerant.

- *Now Is Your Time! The African-American Struggle for Freedom* won the 1992 Coretta Scott King Award. In this YA book, author Walter Dean Myers examines the stories of famous and influential black Americans who pursued freedom despite the hardships and danger they faced. Myers includes the stories of early abolitionists all the way through Martin Luther King Jr.

- *Kiffe Kiffe Tomorrow* (2004), by Faïza Guène, translated by Sarah Adams, is the story of a girl from Morocco who moves with her mother into a housing project in suburban Paris. Doria and her mother are poor and Arab, and Doria is having a hard time fitting in and growing up. Her story illuminates France's "immigration problem" from the viewpoint of the immigrant.

American poet Carl Sandburg (1878–1967) in his anthology of folk songs *American Songbag* (1927). The anthology includes the lyrics and music to over two hundred songs from all regions of the United States and was enormously influential to the folk singers of the 1950s and 1960s. Sandburg writes that he first heard "Dis Mornin' An' Dis Evenin' So Soon" in St. Louis in 1922. The Kingston Trio, an influential group of California musicians who launched the folk revival in the 1950s, included their version of the song, titled "This Mornin', This Evenin', So Soon," on

their 1960 album *String Along* and credited Sandburg as the writer. Many other groups later recorded the song, but it seems likely that Baldwin was thinking of the Kingston Trio's version as he was searching for a title for his story about a man who feels the weight of history on his shoulders as he worries about protecting his family in a racially contentious environment.

Folk revival acts of the 1950s, such as Pete Seeger, Woody Guthrie, and the Weavers, recorded traditional songs that related the African American experience from a first-person

" BALDWIN IMBUES 'THIS MORNING, THIS

EVENING, SO SOON' WITH MUSICAL REFERENCES

THAT, WHEN ANALYZED, ADD TEXTURE AND

CULTURAL WEIGHT TO THE STORY'S THEMES."

viewpoint. These songs told of racial strife, violence, and death at the hands of those in power. Ironically, most folk revival acts were whites, performing for majority white audiences. By singing of the black experience, they raised awareness of racial oppression at a crucial moment in civil rights history. By attaching such a song title to his story, Baldwin is piggybacking on the folk revival to add an American subtext to a story that takes place in France. This was not the first time Baldwin had done this, and it would not be the last. Baldwin's 1953 novel *Go Tell It on the Mountain* is named for a popular African American spiritual that dates back to the Civil War. "Tell Me How Long the Train's Been Gone" is a blues song popularized by Mable Hillery (1929–1976) and is the title of Baldwin's fourth novel, published in 1968.

Within the story Baldwin's musical allusions are most revealing during the flashback in which the narrator sails to the United States for his mother's funeral. The ship's passengers have discovered that he is a singer and invite him to entertain them after dinner one evening. The narrator thinks to himself, "Nothing was more familiar to them than the sight of a dark boy, singing, and there were few things on earth more necessary." He means that white audiences have long accepted African American artists as entertainers, but rarely have they understood the social message of that entertainment. The blues, gospel, and other genres of music invented by African Americans contain an undercurrent of rage directed toward whites. "They did not know, they could not know, what my songs came out of," he says of his shipboard audience.

"Strange Fruit" is the song the narrator would like to sing to his captive audience but does not. He knows that it is his place to give them what they want to hear, not what he wants

to sing. "They were ready to be pleased," he says. Readers of today might not know "Strange Fruit," but Baldwin bet that his readers in the 1960s did. Written by a Jewish teacher from New York in 1937, "Strange Fruit" is a metaphor for the bodies of lynched black men swinging from poplar trees. It is one of the most notable and controversial protest songs of the early civil rights era, made famous by blues singer Billie Holiday (1915–1959), who first sang it in 1939. In 1999 *Time* magazine named it the song of the century. Sung as a ballad, the lyrics are delivered sweetly but full of fury. This is the fury that lies behind the narrator's calm demeanor as he entertains the audience. Instead of protest songs, he belts out a small handful of upbeat numbers: "I'm Coming, Virginia," "Take This Hammer," "Precious Lord," "Swanee River," and "Great Getting-Up Morning." All of these are African American songs lacking any lyrics white people might find controversial.

"I'm Coming, Virginia," dating from 1926, is a song about the singer's happy return to Virginia. The narrator chooses this song ironically. He is not happy to be returning to America or his native Alabama for his mother's funeral. He longs to be in Paris with Harriet, his newfound love. Instead of happily returning to his "Dixieland home," he regards the looming New York skyline as a "murderous beast, ready to devour, impossible to escape." However, the song would have warmed the hearts of other Americans sailing toward their beloved homeland; indeed, it is what they wanted to hear.

"Take This Hammer" is a work song, meaning that African Americans sang it to keep time as they hammered stakes into railroad ties. The song could be adapted for other purposes, such as mining, farming, and building levees—any situation in which a group of men, usually African Americans, could work more efficiently by synchronizing their movements to a steady rhythm. The song exists in many versions; Sandburg's *American Songbag* version is called "My Old Hammah." Another variation is called "Nine Pound Hammer." Legendary folk and blues musician Lead Belly (1888–1949) recorded the song in the 1940s, and it became a staple of the folk revival in subsequent years. With the refrain of the song, the narrator is betting that his shipboard audience pictures black men happily engaged in heavy labor on chain gangs, doing the type of work that seemed appropriate for their station in life. The racist undertones of such a viewpoint and the song's subversive lyrics would have been beyond them.

Next he sings "Precious Lord," a song closely identified with Mahalia Jackson (1911–1972). Also known as "Take My Hand, Precious Lord," this gospel tune would have been familiar to many white passengers owing to its long history in popular music. It was written in 1932 by gospel legend Thomas Dorsey and soon after became associated with Jackson, who had many black and white fans. It was recorded by numerous groups, including Elvis Presley, Ike and Tina Turner, Nina Simone, and Lawrence Welk. Beyoncé even performed it at the Grammy Awards in 2015. The song's lyrics convey complete devotion to and reliance on God and thus bridge the cultural divide between white and black America, both of which share Christian beliefs.

After "Precious Lord," the narrator says, "They wouldn't let me go and I came back and sang a couple of the oldest blues I knew." He does not name these songs, but he then fulfills an audience request for "Swanee River." He sings it, "astonished that I could, astonished that this song, which I had put down so long ago, should have the power to move me." "Swanee River" is also known as "Old Folks at Home" and was written by Stephen Foster (1826–1864), perhaps the country's first hit songwriter, in 1851. The song was written to be performed at minstrel shows, in which white actors dress in blackface and depict gross stereotypes of African Americans.

By the time Baldwin wrote "This Morning, This Evening, So Soon," minstrel shows were considered in very poor taste. That a white audience member would request the narrator to sing "Swanee River" underscores a certain racial insensitivity. The song is sung from the perspective of a slave who is longing for life on the plantation. That such a preposterous thought had the power to "move" the narrator has more to do with the connection he feels to his enslaved ancestors. Even though Foster was an abolitionist, this song has long been criticized for romanticizing slavery and for the use of racist terms, such as "darkies." The song is still widely performed today—and is even the state song of Florida—but the lyrics have been cleaned up, substituting "Swanee River" for "Swanee Ribber" and erasing the offensive slave dialect with proper English.

The narrator closes his set with the classic gospel number "Great Getting-Up Morning," another of Mahalia Jackson's famous tunes. It is an upbeat number with a call-and-response pattern, usually sung with a backing choir, in which the singer looks forward to Judgment Day. How the narrator managed to sing this song without a backing choir he does not say, but once again Baldwin is counting on his audience's familiarity with this crowd-pleasing number. The song is his finale; he has given his audience what they wanted: "I got a big hand and I drank at a few tables and I danced with a few girls."

Interestingly, the narrator expresses no opinions about the gospel message of the songs he sings. Baldwin, who had spent time in his youth as a Pentecostal preacher, had renounced his belief in religion by the time he became a writer. Yet religion, especially in the form of gospel music, has always been an integral part of African American life. It is this cultural link, not the religious message, that is so important to Baldwin and by proxy his narrator.

The next morning the mood on the boat sailing into New York Harbor has changed; the narrator's triumphant feeling of the previous night has slipped away. "Was it my imagination or was it true that they seemed to avoid my eyes?" He disembarks and passes through customs; he is derogatorily called "boy" by a dockworker. He laments that he has forgotten "how to pitch my voice precisely between curtness and servility" in order to escape the "wrath" of white people. He is no longer among friends.

Elsewhere in the story, Louisa, the narrator's sister, mentions Mahalia Jackson, and later the narrator plays one of her records while waiting for Vidal to arrive. Baldwin's choice of Jackson in this story is telling. Louisa, who believes strongly in the colorful flavor of black language, is outraged at blacks who try to scrub dialect from their speech in order to sound more white. These are the black folks who are "*ashamed* of Mahalia Jackson" because she embraces black culture. "*Ashamed* of her," Louisa repeats, "one of the greatest singers alive! They think she's common." The thought prompts her to look "about the room as though she held a bottle in her hand and were looking for a skull to crack." She is the story's voice of black pride. When Vidal arrives, he plays Jackson's "I'm Going to Live the Life I Sing about

The unresolved conflict over the theft reflects the narrator's mixed feelings about his upcoming return to America *(©Pressmaster | Shutterstock.com)*

in My Song," an ode to practicing what one preaches. The song takes on special significance later in the evening as the narrator becomes torn between believing Boona or shunning him because of the alleged theft.

The final nod to gospel music in the story is Pete's rendition of "I'll Meet You on Canaan's Shore," with which the narrator and the four young students serenade passersby outside the Deux Magots. Yet another hopeful gospel song, the narrator notes that it "has come down the bloodstained ages. I suppose this to mean that the song is still needed, still has its work to do." Through this and his other song choices in "This Morning, This Evening, So Soon," Baldwin is telling readers that his writing is part of a long tradition of African American culture. He is hoping that we will see beyond "a dark boy, singing," and find our common humanity on our shared journey "to the new world."

Source: Kathy Wilson Peacock, Critical Essay on "This Morning, This Evening, So Soon," in *Short Stories for Students*, Gale, Cengage Learning, 2017.

Louis H. Pratt
In the following excerpt, Pratt discusses the protagonist's determination to make things better for his son.

. . . IV BREAKING THE CHAIN: STRATEGY, SURVIVAL, AND FREEDOM

Baldwin continues his probe of the estrangement of the black intellectual in "This Morning, This Evening, So Soon." In this story we encounter the artist as singer who functions as first-person narrator in revealing his story of success in Europe. This triumph, however, is contrasted sharply with constant "nightmares" and inner feelings of frustration and alienation, the majority of which can be traced back to the singer's youth.

As we learn through a series of flashbacks, the narrator, like Peter, had been reared by parents whose traditional values served as reinforcements of the *status quo*. This was the facade which had been erected painfully with but one objective in view: survival. Consequently, the artist had inherited a life fraught with anxiety;

> THERE WAS SIMPLY NO WAY TO RECONCILE HIS CHILDHOOD PATTERNS OF TRADITIONAL BEHAVIOR WITH THE FREEDOM THAT HE HAD EXPERIENCED IN PARIS. HE COULD NO LONGER ATTUNE HIS HOPES, FEARS, DESIRES, AND ASPIRATIONS TO THE PREJUDICES OF WHITE SOCIETY."

he had acquired the ability to attune himself emotionally to the demands of white society: "I had once known how to pitch my voice precisely between curtness and servility, and known what razor's edge of a pickaninny's smile would turn away wrath."

His experiences with the police corroborate the encounters with the law which Peter reveals in "Previous Condition," and they serve as a symbol of the thousands of indignities and humiliations which the masses of blacks face on a day-to-day basis. The narrator recalls that in his hometown in Alabama, typically, a police car might pull up to the curb. And, being black, you realize that you have been called to appear before the law—judge, jury, and executioner—to answer the charge of drunkenness. Any defense offered that fails to elicit laughter and manifestations of amusement—any slight deviation from the expected mode of conduct—will literally heap wrath and fury upon your head: "The trick is to think of some way for them to have their fun without beating you up. . . . And they'll do anything at all, to prove that you're no better than a dog and to make you feel like one."

Having "survived" these experiences, the narrator travels to Europe to pursue his career and to escape "the menacing, the hostile, killing world" into which he was born. At this point the autobiographical element becomes evident. Baldwin tells us that "I left America because I doubted my ability to survive the fury of the color problem here," and so he, like the protagonist, escapes to Europe in an effort to recover a sense of his uniqueness, to begin his quest for identity. The author's description of his exhilaration, his sense of freedom, his feeling, "for the

first time in his life—that he can reach out to everyone, that he is accessible to everyone and open to everything," parallels the narrator's jubilation on the April morning, high upon the Pont Royal Bridge, when he discovers his love for Harriet. But as he describes that moment, he reveals a parallel and equally engulfing electrification as the awareness dawns upon him that he is free; the white man is no longer on his back: "There were millions of people all around us, but I was alone with Harriet. She was alone with me. Never, in all my life, until that moment, had I been alone with anyone. . . . During all the years of my life, until that moment, I had carried the menacing, hostile, killing world with me everywhere."

Thus, there is a feeling of release and relief; the tension is gone, and he has found love, peace, and tranquility in Paris, "the city which saved my life . . . by allowing me to find out who I am." The whiteness of Harriet's skin and the darkness of his own were of no consequence. Here, at last, was a society that made no effort to circumscribe his feelings, his behavior, his very existence. He was free to discover the meaning of his life and become a man.

Then came the death of his mother, followed by a three-month return visit to America. During those four years in Europe, he had violated the two basic canons in the code of conduct that he had learned so well as a child. First, he had gone North and to Europe, experienced a different society, and forgotten how to shuffle his feet, scratch his head, and cater to the whims of the white power structure. Secondly, refusing to restrict his amorous inclinations to his own race, he had fallen in love with Harriet. For the first offense, he could be whipped in line, beaten, and "put in his place"; but for the second transgression, the violation of lily-white womanhood, there would have been—had they known—only one possible punishment: castration and death. Intuitively he knew these things.

With the approach of New York, "slowly and patiently, like some enormous, cunning, and murderous beast, ready to devour, impossible to escape . . . " came the realization that the white passengers were moving with the boat toward freedom and safety; only he was approaching the danger and insecurity of his native land. And if one iota of doubt about the cruciality of that impending danger remained, the fat, red-faced cop standing below the plank shouted a grim reaffirmation of that fact: "Come on, boy, . . . come on, come on!"

That summer he had been "lucky" enough to get a job running an elevator in a large department store through the "kindness" of white friends, but it had not worked out because he no longer believed what white people said about him: "People kept saying, I hope you didn't bring no foreign notions back here with you, boy. And I'd say, 'No sir,' or 'No M'am,' but I never said it right. And there was a time, all of them remembered it, when I *had* said it right. But now they could tell that I despised them—I guess, no matter what, I wanted them to know that I despised them. But I didn't despise them any more than everyone else did, only the others never let it show." There was simply no way to reconcile his childhood patterns of traditional behavior with the freedom that he had experienced in Paris. He could no longer attune his hopes, fears, desires, and aspirations to the prejudices of white society. He had forgotten the rules of life and death in the game of survival which the black man in America is compelled to play: "That moment on the bridge had undone me forever."

That had been eight years ago, and yet the horrible nightmare lingers hauntingly as the singer again prepares to make the trip across the Atlantic—this time with his wife and his young son, Paul. He has become famous now, and that fame—like all achievement—requires nourishment by an unbroken line of future successes. The prospect of singing on the nightclub circuit and the beckon of Hollywood lights combined to lure him from his new, secure life in Paris. And yet, neither fame, nor bright lights, nor fortune can dispel the ugly reality of the nightmare, the hatred, the fear.

Harriet jokes with Paul that his father has become worried about the reception which he will receive in New York. She reassures her husband, innocently, that things are never as bad as they seem. But she does not know the unspeakable horror, the degradation, and the humiliation that attend the very survival of the black man in America. And he has good reason to fear—not that they will not like his songs—not even that they will require him to give up his life. What he fears most is that these indignities suffered by him and by his father and his father's father since time immemorial will be

heaped upon the innocent head of his son, working their way into his psyche and corrupting his very being: " . . . I discovered that I did not want my son ever to feel toward me as I had felt toward my own father. . . . I had watched the humiliations he had to bear, and I had pitied him. . . .

But for Paul, I swore it, such a day would never come. I would throw my life and my work between Paul and the nightmare of the world. I would make it impossible for the world to treat Paul as it had treated my father and me." Indeed, this is an ambitious undertaking when one is journeying to a "new world," especially when that new world is America and the color of one's skin is black. . . .

Source: Louis H. Pratt, "The Fear and the Fury," in *James Baldwin*, Twayne Publishers, 1978, pp. 39–42.

SOURCES

Akins, Adrienne, "'I Love America More than Any Other Country': National and Racial Identity in Baldwin's 'This Morning, This Evening, So Soon,'" in *Journal of the Short Story in English*, Vol. 54, Spring 2010, pp. 155–58.

Baldwin, James, "This Morning, This Evening, So Soon," in *Going to Meet the Man*, Vintage, 1995, pp. 143–94.

"Civil Rights Martyrs," Southern Poverty Law Center, https://www.splcenter.org/what-we-do/civil-rights-memo rial/civil-rights-martyrs (accessed February 23, 2016).

Coles, Robert, "James Baldwin Back Home," in *New York Times Book Review*, July 31, 1977, pp. 1, 22–23.

"Constitution of October 4, 1958," Assemblée Nationale website, http://www2.assemblee-nationale.fr/langues/ welcome-to-the-english-website-of-the-french-national-assembly (accessed February 23, 2016).

Donoghue, Denis, "Blues for Mr. Baldwin," Review of *Going to Meet the Man*, in *New York Review of Books*, December 9, 1965, pp. 6–7.

Farnell, David, "(Dis)location and Liberation in James Baldwin's 'This Morning, This Evening, So Soon'," in *Bulletin of Central Research Institute Fukuoka University Humanities, Series A*, Vol. 13, No. 5, 2014, pp. 43–47.

Goodnough, Abby, "Saluting a Songwriter Far from Home," in *New York Times*, January 12, 2004, http:// www.nytimes.com/2004/01/12/us/saluting-a-songwriter-far-from-home.html (accessed February 23, 2016).

Kauffman, Stanley, Review of *Going to Meet the Man*, in *New York Times Book Review*, December 12, 1965, p. 5.

Moore, Edwin, "Strange Fruit Is Still a Song for Today," in *Guardian*, September 18, 2010, http://www. theguardian.com/commentisfree/cifamerica/2010/sep/

18/strange-fruit-song-today (accessed February 23, 2016).

Piechocki, Valerie, Review of *Going to Meet the Man*, in *Library Journal*, Vol. 136, No. 9, May 15, 2011, p. 48.

Pratt, Louis H., "The Fear and the Fury," in *James Baldwin*, Twayne's United States Author Series, No. 290, Twayne Publishers, 1978, pp. 31–49.

Sandburg, Carl, *The American Songbag*, Harcourt, Brace, 1927, pp. 18–19, https://archive.org/details/americansongbag029895mbp (accessed February 23, 2016).

Tomlinson, Robert, "'Payin' One's Dues': Expatriation as Personal Experience and Paradigm in the Works of James Baldwin," in *African American Review*, Vol. 33, No. 1, 1999, pp. 135–48.

Willsher, Kim, "France Remembers Algerian Massacre 50 Years On," in *Guardian*, October 17, 2011, http://www.theguardian.com/world/2011/oct/17/france-remembers-algerian-massacre (accessed February 23, 2016).

Wright, David, "No Hiding Place: Exile 'Underground' in James Baldwin's 'This Morning, This Evening, So Soon'," in *CLA Journal*, Vol. 42, No. 4, June 1999, pp. 445–61.

FURTHER READING

Dyson, Michael Eric, "*Between the World and Me*: Baldwin's Heir?," in *Atlantic*, July 23, 2015, http://www.theatlantic.com/politics/archive/2015/07/james-baldwin-tanehisi-coates/399413/.

    This essay compares Ta-Nehisi Coates's award-winning nonfiction treatise on race in the twenty-first century, *Between the World and Me*, written as a letter to his son, to the best work of Baldwin from a couple of generations earlier in its ability to create a public discussion of how far we have not come in terms of white people's acknowledging institutional racism.

Fabre, Michel, *From Harlem to Paris: Black American Writers in France, 1840–1980*, University of Illinois Press, 1993.

    The author traces France's affection for African American culture back to pre–Civil War New Orleans, which began as a French city with a unique mulatto culture. Ironically, behind France's love for black American culture lies an aversion to both white Americans and black Africans, according to this academic history.

Field, Douglas, ed., *A Historical Guide to James Baldwin*, Oxford University Press, 2009.

    Various scholars consider all forms of Baldwin's writing, from essays to novels to short stories. Of particular interest are specific historical events, music, religion, gay rights, and writing in exile. The book also includes an illustrated chronology of his life.

Hughes, Langston, ed., *The Best Short Stories by Black Writers: The Classic Anthology from 1899 to 1967*, Little, Brown, 1967.

    This thorough, best-selling collection includes "This Morning, This Evening, So Soon" as well as stories by Baldwin's contemporaries Arna Bontemps, Gwendolyn Brooks, Charles W. Chesnutt, Alice Childress, Ernest J. Gaines, Ralph Ellison, and Zora Neale Hurston.

Standley, Fred R., and Louis H. Pratt, eds., *Conversations with James Baldwin*, University Press of Mississippi, 1989.

    This collection of interviews with Baldwin and various intellectuals spans many years and subjects. He discusses mostly race and politics with figures as diverse as British comedian and television host David Frost, British member of parliament Bryan Magee, journalist George Plimpton, and scholar and cultural critic Henry Louis Gates Jr. Included is his last interview in 1987, with African American journalist Quincy Troupe, shortly before he died.

SUGGESTED SEARCH TERMS

James Baldwin AND "This Morning, This Evening, So Soon"

James Baldwin AND Paris

James Baldwin AND France

France AND race

France AND Algeria

James Baldwin AND race

James Baldwin AND exile

African American AND expatriate

African American AND Paris

Tony's Story

LESLIE MARMON SILKO

1969

In Leslie Marmon Silko's "Tony's Story," first published in 1969 in *Thunderbird* and later collected in *Storyteller* (1981), two childhood friends from a Pueblo reservation are stalked across the New Mexico highways by a violent and unpredictable state police officer. While Leon, an army veteran, turns to the government for help, Tony, a lifelong resident of the pueblo, is visited by a disturbing vision of the dark nature of the officer's fixation. Set in the midst of a harsh summer drought on the anniversary of the Pueblo Revolt of 1680, "Tony's Story" explores the intersection of oral tradition and written word, individual perception and indisputable reality, and violence and hate. Silko's powerful prose turns the desperate struggle of two friends against an unknown and unknowable force into a battle for the survival of a culture that rests on the knife's edge of extinction.

AUTHOR BIOGRAPHY

Silko was born on March 5, 1948, in Albuquerque, New Mexico. She attended grade school at the Laguna reservation, where students were whipped for speaking in their native Keresan language, before transferring to a Catholic school. After graduation, she attended the University of New Mexico, earning her bachelor's degree in English in 1969. "Tony's Story" was

Leslie Marmon Silko (©*Chris Felver / Getty Images*)

first published in 1969 in the university's student literary magazine, *Thunderbird*. The story was based on the infamous murder of a New Mexico State Police officer by two Native American brothers that Silko remembered from her childhood.

After initially enrolling in law school at the University of New Mexico in 1970, Silko left school in 1971 after she was awarded a National Endowment for the Arts Discovery Grant for her story "The Man to Send Rain Clouds." She began a career teaching English at the University of Arizona, Tucson, while continuing to write and publish both fiction and poetry. She published her first collection of poems, *Laguna Woman*, in 1974. In 1977, she won a Pushcart Prize for Poetry and published her first novel, *Ceremony*, a critical success that became an American literary classic and landmark of Native American literature.

In 1981, Silko published *Storyteller*, an anthology of short stories, poems, and photographs in which "Tony's Story" is collected. Upon being named the recipient of a MacArthur Foundation "genius" grant, Silko resigned from her teaching job to focus on writing full-time. In addition to writing fiction and poetry, Silko is a successful essayist and outspoken advocate for Native American rights. She writes on historical and current events relevant to the Native American condition in society, such as her 1981 op-ed piece for the *Los Angeles Times*: "America's Debt to the Indian Nations: Atoning for a Sordid Past." Silko received the Native Writers Circle of the Americas Lifetime Achievement Award in 1994. She published her second novel, *Almanac of the Dead*, in 1991, a collection of essays, *Yellow Woman and a Beauty of the Spirit: Essays on Native American Life Today*, in 1996, and a third novel, *Gardens in the Dunes*, in 1999. She published a memoir, *The Turquoise Ledge*, in 2010. A mother of two, Silko lives in Tucson, Arizona as of 2016.

PLOT SUMMARY

"Tony's Story" is set during a drought-ridden summer on a New Mexico Pueblo reservation. At a fair held in honor of San Lorenzo Day, Tony is reunited with his friend Leon. Leon, an army veteran newly returned to the reservation, is drunk on a bottle of wine that he has concealed in a paper bag. He calls too loudly across the crowd to Tony, embarrassing his friend. Leon shakes Tony's hand "like a white man" and admits he is nervous to perform in the corn dance because he has forgotten the steps in his time away. Tony reassures Leon that his memory will return when he hears the sound of the drums. Leon gives Tony a dollar to buy himself a hamburger, but just as Tony turns to leave he sees a big cop pushing through the crowd toward them. Tony is worried that the cop has seen Leon's wine, because it is illegal to possess alcohol on the reservation, but the cop is wearing dark sunglasses that conceal the direction of his gaze.

The big cop does not speak but punches Leon in the face without warning. Leon falls to the ground, unconscious and bleeding. His wine bottle breaks. Bloods flows from his mouth and nose and is quickly absorbed by the dusty, parched ground. Tribal policemen rush to check on Leon, asking the big cop what happened. The big cop, a state police officer, does not answer the tribal policemen, staring at Leon's blood instead. He remains in place until Leon is carried away in a police van.

At a hospital in Albuquerque, Tony waits alongside Siow and Gaisthea as Leon receives stitches around his mouth. Siow and Gaisthea ask if Leon said something to upset the big cop, but Tony can only repeat that they were simply standing by the hamburger stand talking. The medical staff tells Leon he is lucky he only has broken teeth rather than a broken jaw.

Tony is dropped off at his house that night: "Stillness breathed around me, and I wanted to run from the feeling behind me in the dark; and the stories about witches ran with me." He dreams of the big cop threatening him with a long human bone that shines bright white in the moonlight. The big cop wears a black ceremonial mask with small white-rimmed eyes. Tony realizes that the cop is a witch: an unspeakable supernatural force. Upon seeing the bone the witch holds, Tony notes, "They always use human bones."

Leon remains bitter over the big cop's attack, growing obsessed with seeking vengeance. Tony, who believes it is best not to speak about the evil force at work, tries to convince Leon that there is no further action he can take. He wonders why returning army veterans always seem to cause trouble on the reservation.

Before the elders at a pueblo meeting, Leon demands justice for the attack. The old men decide instead that Leon was wrong to be intoxicated. An interpreter reads the laws concerning possession of alcohol on the reservation. Leon and Tony leave the meeting unsatisfied with the results.

Tony travels to Grants with Leon to buy a roll of barbed wire for Leon's uncle. At a gas station on the way, Tony sees the big cop inside the store and quickly rushes to the truck to flee. Leon pulls away, looking back in the rearview mirror. He says, "He can't do it again. We are just as good as them." Tony has heard this kind of talk before, from men who come back to the reservation after long absences, and does not put much stock in the idea of equal treatment by law enforcement.

The big cop catches up with Tony and Leon and pulls them over. He makes them both get out of the car, studies Leon's driver's license, and then asks for Tony's name. Tony, who has been trying to avoid looking into the big cop's eyes, finds himself looking into his sunglasses. He sees himself reflected back, distorted by the lenses. The big cop's voice is high-pitched, which distracts Tony from answering right away. Leon tells the big cop that Tony does not understand English very well. Then Tony tells him his full name, Antonio Sousea.

The big cop asks where they are going. Leon answers that they are going to Grants and asks if they are free to leave. The cop tells Leon he does not like smart guys: "They transferred me here because of Indians. They thought there wouldn't be as many for me here. But I find them." He spits out his gum at Tony's feet before getting back into his patrol car and pulling away.

Leon is furious, saying they have a right to be on the highway. Tony does not understand Leon's obsession with their rights. He feels Leon has been separated from the truth of things because he no longer remembers the old storyteller Teofilo's stories about life. They arrive back at Tony's house at noon. The whole family is there, eating. His grandfather says their trip was fast, but Tony does not tell them what happened on the road. His father tells him that Leon is nothing but trouble, but Tony is too worried about the true nature of the big cop to stand up for his friend. He believes that the truth behind the big cop is unspeakable: "I knew that the cop was something terrible, and even to speak about it risked bringing it close to all of us; so I didn't say anything."

After speaking with the governor, who promises to contact the Bureau of Indian Affairs and the state police chief, Leon seems satisfied. Tony tries to give him an arrowhead necklace to wear as a protective amulet, matching the one that he wears. Leon rejects the necklace, scoffing at Tony's belief in its power. He tells Tony he will take his gun with him in his truck from now on, instead. Tony tells Leon he cannot be sure a gun will kill "one of them." Leon misunderstands him, thinking Tony means bullets cannot kill a white man. He laughs and tells Tony he can wear both amulets.

Tony agrees to look after Leon's uncle's sheep camp for a while. He and Leon get on the road early, and on the way Tony daydreams about what the land was like before highways and horses. As Leon turns onto the treacherous road to the sheep camp, he sees in the rearview mirror that the big cop is following them. Tony starts to shake, proclaiming that there is no place to hide from "it." Leon looks over at him, concerned. Past Leon, Tony sees the cop pull his patrol car up beside them, attempting to force them off the road.

Leon continues to drive, half in a rut, brushing past trees. Tony tells him they have to kill it and burn its body, but Leon is not listening. Tony wishes Teofilo were present to chant the correct words for the killing. When Leon finally stops the car, Tony waits inside with Leon's gun on his lap as Leon confronts the cop. The big cop tells Leon he loves to beat Indians with his billy club. He raises the club, reminding Tony of his dream of the big cop with the white bone.

The shot rings out, though Tony does not remember aiming the gun. The big cop falls to the ground dead. Though the cop bleeds heavily, the ground soaks up the blood just as quickly as it emerges. Leon shouts at Tony that he has killed the cop, but Tony asks Leon to help him set the patrol car on fire.

Leon is skittish, as if he wants to run. They wrestle the cop into the car. His dark sunglasses, still in place over his eyes, blind Tony with their reflection until the cop is fully shoved into the front seat. They set the car on fire, and it explodes once the flames reach the gas tank. Leon asks Tony what is wrong with him, killing a state trooper.

"Don't worry," Tony says, "everything is O.K. now, Leon. It's killed. They sometimes take on strange forms." The heat from the fire causes the air to shimmer before them. In the sky to the west, rain clouds gather.

CHARACTERS

Big Cop
The big cop is a state police officer whose eyes remain hidden behind dark sunglasses throughout the story. When he first appears, he marches through a crowd to punch Leon in the face without provocation. He does not provide an explanation when the tribal policemen ask him what happened. Instead, he stares at Leon's blood in the dust. He next appears in Tony's dream, wielding a long, human bone and wearing a black ceremonial mask with tiny, white eyes. At this point, Tony comes to the conclusion that the big cop is a witch, but he will not speak of it out loud, keeping this knowledge to himself. The big cop sees Tony inside a gas station during his and Leon's trip to Grants and follows the car. He

pulls them over, examines Leon's identification, and tells them he does not like Indians. In their final confrontation, the big cop forces Leon and Tony off the road. When Leon gets out of the car to face him, the cop tells Leon he wants to beat him with his club and raises it to strike him. Tony shoots and kills the cop and then burns his body and the patrol car.

Father
Tony's father disapproves of Leon because he sees him as a troublemaker. Tony's father hates trouble and wishes his son would keep better company. Tony is too frightened of speaking the truth of the big cop's nature out loud, so he does not defend himself.

Gaisthea
Gaisthea waits with Tony and Siow in the emergency room for Leon after the big cop punches him. Gaisthea asks Tony to retell the story of the attack, confused as to whether Leon said something to anger the big cop in order to provoke him to such violence.

Governor
Leon speaks to the governor after the pueblo meeting proves fruitless and after yet another incident of harassment. The governor promises to send letters to the Bureau of Indian Affairs and to the state police chief.

Grandfather
When Tony and Leon return from their trip to Grants, Tony's grandfather says that they made the trip fast. Tony does not tell them the truth of what happened.

Interpreter
The interpreter at the pueblo meeting reads a passage from the pueblo law books about the illegality of possessing alcoholic beverages on the reservation, which spurs Leon and Tony to leave the meeting, having failed their mission of bringing the dangerous actions of the big cop to the group's attention.

Leon
Leon returns to the pueblo from the army. As a veteran, he struggles to reconcile the outside world he has seen while on duty with the insular culture of the pueblo, which he has somewhat forgotten. Drunk on wine he has hidden in a brown paper bag, he greets Tony enthusiastically

at the fair where they are reunited. Only moments later, he is punched in the face by the big cop and knocked unconscious. He is taken to the hospital to receive stitches, but his bitterness does not heal as easily as his mouth. He tries to bring the cop's actions to the attention of the pueblo elders but is told instead that he should not have been drunk.

The big cop continues to harass Leon, who demands that he has rights as an American citizen, the same as anyone else's. Leon refuses Tony's offering of an arrowhead necklace for protection, instead claiming he will rely on his gun. When the big cop forces them off the road on the way to Leon's uncle's sheep camp, Leon gets out to confront him. Just before the big cop can hit Leon with his club, Tony shoots the cop with Leon's gun. Leon, pale and shaken, tries to explain to Tony that he has killed a state cop, implying that he will be in an enormous amount of trouble. He looks as if he wants to run but stays by Tony's side.

Leon's Uncle

Leon's uncle sends Leon to Grants for a roll of barbed wire. Later he asks Tony if he would like to stay at his sheep camp to look over the flock. Each of these requests leads to a run-in with the big cop.

Old Men

The old men are members of the pueblo council. At a meeting, they hear Leon's story of the big cop's attack at the fair and decide only that it was a mistake for Leon to be intoxicated.

Siow

Siow waits with Tony and Gaisthea in the emergency room for Leon after the big cop knocks him out with a punch. He does not understand why the cop would attack Leon without provocation and asks Tony to explain.

Antonio Sousea

See Tony

Teofilo

Teofilo is an old storyteller in the pueblo. Tony holds his stories in high esteem, but Leon does not remember them. When Tony prepares to kill the big cop, he wishes Teofilo could be there to chant the correct words.

Tony

Tony lives on a Pueblo reservation with his family. His life is turned upside down when his friend Leon returns from the army and they find themselves stalked by a violent, racist cop who Tony realizes after a dream is a witch. He refuses to speak of what he has learned out loud, because he is afraid it will bring the danger closer. As Leon fumes about the big cop's violation of his civil rights, Tony remains silent, bearing witness to the mounting evidence that the big cop is a supernatural and immensely evil being. He offers Leon an arrowhead necklace for protection, but Leon rejects it, preferring to rely on his gun in case of more trouble. Tony does not think a gun can necessarily kill a witch. He ends up wearing both his and Leon's necklaces. On their way to Leon's uncle's sheep camp, finding themselves stalked again, Tony begins to shake. When the big cop threatens to strike Leon, Tony shoots him with Leon's gun. He tells Leon that they must burn the body. Leon is panicking as they put the body in the police car and set it on fire, but Tony reassures him that the witch is dead.

Tribal Policemen

The tribal policemen check on Leon after the big cop has punched him in the face to check to see if he is okay. They look up from the ground at the big cop to ask him what caused the altercation. The big cop does not answer them.

THEMES

Justice

"Tony's Story" begins with an inexplicable act of sudden violence as a state police officer attacks a pueblo man without provocation. Many of the characters attempt to understand why the big cop punched Leon, from Siow and Gaisthea's questioning of Tony through the tribal policemen's questioning of the big cop to Tony's worry, when he first sees the officer pushing through the crowd, that the cop has spotted Leon's concealed bottle of wine. The cop, however, provides no explanation for his actions, nor is he held immediately accountable. This begins Leon's fruitless search for justice as he applies first to the pueblo elders, then to the governor to see the big cop punished for the attack. A firm believer in his right as an American citizen to be treated fairly, Leon likewise believes that those

TOPICS FOR FURTHER STUDY

- Read Sherman Alexie's young-adult novel *The Absolutely True Diary of a Part-Time Indian* (2007). Compare Junior's struggles to adapt to his all-white high school with Leon's discomfort at rejoining the pueblo. In what ways do the two characters cope with their new surroundings? What resources are available to them to help them feel more at ease? In an essay, describe the unique difficulties each situation presents and the similarities between them.

- Create an infographic in which you compare and contrast the character traits of Leon and Tony. Use specific quotes from the text when applicable and include an additional paragraph in which you explain the significance of Silko's inclusion of a foil for Tony rather than having him face the big cop alone. Free infographics are available at the easel.ly website.

- What is the significance of the big cop's dark sunglasses? Trace this image through the story, noting when they appear in the text and under what circumstances. How do the sunglasses make Tony feel? What is implied by the fact that the big cop's eyes remain hidden throughout the story? Work with small groups to answer these questions, taking notes in preparation for a class discussion.

- Research Pueblo history and culture online. Create a blog in which you make a minimum of five posts on the topic of the Pueblo, focusing on the details of pueblo life provided in "Tony's Story," such as San Lorenzo Day, tribal law, and religious beliefs. Include photos, maps, articles, and helpful websites as well as relevant quotes from the story. When you are finished, visit a classmate's blog and leave a thoughtful comment on one of the posts. Respond to any comments you receive.

who violate this right should be brought to justice. As the big cop reveals himself to be prejudiced against Native Americans, sent away from his previous district because of his harassment of the Native American population there, no help comes from either the local or the state government. Paperwork moves slowly while the big cop closes in with frightening speed. He stalks Leon and Tony on the highways, detains them without just cause, and threatens to beat them with his club. Leon's version of justice, in which those in positions of authority are held accountable for their actions, fails in the face of the relentless big cop.

Tony views the conflict through a different lens than Leon does and decides the situation can be remedied only through taking justice into his own hands. The big cop's racism, lawbreaking, and abuse of power do not specifically concern Tony. He views the situation as a strictly spiritual battle, outside the petty realm of letters from the governor and community meetings. Approached from Tony's perspective, the big cop is not human but is a monstrous witch who must be not only killed but also burned to ensure their safety from its destructive influence. To match the witch's dark magical powers, Tony must rely on an arrowhead amulet and trance-like spiritual state to accomplish the killing. He wishes, in the moments before he fires the gun, for the presence of Teofilo, an elder storyteller and spiritual leader who could provide the appropriate ceremonial chant.

After the big cop has been killed and burned, Tony is as deaf to Leon's warnings that he will be a wanted man as Leon is to Tony's assurances that they will be safe now that justice has been served. Tony, who has watched Leon's government fail to protect him, has no faith in its ability to function outside of reassuring itself of its own importance. In the life or death situation he and Leon face, reliance on his knowledge of Teofilo's old stories lead the way to safety. By killing the witch, Tony has protected himself, Leon, and their families. He is, from his own perspective, a victor in the battle of good and evil and a bringer of justice to the pueblo.

Oral Tradition

Silko's *Storyteller* is written with the specific goal of expressing the oral tradition of the Pueblo through the written word. "Tony's Story" contributes to this theme through its exploration of two characters who contradict each other through their devotion to the written text and oral traditions in

Tony's friend Leon is punched in the face by a policeman and ends up in the hospital (©*Peter Lang | Shutterstock.com*)

turn. Though they were raised together, Tony remains a passionate student of Pueblo culture and Leon, through his travels in the army, has become a believer in the written word: government documents, laws, and bureaucratic order. Leon, identifying more as an American than as a Pueblo after his years in the army, faces the first significant violation of his rights as a minority member since returning home in the big cop's illegal harassment. This in turn undermines Leon's view of himself as now separated from his tribe through his worldly experience. In response, he seeks justice aggressively, through official channels, as if he were "like a white man"—used to fair and equal treatment— rather than resigned, like Tony, to a degree of inequality.

Tony watches Leon struggle for acknowledgment with weariness, noting mournfully, as Leon takes his case to the tribal meeting: "I wondered why men who came back from the army were troublemakers on the reservation."

Leon's fight for his rights ends in a promise from the governor to write letters to those who can hold the big cop responsible. Though Leon is satisfied by this tribute, the big cop remains at large. Leon has not only wasted his time but also inadvertently left a paper trail that will allow the government to track the pair down with ease after the murder of the big cop. The written word works only for the government in "Tony's Story," not for its people.

Paradoxically, as Leon becomes a loud advocate for his rights, Tony—who relies on the guidance of his culture's oral traditions, retreats into silence. Yet this can be understood by the grave nature of the conflict they face. The cop's sinister identity, which Tony has seen in a dream, is unspeakable. The burden becomes his alone to bear, lest he speak of the witch out loud and bring its evil into the pueblo itself. Though he tries to share his knowledge with Leon, attempting to bring him under the protection of an amulet, Leon refuses. He finds the beliefs of his people provincial—fixated instead on the written word of the government. Tony's silence only emphasizes the danger of the big cop. To be unspeakable in a culture that values storytelling is to be the antithesis of the culture itself. Relying on his knowledge of Teofilo's stories, Tony does what Leon and his paperwork cannot.

STYLE

Foil

A foil is a character whose personality traits or behaviors contrast to those of the protagonist. Leon is Tony's foil in "Tony's Story." Returning to the pueblo as a grizzled army veteran, Leon brings back from his travels a sense of his inalienable rights as an American citizen, a dismissive attitude toward the religious beliefs of his people, and the mannerisms of a white man. Tony, who has stayed within the reservation during Leon's time away, retains the strictest reverence for Pueblo traditions, an awareness of the outside world's indifference toward Native Americans, and a lack of faith in the government's abilities to change the state of affairs. Though Leon and Tony share a cultural heritage, and though they remain friends once they are reunited, they no longer understand each other implicitly, as members of the same close-knit community might. For example, when Tony tells Leon a gun may not be enough to kill "it," Leon incorrectly assumes that Tony has been brainwashed by his fellow Pueblo to believe that a gun cannot kill a white man. Tony, however, is drawing on his knowledge of stories passed down to him from Pueblo elders, and believes that a gun cannot kill a witch. In this way, Silko uses the differences between the two men to illustrate the ways in which perception can shape actions.

Motif

A motif is a repeating word, image, character, or theme that appears throughout a work. In "Tony's Story," images of heat form a motif that builds from the first sentence to the story's explosive conclusion. The story is set in August during a harsh drought: dust soaks up any moisture that touches the ground, the sun hangs in cloudless skies, and its reflection in the big cop's sunglasses is blinding, the plants on the roadside are dead and dried up, and the heat shimmers in waves off the pavement. These images convey to the reader not only heat but also tension and danger, with a sense that there is no relief in sight. Only a sacrifice to the heat itself—Tony's burning of the cop inside his car—brings the first sign of change. As Tony and Leon watch the car burn, rain clouds form in the distance. The heat motif sets the anticipatory mood of the story, adds to the setting, and bears down on the shoulders of the already anxious characters.

HISTORICAL CONTEXT

The Murder of Nash Garcia

On Friday, April 11, 1952, two Acoma Pueblo brothers, Willie and Gabriel Felipe, shot and killed New Mexico State Police Officer Nash Garcia after a high-speed pursuit. Officer Garcia had been sitting in his cruiser on the roadside when he noticed the brothers' pickup truck traveling erratically on Route 66. He gave chase, first along the highway, then onto a dirt road leading into the Acoma Pueblo reservation. The pickup truck slowed and stopped, opening fire on the police cruiser. Officer Garcia fell to the ground as he attempted to exit his vehicle, at which point the brothers beat him with the butts of their rifles to ensure that he was dead.

The Felipe brothers were arrested without incident in the days following the discovery of Officer Garcia's remains inside his police cruiser, which had been set on fire on Sandstone Mesa on reservation land. Willie admitted to the crime, but Gabriel claimed that he had attempted to stop his brother from opening fire. Each was initially sentenced to death but appealed the sentence, pleading insanity. Dr. George Devereux, an anthropologist and psychologist, was responsible for the brothers' medical examinations and found that Willie was insane and Gabriel psychotic when the murder took place, arguing in favor of a reduced sentence. In the spring of 1953, following U.S. District Court Judge Carl Atwood Hatch's ruling that both brothers were sane and fit for trial, they were sentenced to life in federal prison. Willie served twenty years of his sentence before his release, and Gabriel served nineteen.

COMPARE
&
CONTRAST

- **1969:** The publication of N. Scott Momaday's novel *House Made of Dawn* ushers in the Native American renaissance, a time of national and global celebration of artistic works by Native Americans. Silko is one of the movement's most active and respected members.

  Today: Courses in Native American literature, art, and history are taught in colleges throughout the United States. A national effort to promote and publish new works by emerging Native American artists and to preserve the languages and stories of the tribal nations guarantees the voices of Native Americans will not be soon forgotten.

- **1969:** After the election of President Richard Nixon, Silko notices that the words *ancestry* and *heritage* suddenly disappear from government documents, effectively erasing Native Americans' ability to claim their identity on official forms.

  Today: Native Americans are a protected class under federal law through equal opportunity employment and affirmative action measures. Tax exemptions are available to Native Americans at the state level.

- **1969:** The Vietnam War rages overseas while protesters at home demand an end to the needless, unending violence. Counterculture movements flourish as doubt in the effectiveness and moral superiority of the establishment grows. The American Indian Movement (AIM) is founded to fight discrimination against Native Americans and holds protests throughout the country.

  Today: AIM splits into two factions: the AIM Grand Governing Council and the AIM International Confederation of Autonomous Chapters. They are joined in the fight for Native American rights by many other organizations dedicated to protecting Native American rights and cultures, including the Native American Traditions, Ideals, and Values Educational Society and the Women of All Red Nations.

Officer Garcia was the first New Mexico State Police officer to be killed on duty. The crime became infamous, and Silko vividly remembers her father discussing the murder and trial with other members of the pueblo, though she was a child at the time. In addition to "Tony's Story," the murder has been the inspiration for Simon Ortiz's "The Killing of a State Cop" (1974) and N. Scott Momaday's *House Made of Dawn* (1968).

August 10: San Lorenzo Day, the Corn Dance, and the Pueblo Revolt of 1680

"Tony's Story" begins on San Lorenzo Day, August 10, a day especially significant to Pueblo history and religious traditions. San Lorenzo Day is a Catholic feast day celebrated by the Pueblo as a result of Spanish Catholic colonizers' influence on Pueblo religious traditions

(a process known as syncretism). San Lorenzo met his fate on August 10, 258, for defying a Roman emperor's demand that he hand over the riches of the Catholic Church to the government. As punishment for his rebellion, he was raked over hot coals until dead.

The Pueblo corn dance is held alongside San Lorenzo Day, a summer ceremony, according Mary Ellen Snodgrass in *Leslie Marmon Silko: A Literary Companion*, "that propitiates deities to guard the Laguna food supply from drought." While San Lorenzo's likeness is carried past Tony and Leon from the corn altar to its niche in the church in the opening scene of "Tony's Story," Leon worries aloud about his faulty memory of the steps to the corn dance, further emphasizing the Spanish-Pueblo confluence of the day's celebrations.

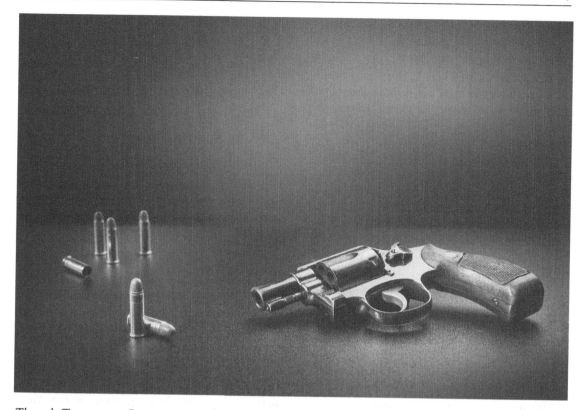

Though Tony urges Leon not to seek revenge, Leon starts carrying a gun (©*Fer Gregory | Shutterstock.com*)

August 10 also marks the anniversary of the Pueblo Revolt of 1680, in which the Pueblo forced the Spanish colonizers from their land after a battle that left four hundred colonizers dead. The Pueblo rebelled in large part because of the oppression of their traditional religious practices by the Spanish colonizers. Silko's decision to set "Tony's Story" on August 10 sets the scene for the violent story that follows, in which confused identities, differences in individual perception, and religious beliefs play an enormous role in the murder of the big cop.

CRITICAL OVERVIEW

From her debut as a young author, Silko has reigned as one of the most influential voices in Native American literature. Larry McMurtry writes in his introduction to *Ceremony*: "When Leslie Marmon Silko began to publish her first stories and poems in the early 1970s, it was immediately clear to discerning judges that a literary star of unusual brilliance had appeared."

Silko was one of the first recipients of a MacArthur Foundation Grant, in 1981, and her experiments with narrative voice have won her wide critical praise. Linda Danielson, in her essay "The Storytellers in *Storyteller*," writes: "The verbal arts sustain cosmic relationships, testify to sources of creative energy, teach young people. . . . Leslie Silko's *Storyteller* is an heir of such tradition and a testimony to verbal art as a survival strategy."

Silko's experiments with writing within an oral tradition bring her closer to her Pueblo origins rather than distancing her from her cultural roots. Arnold Krupat praises Silko's loyalty to Pueblo tradition in "The Dialogic of Silko's *Storyteller*": "For all the polyvocal openness of Silko's work, there is always the unabashed commitment to Pueblo ways as a reference point."

Snodgrass agrees, writing in her introduction to *Leslie Marmon Silko: A Literary Companion* that through the honesty of her fiction, Silko helps heal her tribal nation: "An original voice of the Native American Renaissance, Laguna author and teacher Leslie Marmon

Silko retrieves from neglect and error the history of the American Southwest."

"Tony's Story," was the subject of much critical acclaim. Brewster E. Fitz praises the story's blunt power in *Silko: Writing Storyteller and Medicine Woman*: "'Tony's Story,' the story of the coming together of white and Pueblo, is written and rewritten in blood."

A. LaVonne Brown Ruoff admires the story's originality in "Ritual and Renewal: Keres Traditions in the Short Fiction of Leslie Silko:" "The all-too-familiar story of the brutal policeman out to harass reservation Indians is made far more complex by Silko's use of the witchcraft theme as well as by her use of irony."

Silko is a cherished American author for her ability to reflect the world outside from within the world of the pueblo, for articulating the spirit of an oral culture through the written word without losing its essence. Bernard A. Hirsch writes in "'The Telling Which Continues': Oral Tradition and the Written Word in Leslie Marmon Silko's *Storyteller*":

> It is this sense of life being lived, of life timeless and ongoing, changing and evolving, contradictory and continuous, that Silko expresses with grace and power through her melding of oral tradition and the written word.

CRITICISM

Amy L. Miller

Miller is a graduate of the University of Cincinnati, and she currently resides in New Orleans, Louisiana. In the following essay, she examines the nature of Tony's unspeakable fear of the big cop in Silko's "Tony's Story."

In "Tony's Story," Tony returns home from the hospital the night of the big cop's attack on Leon with a sense of fearful anticipation: "Stillness breathed around me, and I wanted to run from the feeling behind me in the dark; and the stories about witches ran with me." Though this is the only time the word *witch* is explicitly stated in the text, the nearby presence of a witch under the guise of the big cop becomes as much an obsession for Tony as Leon's fixation on seeking legal justice for the big cop's attack. The big cop, too, nurses an unhealthy passion for harassing Leon and Tony, his two latest victims in a string of incidents that led to his transfer to the sparsely

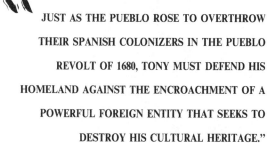

JUST AS THE PUEBLO ROSE TO OVERTHROW THEIR SPANISH COLONIZERS IN THE PUEBLO REVOLT OF 1680, TONY MUST DEFEND HIS HOMELAND AGAINST THE ENCROACHMENT OF A POWERFUL FOREIGN ENTITY THAT SEEKS TO DESTROY HIS CULTURAL HERITAGE."

populated area. Bound by their obsessions, the two protagonists are unable to turn their attention from the conflict in order to seek relief. As the sun stares relentlessly down from the cloudless August sky, unblinking, so are Tony and Leon caught in the big cop's predatory gaze.

Tony receives his vision of the big cop's secret identity at night, alone, and keeps the information to himself. That speaking of the witch would add to its power remains at the forefront of Tony's thoughts throughout the rising action. Fitz writes: "Tony's understanding manifests itself as a special vision, an interpretive insight, which he thinks enables him to see what remains unseen and unheard by Leon." Yet the price of seeing what others cannot see is to be silenced by such terrible knowledge. Unable to raise the alarm, Tony withdraws further into his own mind, to the point at which he cannot answer the big cop's questions because he is too busy adding evidence to his vision: the cop's eerily high-pitched voice and his eyes hidden behind the dark glasses, reflecting a distorted image of Tony back when he peers into the lens. While Tony stands paralyzed in the face of the big cop's witch-like features, Leon is forced to answer for him, until Tony finds his voice again.

Leon is introduced speaking loudly, and his voice remains loud through to the story's conclusion. A veteran who has turned his back on his old pueblo ways, Leon has confidence in the system that is bolstered by the governor's promise to write a pair of letters in response to his brutal victimization by the big cop. The written word means something to Leon now that he has returned from serving in the army and forgotten not only the steps to the corn dance but also the shapes of Teofilo's instructive stories. For Tony,

WHAT DO I READ NEXT?

- N. Scott Momaday's *House Made of Dawn* (1968) was awarded the 1969 Pulitzer Prize in Literature and is credited with beginning the Native American renaissance in art and literature. Able, a World War Two veteran, returns home to the Pueblo reservation but struggles with depression following his experiences overseas. The murder of Nash Garcia plays a role in the novel, as do Pueblo religious traditions and history.

- *Pueblo Nations: Eight Centuries of Pueblo Indian History*, by Joe S. Sando (1992), traces the Pueblo of New Mexico spanning eight hundred years, from their origins as a civilization to the present day. Sando is a Native American author with an intimate understanding of Pueblo culture. The book includes historical photographs and maps.

- In Elizabeth George Speare's young-adult novel *The Sign of the Beaver* (1983), thirteen-year-old Matt is left to fend for himself while his father travels across the country to bring the other members of their family to their new home on the frontier. When Matt meets Attean, a young member of the Beaver clan, the two become friends, bridging the gap between their cultures through teaching each other their unique skills.

- *Love Medicine*, by Louise Erdrich (1984), tells the intersecting stories of two Chippewa families living on a reservation in North Dakota over the course of sixty years. Though both families once were held in high esteem within the tribal leadership, they must work to find a new balance after their way of life is disrupted by their relocation onto the reservation.

- James Welch's debut novel *Winter in the Blood* (1974) follows the self-destructive path of a young Native American living on a reservation in Montana as he suffers an identity crisis in the effort to understand his and his people's place in the modern world. Considered a near-perfect work of literature, *Winter in the Blood* established Welch as a towering voice in the Native American renaissance.

- In Silko's *Ceremony* (1977), Tayo, a war veteran who suffers from posttraumatic stress disorder after witnessing the death of his cousin, returns to the pueblo to heal his mind and spirit through learning and participating in Pueblo ceremonies and stories.

- Simon Ortiz's "The Killing of a State Cop" (1974) is, like "Tony's Story," a fictional retelling of the murder of Nash Garcia by Willie and Gabriel Felipe. Narrated by a young Pueblo boy who has, in turn, been told the story by Felipe, "The Killing of a State Cop" explores the role of racial prejudice in the brothers' murder of Baca, the obsessive officer.

- Chimamanda Ngozi Adichie's *Americanah* (2014) follows Ifemelu and Obinze, two young lovers who are separated when they leave their war-torn homeland of Nigeria. Ifemelu attempts to adapt to a new life in America, but Obinze lives as an undocumented immigrant in England. When conditions in Nigeria stabilize, Ifemelu and Obinze return home to find themselves changed as people but no less in love.

- *The Lone Ranger and Tonto Fistfight in Heaven*, by Sherman Alexie (1993), is a collection of short stories set on the Spokane Indian Reservation in Washington. With interconnected plots and reappearing characters, Alexie's collection paints a portrait of a community uprooted but not defeated, questing but not entirely lost, as its members struggle to define themselves in terms of both ancestral past and present realities.

however, the written word is the idol of another culture and irrelevant to the spiritual battle at hand. Fitz writes: "What Tony sees in his dream is a silent sign pointing to other signs of power, all of which can be construed as long cylindrical instruments of power that can be abused: club, cane, and pen." These instruments merge together in Tony's vision in the moment before he pulls the trigger, as the big cop's billy club becomes "the bone wand," the source of the witch's evil manipulations.

The witch's proximity to the pueblo steals Tony's voice: a metaphor for the power of the written word to eradicate long-standing oral traditions. Just as the Pueblo rose to overthrow their Spanish colonizers in the Pueblo Revolt of 1680, Tony must defend his homeland against the encroachment of a powerful foreign entity that seeks to destroy his cultural heritage. As a loyal student of Teofilo, Tony knows the oral traditions of his people, and his knowledge is invaluable in keeping those traditions alive. Tony holds in his memory the memory of the Pueblo people and passes it down by word of mouth alone. Tony is happy to see Leon returned to the culture of the Pueblo and anxious for him to mesh once again into their shared culture, in part because such a culture gains strength through its active participants. In a society based on oral traditions, every voice is important to the health of the whole. The witch's ability to strip Tony of his voice, then, is a testament to its terrifying destructive potential.

Unable to speak, Tony can rely only on Leon to understand his nervous hints—all of which are lost on Leon, who cannot see past his own prejudice against pueblo ways. Fitz writes, where Tony sees the big cop as "it" "Leon sees 'him', namely . . . a sick, violent bigot, who abuses his legal power, and who personifies blind (in)justice and the written dry law." Though this is an accurate description of the big cop, Leon is all the more vulnerable for his understanding of the world outside the pueblo. Leon rejects Tony's offer of an arrowhead necklace with derision, as if Tony is a naïve Native American of old Hollywood movies rather than his closest ally in a fight for their lives. Because he has lost touch with his heritage, Leon does not predict the direction of Tony's thoughts and does not sense the necessity of the big cop's murder. Even when Tony tells Leon outright that they need to kill the big cop and burn the body, Leon does not listen to him as

he speaks. As Tony is weakened by his inability to articulate the threat of the witch, Leon is weakened by his inability to hear the opinions of others over his own.

Snodgrass writes that the discrepancy between Tony and Leon's perceptions of the big cop "implies the two sides of the Indian psyche, the warrior who refuses to be cowed by a white authority and the traditional Indian who perceives evil as a supernatural force demanding the exorcism of fire." Once Leon secures the governor's promise, his complacency and trust in the written word allow Tony to focus on his own project: the purification of the land through the destruction of the witch. He dresses himself for battle in the arrowhead necklace and, when the big cop next appears, begins to tremble with the certainty of what is to come: "I kept wishing that old Teofilo could have been there to change the proper words while we did it." Whereas Leon, using the tools of his adopted culture, has failed to escape the big cop's reach, Tony triumphs through his faith in the oral traditions in which he was raised. Snodgrass writes: "Left unstated at the end of 'Tony's Story' is the punishment the white world will inflict on the protagonist for murdering a corrupt policeman and sacrificing himself to the needs of his people." The only answer given to Tony's murder of the big cop within the text is the gathering of rain clouds in the western sky: a sign of the end of the drought and the release of the witch's hold over the land.

Ruoff writes: "Silko uses the concept of witchcraft as power used improperly." Whether viewed from the legally oriented perspective of Leon in which the big cop is abusing his authority or through the spiritual lens of Tony in which "it" is an evil set loose upon the land, the big cop is an aberration of power interested only in crushing both men beneath his heel. To defeat the monstrous force, Tony must go beyond the laws rather than working within them, yet, in doing so, Tony may—in doing good—fall to the same laws that failed to stop the big cop from spreading evil. With the witch dead and burned, Tony is released from his silence and can reassure his panicking friend: "Everything is O.K. now, Leon. It's killed. They sometimes take on strange forms." Any punishment brought down on Tony for the big cop's murder will be meaningless against the pride he feels in fulfilling his duty to the tribe.

In presenting Leon and Tony as foils, at once united and divided in their fight against

When the cop tries to drive their car off the road, it is Tony who shoots him and sets fire to the car to hide the body (©*Shi Yali* / *Shutterstock.com*)

the big cop, Silko raises questions of perception, identity, and religion. Both characters are at once vulnerable and self-assured. Tony's unwavering certainty that his is the righteous path is undercut by his inability to speak his convictions out loud. Leon's knowledge of the world outside the pueblo does not separate him from his identity as a Native American and a victim of police aggression. Snodgrass writes: "'Tony's Story' magnifies the tensions in Pueblo natives who attempt to merge their own life episodes with those of the white world." This is Leon's struggle throughout the short story, as he rests uneasily between two cultures without a true sense of belonging. Tony may in fact be too comfortable within the realm of the Pueblo, as his actions will indeed have serious consequences outside the reservation regardless of their spiritual superiority. However, Silko comes down firmly on the side of Tony with her inclusion of the rain clouds, a clear message that

Tony's actions have broken the long, harmful drought. Silko's incredible, unpredictable tale of the struggle of two friends against an unknowable force of violence and evil emphasizes the importance of listening closely, to oneself and others. A story without an audience is soon forgotten, and a culture without stories will soon be silenced.

Source: Amy L. Miller, Critical Essay on "Tony's Story," in *Short Stories for Students*, Gale, Cengage Learning, 2017.

Pauline Morel

In the following excerpt, Morel discusses boundaries and witchcraft in "Tony's Story."

CROSSING BOUNDARIES AND BORDER IDENTITIES: ANCIENT MYTHS IN MODERN GARB IN "YELLOW WOMAN" AND "TONY'S STORY"

. . . Many similarities link the two stories beyond their both incorporating actual occurrences

"

MANY BOUNDARIES OR BORDER SPACES IN
'YELLOW WOMAN' ARE CROSSED AND RECROSSED BY
SILVA AND THE UNNAMED PUEBLO WOMAN, SUCH AS
THE RIVER, THE MOUNTAIN, THE DIFFERENT ROADS
OR PATHS, AND THE DIFFERENT PUEBLOS."

and myths. In both stories, a white figure of author-ity is killed—a white police officer and a white rancher. Both Tony and the unnamed Pueblo woman transgress society's ethics and taboos, although at different levels: Tony kills a police offi-cer in "Tony's Story," in "Yellow Woman" Silva presumably kills a white rancher, and the unnamed protagonist commits adultery while temporarily abandoning her home, husband, and child. The protagonists justify their acts by their belief that they are re-enacting the "old stories" of Yellow Woman and the witchery that their grandfa-thers—old Grandpa and old Teofilo—used to tell. In these two short stories, as in *Ceremony*, Silko posits the need to perpetuate myth and the old stories of the grandparent storyteller generation in the modern-day environment as an answer to the witchery which reappears and brings drought to communities in which power is used improperly, the right order of things is reversed, and the people are forgetting their traditional roles.

Tony and the unnamed Pueblo woman both come to terms with problems of identity in such contexts of destabilized communities by returning to ritual—the re-enactment of myth—as a way of coping with external forces and ordering their anarchical contemporary histories. At first uncer-tain of her identity as Yellow Woman, the unnamed Pueblo woman eventually accepts that identity, which places her in the realm of her grandfather's favourite stories and thereby contin-ues the storytelling tradition. During her first encounter with Silva, she says she is Yellow Woman, then disclaims it: "But I only said that you were him and that I was Yellow Woman—I'm not really her—I have my own name and I come from the pueblo on the other side of the mesa." The protagonist first resists her inscription in the old story of Yellow Woman as an impossibility, claiming that "what they tell in the stories was real

only back then, back in time immemorial, like they say." She is reluctant to equate her adventure with that of Yellow Woman as she cannot yet envision a medium ground, a borderland uniting past and present, modern and ancient, and attempts to draw boundaries between the two worlds: "the old stories about the Ka'tsina spirit and Yellow Woman can't mean us. . . . Because she is from out of time past and I live now and I've been to school and there are highways and pickup trucks that Yellow Woman never saw." According to Hirsch, the protagonist resists her inscription in the timeless and mythic realm of her grandfather's stories because it "is threatening to the narrator, for seeing oneself whole demands eradication of those perceptual boundaries which offer the secur-ity of a readily discernible, if severely limited, sense of self. The narrator clings to that historical, time-bound sense of self like a child to her mother's skirts on the first day of school."

Many boundaries or border spaces in "Yel-low Woman" are crossed and recrossed by Silva and the unnamed Pueblo woman, such as the river, the mountain, the different roads or paths, and the different pueblos. Silva's identity is indeterminate, in flux, neither Pueblo (though he "could speak the Pueblo language so well") nor Navajo, fully human, nor fully spirit. Look-ing out upon the "vast spread of valleys and plains" visible from his home, Silva steps out "on the edge" and describes the boundaries of the surrounding land:

> "From here I can see the world. . . . The Nav-ajo reservation begins over there." He pointed to the east. "The Pueblo boundaries are over here." He looked below us to the south, where the narrow trail seemed to come from. "The Texans have their ranches over there, starting with that valley, the Concho Valley. The Mex-icans run some cattle over there too."

The fact of his rustling the white ranchers' cattle, just as he also "abducts" the Pueblo woman, is metaphorical of the crossing or tres-passing of these boundaries. However, only when the narrator lets these boundaries fall does she come to an epiphany, a sense of self in relation to the stories and to a whole that conjoins myth and reality. As she drowses on a rock in the sun, "surrounded by silence," she claims: "I didn't believe that there were highways or railroads or cattle to steal." She understands that, entering a liminal state, she was impelled by the call for ritual to follow Silva: "This is the way it happens in the stories, I was thinking, with no thought beyond the moment she meets the ka'tsina spirit and they go." When she awakes in Silva's home in the mountains, going home "didn't seem important any more." She sheds her previous "historical, time-bound sense of self," or everyday identity to assume a mythic, timeless sense of identity as the modern embodiment of Yellow Woman. Although the character remains unnamed throughout the story, Silva refers to her, and finally so does the protagonist herself, as "Yellow Woman." The protagonist's adultery therefore carries mythic resonance, and, placed within the mythic realm, is no longer an act of transgression of society's ethics, but inscribed in the mythic hero's quest. Her adulterous adventure is not an illustration of the operation of *id*, in Freudian terms—that part of the subconscious that propels us toward sexual license and antisocial mayhem, (though that is the way it is more likely to be perceived by the other members of the community who have lost touch with the old stories and the older generations)—but rather, as a necessary part of the ritual.

Like Yellow Woman, Tony initially experiences uncertainty regarding the persistence of the old stories within the present, and his inscription in these stories. The policeman's identity as a witch is made clear to him while also in a liminal state, caught between past and present, sacred and secular, myth and reality, as is the case in "Yellow Woman." Sources of division in the "real" world disappear as well as he enters this boundless realm; minutes before killing the police officer/witch, Tony "imagin[es] what it had been like before there were houses or even horses." In Tony's dream, the police officer points a human bone at him, a traditional symbol which serves to identify him as a witch. As Edith Swan explains, "Witches use ghosts and materials connected to the dead to contaminate and ruin the living." According to A. LaVonne Ruoff, "Tony's dream serves as a form of clairvoyance, a technique used by many Pueblo tribes for detecting witchcraft or witches." As the policeman's identity is made clear to him, so is his responsibility, as self-appointed War Captain or Monster Slayer figure, to fight the witchery embodied by the white police officer for the continuation of the community. As Tony realizes they will have to kill the police officer/witch to complete the restoring ritual, he says: "I kept wishing that old Teofilo could have been there to chant the proper words while [they] did it." In Bell's terms, which he applies to *Ceremony*, but which are also relevant

here, "The act of telling and retelling traditional stories is itself part of prescribed rituals. Repetition of story is comparable to recapitulation of ritual." The rituals in "Yellow Woman" and "Tony's Story," like the healing ritual in *Ceremony*, establish the re-enactment of mythological events as a necessary means of identification. The unnamed protagonist in "Yellow Woman," and Tony in "Tony's Story," like Tayo in *Ceremony*, are impelled to achieve or reappropriate their own identities through ritual, by repeating the original acts of Yellow Woman and Monster Slayer—archetypal characters, not in the Jungian sense of the term (structures of the collective unconscious), but in Mircea Eliade's sense of the term—a synonym for "exemplary model" or "paradigm." The events of their lives run parallel to the mythological events which both protagonists re-enact without fully deciding to, "with no thoughts beyond the moment" ("Yellow Woman"), urged along by the powerful spiritual forces embodied by Silva and the witch. By retelling and re-enacting myth through ritual, by returning to the old ways, the protagonists in these two stories give sense to the new, gain a sense of their own identity within the community, as there occurs a blurring of boundaries, as time becomes eternal recurrence rather than linear progression, and myth persists within reality, as past persists within the present.

Like all of the short stories in *Storyteller*, "Tony's Story" and "Yellow Woman" take place within a contact zone, where different cultures lay claim to the same space, a psychological/intellectual/physical borderland. Identity is conceived here not along ethnically absolute lines, but as something intrinsically fluid, unfixed, unstable, porous, and hybrid. Tony and Yellow Woman, like many other characters in Silko's texts, construct what Henry Giroux terms "border identities," that is, identities "that challenge any essentialized notion of subjectivity while simultaneously demonstrating that the self as a historical and cultural formation is shaped in complex, related, and multiple ways through its interaction with numerous communities." Many elements of Anglo-Indian interplay punctuate Silko's texts, which portray the old stories, ways, and mythic figures interacting with objects of contemporary consumer society, such as Kool-Aid ("Tony's Story"), Jell-O ("Yellow Woman"), highways and pickup trucks. In "Yellow Woman," Silva, the ka'tsina spirit, wears Levi's and carries a .30–30. In "Tony's Story," as illustrated in Table 1.2,

Silko also accommodates certain elements of modern society by placing them in a more mythic context: the billy club with which the police officer claims to "like to beat Indians" becomes, in Tony's mind, first a stick, then is likened to "the long bone" in Tony's dream: "a human bone painted brown to look like wood, to hide what it really was; they'll do that, you know—carve the bone into a spoon and use it around the house until the victim comes within range." The red light on the patrol car is whirling upon itself replicating the movement of the witchery, and the officer's dark sunglasses prevent Tony from looking into the eyes of the witch. Leon's protection is his .30–30, not Tony's amulets, the arrowheads (a Pueblo protection against witchcraft), to wear around the neck "for protection"; however, Tony is the one who ends up killing the witch with Leon's .30–30. By having these objects of modern white society coexist in the context of ancient Indian culture, Silko is again, through Anglo-Indian interplay, blurring the boundaries between past and present, sacred and secular. Moreover, she is, as Betonie in *Ceremony*, positing the need for the traditional heritage to accommodate change if it is to survive and grasp contemporary imaginations. . . .

Source: Pauline Morel, "Counter-Stories and Border Identities: Storytelling and Myth as a Means of Identification, Subversion, and Survival in Leslie Marmon Silko's 'Yellow Woman' and 'Tony's Story,'" in *Interdisciplinary and Cross-Cultural Narratives in North America*, edited by Mark Cronlund Anderson and Irene Maria F. Blayer, Peter Lang, 2005, pp. 35–38.

A. LaVonne Brown Ruoff

In the following excerpt, Ruoff explores how "Tony's Story" reflects elements of Native American ritual.

. . . "Tony's Story" deals with the return to Indian ritual as a means of coping with external forces. However, here the ritual concerns the shooting of a state policeman by a traditional Pueblo who becomes convinced that the policeman harassing him and his friend is a witch. Regarding her own views on the presence of witch stories in Laguna oral tradition and on the nature of witchery, Silko says that she never heard such stories until she went to Chinle on the Navajo Reservation. In expressing her agreement with Simon Ortiz, from Acoma Pueblo 20 miles south of Laguna, Silko states that when "everything is in good shape within the pueblo view, then there's not going to be any

> TONY'S DREAM SERVES AS A FORM OF CLAIRVOYANCE, A TECHNIQUE USED BY MANY PUEBLO TRIBES FOR DETECTING WITCHCRAFT OR WITCHES."

witchcraft. . . . Witchcraft is happening when the livestock are skinny"; instances are rare; but when they do occur, they are handled by everyone (Evers and Carr). The treatment of witchery in this story is especially significant in view of Silko's later treatment of the theme in *Ceremony*.

Parsons defines the Pueblo concept of witchcraft simply as "power used improperly" (*Pueblo*). A witch may injure individuals or the entire community: "He may send an epidemic upon the town or he may sicken or kill a person by stealing his heart which is his life or by sending . . . into his body injurious things: insects, a piece of flesh from a corpse or a shred of funeral cloth or a splinter of bone, thorns, cactus spines, glass, anything sharp. . . . He is a potential murderer, a grave-robber, and a perpetual menace" (*Pueblo*). She emphasizes that to Pueblo Indians, witchcraft and immorality or crime are almost synonymous and that the witch possesses the traits people consider antisocial: envy, jealousy, revenge, quarrelsomeness, self-assertiveness, uncooperativeness, and unconventionality. Fear of witchcraft affects manners. You offer a visitor food or anything he may admire lest he take offense; you keep your affairs to yourself, do not meddle, and avoid quarrels. Particularly relevant to "Tony's Story" is Parsons's example of the Laguna war captains' shooting a woman thought to be a witch (Parsons, *Pueblo*). Parsons concludes that at the time she was writing (about 1920), the right of a war captain to perform such an act would not be questioned in most Keresan or Tewan pueblos or in Zuni.

In "Tony's Story," Silko uses the concept of witchcraft as power used improperly. She also uses many of the circumstances associated with witchcraft described above. The all-too-familiar story of the brutal policeman out to harass reservation Indians is made far more complex by Silko's use of the witchcraft theme as well as by her use of irony. Leon, the character beaten and hounded by the policeman without real provocation, is an ex-serviceman whose behavior sets him apart from the others of his pueblo. Although Leon, through his drinking and bold manner, inadvertently triggers the policeman's violence and although he threatens over and over to kill his attacker, he is nevertheless only a passive witness to the final shooting of the policeman. On the other hand, his friend Tony, a traditional Pueblo only wishing to avoid trouble, becomes so convinced that the policeman is a witch that he shoots his adversary and then burns the body by setting fire to the police car. Silko makes clear that the times and the circumstances are such that a young man like Tony could become convinced that witchery is present. The ordinary life of the pueblo has been disrupted by the presence of the returning ex-servicemen, who always seem to cause trouble. Further, there has been a long dry spell—a sure sign in pueblo mythology that something has gone wrong.

The fact that Leon acts differently from Tony and from the others of his tribe indicates how far his experiences outside his pueblo have changed him. As the story opens he is oblivious to the danger of openly drinking in the midst of a festival crowd. Tony's comment that Leon now shakes hands hard like a white man demonstrates that the changes are not merely the result of his drinking. Leon himself admits both his separation from his past and his desire to regain it when he wonders whether he has forgotten what to do during the Corn Dance, in which he plans to participate. Tony's anxiety about Leon's drinking turns to fear when he sees a policeman in the crowd. Without provocation, warning, or explanation, the policeman smashes his fist into Leon's face, knocking him down, cutting his mouth, and breaking some of his teeth. The policeman's sudden violence vividly illustrates the misuse of power associated with witches.

The theme of witchcraft and the identification of the policeman as a witch is explicitly introduced in Tony's dream the night of the attack, when he sees the man point a long bone at him and when the man appears to have not a human face but "only little, round, white-rimmed eyes on a black ceremonial mask" (Rosen). Tony's dream serves as a form of clairvoyance, a technique used by many pueblo tribes for detecting witchcraft or witches. As

the harassment continues, the difference between the reactions of Leon and Tony becomes increasingly clear: Leon's non-pueblo dependence on verbal bravado and insistence on his legal rights seem to Tony to be dangerous ways to deal with witchery, which can only be overcome by dependence on Pueblo ritual. While Leon threatens to "kill the big bastard if he comes around here again," Tony tries to persuade him to forget the incident (Rosen). Leon's subsequent attempt to get redress from the pueblo council results only in an admonishment for drinking on the reservation. As Leon's methods for dealing with the policeman prove ineffective, Tony becomes more and more convinced of the power of witchery. The second confrontation with the policeman takes place after he has forced them off the road. Tony's fear of the policeman's power is so great that he cannot look into the man's eyes—just as, when a child, he was afraid to look into the eyes of the masked dancers lest they grab him. During this episode, the policeman gives his only explanation for tormenting Leon: "They transferred me here because of Indians. They thought there wouldn't be as many for me here. But I find them" (Rosen). Still trying to avoid the power of this supernatural force, Tony persuades Leon to go back home and rejects his friend's anger about the violation of his rights, which is not what the policeman was after: "But Leon didn't seem to understand; he couldn't remember the stories that old Teofilo told" (Rosen).

In his fear and anguish, Tony becomes increasingly isolated. He does not go to a *shaman* for help nor does he feel he can seek outside help. Old Teofilo, whose knowledge he trusted, is dead, and he is afraid to tell his family for fear he might subject them to harm. In fact, he ignores his father's warning to stay away from Leon, who is regarded as a troublemaker. Tony's attempts to communicate to Leon his perception of the nature of the danger represented by the policeman end in failure. When Tony offers his friend an arrowhead, a Pueblo protection against witchcraft, Leon rejects it, choosing instead to put his faith in his request for help from the pueblo governor and in his own rifle.

The final confrontation takes place when Leon and Tony are driving toward a remote sheep camp. The role reversal, which dominates the final scene, is first indicated by the fact that this time it is Leon who spots the policeman, who is following them in his patrol car. The news interrupts Tony's reverie of what the land was like before the coming of the white man and convinces him that the witch must be destroyed. When the policeman forces them off the road and gets out to beat them with his billy club, he becomes for Tony the witch of his dream and the club, a camouflaged human bone.

Ironically, Tony, who advocated avoidance of trouble and who had objected to Leon's murder threats, shoots the policeman with Leon's gun and then takes charge of burning the police car and body. Tony calmly reassures the panic-filled Leon with the words, "Don't worry, everything is O.K. now, Leon. It's killed. They sometimes take on strange forms" (Rosen). As the car burns, rain clouds form, signaling the end of the drought.

At the moment that Tony decides to destroy the witch, he becomes a self-appointed pueblo war captain—a role in which he later involves Leon. The war captains represent the twin heroes Ma'sewi and Uyuyewi, who appear in many Keres stories. The theme of the destruction of a witch by two young men is based on the exploits of these twins, such as their jointly killing two giantesses or as Ma'sewi's single-handedly drowning Pa'cayani, whose tricks brought drought and famine (Boas; Parsons, *Pueblo*; Gunn Lummis). Although Ma'sewi, the elder twin, appears most frequently in Laguna stories as a monster slayer, here the younger man is given this role. The hero twins in the mythic past would have been praised for their witch killing. The formation of rain clouds immediately after the murder seems to indicate that nature approves of Tony's act, which has rid the pueblo of a menace. Nevertheless, Tony will be judged by neither Keres nor natural law but rather by non-Indian civil law. The conclusion of the story makes clear that the exorcism ritual is complete. What the conclusion leaves unclear are the consequences Tony will suffer for carrying out the ritual. . . .

Source: A. LaVonne Brown Ruoff, "Ritual and Renewal: Keres Traditions in the Short Fiction of Leslie Silko," in *Leslie Marmon Silko: A Study of the Short Fiction*, edited by Helen Jaskoski, Twayne Publishers, 1998, pp. 154–58.

Laura Coltelli

In the following interview excerpt, Silko talks about the importance of storytelling in Native American culture and its influence on her work.

> WHEN I WAS WRITING *CEREMONY*, I JUST HAD THIS COMPULSION TO DO HELEN-JEAN. BUT THE OTHER PART, ABOUT GALLUP, IS THE ONLY SURVIVING PART OF WHAT I CALL STILLBORN NOVELS; AND THE GALLUP SECTION IS FROM ONE OF THE STILLBORNS."

. . . *LC: In* Ceremony, *Thought-Woman thinks and creates a story; you are only the teller of that story. Oral tradition, then: a tribal story-teller, past and present, no linear time but circular time. Would you comment on that?*

SILKO: The way I experienced storytelling as a young child, I sensed that people—the person you know or loved, your grandma or uncle or neighbor—as they were telling you the story, you could watch them, and you could see that they were concentrating very intently on something. What I thought they were concentrating on was they were trying to put themselves in that place and dramatize it. So I guess as I wrote those words, Ts'its'tsi'nako, Thought-Woman, and the Spider, I did not exactly mean in the sense of the Muse, at least as I understand the Muse with a capital "M." What was happening was I had lived, grown up around, people who would never say they knew exactly, or could imagine exactly, because that's an extremely prideful assertion; they knew what they felt, but you could try those words and all that follows about Thought-Woman, the Spider, as being a story-teller's most valiant—and probably falling short at the same time—attempt to imagine what a character in a story would be like, and what she would see, and how in the logic of that old belief system, then, things would come into creation.

LC: As is said of some archaic societies, there is a revolt against historical time? What about the concept of time?

SILKO: I just grew up with people who followed, or whose world vision was based on a different way of organizing human experience, natural cycles. But I didn't know it, because when you grow up in it, that's just how it is, and then you have to move away and learn. I think that one of the things that most intrigued me in *Ceremony* was time. I was trying to reconcile Western European ideas of linear time—you know, someone's here right now, but when she's gone, she's gone forever, she's vaporized—and the older belief which Aunt Susie talked about, and the old folks talked about, which is: there is a place, a space-time for the older folks. I started to read about space-time in physics and some of the post-Einsteinian works. I've just read these things lately, I should tell you, because in Indian school, in elementary school, I got a very poor background in mathematics and science. So it has only been recently that I've ventured, because I'm so curious. And why am I interested suddenly in the hard, hard, cold, cold (something I thought I would never be) so-called sciences? Because I am most intrigued with how, in many ways, there are many similarities in the effect of the so-called post-Einsteinian view of time and space and the way the old people looked at energy and being and space-time. So now I am doing reading and what I am finding is that if the particular person, the scientist, is a good writer—can write in an expository manner clearly—then I'm finding if I read along doggedly, reading it as you would poetry, not trying to worry if you're following every single line, I'm starting to have a wonderful time reading about different theories of space and distance and time. To me physics and mathematics read like poetry, and I'm learning what I try to tell people from the sciences: you know, don't get upset, don't demand to follow it in a logical step-by-step [fashion]. Just keep reading it. Relax. And that's what I did. I just went with it. I would get little glimmers of wonderful, wonderful points that were being made. I got so excited. I told somebody: "I'm only understanding a fifth of it, because I never had very good mathematics or physics or anything. But, you know, I really like to keep on learning." That's what I'm doing right now. In some ways you would say what I'm reading and thinking about and working on is many light-years away from the old folks I grew up with, and how they looked at time. But not really. Really what I'm doing now is just getting other ideas about it. Although you might not notice it from the books you would see around, I am working on just that right now. And of course this new book I'm working on is also about time, so it's very important to me.

LC: Ceremony *has a male protagonist, but it is a story created by a woman, told by a woman [but a story] already known by another woman,*

Tayo's grandmother, whose words conclude the novel. Does it stress women's role and importance in the Pueblo society?

SILKO: Certainly, that's part of it, just because women hold such an important position in temporal matters—the land-title, the house, the lineage of the children; the children belong to the mother's line first, and secondarily of course to the father. There is not any of this peculiar Christian, Puritan segregation of the sexes. So there is very much wholeness there. Women remembering, listening, hearing the things that are said and done. There's no prohibition against a woman repeating a funny story that's basically about the copulation of say, two coyotes, any more than a man. There's no difference, but you do find that in different cultures. Therefore, a girl has as much of a chance, as she grows up, to be a teller, to be a storyteller, as a boy-child. And as we always like to say, the women are tougher and rougher and live longer, so chances are we'll live to tell our version last, because of course we all know that there are different versions. I can say I will outlive so-and-so and then I will tell that story one time when she cannot be around, or later whisper it to somebody. But the viewpoint in the novel wasn't intentional; I mean, I didn't sit down and say, "This is what I'm going to do." About two-thirds of the way through I was pleased for what I knew then; I was pleased with those characters. I'm not really pleased with some of them now, especially the women. I think I understand why they're not as fully realized as the men.

LC: There are three women who play a very important role in the novel: Night Swan, Ts'eh, Betonie's grandmother; all associated with the color blue, the color, by the way, which is associated also with the West, yet their relationship with each other is somehow mysterious, even if Night Swan seems to be an anticipation of Ts'eh. Is that correct?

SILKO: I am interested in certain convergences and configurations, where many times the real focal point is the time. I'm interested in these things that aren't all linked together in some kind of easy system. For example, the Ute woman, Helen-Jean, appears very briefly. She's in the bar when Rocky's friends, the drunks he hangs around with, Harley and Emo, are there. She is telling herself, "pretty soon I'm going to go home" and she does try to send money back to this poor, poor reservation. She's just there, and she goes. In one way, if you were judging her by more conventional structural elements of a novel, she just sort of comes and goes. But I would rather have you look at her, and get a feeling for her, so that when we make a brief reference to Tayo's mother, the one who dies early and is disgraced and so on, then I don't have to tell you that story. I'm trying to say that basically what happened to Tayo's mother is what happened to Helen-Jean, is what happened to—on and on down the line. These things try to foreshadow, or resonate on each other.

LC: Actually, the Gallup story and the Helen-Jean story at first seem to be separate stories within the main plot. Do you relate them to the story-within-a-story technique of the old storytellers?

SILKO: When I was writing *Ceremony*, I just had this compulsion to do Helen-Jean. But the other part, about Gallup, is the only surviving part of what I call stillborn novels; and the Gallup section is from one of the stillborns. And you have to remember that when I was writing *Ceremony* I was twenty-three, maybe twenty-four, years old; I really didn't expect anything to happen. So I figured nothing's going to happen with this anyway, and I really like the Gallup section, and in a strict sense it sort of hangs off like feathers or something. It's tied to it, and it belongs there, but its relationship is different. I put that in for exactly the same reason, vis-à-vis structure, as I did the Helen-Jean part. Again, it was important to see a woman caught somewhere—I wouldn't even say between two cultures—she was just caught in hell, that would be the woman who was Tayo's mother, or the woman who is Helen-Jean, or the woman who was down in the arroyo with the narrator of the Gallup section. And the reason I did this— which in a way only storytellers can get away with, narratives within narratives within narratives—is that [the stories] are in the ultimate control of the narrator. But for me there was something necessary about taking a perspective which pulled me and the listener-reader back always. It's tough to write about humans living under inhuman conditions; it's extremely difficult just to report it; one gets caught up in one's own values, and politics, and so forth. And I think I fear too much a kind of uncontrolled emotion. And so it had to be done like that. But it's the old theme, which the old lady at the end articulates: "Seems like I've heard these stories before."

One of the things that I was taught to do from the time I was a little child was to listen to the story about you personally right now. To take all of that in for what it means right now, and for what it means for the future. But at the same time to appreciate how it fits in with what you did yesterday, last week, maybe ironically, you know, drastically different. And then ultimately I think we make a judgment almost as soon as we store knowledge. A judgment that somehow says, "I've heard stories like that" or "I would tend to judge her harshly except I remember now . . ." All of this happens simultaneously. When I was working on *Ceremony*, these were deliberate breaks with point of view. And I agonized over them, because after all I knew that those kinds of shifts are disturbing. But ultimately the whole novel is a bundle of stories.

LC: In a story there are many stories.

SILKO: Right. You can get away with it. I was aware of that. What caused those first two attempts at the novel to be stillborn was that I had a narrator who was a young woman, about my own age. And it just did not work. It just becomes yourself. And then you have to look at how limited you are, and so the only way you can break out of your personal limitations is to deal with a fictional character. Fictional characters are very wonderful. They are parts of ourselves, but then you get to fix up the parts that don't work so well for you in your mind. . . .

Source: Laura Coltelli and Leslie Marmon Silko, "Leslie Marmon Silko," in *Winged Words: American Indian Writers Speak*, University of Nebraska Press, 1990, pp. 137–41.

SOURCES

Barnes, Kim, "Background to the Story: A Leslie Marmon Silko Interview," in *Leslie Marmon Silko: "Yellow Woman*," edited by Melody Graulich, Rutgers University Press, 1993, pp. 47–65.

Bullis, Don, "Officer Nash Phillip Garcia," New Mexico Law Enforcement Memorial website, http://www.nmlememorial.org/record.php?id = 107 (accessed February 19, 2016).

Danielson, Linda, "The Storytellers in *Storyteller*," in *"Yellow Woman": Leslie Marmon Silko*, edited by Melody Graulich, Rutgers University Press, 1993, pp. 201–12.

Fitz, Brewster E., "Dialogic Witchery in 'Tony's Story'," in *Silko: Writing Storyteller and Medicine Woman*, University of Oklahoma Press, 2004, pp. 115–31.

———, "Undermining Narrative Stereotypes in Simon Ortiz's 'The Killing of a State Cop'," in *MELUS*, Vol. 28, No. 2, Haunted by History, Summer 2003, pp. 105–20, http://www.webpages.uidaho.edu/engl484jj/Undermining. pdf (accessed February 19, 2016).

Garulich, Melody, "Introduction: Remember the Stories," in *"Yellow Woman": Leslie Marmon Silko*, Rutgers University Press, 1993, pp. 3–25.

Hirsch, Bernard A., "'The Telling Which Continues': Oral Tradition and the Written Word in Leslie Marmon Silko's *Storyteller*," in *"Yellow Woman": Leslie Marmon Silko*, edited by Melody Graulich, Rutgers University Press, 1993, pp. 151–83.

Krupat, Arnold, "The Dialogic of Silko's *Storyteller*," in *"Yellow Woman": Leslie Marmon Silko*, edited by Melody Graulich, Rutgers University Press, 1993, pp. 185–200.

"Leslie Marmon Silko," Poetry Foundation website, http://www.poetryfoundation.org/bio/leslie-marmon-silko (accessed February 19, 2016).

McMurtry, Larry, Introduction to *Ceremony*, by Leslie Marmon Silko, Penguin Classics, 2006, pp. xxi–xxiii.

Ruoff, A. LaVonne Brown, "Ritual and Renewal: Keres Traditions in the Short Fiction of Leslie Silko," in *American Women Short Story Writers: A Collection of Critical Essays*, edited by Julie Brown, Garland Publishing, 2000, pp. 167–90.

Sharp, Jay, "Pueblo Rebellion," desertUSA website, http://www.desertusa.com/ind1/pueblo-rebellion.html (accessed February 19, 2016).

Silko, Leslie Marmon, Introduction to *Storyteller*, Penguin Books, 2012, pp. xvii–xxvi.

———, "Tony's Story," in *Storyteller*, Penguin Books, 2012, pp. 116–21.

Snodgrass, Mary Ellen, *Leslie Marmon Silko: A Literary Companion*, McFarland, 2011, pp. 3–36, 177, 277–78, 290–93, 316, 319.

FURTHER READING

Corbett, Tom, and Lee Marmon, *Laguna Pueblo: A Photographic History*, University of New Mexico Press, 2015.

> Corbett and Marmon's history of the Laguna Pueblo combines archival images from 1872 to the present day with oral accounts from tribe members themselves on such topics as their history, religious beliefs, ceremonies, and daily lives. Lee Marmon is Silko's father.

Lee, A. Robert, and Alan R. Velie, *The Native American Renaissance: Literary Imagination and Achievement*, University of Oklahoma Press, 2013.

> The Native American renaissance movement in art and literature, sparked by the 1968 publication of N. Scott Momaday's novel *House Made of Dawn*, is examined at length in Lee and Velie's compilation of scholarly essays on such authors as Silko, James Welch, and Louise Erdrich.

Moore, MariJo, *Genocide of the Mind: New Native American Writing*, Nation Books, 2003.

> This collection of essays, poems, art, and fiction on the subject of the disappearance of Native American cultural identity within the past century includes work by Silko, Paula Gunn Allen, Maurice Kenny, Simon Ortiz, and many others representing twenty-five tribal nations.

Page, Jake, *Uprising: The Pueblo Indians and the First American War for Religious Freedom*, Rio Nuevo Publishers, 2013.

> *Uprising* presents the events of the Pueblo Revolt of 1680, also known as Popé's Rebellion, from the perspective of the Pueblo rebels as they successfully fought the Spanish colonizers who had settled on their land, forcing them to flee New Mexico.

SUGGESTED SEARCH TERMS

Leslie Marmon Silko

"Tony's Story"

Silko AND "Tony's Story"

San Lorenzo Day

Native Americans AND prejudice

Laguna Pueblo AND witches

Laguna Pueblo AND oral tradition

returning veterans AND mental health AND addiction

What You Pawn I Will Redeem

SHERMAN ALEXIE

2003

"What You Pawn I Will Redeem" first appeared in the *New Yorker*, to which Sherman Alexie is a frequent contributor. The story was then published in his 2003 collection, *Ten Little Indians*, nine stories about the plight of modern urban Indians. It also appears in his latest collection of stories, *Blasphemy: New and Collected Stories* (2012). Alexie has referred to "What You Pawn I Will Redeem" as one of the best things he has written, and this in spite of the fact that he considers himself primarily a poet.

Alexie is perhaps the most well-known and controversial Indian writer today. He deals in postcolonial themes and images in his poetry, novels, short stories, and films, portraying centuries of American Indian genocide and persecution with a mixture of anger and humor. His own formula, "Survival = Anger × Imagination" explains how he turns his anger to profit with satire. Over the years, his compassion for his characters and all people, including whites, has grown, as reflected in the story "What You Pawn I Will Redeem." The main character, Jackson Jackson, a Spokane Indian, is a homeless man in Seattle. He tells his own first-person account of wandering the streets, trying to find enough money to buy back his grandmother's powwow regalia from a pawnshop.

Alexie's poems and stories pack a punch, seeking to destroy stereotypes of Indians. He scorns the school of Indian writing that looks

Sherman Alexie *(©Chris Felver / Getty Images)*

back in nostalgia to past lost tradition. He also satirizes white portrayals of Indians as environmentalists close to nature. He tells it like it is for Indians of his generation who grew up on the reservation but still addicted to television and white pop culture. Alexie carves his own niche as he dances between Western and Indian ways of looking at the world.

AUTHOR BIOGRAPHY

Sherman Joseph Alexie Jr. was born on October 7, 1966, in Spokane, Washington, one of six children of Lillian Agnes Cox (Spokane, Flathead, and Colville tribes) and Sherman Joseph Alexie (Coeur d'Alene tribe). He was a hydrocephalic baby and underwent brain surgery at six months. The doctors expected him to be mentally retarded, but instead he was exceptional, learning to read by the age of three and becoming an avid reader. His childhood was unhappy, as he grew up in poverty with an

alcoholic father on the Spokane Indian Reservation in Wellpinit, Washington, where he went to primary school. The other children rejected him. To prepare for college, Sherman transferred to Reardan High School, a primarily white school, in 1981. He excelled and flourished, becoming captain of the basketball team, class president, and a debater.

In 1985, Alexie enrolled in Gonzaga University in Spokane, planning to become a doctor. However, he felt overwhelmed by his studies and began drinking to excess. In 1988, he transferred to Washington State University in Pullman, receiving a bachelor's degree in American studies in 1994. While there, he took creative writing under Alex Kuo, his mentor. He began publishing his poems and stopped drinking to become serious about writing. *The Business of Fancydancing* (poems and stories) and *I Would Steal Horses* were published in 1992, and Alexie's success was immediate. Two more books of poetry, *Old Shirts and New Skins* and *First Indian on the Moon*, came out in 1993, as well as a book of short stories, *The Lone Ranger and Tonto Fistfight in Heaven*.

In 1994, Alexie married Diane Tomhave (of Hidatsa, Ho-Chunk, and Potawatomi tribes) and moved to Seattle. *Reservation Blues*, his first novel, came out in 1995, along with *Reservation Blues: The Soundtrack*, a musical collaboration between Alexie and Jim Boyd. The novel won the Before Columbus Foundation American Book Award and a Granta award. A second novel, *Indian Killer*, was published in 1996, as well as *Water Flowing Home* (poetry chapbook) and *The Summer of Black Widows* (poetry). Alexie premiered his award-winning film *Smoke Signals* at the Sundance Film Festival in 1998. He began his career as a stand-up comedian, a poetry performer, and TV guest at this time and won the heavyweight title four times at the Heavyweight Poetry Bout Championship in Taos, New Mexico. *The Toughest Indian in the World* (short stories) and *One Stick Song* (poetry) came out in 2000, the former book winning the PEN/Malamud Award for Short Fiction. A second film, which he wrote and directed, *The Business of Fancydancing*, was shown at the Sundance Film Festival in 2002. *Ten Little Indians* (short stories) in 2003 includes "What You Pawn I Will Redeem," which was reprinted in *The Best American Short Stories* (2004).

In 2005, the poem "Avian Nights" from *Dangerous Astronomy*, a poetry chapbook, won the

Pushcart Prize. *Flight* (a novel) and *The Absolutely True Diary of a Part-Time Indian* (young-adult book) came out in 2007. *True Diary* won a National Book Award for young-adult literature and an American Indian Youth Literature Award. *Face* (poetry) was published in 2009. In 2010, *War Dances* (stories) won a PEN/Faulkner Award. *Blasphemy* was printed in 2012 and gathers Alexie's stories, old and new, including "What You Pawn I Will Redeem." As of 2016, Alexie and his wife live in Seattle with their two sons.

PLOT SUMMARY

Noon

The story is a day in the life of a homeless Native American man in Seattle, Washington, marked off in segments. Jackson Jackson, the first-person narrator, is an Interior Salish Indian whose ancestors have lived within a hundred-mile radius of Spokane for the last ten thousand years. He does not want to explain all the details about his homelessness because Indians like to keep some secrets. He does say that he dropped out of college, worked at blue-collar jobs, married two or three times, fathered two or three kids, and then became crazy. Although he has never hurt anyone, he has broken other hearts and is now disappearing bit by bit.

He has become expert at homelessness in the last six years, having found the places with the best bathrooms and the best free food. He tells the stories of other homeless Indians on the streets of Seattle, some of whom are his buddies and teammates, such as Rose of Sharon and Junior. The narrator tells about serious sufferings of Indians, but he has an unquenchable sense of humor, putting himself forward as an example of the damage of colonialism. He and his buddies panhandle enough money from people on the street to buy some liquor at lunchtime. As they pass a pawn shop, Jackson declares that the powwow dance regalia in the window belonged to his grandmother. They go in and speak to the white shopkeeper.

Jackson claims it is his grandmother's dance regalia that had been stolen fifty years ago, and he proves it by identifying the hidden yellow bead that is always in his family's gear. The pawnbroker says it will cost him one thousand dollars to redeem it. Jackson has only five dollars. The pawnbroker says he will sell it for

MEDIA ADAPTATIONS

- On "Living outside Tribal Lines," an interview with Bill Moyers from April 12, 2013, Alexie explains his change of heart after 9/11 and how it affected his writing. He reads a few poems and a passage from his short story "War Dances." The interview can be found at http://billmoyers.com/segment/sherman-alexie-on-living-outside-borders/.

nine hundred and ninety-nine dollars if he comes with the money by noon tomorrow. To show his goodwill, the pawnbroker gives him twenty dollars to get started raising the money.

1:00 P.M.

Rose of Sharon, Junior, and Jackson spend all the money on liquor at the nearest 7-Eleven and sit under a viaduct drinking.

2:00 P.M.

Rose of Sharon is gone when Jackson wakes up. He never sees her again but hears she hitchhiked home to the reservation. Junior is passed out, and Jackson goes to the ocean. On the wharf, he meets three Aleut Indians who are crying. They have been homeless in Seattle for eleven years. They have no money to give Jackson.

3:00 P.M.

Jackson makes sure Junior is still breathing. He takes a cigarette butt from Junior's jeans and while he smokes it thinks of his grandmother, Agnes, who died of breast cancer when he was fourteen. He wonders if she got the cancer when her regalia was stolen, but his father thought she got it from the uranium mine on the reservation. He has the idea that he might bring his grandmother back to life by retrieving her regalia and dancing in it.

4:00 P.M.

Jackson goes to the Real Change office set up to help the homeless. There, the homeless can buy newspapers for thirty cents apiece and sell them on the street for a dollar, keeping the profit. He asks the Big Boss for one thousand four hundred and thirty papers. The Big Boss who is a kind man says it will cost him four hundred and twenty-nine dollars. Jackson explains he is on a quest to get his grandmother's dancing regalia. When the Boss says he should call the police if it was stolen, Jackson says no, he has to do this by himself. The Big Boss gives Jackson fifty papers for free and hugs him.

5:00 P.M.

Jackson tries to sell the newspapers to commuters at the ferry, sells five, and throws the rest away. With the money he earned, he goes to McDonald's, buys four cheeseburgers, and then throws them up when he leaves because his alcoholic stomach is bad.

6:00 P.M.

Jackson walks back to Junior with one dollar in his pocket, takes off Junior's shoes and socks, and finds his hidden cash. Now with two dollars and fifty cents, Jackson sits by Junior and remembers stories about his grandmother, who served with the American military during World War II as a nurse in Australia.

7:00 P.M.

In a Korean grocery store, Jackson buys a cigar and two scratch lottery tickets. He flirts with Kay, the young Korean at the register, saying he loves her, which he does every time he comes in. He then sits on a bench in Occidental Park, smoking the cigar and scratching his tickets. He wins a free ticket and goes back to Kay. With this ticket, he wins a hundred dollars. He gives her one of the twenty-dollar bills, explaining that it is a tribal custom to share when you win.

8:00 P.M.

With his remaining eighty dollars, he goes to find Junior, but he is gone. He later hears Junior hitchhiked to Portland and died of exposure behind the Hilton Hotel.

9:00 P.M.

Jackson is lonely for other Indians and goes to Big Heart's Indian bar in South Downtown. He sees fifteen Indians there and spends his lottery winnings for five shots of whiskey apiece. He makes friends with Irene Muse and Honey Boy, a bisexual, who jokes with Jackson and tries to

seduce him. Jackson is out of money, but Honey Boy uses his credit card for more drinks and dances to a Willie Nelson song. Irene and Jackson laugh.

10:00 P.M.

Irene pushes Jackson into the women's bathroom for a quick romantic encounter.

Midnight

Jackson vaguely notices Irene and Honey Boy are gone, but he keeps asking for them.

2:00 A.M.

The bartender shouts closing time, and when Jackson refuses to leave, gets in a fight with him.

4:00 A.M.

Jackson finds himself walking in the dark behind a warehouse. He hurts from having been beaten up. He pulls a tarp from a truck and, wrapping in it, falls asleep on the ground.

6:00 A.M.

Officer Williams, a white cop, wakes Jackson, asking what he is doing. Jackson likes Williams because he has been good to Jackson over the years. Williams points out that Jackson is sleeping on the railroad tracks, and he has never been this stupid before. Jackson blames it on his grandmother's death but then has to admit she died in 1972. Jackson also tells him about the death of his grandfather, who was a reservation cop. He died in the line of duty when his own brother shot him in a domestic dispute. Williams wants to take Jackson to detox, but Jackson objects, saying he is on a quest. He explains the quest to Williams, who ends up giving Jackson his last thirty bucks, though he knows he will spend it on booze. He wants to believe Jackson can turn it around and make the thirty into a thousand dollars, by magic.

8:00 A.M.

Jackson sees the three Aleut Indians on the wharf, and they sing their songs to him.

10:00 A.M.

Jackson invites the Aleuts to breakfast, planning to use the cash Officer Williams gave him.

11:00 A.M.

The Indians go to Mother's Kitchen, a greasy diner that serves homeless Indians. There, they feast.

Noon

Jackson says goodbye to the Aleuts and never sees them again. Jackson finds the pawn shop and tells the pawnbroker he does not have the money. He shows him his five dollars. The pawnbroker asks if it is the same five dollars as yesterday. Jackson says no. The pawnbroker asks if he earned that money, and Jackson says yes. The pawnbroker decides to give Jackson the regalia for free. Jackson is jubilant as he goes out of the shop, proclaiming there are many good men in the world. He dances in his grandmother's pow-wow regalia in the intersection, feeling that he is his grandmother, while traffic stops.

CHARACTERS

Agnes

Agnes is the name of Jackson Jackson's grandmother, who died of cancer when he was fourteen. His mother told him the cancer started when the grandmother was run over by a motorcycle on the way home from a powwow, breaking three of her ribs. Jackson thinks she got cancer from a broken heart when someone stole her dance regalia. His father thinks she got cancer from the uranium mine on the reservation. His grandmother is important to Jackson as a person and as a representative of his tradition. He makes it a quest to redeem her stolen powwow regalia from the pawn shop, feeling somehow he can bring her back to life. He remembers her stories as a nurse in World War II when she served in Sydney, Australia. Her mingling with other people of color all over the world has given Jackson a bigger perspective on the problem of racism. Jackson holds his grandmother in high esteem, and it is a matter of family and tribal honor for him to get her gear back. When he does, he dances in it, becoming her, he says, in something like the traditional Ghost Dance of resurrection.

Aleuts

Jackson meets three Aleut Indians from Alaska who are cousins, sitting on the wharf and crying. They were fishermen and had come down from Alaska and were stranded as homeless men in Seattle for eleven years. After they sing their songs for Jackson and he feeds them breakfast on the money Officer Williams gave him, they disappear, apparently going back to Alaska.

Big Boss

Big Boss is the white manager at the Real Change Center that helps homeless people. He likes Jackson and tries to help him by giving him fifty free Real Change papers to sell on the street. Normally, a homeless person purchases them at a low price and sells each for a dollar, keeping the change. Jackson cannot afford to buy the papers, but after he explains his quest to the Big Boss, he hugs Jackson and gives him free papers. Jackson likes him because he is funny and calls him Jackson-to-the-Second Power.

Mr. Grief

The fat white bartender, whom Jackson names "Mr. Grief," serves the mostly Native American patrons at Big Heart's bar. When Jackson is drunk and will not leave at closing time, Mr. Grief beats him up and throws him out.

Honey Boy

Honey Boy is a dark-skinned Crow Indian whom Jackson meets at Big Heart's bar. He is a companion of Irene Muse and is bisexual or "two-spirits," so he flirts with Jackson, hoping to seduce him. Honey Boy dances to the juke-box song "Help Me Make It through the Night," by Willie Nelson, as Irene and Jackson laugh. When they run out of liquor, Honey Boy pays for more with his credit card.

Jackson Jackson

Jackson Jackson (family nickname, "Jackson squared") is the main character in the story and its first-person narrator. He is a homeless Spokane Indian in Seattle, probably middle-aged. He says he will not divulge why he is homeless, but he does tell us that he has tried respectable life. He flunked out of college, became a blue-collar worker, was married two or three times, had two or three kids, and has broken other hearts. Now he is a diabetic alcoholic, slowly disappearing, like the other Indians he meets in the story, all of whom then vanish. He calls himself the "After Columbus Arrived Indian," an example of the race disappearing because of the damage of white colonialism.

Although the story indicts the Anglos in American history, Jackson is not angry. Rather, he is sad and funny. He makes jokes about racism, poverty, and genocide but makes friends wherever he goes, finding and spending money as soon as he gets it. He has a generous heart because whatever he gets, he shares with others. He flirts with Kay in the grocery store and jokes with the white policeman. He could seem pathetic, but Jackson has spirit and is able to command some degree of respect from others. He believes in his own quest to redeem his grandmother's regalia and persuades others to help him on this quest.

When Jackson dances in his grandmother's outfit, he believes that he is bringing her back to life, as in the traditional Native American Ghost Dance. He does not apologize for his life or give in to conventional ways. He is stuck between the old Indian ways and mainstream urban life, fitting in to neither but not complaining. His stoicism, humor, and humanitarian values make him lovable in spite of his behavior. He appreciates the whites who are kind to him—the Big Boss, Officer Williams, and the pawnbroker. He sees that good and evil go beyond racial boundaries.

Junior

Junior is one of Jackson's homeless street buddies, a very handsome Colville Indian. Jackson says he looks like the "Before Columbus Arrived Indian," meaning, a traditional looking Indian, with prominent cheekbones. Jackson says he is jealous of him. Junior is an alcoholic, like Jackson, and during most of the story, he is passed out under the Alaska Way Viaduct. Periodically, Jackson checks to see if Junior is alive and takes his cigarettes and money from his pockets while he sleeps. Junior is one of the disappearing Indians in the story. Jackson hears that Junior hitchhiked to Portland, Oregon, where he died of exposure in an alley behind the Hilton Hotel.

Kay

Kay is the young clerk in the Korean grocery store where Jackson buys the lottery tickets. (In some printed versions, her name is Mary.) Kay is the daughter of the owners and attractive, so Jackson flirts with her and tells her he loves her. She flirts back, but it is all innocent, as she is very young, and he is older. When Jackson wins one hundred dollars, he gives Kay a twenty-dollar bill, saying it is Indian tradition to share, and she is his family.

Irene Muse

Irene Muse is the chubby, light-skinned Duwamish Indian in Big Heart's Indian bar downtown where Jackson Jackson spends his eighty dollars on whisky for everyone. Irene is intelligent and funny, so Jackson spends time with her and her companion, Honey Boy. After they are drunk, Irene pushes Jackson into the women's bathroom and makes love to him. Then she leaves the bar, and Jackson keeps looking for her, but she is gone.

Pawnbroker

The old white pawnbroker gives Jackson Jackson twenty-four hours to come up with nine hundred and ninety-nine dollars to redeem what he claims is his grandmother's stolen pow-wow dance regalia. The pawnbroker generously gives him twenty dollars as seed money, which Jackson immediately spends on booze. When he comes back the next day without the money, the pawnbroker gives him the regalia anyway for free, causing Jackson to declare there are good people everywhere.

Rose of Sharon

Rose of Sharon is one of Jackson's homeless street buddies. She is five feet tall, but her personality is seven feet tall. She is a Yakama Indian of the Wishram variety. She disappears after the drinking binge under the Alaska Way Viaduct. Jackson hears that she hitchhiked back to Toppenish to the reservation.

Officer Williams

Officer Williams is a nice cop who has known and helped Jackson over the years, giving him candy bars to keep him from starving, not knowing Jackson is a diabetic. Jackson says Williams is good because he helps people instead of arresting them. He finds Jackson passed out on the railroad tracks and scolds him for his stupidity. Jackson understands that Williams is genuinely sad for his life. When he offers to take Jackson to detox, Jackson says he is on a quest, and so Williams gives him his last thirty dollars. Jackson is interested in Williams's life as a cop and sympathizes with the danger of the job. He tells him how his grandfather, a reservation cop, died in the line of duty as he was shot by his own brother in a domestic dispute.

THEMES

Native American Culture

Even though the story takes place in a city, far from any reservation or nature, Jackson and the Indians in the story exhibit traits of Native American culture and behavior. First of all, they are aware of their tribal identity and past history. Jackson Jackson points out that his ancestors have lived on this land for ten thousand years. Though they are displaced, they still identify with their origins and relationship to the land. The Indian religions placed them as stewards of the land. They had direct interactions with the gods or powers of nature, especially during ceremonies and vision quests. Jackson is on a self-proclaimed quest to bring his grandmother back to life by redeeming her gear from the pawnshop. His dance in her regalia is an allusion to the Ghost Dance practiced by certain tribes to resurrect the dead.

Jackson is liked by everyone in the story, though he is a homeless alcoholic. He manages to get his way, despite being an marginal figure offensive to mainstream society. In fact, he carries a lot of the trickster archetype, a recurring figure in Native American culture, like Coyote. He is able to con money and favors but then loses them again in bizarre ways, refusing to give in to white values, such as working, abstinence, and saving or accounting for one's money. In the Indian world, even on the street, it is a culture of singing, dancing, sharing, celebration, and warrior values. Jackson is half trickster, half warrior, as he refuses to back down or bend to the ideas of others for what he should do. He never apologizes but accepts stoically conditions as they are. He gives voice to what the tribal people have suffered, becoming a witness for their plight, without being sentimental, strident, or militant. Instead, his humor and humanitarian love are the Indian values that he puts forth as an answer to white crimes.

On the other hand, the author is honest about the unpredictability and unreliability of Indians, even to each other. The narrator swears Junior and Rose of Sharon are his street family who have each other's backs, but they leave without farewells, and Jackson does not hesitate to steal cigarettes and money from Junior's pants when he has passed out. Jackson proclaims Indians are peaceful, but he gets in a fight with the bartender. He shares his last dollars with other Indians, enjoying their company and stories. As he says, "Indians are great storytellers and liars and mythmakers," so although he enjoys hearing other Indian stories, he does not necessarily believe them.

Colonialism

Alexie is a skillful and entertaining postcolonial author dealing with what he shows vividly are the historical results of white colonialism in the United States. Jackson Jackson explains his ancestors have been on the surrounding land for ten thousand years. The moving paradox of the once powerful fishermen and hunters of the land now moving around the city streets as beggars in their own country is the opening image that tells the whole story of colonialism. The drunken Indian may be a stereotype of contemporary Indian life, but it is also a telling result of the physical and spiritual displacement borne by tribal peoples. Jackson Jackson juggles two cultures and two sets of ethics in his everyday life. He explains that he tried being mainstream, going to college, getting married, working at a job, and being a father. He could not do that, and neither can he live like his ancestors. He does not apologize. Instead, he documents the situation with heart and humor. He calls his friend Junior the picture-perfect "Before Columbus Arrived Indian," whereas Jackson himself is the "After Columbus Arrived Indian," "living proof of the horrible damage that colonialism has done to us Skins."

Jackson's grandmother becomes the main focus of Native American history. Seeing her dance regalia in the pawnshop sets off a spiritual crisis for him. The grandmother's traditional dance gear displayed and auctioned off in public is another reminder of foreign occupation. His grandmother was a nurse in World War II, taking care of wounded soldiers in Sydney, Australia. Jackson remembers one of her stories of nursing a Maori man who lost both legs at Okinawa, mentioning how strange it was that brown people were fighting each other so the white people could be free.

The final indignity is his grandmother's death from breast cancer because of the uranium mine on the reservation, a symbol of ongoing economic colonialism and ongoing genocide. This idea of the genocide of Indians as continuing is one of Jackson's more potent points. He is casual about it. He keeps mentioning the disappearance of the other Indians in the story: Rose

TOPICS FOR FURTHER STUDY

- In a group, do a study on homelessness in the United States. Have individual reports cover topics such as how the problem appears in various big cities across the country, like Seattle, Los Angeles, Chicago, New York, and Washington, DC. Describe the programs available to help. Include the reasons people become homeless and whether social programs can eliminate or lessen the problem. Include in the discussion probable reasons why Jackson Jackson is homeless. Could he be helped to live a different life? Is he ashamed of being homeless? Does he fit any profile? Use PowerPoint or other visual aids, like film clips, to illustrate the problem and solutions that have been tried.

- Read a novel about life on the reservation, such as Janet Campbell Hale's *The Jailing of Cecelia Capture* (1987). She, like Alexie, had a Coeur d'Alene father and grew up on a reservation. Discuss as a group the life of Indians on the reservation as she depicts it, using examples that you can later write up in a short critical paper. Broaden the scope of the discussion and paper by doing research on the Internet on the reservations of different tribes. Do they face similar issues? Be sure to include examples from the book and your research to validate your assertions.

- Work with a group of your classmates. Each student should read one or two of the major works of the Native American Renaissance, such as Joy Harjo's *The Last Song* (1975), Leslie Marmon Silko's *Ceremony* (1977), James Welch's *Winter in the Blood* (1974), and Louise Erdrich's *Love Medicine* (1984). Record impressions of their messages and styles in a class blog, with each person responsible for a different author. Alexie began publishing in the 1990s. How does his style and message in this short story and in any other fiction of his you have read seem different from those of earlier writers? Make a class web page that includes great novels and short stories of Native American writers, highlighting Alexie, how he might have been influenced by other Indian writers, and how his work differs from theirs.

- Many books and novels have been written about homeless children and teens, starting with the famous *Box Car Children*, by Gertrude Chandler Warner (1924). Read a young-adult novel about a homeless teen, such as *Tyrell* (2007), by Coe Booth, which is about an African American boy living in a shelter, or Virginia Hamilton's *The Planet of Junior Brown* (1971), about two African American boys hidden by a janitor in the school. Gary Paulsen's *The Crossing* (1987) tells of a Viet Nam veteran helping a homeless Mexican teen to escape the streets and cross the Rio Grande. There is also the homelessness caused by war, such as that in *The Diary of Anne Frank* (1947), about a Jewish teen who had to go into hiding during World War II. After reading one or more novels about a homeless youth, write a personal essay on your reflections of that youth's story, including details from the book. Have you ever been or ever felt homeless? What feelings does a homeless person have that most people do not?

---

of Sharon, Junior, the three Aleuts, his grandmother, all the fifteen Indians in the bar, especially Irene and Honey Boy, leaving him alone at the end, recalling the counting out rhyme of "ten little Indians." Jackson admits at the beginning that he too is disappearing, bit by bit, as an alcoholic. Officer Williams is sad for Jackson's life and cannot understand how he can joke about it. Jackson replies, "The two funniest tribes I've ever been around are Indians and Jews, so I guess that says something about the inherent humor of genocide."

Jackson's literal homelessness reflects the displacement of his people from their native lands (©*iofoto | Shutterstock.com*)

Redemption

Though the story is tragic, it is also funny and hopeful. Jackson uses his humor not only as a defensive weapon of irony but also as a method of redemption. The fact that he can joke proves he is still alive, still in control of his own response to life. His humor is a lot like the African American blues that Alexie admires and celebrates in *Reservation Blues*. It is an art form of hope. Alexie once called humor his green card that admits him to any group. Humor can break down walls and create understanding. Jackson's humor about his own predicament tells us he is not a victim. He retains his identity as Indian warrior/trickster.

Alexie also creates a feeling of redemption in the story through sympathy with the characters and through Jackson's big-hearted love for everyone. He does not judge people, white or Indian, and in turn, others do not judge him. Everywhere he goes, he creates love and goodwill. He makes

friends, and they give him money and favors. They wish him well. Many of the people who help Jackson are white: the Big Boss at Real Change, Officer Williams, and especially the pawnshop broker, who gives him his grandmother's regalia for free, prompting Jackson to proclaim how many good people there are in the world. Good people become a tribe of their own, composed of different races.

The final redemption is getting the regalia and dancing in it. Jackson says he is his grandmother. This mystical image refers to the Ghost Dance in which the spirits of ancestors could be resurrected or redeemed to help the tribe. Jackson may be drunk and homeless, but he goes on his quest and redeems his grandmother.

STYLE

Postcolonial Short Story

The modern American short story gained popularity in the nineteenth century with the stories of Nathaniel Hawthorne and Edgar Allan Poe. They gave the short narrative its modern form as a compressed story with a unified plot striving for a single effect. The modern short story is a highly polished form, with surprise turns and philosophical depth, usually ending with some character revelation.

After World War II, postmodern authors did not feel compelled to stick to realism. With more awareness of a multicultural and postcolonial world, authors, especially from various ethnic backgrounds, began to include more traditional forms of storytelling interspersed with modern technique. They might use dream, surrealism, magic realism, mixed genres, and plots that are not sequential or do not have closure. Postcolonial fiction, in particular, makes reference to the consequences of European colonialism on nonwhite communities, such as the Chicana stories of Sandra Cisneros (*Woman Hollering Creek*, 1991) or Jamaica Kincaid's stories of Caribbean upbringing in her 1983 collection *At the Bottom of the River*.

"What You Pawn I Will Redeem" is a postcolonial short story expressing sorrow for the genocide of the American Indian. Alexie does not use a tight plot structure but follows the meandering movements of Jackson Jackson over a twenty-four-hour period. His seemingly random actions go in the opposite direction of his purpose. There is an element of magic realism in that Jackson gets the powwow regalia, but not in any logical way. The story ends in surprise and revelation, but not the kind of ironic turn typical of modern short stories in which the protagonist confronts limitations. Jackson is rather surprised by human goodness and his ability to get the regalia. Alexie uses many postmodern techniques in his work, including surrealistic images, absurdity, pastiche, irony, exaggeration, and the blending of different cultures and literary genres. Much of the humor derives from the juxtaposition of Indian tradition and pop culture; for instance, Honey Boy dancing to Willie Nelson's "Help Me Make It through the Night."

Native American Fiction

Most Native American fiction writers combine traditional elements of Western fictional storytelling, such as realistic character and plot development with elements of American Indian storytelling that include tribal history, tales, and mythical characters and references. The characters, even if they are living in a modern world, tend to look back to the Indian tradition of a more direct relationship with nature. Fiction often shares with Native American poetry references to tribal beliefs and customs and shows characters on a quest or journey to integrate native heritage within modern conditions. Examples include N. Scott Momaday's character Abel in *House Made of Dawn* (1969) and Nanapush in Louise Erdrich's *Tracks* (1988). The vision quest or personal quest as part of native ceremony to find one's identity and relationship to the gods is often used as plot structure, as in Leslie Marmon Silko's *Ceremony* (1977), with Tayo given a quest by a medicine man to help him heal his war stress. The short stories of Simon Ortiz use humorous anecdotes about the trickster figure of Coyote to express Indian values and ethics of survival. "What You Pawn I Will Redeem" is a quest story, with Jackson given the almost impossible task of raising the money to redeem his grandmother's powwow regalia within twenty-four hours. Jackson does gets the regalia, but more through trickster tactics and his openhearted outlook than heroic effort. The point of the story is not to highlight action or character but to validate Indian identity.

Ceremony

Native American ceremony is at the heart of native religion. It assumes that there is a close relationship between humans and the powers of nature and that the secret ceremonies of the tribes, including chanting, dancing, singing, drumming, and offerings, could influence the fortune of the people. In spite of the fact that most Indian writers today are educated at universities, their poetry and fiction retain the ancient context of language used in a magical and ceremonial way, evoking the powers, rather than simply describing reality.

Though Alexie's work is strongly influenced by Indian writers like Simon Ortiz, Joy Harjo, N. Scott Momaday, Linda Hogan, and Adrian C. Louis, his poetry and fiction have gone in a more satirical and political direction rather than in a lyrical direction. Nevertheless, Jackson Jackson's crazy twenty-four hours of wandering in Seattle as a drunken homeless Indian has elements of being a ceremony to resurrect his dead grandmother. By redeeming the regalia and dancing in it, he feels he has done something to revive his Indian heritage. Alexie, like other Indian writers, regards language as having almost magic properties. He goes beyond lyricism to enjoy language as a humorous and ironic weapon that moves the audience to realization.

HISTORICAL CONTEXT

Colonization and Genocide

Alexie is from the Spokane and Coeur d'Alene tribes. He grew up on the Spokane Reservation in Wellpinit, Washington, about fifty miles from Spokane. For centuries, the Spokane occupied the land in northwestern America—what is now Washington, Idaho, and Montana—living off salmon fishing and hunting. The Europeans brought horses, guns, and alcohol in the fifteenth and sixteenth centuries, thus changing tribal life. Though there was some fruitful trade among indigenous Americans and Europeans, as with the Spokane and French fur traders, the supposedly civilizing influence of the whites was largely destructive to the Indians.

The Spokane originally accepted the white men. They traded, and many converted to Christianity. The discovery of gold in Spokane country in the 1840s and 1850s, however, disrupted the delicate balance. The intrusion of the miners, the settlers, and the railroad demanded the Indians be removed to reservations. The last military defeat of the Spokane by US Army Colonel George Wright in 1858 ended in his

COMPARE
&
CONTRAST

- **2003:** Alexie shows the problem of Native American homelessness in urban life.

  Today: Eight federal agencies sign a memorandum on February 16, 2016, to focus on alleviating Native American veteran homelessness in the United States.

- **2003:** Alexie shows Indian alcoholism with compassion, but the story does not try to dispel the idea that Indians have a problem holding their liquor.

  Today: A study published by University of Arizona researchers in *Drug and Alcohol Dependence*, dispels the stereotype that Native Americans have more problems with liquor than other groups. The study shows Native Americans are more likely to avoid alcohol in the first place, but if they drink, they have the same rate of abuse as whites.

- **2003:** Jackson Jackson depends on the good will of the local policeman and social agencies who know him and try to help him. The National Congress of American Indians, the unified voice of tribal nations since 1944, depends on the individual goodwill of various administrations to help secure their right to keep their lands and traditional ways.

  Today: The Embassy of Tribal Nations is a physical building in Washington, DC, reminding the public that tribal nations have sovereignty and an ongoing legal negotiation with the federal government, as other nations do. President Obama has endorsed the UN Declaration of the Rights of Indigenous Peoples, and the National Congress of American Indians has expanded to engage in collaborations with indigenous people around the world.

---

notorious slaughter of eight hundred Indian horses, shot and left to rot, so the Indians could not use them. This cruel act is mentioned in many of Alexie's poems ("Sonnet: Tatoo Tears"), and Wright became a satirical character in *Reservation Blues*.

Indians were treated as heathens without moral or legal rights. Westward expansion and the passage of the Indian Removal Act in 1830 relocated one hundred thousand Indians from eastern to western lands, leading to the Indian Resistance, or the Indian Wars. American Indians were romanticized by nineteenth-century American writers as a noble but vanishing people (for example, in James Fenimore Cooper's *The Last of the Mohicans*, 1826). This sentimental but dismissive view of American Indians is a stereotype satirized by Alexie in *The Lone Ranger and Tonto Fistfight in Heaven*.

Assimilation

After the Civil War, boarding schools run by Christian missionaries were set up to convert and educate Native Americans. Children were taken from their parents and were not allowed to speak their native language or practice their religion. In 1894, all Indian religion was banned by the Bureau of Indian Affairs, even on the reservations, and Indians were prosecuted for singing or performing religious dances. Alexie emphasizes Indian dancing in his writing as an act of rebellion and authentication of identity. He grew up in poverty on the Spokane Reservation, where he witnessed the tragedy of the notorious Midnite Uranium Mine, where many Spokane were forced to work. The white owners took most of the profit, and the Spokane were exposed to lethal radiation doses from the open pit. When the mine was abandoned in 1981, no attempt was made to clean up the waste that continued to flow into the Spokane and Columbia Rivers and decimated the tribe with radiation poisoning. Alexie's outrage for the genocide of his people, the banning of their religion, and destruction of the land are potent themes in his work.

When his grandmother's ceremonial powwow clothing is stolen, Jackson goes on a quest to find it
(©Nina Henry | Shutterstock.com)

Native American were granted US citizenship by the Indian Citizenship Act of 1924, although they were not allowed to vote in local elections. The policy of Termination in the 1950s and 1960s was another attempt to assimilate the natives by taking away their land. It called for taking all natives off the reservation and relocating them to cities, thus disbanding their tribal groups and taking their lands for their natural resources. Native American activist groups fought Termination. In 1975, the Indian Self-Determination and Education Assistance Act allowed Native Americans to form their own governing bodies and to keep their reservations. In 1978, the American Indian Freedom of Religion Act was passed.

Contemporary Indian Life and Seattle

Many tribes have sued the government for land compensation. For example, the Spokane have successfully sued for the flooding of their hunting grounds by the Grand Coulee Dam. Gambling casinos, such as the Two Rivers Casino run by the Spokane, are one economic strategy for tribes to survive. Alexie suffered many of the native problems such as alcoholism, depression, and poverty, until he was inspired by the literature of the first generation of writers in the Native American Literary Renaissance of the 1970s and 1980s. He began writing himself, creating a profile of Indian success within the mainstream culture.

More than half of the American Indian population today lives in cities. Alexie plays on the counting-out rhyme "Ten Little Indians" in many stories and poems to refer to the genocide in which Indians systematically disappear. Another problem is loss of identity through intermarriage and mixed blood, resulting in difficulty establishing legal identity with the government to obtain tribal rights. The high rate of alcoholism, poverty, heart disease, and drug addiction and the low rate of college attendance among Indians testify to an ongoing struggle to find a place in the modern world. Jackson Jackson symbolizes this plight in his homeless wandering urban existence in Alexie's story "What You Pawn I Will Redeem."

Jackson is homeless in Seattle, where, ironically, Native American tribes lived for four thousand years before whites came. The city is named for an Indian chieftain, and though Seattle has a racially diverse population, it has been predominantly white and is known for its large homeless population. It is a liberal city that in 2014 replaced Columbus Day with Indigenous Peoples' Day. Many local Seattle places are mentioned in "What You Pawn I Will Redeem," such as Occidental Park; the Real Change headquarters for the street newspaper that supports the Homeless Empowerment Project; Safeco Baseball Field; Pike Place, a farmer's market on the ocean shore; the Alaska Way Viaduct; and South Downtown, where the Indian bars are located.

CRITICAL OVERVIEW

Alexie is an acknowledged master of multiple literary forms: poem, novel, short story, and film. His story "What You Pawn I Will Redeem" was first published on April 21, 2003, in the *New Yorker*, which had also named him as one of the twenty best American writers for the twenty-first century in 1999. When this story was collected with eight others in *Ten Little Indians* (2003), the book became a national best seller.

In a review of *Ten Little Indians* for *Library Journal*, Marc Kloszewski notes Alexie's "compassion for his characters, directness in storytelling, and wry and cautiously optimistic worldview." However, Kloszewski describes the form of the stories as "loose and ragged," not the tight form of a traditional short story; even so, the sketches contain heart. Steve Brzezinski, in a review of the book for *Antioch Review*, calls Alexie's storytelling voice "distinctive, idiosyncratic, and disarmingly compelling." He is struck by Alexie's portraits of Native American character: Indians are "perceptive" but have a "deeply conflicted sensibility" and seem "often clueless about their own motives." They are also "brutally frank about their own failings."

Eric Weinberger in the *New York Times Book Review* finds three of the nine stories in *Ten Little Indians* outstanding, a good batting average, he feels. He finds an homage to the writer Raymond Carver in some stories but feels overall, though Alexie has characters, he lacks themes. In a review of the collection in *Book*, Beth Kephart sees life in Alexie's stories

"portrayed as paradoxical and raw, as a maze of questions not even the smartest Spokanes know how to answer." She calls the author "fearless in his exploration of character and culture." *Publishers Weekly* praises Alexie as at the height of his powers in *Ten Little Indians*. Again the loose form is noted, but positively, because these "powerful narratives" contain "long, hilarious, inspired riffs."

Alexie began as a voice for the American Indian and was honored with a lifetime achievement award from the Native Writers' Circle of the Americas in 2010. He also won national celebrity and a place in mainstream American literature, becoming a sought-after speaker and a regular contributor to the *New Yorker*. His territory expanded further as he achieved acclaim as a world author. An article in *World Literature Today* celebrates Alexie's being chosen as the first American Puterbaugh Fellow at the Puterbaugh Festival for World Literature in 2010, an honor putting him in company with other great international authors who had won the distinction over the years: Jorge Guillén from Spain, Jorge Luis Borges from Argentina, Octavio Paz from Mexico, Michel Butor from France, and Kenzaburo Oe from Japan.

CRITICISM

Susan K. Andersen

Andersen is a writer and teacher with a PhD in English literature. In the following essay, she considers Alexie's short story "What You Pawn I Will Redeem" as a change of heart from his earlier message of anger after the national tragedy of 9/11.

In a 2012 negative review of Alexie's *Blasphemy: New and Selected Stories*, which includes Alexie's own favorite, "What You Pawn I Will Redeem," Jess Row, writing for the *New York Times Book Review*, claims that Alexie's jokes have not changed in over twenty years and that his writing represents "arrested development" because "Alexie's world is a starkly limited one." This essay argues with that conclusion by taking into account Alexie's change of heart after 9/11, when he understood the destroyers of the Twin Towers were tribal terrorists. He claims that in this revelation, he no longer wanted to identify himself as simply a tribal member whose anger over Indian genocide and the rape of the land poured out in verbal revenge.

WHAT DO I READ NEXT?

- Alexie's *Reservation Blues* (1995) is his famous novel satirizing life on the reservation. Alexie uses realism and humor to counter romantic images of the American Indian. Through an Indian rock-and-roll band, he shows the alcoholism, poverty, and lost dreams and also the community solidarity that allows life to continue.

- Rudolfo Anaya's *The Man Who Could Fly and Other Stories* (2006) is a collection of eighteen short stories by one of the masters of Chicano literature. His stories contain elements of folktale and magic realism.

- Raymond Carver's short stories, with their gritty realistic minimalism, find an echo in Alexie's style. *The Complete Collected Stories of Raymond Carver* (2009) detail the loneliness, despair, poverty, and marginal position of social outcasts.

- Vine Deloria Jr., a Sioux professor of political science at the University of Arizona until his death in 2005, wrote *Custer Died for Your Sins: An Indian Manifesto* (1969), indicting white Americans for genocide and continuing social injustice, pointing out what had been unacknowledged in American history, and demanding political rights and cultural integrity for Indians.

- Distinguished historian Alvin M. Josephy Jr. edited *500 Nations: An Illustrated History of North American Indians* (2002) as a companion to a CBS television series. The volume includes oral history, native stories, archaeological evidence, and historical documents that show a large picture of the many tribes that flourished before European colonization.

- N. Scott Momaday's *The Man Made of Words: Essays, Stories, Passages* (1998) tells in stories and essays how he became the first great author of the Native American Renaissance in the 1960s, negotiating between his Kiowa and American backgrounds.

- Leslie Marmon Silko's *Storyteller* (1981) is an autobiographical memoir, a collection of poems, short stories, and tribal tales, with memories of life on the Laguna Pueblo reservation in New Mexico. This multigenre format has become popular with postcolonial ethnic writers.

- *American Dragons: Twenty-Five Asian-American Voices* (1993), edited by Laurence Yep, is a collection of short stories for young adults about Asian American teens trying to find their place.

Alexie's satirical anger has delighted audiences through the years because of his humor and wild imagination. His formula from the 1993 collection of stories *The Lone Ranger and Tonto Fistfight in Heaven*, "Survival = Anger × Imagination," has been fruitful in making Alexie the leading postcolonial postmodern Native American author. His bold mixture of contradictory materials, from traditional Indian beliefs to pastiche using pop culture, basketball, and characters like Marilyn Monroe, Walt Whitman, and Crazy Horse in unlikely scenes registers the enormity of the loss of Native American culture. The Indians in his work fight for an identity. Far from simply repeating his earlier rampages, however, "What You Pawn I Will Redeem," written after 9/11, moves Alexie's message forward towards a sort of reconciliation—an imagined scene of redemption. This point can be illustrated by contrasting his 1996 poem "The Powwow at the End of the World" to the 2003 story "What You Pawn I Will Redeem." Both pieces use some of the same themes and images, though the poem's anger is never softened. The story, on the other hand, is full of a wondrous compassion, accepting the goodness of whites who help Jackson Jackson's attempt to redeem his grandmother's tribal dance gear out of the pawnshop.

> FAR FROM SIMPLY REPEATING HIS EARLIER RAMPAGES, HOWEVER, 'WHAT YOU PAWN I WILL REDEEM,' WRITTEN AFTER 9/11, MOVES ALEXIE'S MESSAGE FORWARD TOWARDS A SORT OF RECONCILIATION—AN IMAGINED SCENE OF REDEMPTION."

In the poem, the speaker addresses a hostile white audience, complaining they want him to exercise Christian forgiveness for their crimes on his people. He asserts he will never forgive until the atrocities are undone and he can dance at a powwow with his resurrected ancestors at the end of the world. The poem names the atrocities to the land, besides the decimation of the people. The Grand Coulee Dam was built on the Columbia River between 1933 and 1942 for hydroelectric power. It flooded more than twenty thousand acres where Indians lived and hunted for thousands of years. It ended traditional ways for Alexie's Spokane tribe, such as salmon fishing, mourned by thousands of Northwest Indians gathered at the Ceremony of Tears at Kettle Falls in 1940. The speaker of the poem says he will not forgive until all the dams are burst and the waters find their way to the mouth of the Columbia and to the ocean, so the salmon can return. He calls for the nuclear reactors of Hanford to be destroyed. There are similar references in "What You Pawn" as Jackson speaks of the Aleut Indians, once fishermen, sitting on a bench by the ocean and crying for their lost way of life. Jackson also insinuates that his grandmother, Agnes, was killed by nuclear poisoning from the uranium mine on the reservation. The poem "The Powwow" is a dramatic verbal ceremony by the last tribal man with the purpose to destroy white civilization and to bring back the salmon and ancient ways. It ends with an evocation of the Ghost Dance, or Prophet's Dance, to resurrect the dead.

"What You Pawn" takes place in the city, and Jackson Jackson seems to be the last Indian standing in the story. He performs a miracle by getting his grandmother's regalia from the pawnshop without money and dances his grandmother back to life, in a sense,

once again evoking the image of the Ghost Dance that can resurrect ancestors. Like other Indian authors, Alexie understands the arts in both cultural and ceremonial ways. Poetry (language) and dance are therefore references to the way the persona of the poem and narrator of the story can correct the wrongs done to Indians, through ceremony. There is power in Native American language and dance that can subvert white dominance and change things through sympathetic magic. For a moment, Jackson Jackson brings back the tribal power as he dances and becomes his grandmother.

The difference in "What You Pawn" is that it is not a story of revenge or reversal, as in the poem "The Powwow at the End of the World." The story is not about Indian versus white, but people helping other people. The whites—the pawnbroker, Big Boss at the homeless center, and Officer Williams, whom Jackson names as a good cop—come forward with genuine goodwill to give him money, encouragement, and friendship. In his grief, Jackson is still able to find faith in the human race at large. In this story, Alexie's anger has shifted to sorrow mixed with hope. There *is* a sense of forgiveness.

Jackson's journey is a quest not only to find his grandmother's regalia and legacy but also to find a new, more universal tribe that transcends race. His found tribe includes Indians from other tribes, like Junior and Rose of Sharon, the Aleuts, Irene and Honey Boy, but also Kay, the Korean store clerk, and the white characters. All of these people accept each other without judgment. They may not live in the best of worlds, but they are trying to make the best of it. This was the moral of the 9/11 tragedy for many Americans as they watched a multicultural New York City come forward together in courageous and unselfish solidarity during the crisis. Daniel Grassian in *Understanding Sherman Alexie* finds the collection of stories in *Ten Little Indians* to be "somewhat postethnic" because they describe Indians in between white and native cultures, perhaps going in the direction of mainstream life, as Alexie himself did. Margaret O'Shaughnessy agrees in "Sherman Alexie's Transformation of 'Ten Little Indians'": "The stories in *Ten Little Indians* are less about what makes one distinctively Indian than being human and alive."

Some readers have struggled with the question of whether Alexie has a moral vision beyond anger. He is known for portraying poverty, drug and alcohol abuse, profanity, violence, death, and explicit sexuality and homosexuality. Both white and Native American readers have been offended, for many Indians are incensed at his negative portrayal of Indians. Certainly, the homeless and alcoholic Indians in this story are no role models. Heather Bruce, Anna Baldwin, and Christabel Umphrey, authors of *Sherman Alexie in the Classroom*, are high school teachers who teach Alexie both on and off the reservation. They claim that "Alexie's blend of anger, humorous disregard, and imaginative creativity gives [students] reason to hope for survival in a dangerous world, gives them reason to speak up and be counted." Most teens of any ethnic group find him appealing because of his use of pop culture and sports like basketball as a common language. He speaks of life's darker challenges with honesty. His style also makes him accessible to a wide variety of readers. According to Bruce, Baldwin, and Umphrey, "Alexie is a master satirist who provides poignant and humorous access to his described Indian worlds." These teachers help students see his in-your-face style as a challenge to mainstream culture. The poverty of his characters, for instance, is turned around as a condition that creates community: "Alexie portrays American Indians as battered but resilient survivors of an unacknowledged American genocide."

In "Survival = Anger × Imagination: Sherman Alexie's Dark Humor," Philip Heldrich writes of Alexie as a black humorist in company with other postmodern authors registering the absurdity of life. For a black humorist, no subject is taboo for satire or blasphemy. In his famous formula, "Survival = Anger × Imagination," it is the imagination ingredient that has made Alexie successful rather than the anger, as Alexie himself has acknowledged. Anger may supply a certain fuel, but unless it can be transformed to something useful, it is destructive. He himself gives the credit to art as opening doors that have been closed owing to the cruelty of the past. Jeff Berglund, in "The Business of Writing," mentions that Alexie "has fashioned and refashioned his authorial persona" to be an ongoing voice for Indian culture: "He has bridged the pop, academic, and literary divide." Alexie's short stories are best sellers; he produces popular films like "Smoke Signals"; he has been a stand-up comedian on the Jon Stewart and Stephen Colbert shows; he is a model performer for students in poetry slams; and he is taught as a serious author in college classrooms.

But more than this, one could argue that Alexie is a sort of moral leader in not being ashamed either of pointing out social injustice or rejecting his own narrow thinking. In many interviews, such as the one with Tanita Davis and Sarah Stevenson in 2007, he has expressed his epiphany during 9/11 that tribalism in certain of its aspects must be transcended for a larger humanitarian view. He has gone so far as to disown his novel *Indian Killer* (1996) for its racism. Art and humor, on the other hand, create bridges and understanding. Grassian claims Alexie is a "serious moral and ethical writer." Jackson Jackson is not a recognizable hero type with whom most readers can identify, but his funny, Coyote trickster-like character, getting himself in and out of trouble with his clever wit, and his humanitarian vision of love and sharing are appealing. Alexie told interviewer Ase Nygren that his religion is now art and that he regards his own stories as a kind of prayer. "What You Pawn I Will Redeem" is certainly a kind of prayer for transcending the anger and thinking of the past.

Source: Susan K. Andersen, Critical Essay on "What You Pawn I Will Redeem," in *Short Stories for Students*, Gale, Cengage Learning, 2017.

Jeff Berglund

In the following excerpt, Berglund explains that Alexie challenges stereotypes about Native Americans in his work.

. . . Nonetheless, he knows that he will always be labeled an "Indian writer," no matter what his focus is. Instead of worrying about limits imposed from without, including the critique that he is obsessed with popular culture, Alexie parodies the expectations of Native writers in poems such as "How to Write the Great American Indian Novel" and his essay/memoir "The Unauthorized Autobiography of Me," and through characters like Jack Wilson in the novel *Indian Killer*. In later works such as "The Search Engine" from *Ten Little Indians* and his film *The Business of Fancydancing*, he continues to question expectations placed on Indigenous writers, something considered explicitly in my essay, "The Business of Writing: Sherman Alexie's Meditations on Authorship," included in this collection.

The story takes place over a single day in Seattle as Jackson tries to come up with the money to retrieve the family heirloom from a pawn shop (©TomKli / Shutterstock.com)

In most of his writing, Alexie reshapes readers' attitudes about Native people, particularly notions based on stereotypes and misinformation. Taking on all the wannabe Indians out there, the Hollywood stereotypes, and the pop-culture heroes, he has the narrator of the first poem in his first collection of poems, *I Would Steal Horses*, declare to the world: "I got eyes, Jack," eyes that can see and a voice that can decry five hundred years of injustice. More recently, his poetry and fiction dismantle stereotypes by their subject matter—subject matter that has no overt, stereotypical, or exclusive connection to Indigenous culture—whether it be the father-son relationship in "The Senator's Son," or the ethnically unidentified owner of a lucrative used-clothing business who is a serial adulterer in "The Ballad of Paul Nonetheless," or the poems dedicated to now-antiquated fixations of the poet's young adulthood in the 1980s: "An Ode to Pay Phones" or "Ode to Mixed Tapes," all in *War Dances*.

Over the years, scholars such as Elizabeth Cook-Lynn (Dakota), who is often the target of

Alexie's critique of the contemporary state of academia, have criticized him for not appropriately focusing on issues related to Native sovereignty. Alexie continues to confront such critiques directly and indirectly by finding a unique way to view subjects that compel him as an Indian man, an artist, a U.S. citizen living in the media-saturated early twenty-first century and discovering what may be called the "sovereignty of self": "My sobriety does give me sovereignty. Most Indians use 'sovereignty' to refer to the collective and tribal desire for political, cultural and economic independence. But I am using it here to mean 'the individual Indian artist's basic right to be an eccentric bastard'" (*Face*). He suggests that the critics who chastise him for not writing in the service of sovereign nationalism—and he includes Cook-Lynn in this group—are "dying of nostalgia. She had taken nostalgia as her false idol—her thin blanket—and it was murdering her" (*WD*).

While Alexie's characters and subject matter are most often rooted in lives that have been influenced by the Spokane or Coeur d'Alene cultural experience, on the reservation or off, his artistic reach is pantribal. For example, his repeated references to Crazy Horse, the Ghost Dance, Sand Creek, or Wounded Knee—to name several associations—assert a shared history among Native peoples across space and time. For example, the speaker—perhaps Alexie himself in "Looking Glass" from *War Dances*—represents the well-known Nez Perce leader, Chief Joseph, as a family familiar, one of his grandmother's favorite babysitters, and a loving man whose famous words of surrender were taken out of context. And, in the same collection, Alexie offers a correction to American history's remembrance of the Lincoln who signed the Emancipation Proclamation: a year before in 1862, he had approved "the largest public execution" in United States history; "Another Proclamation" remembers the thirty-seven Sioux hung in Minnesota and vividly calls on readers to imagine the "cacophony of thirty-seven different death songs" (*WD*). Alexie—being Alexie—asks us to imagine the one pardoned survivor's mourning song and poses the question, "If he taught you the words, do you think you would sing along?" (*WD*). In other words, will you honor his memory and sense of injustice, or will you sustain the historical fiction and comfortable myths about a leader such as Lincoln?

Alexie acknowledges a responsibility to other American Indian people to build a better, less-factionalized America, but he's not interested in making his readers feel comfortable or complacent or fulfilling anyone's expectations. He knows that even poets suffer from illusions about possibility: "Why do poets think / They can change the world?" Alexie's speaker asks at the outset of his twenty-first book (*WD*). If anything, he works to frustrate complacency, even in his view about the role of writing and art: "The only life I can save / Is my own" (*WD*). His series of poems—"The Alcoholic Love Poems"—from *First Indian on the Moon* (1993) is just one example of the way his writing confronts readers without pretense. Readers see the poet trying to come to terms with his family legacies, his own personal demons, and internal conflicts difficult to resolve easily. In "Shoes" from his book *Old Shirts and New Skins* (1993), Alexie asks, "How do you explain the survival of all of us who were never meant to survive?"

In other contexts, Alexie offers a personal answer to this rhetorical question. For example,

in "Imagining the Reservation" from *The Lone Ranger and Tonto Fistfight in Heaven*, he writes, "Survival = Anger × Imagination. Imagination is the only weapon on the reservation." By the time "The Unauthorized Autobiography of Me" was published in *One Stick Song*, this formula had been transformed into "Poetry = Anger × Imagination," leading to the conclusion that "Survival = Poetry." Anger is a likely reaction to deep economic, social, and political inequities, but it is a self-destructive force if left to fester. If mediated through the creative process of poetry making, though, anger can be transformed into survival.

> *How can we imagine a new language when the language of the enemy keeps our dismembered tongues tied to his belt?*—Sherman Alexie, "Imagining the Reservation," *The Lone Ranger and Tonto Fistfight in Heaven*

Sherman Alexie's transformative imagination and the vivid contrasts in the range of his writing to date have kept scholars and teachers racing to keep pace with his literary output. Anyone who has taught Alexie's writing knows that it energizes students and provokes deep thought about complex subjects. His work appeals to readers who are interested in mining the dimensions of our human experiences, but it also demands a different kind of literary analysis than that currently practiced in the academy. Over the years, Alexie has criticized how out of sync contemporary criticism is from the real world that readers—Native and non-Native alike—inhabit. This collection asks readers to rise to the challenge of finding a meaningful intersection with Alexie's writing through the various scholarly points of entry into the world of his characters and poetic vision. . . .

Source: Jeff Berglund, "An Introduction to Sherman Alexie," in *Sherman Alexie: A Collection of Critical Essays*, edited by Jeff Berglund and Jan Roush, University of Utah Press, 2010, pp. xxvii–xxx.

Daniel Grassian

In the following excerpt, Grassian asserts that the stories in the collection Ten Little Indians *reflect a specifically post-9/11 view of America.*

With his recent collection *Ten Little Indians* (2003), Alexie continues the exploration of urban Indians that he began with *The Toughest Indian in the World*. *Ten Little Indians* has much in common with *The Toughest Indian in the World*: an emphasis placed on sexuality, for instance, although not on homosexuality this time.

> ONE EITHER COMPLETELY GRIEVED FOR
> ALL THE VICTIMS AND WHOLEHEARTEDLY
> SUPPORTED THE COUNTRY OR ONE WAS BRANDED
> UNPATRIOTIC, A SUPPORTER OF TERRORISM
> AND OSAMA BIN LADEN."

However, the characters in *Ten Little Indians* are more comfortably situated between the Indian and white worlds. Whereas in *The Toughest Indian in the World* Alexie's characters tended to obsessively question the codes of Indian authenticity, in *Ten Little Indians* the major characters are less concerned with their ethnic identity. Being "Indian," while still important, is not the primary determinant of these characters' identities. This is not to suggest that Alexie or the characters themselves have found some happy medium between the reservation and city. Rather, most are socially isolated. However, their isolation is just as often caused by nonethnic reasons as ethnic reasons: poor family relations, psychological problems, and a patriarchal American culture.

. . . That many of the characters in *Ten Little Indians* are more generically American and less specifically Indian may in part be due to the fact that some, it not all, of the stories were written shortly after the events of September 11, 2001, which at least temporarily seemed to efface ethnicity in America. In the story "Can I Get a Witness?" a disgruntled, near-suicidal Spokane Indian woman/wife/mother survives a post-9/11 restaurant bombing in Seattle. The woman, who works as a paralegal, feels she is merely floating through her assigned roles in life as a mother, wife, and worker: "She was a parawife and a paramother and a parafriend." The bombing helps jar her from her routine and provides her with an escape route from her dreary life. Later in the story, she admits that she was happy when she first saw the bomber because, "I knew I was going to survive. I was going to live, and I was going to crawl out of the ruins, and I was going to walk away from my life. I knew they'd never find me and would figure I was dead." With the aftermath of the bombing, Alexie also makes some

connections between violence and sexuality. The woman immediately thinks of having sex with a middle-aged white man who inquires after her. While she immediately labels herself "perverse" for having erotic thoughts, she then considers that it might be a "reflexive and natural reaction." If her thoughts are abnormal and perverse, then her "perversity" may be a by-product of the media. Indeed, the woman recalls how her colleagues seemed to be erotically charged when they watched the twin towers collapse during 9/11. Therefore, she concludes, "We're so used to sex on TV that everything on TV becomes sexy, she thought." It is more likely a natural reaction, however, and the woman offers some support for that theory with a half-in-jest proposition, but one that points to the importance of sexuality in virtually every human activity. Considering that most Islamic suicide bombers believe they will be rewarded in an afterlife with willing, submissive virgins, the woman concludes: "Political posturing aside, didn't a few thousand stupid men believe terrorism was another way to get laid? What would happen if the United States offered seventy-three virgins to each terrorist if he would abstain from violence? Instead of deploying an army of pissed-off U.S. soldiers to Afghanistan and Iraq, we could send a mercy team of patriotic virgins." While this is hardly a realistic solution, it does identify how repressed sexuality may be a catalyst for terrorism, an idea rarely if ever discussed in contemporary society.

Still, this story is not so much about sexuality as it is a criticism of the post-9/11 atmosphere of American nationalism, which considered all victims to be saintly heroes, the country to be virtually without fault, and sparked a desire for retribution. The middle-aged man, a rather arrogant person whose ex-wife called him "Mr. Funny," for his constant joke telling, represents an archetypal American, too self-assured and materialistic. Alexie exposes his hidden faults with the fact that he was working on a computer game right before September 11, in which a person could play a terrorist who attacks American interests. After changing the game so that the players take the role of cops hunting terrorists (instead of vice versa), the game becomes hugely successful. The man suffers bouts of guilt due to his materialism, sometimes wondering "if he was a monster, making the games he made and earning the money he earned." His extreme arrogance wins out, concluding that "I'm the highlight of every party. I'm the best dinner guest in the history of the world. I can make any woman fall in love with me in under five minutes and alienate her five minutes later."

Reacting against what she believes to be the "grief porn" of the post-9/11 media coverage, the woman insists that the attacks may not have been a complete tragedy in the sense that not all the victims were saintly and some, in fact, may have been despicable. Thereby, she argues that it is wrong to idealize all the victims of the attacks. She asks the man to consider that some "victims" might have been amoral and vicious individuals who physically abused their families and therefore "maybe . . . did deserve to die." While the woman's reasoning doesn't in any way justify the actions of the terrorists, it does identify that there was a post-9/11 either/or dichotomy in America. One either completely grieved for all the victims and wholeheartedly supported the country or one was branded unpatriotic, a supporter of terrorism and Osama bin Laden. A person who tried to take a middle stance, like this woman, would have been considered by most to be in cahoots with the terrorists. This either/or dichotomy helped turn the woman's Indian husband and sons into flag-waving patriots and led her sons to want to be Marines, unaware or choosing to ignore that their purported love of America clashes with this country's treatment of Indians. The woman notes, "How could any Indian put on an U.S. military uniform and not die of toxic irony?"

Furthermore, through the woman, Alexie also suggests that the roots of 9/11 may also be entrenched in the codes of male authenticity, stemming from the desire to prove one's superiority through aggression and violence. If the main culprit behind the terrorist attacks is masculinity, then the man, "Mr. Funny," suffers from deficiencies similar to those of the terrorists, except that he does not seek to prove his manhood through killing others but through saving, even loving, the woman. Furthermore, the man's huge, unfounded self-confidence and arrogance are dangerous in the sense that he perceives himself to be better than virtually everyone else. "He wanted his love to be different than everybody else's," Alexie writes. "He wanted his love to be the only true image of God. He wanted his love to be the tyrant that saved the world no matter if the world desired to be saved." Still, his encounter with the woman helps change his perspective. When he goes

outside with the woman, instead of seeing benevolent passersby, he imagines the horrific secrets each holds: "He knew that man cheated on his wife with her sister and that woman pinched her Alzheimered mother's arms until they bled. And that teenage boy set dogs on fire and that pretty teenaged girl once knocked down a fat ugly girl and spit in her mouth." The man finally concludes, "We're all failures." Due to his revelation, the man begins to shed his arrogant, ultraconfident facade, evidenced by the fact that he no longer feels that he can save the woman but that if he loves the woman "he might be saved." The fact that he lets the woman go after she breaks away from him also shows a newfound resignation in his character.

. . . Whereas most of the characters in *Ten Little Indians* are urban professionals, the main character, Jackson Jackson, in "What You Pawn I Will Redeem" is a homeless, Spokane Indian alcoholic who lives in Seattle. Jackson, although certainly troubled, is far from defeated and goes on a mission to recover his grandmother's fancydancing regalia, which he discovers in a pawnshop. The pawnbroker initially agrees to sell it to Jackson if he can come up with the thousand dollars that it cost the pawnbroker to buy it. The extent to which family is important to this character is apparent in his monomaniacal, twenty-four-hour hapless pursuit of the money. He insists, "I know it's crazy, but I wondered if I could bring my grandmother back to life if I bought back her regalia." The good-hearted Jackson does scrounge together some money, but ends up spending most of it on alcohol and food for other hungry and alcoholic Indians. When he comes back to the pawnshop, however, it is the white pawnbroker who selflessly gives him the fancydancing regalia for free. The narrator concludes, "Do you know how many good men live in the world? Too many to count!" The narrator "redeems" himself by taking the regalia and dancing it in the street, with the narrator concluding, "I was my grandmother, dancing." This story is a first for Alexie, in which a white man is ultimately the hero of the story, suggesting that Alexie's perspective toward non-Natives may have softened. . . .

Source: Daniel Grassian, "*Ten Little Indians*," in *Understanding Sherman Alexie*, University of South Carolina Press, 2005, pp. 173, 178–82, 187–88.

Steve Brzezinski

In the following review, Brzezinski describes Alexie's style as "disarmingly compelling."

This volume of short stories, which begins and ends with two novella-length stories, is the third book of stories written by one of the most distinctive and original young voices in contemporary American literature.

Alexie's literary voice is distinctive, idiosyncratic, and disarmingly compelling. Born on a reservation near Spokane, he pokes cynical but deadly serious fun at all labels describing what he and his people should be called and is equally dismayed by the inaccuracy of both "Indian" and "Native-American." All ten stories are about "Indians," if he is forced to choose a label to describe the ethnicity of his characters, both men and women, from deeply impoverished street people to up-scale Seattle lawyers. What unites them is their deeply conflicted sensibility: perceptive about many things, but often clueless about their own motives; cynical about the world and their place in it but often sentimental and deeply emotional; outraged by the discrimination and damage inflicted on them, but caustically and brutally frank about their own failings and shortcomings as a culture.

The two novellas are in many ways the most notable efforts in a uniformly impressive achievement. The first, *The Search Engine*, is the story of a college student who tracks down and finds an obscure and forgotten Reservation poet on whom she is fixated; she finds both more and less than what she expected from her quest. The second, *What Ever Happened to Frank Snake Church*, is the story of a legendary Indian high school basketball player who gives up the game altogether after graduation and then, in his 40s, decides to rededicate himself to basketball with a zeal that verges on obsession. It is an unusual and deeply felt story and the author's own passion for basketball is clearly evident in the writing. This is a wonderful book that could have been written only by Sherman Alexie.

Source: Steve Brzezinski, Review of *Ten Little Indians*, in *Antioch Review*, Vol. 62, No. 3, Summer 2004, p. 581.

SOURCES

Alexie, Sherman, "What You Pawn I Will Redeem," in *Blasphemy: New and Selected Stories*, Grove Press, 2012, pp. 437–64.

Berglund, Jeff, "The Business of Writing: Sherman Alexie's Meditations on Authorship," in *Sherman Alexie: A Collection of Critical Essays*, edited by Jeff Berglund and Jan Roush, University of Utah Press, 2010, pp. 245, 249, 258.

Bruce, Heather, Anna E. Baldwin, and Christabel Umphrey, *Sherman Alexie in the Classroom*, NCTE High School Literature Series, National Council of Teachers of English, Urbana, Illinois, 2008, pp. xvii, xvi, 8.

Brzezinski, Steve, Review of *Ten Little Indians*, in *Antioch Review*, Vol. 62, No. 3, Summer 2004, p. 581.

Davis, Tanita, and Sarah Stevenson, "Sherman Alexie," in *Conversations with Sherman Alexie*, edited by Nancy J. Peterson, University Press of Mississippi, 2009, p. 190.

Fogarty, Mark, "Ending All Native Homelessness Next Federal Target," in *Indian Country Today*, February 4, 2016, http://indiancountrytodaymedianetwork.com/2016/02/04/ending-all-native-homelessness-next-federal-target-163302 (accessed May 21, 2016).

Grassian, Daniel, *Understanding Sherman Alexie*, University of South Carolina Press, 2005, pp. 56, 191.

Heldrich, Philip, "'Survival = Anger × Imagination': Sherman Alexie's Dark Humor," in *Sherman Alexie: A Collection of Critical Essays*, edited by Jeff Berglund and Jan Roush, University of Utah Press, 2010, pp. 26–27, 32–33.

Izadi, Elahe, "Your Assumptions about Native Americans and Alcohol Are Wrong," in *Washington Post*, February 12, 2016, https://www.washingtonpost.com/news/post-nation/wp/2016/02/12/your-assumptions-about-native-americans-and-alcohol-are-wrong/ (accessed May 21, 2016).

Kephart, Beth, Review of *Ten Little Indians*, in *Book*, July–August 2003, p. 79.

Kloszewski, Marc, Review of *Ten Little Indians*, in *Library Journal*, Vol. 128, No. 9, May 15, 2003, p. 129.

McNally, Joelly, "Sherman Alexie," in *Writer*, Vol. 114, No. 6, June 2001, p. 28.

Nelson, Joshua B., "'Humor Is My Green Card': A Conversation with Sherman Alexie," in *World Literature Today*, Vol. 84, No. 4, July–August 2010, pp. 39–45.

Nygren, Ase, "A World of Story-Smoke: A Conversation with Sherman Alexie," in *MELUS*, Vol. 30, No. 4, 2005, p. 149.

O'Shaughnessy, Margaret, "Sherman Alexie's Transformation of 'Ten Little Indians'," in *Sherman Alexie: A Collection of Critical Essays*, edited by Jeff Berglund and Jan Roush, University of Utah Press, 2010, p. 222.

Review of *Ten Little Indians*, in *Publishers Weekly*, Vol. 250, No. 18, May 5, 2003, p. 198.

Row, Jess, "Without Reservation," in *New York Times Book Review*, November 25, 2012, p. 20.

"Sherman Alexie: The 2010 Puterbaugh Fellow," in *World Literature Today*, Vol. 84, No. 4, 2010, p. 35.

Tatonetti, Lisa, "Dancing That Way, Things Began to Change: The Ghost Dance as Pantribal Metaphor in

Sherman Alexie's Writing," in *Sherman Alexie: A Collection of Critical Essays*, edited by Jeff Berglund and Jan Roush, University of Utah Press, 2010, p. 16.

Weinberger, Eric, "Off the Reservation," in *New York Times Book Review*, Vol. 108, June 15, 2003, p. 13.

FURTHER READING

LaDuke, Winona, *Recovering the Sacred: The Power of Naming and Claiming*, South End Press, 2005.

> Ojibwe writer LaDuke, who ran for vice president with the Green Party in 2000, shows how traditional Indian beliefs inform the philosophical ground for political action on behalf of the land. She points out the difference between Native American and mainstream thinking about nature.

Lincoln, Kenneth, *Ind'n Humor: Bicultural Play in Native America*, Oxford University Press, 1993.

> Lincoln argues that Indians have used humor to combat genocide, as have the Jews. He shows how their humor was developed as a skill in colonial oppression by looking at folktales, psychology, and the arts.

Ortiz, Simon, *Men on the Moon: Collected Short Stories*, University of Arizona Press, 1999.

> Ortiz is an Acoma Pueblo Indian of the generation that established the Native American Renaissance in the 1960s, one of Alexie's inspirations for writing as a young man. This is a collection of Ortiz's short stories whose strength is based on the oral tradition he grew up with in the pueblo, speaking the language.

Treuer, David, *Native American Fiction: A User's Manual*, Macmillan, 2006.

> Ojibwe short-story writer and critic Treuer claims Native American fiction does not exist. Instead, he asserts that the many ethnic strands in the country are part of the total body of American literature. He criticizes Sherman Alexie and Louise Erdrich for perpetuating stereotypes of Indians as a separate and special culture.

SUGGESTED SEARCH TERMS

Sherman Alexie

"What You Pawn I Will Redeem" AND Sherman Alexie

Ten Little Indians AND Sherman Alexie

Native American Renaissance

Spokane tribe

Grand Coulee Dam AND Native Americans

Native American fiction

postcolonial fiction

fancydancing

Native American powwow

Ghost Dance

Who's Irish?

GISH JEN

1999

In an interview with Bill Moyers, Gish Jen discussed Philip Roth's concept of the amiable irritant—a difficulty or annoyance that, according to Roth, "arouses whatever is stubborn, elusive, or even defiant in the writer's nature." Jen tells Moyers, "Growing up Asian American, having been a child of immigrant parents—all of that difficulty did serve as a kind of amiable irritant, the grain of sand that hopefully produces the pearl." Without this irritant, Jen says, "I'm not even sure I would have become a writer." She continues, "Part of my writing has been an effort to claim my American-ness in a way that does not deny my Chinese heritage." With her novels and stories, Jen explores,

> the whole business of trying to make sense of two very different worlds that I was living in. . . . It really just wasn't a matter of: you ate with chopsticks and they ate with forks but the whole difference in the way that people thought.

This explains why her work so often focuses on themes of immigrant life. However, Jen also feels that it is not at all necessary "to erase all the particulars of the Chinese American experience in order to capture the essential American experience." Though her characters are often Asian American, their experiences are universal. For example, though most of the stories in the collection *Who's Irish?* (1999) examine the immigrant experience, the title story goes beyond that theme to show generational conflict between a mother and a daughter, the struggles of a young couple

Gish Jen (©*Boston Globe* / *Getty Images*)

to handle their unruly child, and the strain unemployment puts on a family and a marriage.

AUTHOR BIOGRAPHY

Jen was born in New York City on August 12, 1955. She is the second of five children and grew up in the New York suburbs Yonkers and Scarsdale. Her given name is Lillian, but while in high school she adopted the name Gish after the actress Lillian Gish. She credits this personal renaming as part of her path to becoming a writer because it was one of the first times she made a conscious choice about who she was rather than conforming to the path her family expected her to follow.

Jen's parents were not typical immigrants who came to America in search of a new life. Both of her parents arrived in the United States in the 1940s intending to stay only temporarily. Her father arrived near the end of World War II to work on a joint American-Chinese project against Japan, and her mother came to the United States for graduate school. The Chinese Communist revolution in 1949 left both parents effectively exiled. They met in the United States and started a family.

After enrolling at Harvard University and studying both premedical and prelaw courses, Jen changed her major to English, another step toward her writing career. She graduated in 1977 and started in the business program at Stanford University. This practical choice was another effort to please her parents, but she was unhappy and left Stanford to work in China as an English teacher for a short time. Upon her return to the United States, Jen studied at the Iowa Writers' Workshop and in 1983 earned her master of fine arts degree.

Jen married and followed her husband to California and then Massachusetts when his work required him to move. In Massachusetts, she received a fellowship from the Bunting Institute of Radcliffe College. The fellowship allowed her the freedom to write without having to earn a wage, and she completed her first novel, *Typical American* (1991), which was a *New York Times* Notable Book of the Year and a finalist for the National Book Critics Circle Award. Jen's second novel, *Mona in the Promised Land* (1996), is a sequel to *Typical American* and was followed by her short-story collection *Who's Irish?* (1999), which includes the story of the same name. Jen's other novels include *The Love Wife* (2004) and *The World and Town* (2010).

Jen's unique and humorous take on immigrant life has earned much praise from critics and numerous awards, honors, and fellowships, notably a National Endowment for the Arts fellowship and a Fulbright Fellowship to the People's Republic of China. In 2009, she was made a fellow of the American Academy of Arts and Sciences, and her work has been included in the prestigious Best American Short Stories volumes more than once. As of 2016, Jen was writing and living in Massachusetts with her husband and children.

PLOT SUMMARY

"Who's Irish?" is told by a nameless first-person narrator. She is a Chinese American widow, mother, and grandmother who lives with her daughter, Natalie Shea; her Irish American son-in-law, John Shea; and their young daughter, Sophie. Natalie has a good job at a bank, but John is unemployed. However, even though he does not have to go to work every day, he says he cannot take care of Sophie because he is a man. Natalie makes excuses for him, explaining to her mother that he must keep up with his workouts at the gym or he will become depressed.

The narrator compares herself, who with her husband owned a successful restaurant, with her son-in-law. She points out that all three of his brothers are also unemployed. Though she respects John's mother, Bess, for raising four sons on her own and holding down a good job, the narrator chalks some of the problem up to heritage, claiming that the Chinese beat the Irish. John's family members have their own prejudices; they are continually surprised at Sophie's

dark skin, though they insist that there is "nothing the matter with brown."

Though the narrator asserts that in China, she would be taken care of by her daughter in her golden years, she wants to help Natalie, who is under a lot of strain with John out of work. Therefore, the grandmother babysits for young Sophie, providing the financially strapped family with free child care. Sophie is an unmanageable child. She takes off her clothes in public and does not listen to her parents or grandparents. The narrator makes it clear that she thinks that Natalie and John and Sophie's former babysitter, Amy, may have been too lenient. The grandmother believes that for Sophie to become obedient, she needs to be spanked. Her parents, however, believe that physical punishment is harmful to children and instead encourage the grandmother to use her words, as if she herself is a toddler.

The grandmother tries to discipline Sophie in other ways, such as taking away snacks and trips to the park, but in the end, she does spank her. After the spanking, the child does keep her clothes on, and John and Natalie are amazed. The narrator does not tell them that she has spanked Sophie, instead allowing them to believe that the girl was going through a phase that has now passed. However, Sophie's basic behavior is unchanged. She still does not obey her grandmother and calls her Meanie when she does not get her way.

The narrator often takes Sophie to the park, where she plays with her friend Sinbad, who is a bad influence. He teaches Sophie to kick his mother and other parents, and after playing with him, Sophie throws a shovel load of wet sand at her grandmother. Sinbad's favorite game is to play war, digging a deep foxhole under the playground equipment.

One afternoon at the park, Sophie crawls into Sinbad's deep foxhole and refuses to come out. There is a standoff, and the grandmother is not able to physically remove Sophie from the hole or to coax her to obey. As it grows dark, the grandmother panics and tries to use a stick to chase Sophie out of the hole. She also threatens to leave without her and then bribes her with candy, but Sophie does not respond.

John and Natalie arrive. John crawls into the hole to retrieve Sophie, who has fallen asleep but begins to cry when she sees her parents. Everyone is relieved until they return home and see that Sophie has bruises and a swollen eye. Natalie is furious that her mother poked at Sophie with a stick. While eating ice cream, Sophie tells her parents that her grandmother "hits me all the time." Natalie and John are exasperated.

At John's insistence, Natalie looks for another place for her mother to live. Though they cannot afford the extra expense, they will hire a babysitter because they no longer trust the narrator to watch Sophie. In the end, John's mother invites the narrator to live with her because she herself is lonely. The narrator is glad to find a comfortable home with Bess, who makes her feel like an "honorary Irish," but there is a lingering sadness that she is still somewhat estranged from Natalie and not allowed to see Sophie very often.

CHARACTERS

Amy

Amy is Sophie's former babysitter. The narrator does not approve of Amy's child-rearing methods or of anything else about her. Natalie calls Amy creative, but the narrator dismisses the importance of creativity, explaining that it is a "word we do not talk about in China. In China, we talk about whether we have difficulty or no difficulty." She also disapproves of Amy's cropped shirt that leaves her navel showing. Most important, the narrator does not like that Amy has allowed Sophie to do as she likes rather than enforcing basic rules like having to wear clothes. Although the narrator sees Sophie's behavior originating in "her wild Shea side," she believes that Amy's indulgence has only made matters worse.

Narrator

The first-person narrator of the story is a sixty-eight-year-old woman who was born in China but moved with her husband and daughter, Natalie, to America in search of a better life. Although she is clearly fond of her daughter, remembering affectionately when she "took care of her when she could not hold her head up" and "when she was a little girl with two pigtails, one of them always crooked," the narrator has trouble with her living situation. Although in China it is a daughter's job to take care of her mother, in America, "it is the other way around. Mother help daughter, mother ask, Anything else I can do? Otherwise daughter complain mother is not supportive." However, the narrator does her best

to help, babysitting her granddaughter, Sophie, while Natalie is working, even though the child's father, John, is out of work and home when he is not at the gym.

The narrator and her daughter disagree about methods of child rearing, especially in terms of discipline. Sophie is a high-spirited three-year-old—her grandmother calls her wild—and she acts inappropriately, taking off all of her clothes in public, not obeying her grandmother, throwing sand on the playground, and kicking people. Natalie and John are firm that Sophie is not to be spanked for this behavior, but they do not seem to offer any more appropriate punishment to curb her disobedience. When the narrator ignores her daughter and son-in-law and spanks Sophie, she is finally able to make her keep her clothes on, but the child remains defiant in other ways.

In the climax of the story, the narrator cannot make Sophie emerge from a huge hole another child digs in the playground sand. Though she does not intend to harm Sophie, she prods her with a stick to make her come out. Because of the resulting injuries, John insists that his mother-in-law live elsewhere. Natalie is saddened to make her mother move out, but she feels she has to go along to save her marriage.

The narrator moves in with Bess, John's Irish American mother, and the two women settle in well together. Bess considers the narrator a member of the family and honorary Irish. This gives the narrator a sense of belonging that was lacking when she lived with her daughter.

Bess Shea

Bess is Sophie's other grandmother, John's mother, and Natalie's mother-in-law. She is recovering from an unnamed illness and must use a walker. The narrator seems to like Bess. Before becoming ill, Bess worked as an executive assistant for a large company, and the narrator respects that she has worked hard all her life. Bess has four sons, none of whom seem to be able to hold down a job, and she craves female company. She confides in the narrator that "raising four boys with no father is no picnic."

Jim Shea

Jim is one of John's brothers and one of Bess's sons. Like his brothers, he does not have a job at the time of the story. Rather than feeling ashamed of their unemployment, all four brothers blame it on forces beyond their control:

"They say they cannot find work, this is not the economy of the fifties."

John Shea

John is Natalie's husband, Sophie's father, the narrator's son-in-law, and Bess's son. While Natalie works hard and has an important job at a bank, John is unemployed throughout much of the story. Though he is home during the day, he cannot be bothered to look after Sophie. It has to be assumed that he spends at least some of his time looking for work, but he also has to "go to the gym to be a man," the narrator explains. Natalie justifies his workouts by saying they keep John from being depressed. The narrator resents that her daughter works so hard while John spends time at the gym and refuses to care more for Sophie.

Because of the narrator's faithfulness to a more traditional view of the world, it would be easy to assume that she resents John's not working in part because of old-fashioned gender roles. However, she herself worked hard in the family's restaurant, and she also respects Bess's former job. Therefore, it is not that she believes that women should only be homemakers and provide child care but that she wants John to be an equal partner to Natalie in supporting the family financially and in caring for Sophie.

During the brief time in which John has a job, he is rather dramatic about the weight of responsibility on his shoulders. While Natalie was the sole breadwinner, she did her job without fuss and even made allowances for John so that he could go to the gym. John, however, says that he needs to concentrate and focus because he feels pressure in his new position.

Mike Shea

Mike is another of John's brothers and Bess's sons. Like his brothers, he is unemployed. During Thanksgiving dinner, he jokes that he will start selling pad thai—"It's going to be the new pizza," he says—to make his fortune.

Natalie Shea

Natalie is the narrator's daughter, John's wife, and Sophie's mother. She was very young when her parents immigrated to America and seems to be fully acclimated in mainstream society with little regard for the traditional Chinese ways of doing things. The narrator describes her daughter as fierce and seems proud that she works as a vice

president in a bank. However, there are many times when Natalie seems unable to assert herself. She is caught in the middle when her mother's ideas about raising Sophie clash with John's. Although Natalie agrees that her mother did not handle the situation of Sophie's hiding in the foxhole appropriately, she reveals sadness and guilt about making her mother move out of the house and not letting Sophie visit. She is afraid that if she does not take John's side and force her mother out of the house, she will end up divorced. Natalie is firm, however, about not wanting Sophie to be spanked.

Sophie Shea

Sophie is Natalie and John's three-year-old daughter and the narrator's granddaughter. She is high-spirited, and the narrator believes she has been spoiled by her former babysitter, Amy, whom Natalie considers creative but the narrator considers crazy, and by her parents' permissiveness. Although Natalie and John are exasperated by Sophie's tendency to take off her clothes and diaper in public places, they have no idea how to stop her. They refuse to use stern punishments, like spanking, because they believe that it leads children to have low self-esteem, which causes problems later in life. The narrator tries to follow Natalie and John's rules about spanking by first punishing Sophie for taking off her clothes by denying her snacks and trips to the playground. However, these consequences do not seem to have any effect on Sophie. Her grandmother despairs and eventually spanks Sophie, and the child does stop stripping off her clothes.

Sinbad

Sinbad is a four-year-old boy whom Sophie befriends on the playground. He wears army clothes, and his favorite game involves digging a deep foxhole under the playground equipment and ambushing his mother with a shovel full of sand. Sophie copies him, throwing wet sand at her grandmother and kicking Sinbad's mother when he tells her to.

Sinbad's Mother

Sinbad's mother makes excuses for the children's questionable behavior. When Sinbad throws a shovel of wet sand at her, she says, "Oh, it's all right. . . . You can't get rid of war games, it's part of their imaginative play. All the boys go through it." Similarly, when Sophie kicks her leg, she dismisses the problem because she says it

TOPICS FOR FURTHER STUDY

- Reread "Who's Irish?" and pay careful attention to characters other than the narrator. Then rewrite the story from another character's point of view. Use clues from the original story to make sure your interpretation fits Jen's original characterization. For example, what about the narrator's behavior makes John see scary family patterns? Why does Sophie think her grandmother is a meanie? Why does Natalie call her mother crazy but cry when she tries to get her to move out of the house?

- Read several of the stories in the collection *Mrs. Spring Fragrance* (1912) by Sui Sin Far (the pen name of Edith Maude Eaton), which relates the lives of Chinese American immigrants in the early part of the twentieth century. The volume is divided into a section for adults and a section for children. Write an essay that examines how the stories differ between the two sections. Discuss how the author may communicate different information to children and adults and whether the stories intended for adults seem like more realistic portrayals. Devote part of your essay to analyzing how this book, written at the

beginning of the twentieth century, interprets the immigrant experience compared with Jen's representation in "Who's Irish?" at the close of the century.

- Using print and online resources, research trends in child psychology about discipline in the twentieth and twenty-first centuries. Create a website that explains various debates and theories on the subject of discipline. For example, when was it first recommended that parents stop using spanking as a punishment? Research whether more recent studies indicate that physical punishments damage a child emotionally. What is currently recommended for teaching children socially acceptable behavior without stifling their creativity or damaging their self-esteem?

- Read another story from *Who's Irish?* and think about how the experience of the story's protagonist is similar to and different from that of the narrator in "Who's Irish?" Write an essay comparing the two characters, their worldviews, and how Jen uses the narrative structure of each story to best capture the main character's essence.

---

doesn't hurt. This bothers the narrator, because it teaches Sophie that it is acceptable to attack parents at the playground.

THEMES

Prejudice

Jen realistically depicts the prejudices her characters feel through the dialogue related by the narrator. The first jarring example comes when she describes Sophie's appearance, which the narrator appreciates as mostly Chinese with black hair and black eyes. To Sophie's father's family, however, "her skin is a brown surprise." They, even her father, seem unable to ignore

her skin color and try to lessen the racist nature of the comments by saying there is nothing the matter with it but that it is a surprise. Jen repeats two sentences to emphasize how often the Irish side of the family expresses the sentiment: "There's nothing the matter with brown. They are just surprised."

Though the narrator notices the prejudices of those around her and comments on them, she seems oblivious to her own prejudices or at least blind to why they are no less acceptable. As soon as she mentions that her son-in-law is Irish American, she says, "I always thought Irish people are like Chinese people, work so hard on the railroad, but now I know why the Chinese beat the Irish." She bemoans the fact that her granddaughter is wild and blames that wildness on her Irish blood. When the narrator's daughter tells her she "should not say Irish this, Irish that" and points out, "How do you like it when people say the Chinese this, the Chinese that," she insists that she is not embarrassed about the generalizations she makes about the Irish. She continues her complaints about John's Irish family, reminding her daughter that John and all three of his brothers are out of work, as if that is somehow related to their heritage.

American Dream

The narrator of "Who's Irish?" is proud of the success she and her husband have achieved—their own version of the American dream. She compares herself to her daughter's in-laws: "When I come to this country, I have no money and do not speak English. But my husband and I own our restaurant before he die. Free and clear, no mortgage." She uses her own success to highlight the failings of her son-in-law, John, and his brothers, all of whom are unemployed. At Thanksgiving dinner, she berates them, "At least my husband and I can say, We made it. What can you say? Tell me. What can you say?" She is also justifiably proud of what she achieved on her own after her husband's death, taking care of their only child.

In many ways the narrator's family has attained the American dream. She and her husband have achieved a measure of financial success, and now their daughter, Natalie, has a good job and a big house. However, the story also shows that in spite of these measures of success, the characters are not truly happy. The narrator is somewhat estranged from Natalie and not allowed to see Sophie as often as she would like after the episode on the playground. By the end of the story, Natalie herself is overworked trying to pay for her large house on her own, and her marriage to John, who is once again unemployed and depressed, is strained. The narrator is worried for her daughter and laments that she can do nothing to help now that she has been forced out of the house. She quotes Natalie:

> I have a family to support, she say, and her voice is heavy, as if soaking wet. I have a young daughter and a depressed husband and no one to turn to. When she say no one to turn to, she mean me.

By showing the emotional distance between the members of the family, Jen may be subtly pointing to a new definition of the American

Although the narrator remarks that in China the daughter would take care of her, she tries to help her daughter by babysitting (©Jack.Q / Shutterstock.com)

dream all can strive toward, in which personal happiness and healthy relationships are more important than financial success.

STYLE

Unreliable Narrator

In "Who's Irish?" Jen uses the literary convention known as the unreliable narrator. An unreliable narrator is one whose story cannot be completely trusted. Readers receive subtle clues that they must take what is on the page with a grain of salt and interpret the events of the story in their own way. Some of the narrator's remarks show her own prejudices, which may cue the reader to question her interpretation of what is going on. For example, when she disapproves of the fact that her son-in-law and his brothers are all out of work, she says, "Why the Shea family have so much trouble? They are white people, they speak English." She seems to believe that the problems she has encountered—the racial prejudice she faced as a Chinese American, her immigrant status, and her lack of knowledge of English—are the only obstacles worth considering. Also, when she complains about her granddaughter's wild behavior, she insists, "I am not exaggerate: millions of children in China, not one act like this." Perhaps during the narrator's childhood in China, discipline was more strictly enforced, and Sophie is being raised with leniency, but the narrator's implication that no child in China has ever been wild or disobeyed is a gross generalization. Such instances show how Jen uses her unreliable narrator to add humor to the story. The narrator provides only the information that will support her own point of view, and the disparity between her representation of events and what can be read between the lines is amusing to the reader.

Imperfect English

Throughout the story, Jen writes in the first-person point of view of the unnamed narrator. Because she immigrated to the United States as an adult, she has never completely mastered American English. Perhaps for most of her life, running the family's Chinese restaurant with many Chinese American patrons, she was not required to speak English often. Now, however, living with her daughter, her Irish American son-in-law John, and her granddaughter, the narrator must speak English much of the time.

The story is full of examples of her imperfect grammar. In describing John's mother's job as an executive assistant, she says, "She is handle everything for a big shot." When the narrator gives the highlights of Sophie's wild behavior, she says, "When Sophie take off her shoes, Amy say bare feet is best, even the pediatrician say so." Her indignant feelings about her unemployed son-in-law also cause her language to deteriorate: "But, okay: so my son-in-law can be man, I am babysitter" and "But my daughter too busy to listen, she has to go to meeting, she has to write memo while her husband go to the gym to be a man."

Jen's use of imperfect English for the narrator is realistic in contrast to quotations from other characters, whose use of English is more traditionally grammatical, especially in light of her immigrant status. However, it never seems that Jen is mocking the narrator for her language skills—the grandmother is not portrayed

as a pathetically comic figure or as unintelligent. The rhythms of the narrator's speech are also conversational, making it seem as though the narrator is speaking directly to the reader.

HISTORICAL CONTEXT

Multigenerational Households

The profile of the American family is in constant flux. In addition to marriage equality, single-parent households, and recent college graduates' returning home to live with their parents, other factors have altered the definition of a family. For example, the number of multigenerational families, in which grandparents are full-time residents, has increased.

Most of the twentieth century saw the number of multigenerational households declining. Whereas 57 percent of adults sixty-five years old or older lived in a multigenerational household in 1900, by 1980 that statistic had declined to only 17 percent. This reduction is attributed to improvements in health care and the greater financial security of retirees through programs like private pension plans and Social Security. These factors allowed older people to live independently longer.

However, the number of multigenerational households began to increase at the close of the twentieth century, and the increase continued into the twenty-first. The Great Recession of 2008 drove many families to cut corners by combining households. Financial problems were not the only factor that led to the increase in multigenerational households. Many experts found that the increase was heavily influenced by the Immigration and Nationality Act of 1965. This piece of legislation reformed immigration laws, encouraged skilled workers to immigrate, and allowed family members to sponsor relatives in the immigration process, which promoted family unity. The act also did away with quotas based on country of origin, and new immigrants came increasingly from Africa, Asia, and Latin America rather than Europe.

Households headed by immigrants rather than US-born Americans were more likely to be multigenerational. Because of the increase in immigration since the Immigration and Nationality Act, the number of households headed by an immigrant has increased. In 1980, 7 percent of US households were headed by an

COMPARE & CONTRAST

- **1990s:** In a 1995 publication, the American Academy of Pediatrics reiterates its statement that spanking is not a recommended punishment because it is emotionally harmful to both child and parent. Although spanking may temporarily stop the unwanted behavior, experts say, spanking does not teach an alternative, acceptable behavior. It also sets the example for children that physical violence is an acceptable means of expressing anger.

  Today: A 2012 study indicates that nearly 50 percent of American adults report having been physically punished (grabbed, shoved, pushed, or spanked) when they were children. Researchers question more than thirty thousand adults and learn that in comparison with those who never experienced physical discipline, those punished physically are 24 percent more likely to have panic disorder, 41 percent more likely to have depression, and 59 percent more likely to be dependent on alcohol. However, the study shows only an association—not a direct cause-and-effect link—between these mental disorders and physical punishment.

- **1990s:** The proportion of preschool-aged children cared for by a grandparent while their parents work increases during the 1990s from less than 15 percent to almost 20 percent. The proportion of preschool-aged children cared for by their father while their mother works increases slightly during the decade, from approximately 16 percent to 18 percent.

  Today: The proportion of preschool-aged children cared for by a grandparent has held steady over fifteen years or so, hovering at or just below 20 percent. The proportion of preschool-aged children cared for by their fathers has grown to approximately 20 percent.

- **1990s:** By the close of the twentieth century, approximately 7 percent of American marriages are between people of different races. This statistic reflects a 65 percent increase since 1990.

  Today: The 2010 US Census shows that approximately 8 percent of American marriages are mixed race. This is an increase of only 20 percent since 2000, showing that though numbers are rising, the increase has drastically slowed. Although African Americans are substantially more likely than before to marry white Americans, the growth of mixed-race marriages has drastically slowed for American-born Asians and Hispanics. Experts theorize that recent immigration has provided more ethnically similar partners.

---

immigrant, and that statistic grew to 14 percent by 2012. This trend is reflected in the 2009 statistics regarding multigenerational households: 10 percent of households with a US-born head were multigenerational, but 16 percent of households headed by an immigrant were multigenerational.

As illustrated by Jen in "Who's Irish?," there is a cultural preference for many immigrants to have the family living together. Some immigrant families also opt to share households for convenience: members of the family who have recently arrived have longer-term residents as guides and helpers; the youngest and oldest family members have others around to care for them; and sharing living costs reduces the financial burden on the entire family, especially in expensive urban areas where immigrants are more likely to settle.

The multigenerational population (the number of people living in a multigenerational household) increased by more than two million people per year in 2007–2010. More recent numbers show that the trend has slowed but

Sophie is a difficult child, and the grandmother spanks her for not staying properly dressed
(*©Ronnachai Palas | Shutterstock.com*)

has by no means stopped. Since 2010, the multi-generational population has continued to grow by approximately one million people per year.

CRITICAL OVERVIEW

Jen's work has received mostly positive responses from critics, who especially praise her deft handling of issues central to the lives of immigrant families. In the *Women's Review of Books*, Carol Anshaw discusses Jen's novel *The Love Wife*, which touches on similar themes to those Jen tackles in "Who's Irish?" Anshaw writes:

> There is weight to the way Jen deals with cultural chasms, with the identity issues inherent in race and affiliation, abandonment and adoption, and with the currently unfashionable idea of a woman chafing within the demands of marriage and motherhood.

Esra Sahtiyanci Oztarhan, in a review of *Mona in the Promised Land* for *Interactions*, agrees that Jen is a master of "humorous stories about serious issues like racism and identity quest of Chinese Americans." She notes that Jen's "characters try to adapt to the American Dream while trying to hang on to their Chinese roots." Jean Thompson of the *New York Times* points out that Jen handles these serious matters with a light touch and a sense of fun. "If the American immigrant experience is most often construed as a process of merging and gradual assimilation, like traffic on a freeway," Thompson writes, "then Gish Jen's version resembles a busy intersection with everybody laying on the horn." Thompson marvels at Jen's "clear-eyed affection for people who struggle to find their places in the world" and her ability to capture "comedy that resonates, and sadnesses that arise with perfect timing from absurdities."

Though Jen makes frequent use of humor, she accomplishes important goals, breaking down stereotypes with her quirky characters. According to Oztarhan, "Jen changes the standard notion of Americanness . . . and Chineseness completely by her work. Being a Chinese American wom[a]n writer herself, she deconstructs all existing stereotypes." By "intentionally creat[ing] unconventional and unrepresentative characters in her novel," explains Oztarhan, Jen "reinvent[s] Chinese Americanness to the same extent as she reenacts her Americanness."

Thompson did find some unevenness in the collection *Who's Irish?* She sees in some of the stories "a sense of material struggling to find its proper form, sketches that have grown or novels that have been recast or perhaps never made it off the ground." However, the overall critical reaction to the collection is positive. As a *Publishers Weekly* review indicates, the stories contain "as always with Jen, a multitude of details, domestic and behavioral [that] are acutely observed," and the stories have "the impact . . . of a much longer work."

CRITICISM

Kristen Sarlin Greenberg
Greenberg is a freelance writer and editor with a background in literature and philosophy. In the following essay, she discusses whether Jen's "Who's Irish?" can be classified as immigrant literature.

WHAT DO I READ NEXT?

- In *Call Me Maria* (2004), Judith Ortiz Cofer portrays a teenage girl caught between worlds when she and her father move from Puerto Rico to an American barrio. She struggles to fit in without giving up her heritage.

- Eddie Huang's memoir *Fresh Off the Boat* (2013) is a modern immigrant story. As skillfully as Jen deconstructs those stereotypes with her work, Huang defies racial stereotypes with his behavior, creating for himself a unique definition of what it means to be American.

- John Son's young-adult novel *Finding My Hat* (2003) is based on his own life story. For the protagonist, Jin-Han, the struggles of adolescence are complicated by his Korean name, his imperfect English, and the family's moves from Chicago to Memphis to Houston as his father pursues his version of the American dream.

- Jen's first novel, *Typical American* (1991), features Ralph Chang, his wife, Helen, and his sister, Theresa, as they flee Communist China in 1949 and try to settle into a new home in America. Jen's trademark humor makes readers laugh even as the characters struggle to blend their old ideas with their new lives.

- The title of An Na's 2001 novel, *A Step from Heaven*, comes from the uncle of the protagonist, Ju Park. He tells her that life in America will be close to paradise. However, Ju's new life is far from heavenly. Struggling to adjust to a foreign culture and find work to support themselves makes the adult members of the Park family angry, depressed, and even violent.

- In *Understanding Gish Jen* (2015), Jennifer Ann Ho examines all of Jen's work, both fiction and nonfiction. Ho describes the development of Jen's style and the arc of her career and highlights common themes in her work in this detailed but approachable study.

Jen is praised by critics for creating detailed portrayals of immigrant life with humor and emotional realism. Many of the short stories in *Who's Irish?* fit this pattern. The characters are either themselves immigrants or the children of immigrants. In the title story of the collection, the unnamed narrator is a Chinese American widow, mother, and grandmother who lives with her daughter's family and marvels at the wild behavior of her three-year-old granddaughter. The narrator's broken English and focus on the difference between her background and that of her Irish American son-in-law suggest that her immigrant status is important to who she is and how she sees the world, but is "Who's Irish?" truly immigrant literature?

The very first page of the story is full of clues that an immigrant is telling the story. The first two words, "In China," suggest that everything the narrator experiences in her day-to-day life is filtered through her early experiences in another country and culture. She is sharply contrasted to her daughter, Natalie, who is fully assimilated into mainstream American culture, and to the family of her son-in-law, John Shea, who are of Irish heritage but seem to think of themselves as simply American. The narrator mentions the influential Chinese philosopher Confucius—even if she invents a quote to suit her own opinions and purposes—and compares Chinese people with Irish people. Also, her imperfect English indicates that she is not a native speaker. With all of these details, Jen characterizes the narrator as someone always conscious of her status as an outsider, in spite of having lived in the United States for decades.

Although the trappings of the story categorize it as immigrant literature to some extent,

> THE NARRATOR'S BROKEN ENGLISH
> AND FOCUS ON THE DIFFERENCE BETWEEN
> HER BACKGROUND AND THAT OF HER IRISH
> AMERICAN SON-IN-LAW SUGGEST THAT HER
> IMMIGRANT STATUS IS IMPORTANT TO WHO SHE IS
> AND HOW SHE SEES THE WORLD, BUT IS 'WHO'S
> IRISH?' TRULY IMMIGRANT LITERATURE?"

the plot is truly about family. For example, in the climax of the story, the narrator takes her granddaughter, Sophie, to the park. Sophie crawls into a deep hole dug under the playground equipment and refuses to come out. The grandmother panics. She is not physically able to go into the hole and bring Sophie out by force, and neither verbal threats nor coaxing has any result. The narrator finally resorts to poking into the hole with a stick, which is perhaps not the best solution, but it has nothing to do with the narrator's immigrant status. It is merely the struggle of a grandparent to make her grandchild obey and respect her.

Jen includes some of the narrator's frustrated thoughts. She cannot fathom Sophie's disobedience, insisting "millions of children in China, not one act like this." She also imagines that "a Chinese mother would help," whereas "American mothers, they look at you, they shake their head, they go home." Although these details add richness and humor to the story, there is no indication that the battle between grandmother and stubborn granddaughter would play out any differently in China or had the grandmother been born in America. The conflict is simply family drama.

Perhaps the most interesting relationship in the story is that between mother and daughter. Jen includes details that indicate the narrator is an immigrant. She explains that "in China, daughter take care of mother. Here it is the other way around. Mother help daughter, mother ask, Anything else I can do? Otherwise daughter complain mother is not supportive." Though the cultural tradition she was raised with is very different from what she sees in mainstream American culture, the narrator does her best. She tries to help her overworked daughter, giving up the leisure of her retirement to babysit Sophie.

Jen also shows the mother and daughter arguing about issues of race. The narrator describes how "My daughter tell me I should not say Irish this, Irish that." Her tendency to judge people on the basis of heritage again highlights her immigrant mindset, but the conversation with Natalie is mostly bickering. The squabble illustrates a daughter embarrassed by her mother's dated stereotypes rather than a major ideological disagreement about race.

Many of the disagreements between the narrator and Natalie are perfect examples of typical mother-daughter arguments. Natalie needs her mother's help, but mother and daughter disagree about the how things should be done, especially on the subject of disciplining Sophie. "I don't want you to touch Sophie," Natalie says. "No spanking, period." The narrator is insulted, saying, "Don't tell me what to do. . . . I am not your servant. . . . Don't you dare talk to me like that." However, Natalie is not being intentionally disrespectful. "I'm not telling you what to do," she explains. "I'm telling you how I feel." This conversation has occurred a million times over—it shows the typical generation gap: the older family member becomes frustrated, and the younger generation has its own way of doing things and asserting its independence.

Jen further complicates the mother-daughter relationship by adding John, Natalie's unemployed, depressed husband. Natalie is torn between loyalty to and affection for her mother and the love and duty she feels toward John. After the incident on the playground, Natalie must find a new place for her mother to live. The narrator knows that Natalie "is sorry. Sometimes she cry, I am the one to say everything will be okay. She say she have no choice, she doesn't want to end up divorced." The narrator understands that Natalie needs to go along with her husband to save her marriage.

The relationship between John and Natalie is another important thread running through the story. Jen portrays the strain put on a marriage when one partner is unemployed. Like the narrator, readers may sympathize with John, who suffers from depression, but also see that his insistence on maintaining his time at the gym rather than caring for Sophie puts extra

Sophie hides in a tunnel under the playground, protesting her grandmother's punishment
(© Vintage Tone | Shutterstock.com)

pressure on Natalie. She is exhausted and frustrated at being left to carry the financial burden of the family.

At the close of the story, the narrator moves in with John's mother, Bess. John and his brothers do not understand why their mother has invited the narrator to live with her, but Bess tells them, "Get lost. She's a permanent resident. . . . She isn't going anywhere." This declaration gives the narrator the feeling that she has become honorary Irish. She appreciates the sense of belonging Bess's words give her. Jen is suggesting that even more important to this story than the narrator's becoming a permanent resident of the United States is that she finds a true home living with Bess.

When these intricate relationships are studied, it becomes clear that family is the focus of "Who's Irish?" The struggles the family faces are problems every family can encounter, not just immigrants. This is where Jen shows her mastery as a writer. She makes the immigrant story universal. She uses her personal experience as a Chinese American and the child of

immigrants to give readers a detailed and realistic picture of immigrant life but does not stop there. In this story, she examines what it means to be a family, and in an American family, there is often the need to navigate around the misunderstandings and disagreements that result from mixed heritage and different traditions.

So can "Who's Irish?" be called immigrant literature? The short answer is yes. Much of Jen's work falls into that category. However, looking at Jen's stories and novels only through that lens can blind a reader to the depth of her characters and the complex relationships she creates between them. With "Who's Irish?" Jen tells an immigrant story that is also a quintessentially American story.

Source: Kristen Sarlin Greenberg, Critical Essay on "Who's Irish?," in *Short Stories for Students*, Gale, Cengage Learning, 2017.

Esra Sahtiyanci Oztarhan
In the following review, Oztarhan highlights Jen's common theme of immigrant life.

GISH JEN INTENTIONALLY CREATES UNCONVENTIONAL AND UNREPRESENTATIVE CHARACTERS IN HER NOVEL TO REINVENT CHINESE AMERICANNESS TO THE SAME EXTENT AS SHE REINACTS HER AMERICANNESS."

Mona in the Promised Land is Asian American writer Gish Jen's novel about the identity quest of a Chinese American girl heroine Mona. The story takes place in early 1970's where Mona lives in a Jewish suburbia in Scarshill, NY, with her China born parents and her American born sister. The novel centers on the conversion of Mona into Judaism, thus reconstructs notions such as nationalism, assimilation, multiculturalism and identity that are the common themes of immigrant literature. Jen's novel brings new approaches to these notions by her choice of a young protagonist and her humorous style.

All the novels of Gish Jen are humorous stories about serious issues like racism and identity quest of Chinese Americans. Her first novel *Typical American* (1991) follows the lives of Ralph Chang, his sister and his sister's roommate who later becomes his wife. The novel is a satirical account of the family's various efforts of fulfilling the American dream, of becoming a "typical American" and the obstacles they face. The first line of the novel makes it clear that "it's an American story" in which the characters try to adapt to the American Dream while trying to hang on to their Chinese roots. Jen has also written a collection of short stories entitled *Who's Irish?* (1999), about the immigrant experiences of Chinese Americans, but also of Jewish Americans, African Americans, Irish Americans, etc.

Her latest book of 2004, *Love Wife*, explores similar issues such as being Chinese American in white mainstream society by portraying a racially mixed family. The family consists of Carnegie Wang, his WASP wife, whom Carnegie's mother refers to as "Blondie," their two adopted children and one biological son. Their family life is disturbed by the arrival of a Chinese cousin, who is arranged by Carnegie's mother to work as a nanny to the children. It becomes quite clear early on,

however, the Carnegie's mother brings the Chinese cousin into the family with the intension of presenting "an ideal wife" for her son. The Chinese cousin not only disturbs the relations of the couple as a "love wife," she also brings with her stories and traditions of China. Thus she enables the characters', mainly Carnegie's rediscovery of his Chinese roots. Jen's novel discusses concepts like what is real, what is constructed or what is natural, which will construct the basic problematic themes in her other novels as well.

Mona in the Promised Land is the continuation of her literary tradition of exploring the Chinese American experience in contemporary United States. The novel is the story of the Chinese American family Changs (who came to America in her first novel *Typical American*) that is told through the eyes of their daughter Mona. Mona is a typical adolescent having problems with her family and her peer group, who finds herself being converted to Judaism amidst these cultural controversies. The novel is a good example of ethnic bildungsroman with a clearly defined identity search. The bildung of the novel is reached when Mona, the rebellious adolescent, comes to a final reconciliation with her mother, and by so doing with her ancestry and roots and, paradoxically enough, it is precisely through Jewish rituals and conversion that Mona comes to understand her Chineseness. It is stated in the novel as such: "Now that she is Jewish, she feels more of a Chinese than ever"; or she says: "The more Jewish you become, the more Chinese you'll be." Gish Jen, therefore succeeded in portraying the pain of finding oneself in adolescence as a communal representation for the larger identity quest struggle of Chinese American immigrants as a whole. Therefore Jen defends the irresistible charm of returning to one's roots in coping with the racist and multicultural atmosphere of United States.

The novel apart from being an adolescent narrative, just like any immigrant story, reflects the in between situation of Chinese American Mona split between the Chinese and the American cultures. Jen depicts Mona's uneasiness as being like "a sore thumb . . . sticking out by herself." Being born and raised in America, she is under constant pressure from her parents who are still tied to their Chinese roots. She is also surrounded by her peer group, which pushes her to be like "an American girl." Mona has to find her own identity as opposed to her hyphenated one determined by the dominant culture, free from the identity her parents and peer group design for her. In this sense, Gish Jen's novel has so many common features with the Asian American women's fiction of 70's and 80's like Kingston, Ng and Tan's works. These works of Chinese American women with Jen's focus on the situation of the Chinese daughters born in United States torn between their parent's world and the new world. These novels reflect the ongoing generation struggle between "the swan feather mothers" and "Coca Cola daughters" so to say.

At the same time, Jen brings a fresh insight to Asian American women literature in the 1990s to "what it means to be an Asian American girl in 70's." Her novel is quite revolutionary by portraying a purely postmodern identity model for the new immigrants. It is Mona's solution to be torn between two cultures. As Mona summarizes by saying: "American means being whatever you want, and I happened to pick being Jewish." Mona with her new chosen identity of a "Catholic Chinese Jew" differs from the hybrid characters of the earlier literary examples. In her depiction of Mona's active claiming of Judaism, Jen criticizes the American Dream in the earlier immigrant literature by choosing to portray a character who claims fluid identities. The new American experiment is about the naturalness of choices. A possible reason why Jen used conversion to Judaism in the novel is because in the United States, the Chinese are called the "New Jews." That is because they seem to be the living proof of the American Dream, the "model minority." And it is exactly what Jen criticizes in her novel.

Mona's choice of changing her identity is a practical reflection of Homi Bhabha's "third space" concept of immigrant experience. It is defined as an empowering position, which enables the subject to choose among the various possibilities. Thus, Mona being in the third space, being neither a pure Chinese nor a typical American, feels free to choose whichever she likes. Belonging to neither culture is not a disempowering situation, but an interplay of identity for Mona. She tells her friends that she "just have to switch and that's all." From time to time when her exoticism attracts attention in class, she acts as if she knows Chinese and Chinese civilization. She tells her friends that: "[S]he knows karate . . . she can make her hands like steel by thinking hard . . . she knows how to get pregnant by tea . . . she knows Chinese." But in

fact all she knows in Chinese is how to say: "Stop acting crazy. Rice gruel. Soy sauce" which becomes enough to impress her friends. And from time to time she can reject her Chinese culture and roots entirely when she felt being oppressed by Chinese traditions. Mona converts to Judaism, because she believes it to be about "ask, ask, instead of just obey, obey" which is exactly the opposite of what she always hears at home about being the oppressed minority. These identity switches are predominant throughout the whole novel in other characters as well like her Jewish friends who decide to be a WASP, and back again at their convenience. Also for example her sister decides to become more Chinese than her parents all of a sudden. Mona's boyfriend joining the black power although he is white is another example of identity switch in the novel. This postmodern sense of unfixed identity is a criticism to Orientalist discourses and essentialist theories.

Jen changes the standard notion of Americanness, Jewishness and Chineseness completely by her work. Being a Chinese American women writer herself, she deconstructs all existing stereotypes. That is to say she criticizes the model minority myth of the previous generations. Some critics like Frank Chin label the works of Kingston, Ng and Tan as a continuation of the Western myth of "the model minority." In this respect Jen unlike the previous Asian American women writers subverts this existing tradition. Gish Jen intentionally creates unconventional and unrepresentative characters in her novel to reinvent Chinese Americanness to the same extent as she reinacts her Americanness. Jen says: "This book is not a denial of my heritage, but [America] is the place where I grew up. This is my country; this is what I know. And, in this book, I lay claim to that." In the same interview of the *Asian Week*, Jen confesses that she created her own definition of American. She says: "It is not something that you come into [and] particularly does not involve abandoning where you came from. I think of Americanness as a preoccupation with identity. It is the hallmark of the New World because we live in a society where you are not only who your parents were, and you don't already know what your children will be. That is not to say that I am blond and eat apple pie, but any definition that finds me less American—well, all I can say is that something is wrong with the definition." This reaction against essentialist definitions of identity brings out one of the best examples of a protagonist with a fluid identity in *Mona in the Promised Land.*

Despite its many strengths, there are a number of small weaknesses in the novel, like the plot being a bit erratic. The coming of age story of Mona ends too quickly at the end of the novel. The final bildung of reconciliation with her mother and her marriage are mentioned at the last two or three pages of the book before we understand how she grew up that fast. However, *Mona in the Promised Land* is an important and timely novel on postmodern identity. It opens new horizons in the minds of the reader in bringing forward brand new definitions to Asian American identity. Jen's criticism of Oriental identity and stereotypes provides new meanings to contemporary Chinese American and contemporary immigrant fiction. Moreover the story of Mona—often very humorous—offers new dimensions to many concepts of American culture like assimilation and discrimination. Academicians who are interested in ethnic studies, Asian American literature, identity theory, girl studies and contemporary women's literature can find Gish Jen's *Mona in the Promised Land* worth reading to witness the experiences of the new immigrants like Mona.

Source: Esra Sahtiyanci Oztarhan, Review of *Mona in the Promised Land*, in *Interactions*, Vol. 15, No. 2, Fall 2006, p. 165.

Publishers Weekly
In the following review, the anonymous reviewer writes that Jen's relatively short collection has the "impact . . . of a much longer work."

The Chinese-American author (*Typical American, Mona in the Promised Land*) is a known quantity by now, though her sometimes uproarious but just as often compassionate tales of culture clash always manage to find some new and surprising angles from which to ambush the reader. There are two novella-length tales in this breezy, assured collection: "Duncan in China" tells of a young man, a dropout at home, who achieves a certain bizarre status on a prolonged visit to contemporary China, and of the perplexing choices he has to make when all his usual assumptions are turned on their heads. "House, House, Home" is the account of Pammie's two marriages, to wry; eccentric Scandinavian Sven and, later, to massively laid-back Carver from Hawaii, and the sorts of space these very different men give her to move in. As always with Jen, a multitude of details, domestic and behavioral, are acutely observed, and the impact, in barely 80 pages, is that of a much longer work. The title story is a delightfully rueful account of a Chinese grandmother trying to come to terms with her spoiled Irish grandchild, "Birthmates" is a cunningly woven mixture of farce and pathos about a born loser looking for a job at a convention and "In the American Society" portrays the mixed dignity and foolishness of a traditional Chinese man trying, and failing, to adapt to our mores.

Source: Review of *Who's Irish?*, in *Publishers Weekly*, Vol. 246, No. 17, April 26, 1999, p. 52.

SOURCES

Amano, Kyoko, "Gish Jen," in *Oxford Bibliographies*, http://www.oxfordbibliographies.com/view/document/obo-9780199827251/obo-9780199827251-0129.xml (accessed March 1, 2016).

"America's Children: Key National Indicators of Well-Being, 2015," http://www.childstats.gov/americaschildren/family3.asp (accessed March 6, 2016).

Anshaw, Carol, Review of *The Love Wife*, in *Women's Review of Books*, Vol. 22, No. 2, November 2004, p. 8.

El Nasser, Haya, "More Multigenerational Households in Immigrant Areas," in *USA Today*, October 25, 2012, http://www.usatoday.com/story/news/nation/2012/10/25/census-multigenerational-households/1653159 (accessed March 6, 2016).

Fry, Richard, and Jeffrey S. Passel, "The Growth in Multigenerational Family Households," Pew Research Center website, July 17, 2014, http://www.pewsocialtrends.org/2014/07/17/the-growth-in-multi-generational-family-households (accessed March 6, 2016).

"Gish: Q&A," Gish Jen website, http://www.gishjen.com/?page_id=16# (accessed March 1, 2016).

Jen, Gish, "Who's Irish?," in *Who's Irish? Stories*, Vintage Contemporaries, 1999, pp. 3–16.

Moyers, Bill, "Interview with Gish Jen," in *Becoming American: The Chinese Experience*, http://www.pbs.org/becomingamerican/ap_pjourneys_transcript1.html (accessed March 1, 2016).

Oztarhan, Esra Sahtiyanci, Review of *Mona in the Promised Land*, in *Interactions*, Vol. 15, No. 2, Fall 2006, p. 165.

"Physical Punishment," http://www.nospank.net/aap4-b.htm; originally published in *Caring for Your School-Age Child: Ages 5 to 12*, Bantam, 1995.

Review of *Who's Irish?: Stories*, in *Publishers Weekly*, Vol. 246, No. 17, April 26, 1999, p. 52, http://www.publishersweekly.com/978-0-375-40621-8 (accessed March 1, 2016).

Roth, Philip, "Reading Myself," in *Conversations with Philip Roth*, edited by George J. Searles, University Press of Mississippi, 1992, p. 66; originally published in *Partisan Review*, Vol. 40, 1973, pp. 404–17.

"Spanking Children & Mental Health: Punishment Linked to Disorders Later in Life," in *Huffpost Parents*, July 2, 2012, http://www.huffingtonpost.com/2012/07/02/spanking-children-linked-to-mental-health-disorders_n_1643422.html (accessed March 6, 2016).

Thompson, Jean, "Typical Americans," in *New York Times*, June 27, 1999, http://www.nytimes.com/books/99/06/27/reviews/990627.27thom.html (accessed March 1, 2016).

"U.S. Immigration since 1965," in *History.com*, http://www.history.com/topics/us-immigration-since-1965 (accessed March 6, 2016).

Yen, Hope, "Interracial Marriage Still Rising but at a Slower Pace than 1990s," in *Diverse Issues in Higher Education*, May 28, 2010, http://diverseeducation.com/article/13836/ (accessed March 6, 2016).

FURTHER READING

Crew, Linda, *Children of the River*, Perfection Learning, 1991.
> When she is thirteen years old, Sundara is forced to leave her home and her family behind to escape the Khmer Rouge army. Living in Oregon four years later, she struggles to balance the traditions and expectations of her Cambodian upbringing with her life as an American high school student.

Gallo, Donald R., ed., *First Crossing: Stories about Teen Immigrants*, Candlewick, 2007.
> This edition is a reprint of the popular original volume. Eleven well-known authors offer tales

of the immigrant experience across a wide range of economic and cultural backgrounds.

Houston, Jeanne, and James Houston, *Farewell to Manzanar*, HMH Books for Young Readers, 2002.
> Jeanne Wakatsuki Houston cowrote this memoir with her husband. It recounts her experiences in the Manzanar internment camp during World War II. Although the imprisonment of thousands of Japanese Americans is an extreme example, the book reflects the alienation many immigrants and children of immigrants feel even after deciding to make the United States their home.

Jen, Gish, *Tiger Writing: Art, Culture, and the Interdependent Self*, Harvard University Press, 2013.
> This nonfiction volume comprises transcripts of a lecture series Jen gave at Harvard, her alma mater. She draws from a variety of sources, from academic studies and philosophy to personal family stories, to discuss the differences in narrative literature in the East and the West and in the process explains her own background and development as a writer.

SUGGESTED SEARCH TERMS

Gish Jen AND "Who's Irish?"

Gish Jen AND Asian American writer

Gish Jen AND immigrant life

Gish Jen AND interview

research about spanking

methods of child discipline

multigenerational households

Chinese American family values

The Wide Net

EUDORA WELTY

1943

"The Wide Net" is a story by Eudora Welty, first published in 1943 in her short-story collection *The Wide Net and Other Stories*. The story is about a young couple, William Wallace Jamieson and his wife, Hazel, who is three months pregnant. After they have a quarrel, William Wallace stays out all night drinking with his friends, and when he returns, he finds a note from Hazel saying she is going to drown herself in the nearby river. William Wallace rounds up some neighbors, and they all go to drag the river in search of Hazel. The tale that unfolds, despite what appears to be a rather desperate situation, has a largely comic tone, and it combines realism with myth and symbolism. In the end, William Wallace gains deeper insight into the natural cycles of life and the role of the feminine, and he and Hazel are eventually able to restore harmony in their relationship.

AUTHOR BIOGRAPHY

Eudora Alice Welty was born April 13, 1909, in Jackson, Mississippi, the daughter of Christian Welty, an insurance executive from Ohio, and Chestina, a homemaker from West Virginia. As a young girl, she was an enthusiastic reader, particularly enjoying the work of Charles Dickens, Sir Walter Scott, Robert Louis Stevenson, and Mark Twain. She also showed an early

Eudora Welty (©*Ulf Andersen / Getty Images*)

talent for writing, publishing several stories in children's magazines before she entered her teens. At Central High School in Jackson, she published poems and sketches in the school newspaper. In 1925, she entered Mississippi State College for Women in Columbus, knowing even then that she wanted to be a writer. For her final two years of college, she transferred to the University of Wisconsin, Madison. She graduated in 1929 with a bachelor of arts degree. She then spent an academic year in New York City at Columbia University's Graduate School of Business.

In 1931, Welty worked in Jackson, doing a variety of jobs and editing news stories for the local radio station. Several years later, she worked as publicity agent and photographer for the Works Progress Administration, part of the government's New Deal program. In 1936, her first short story was published, in the magazine *Manuscript*. More success followed, and her stories soon began to appear in literary magazines such as *Southern Review*. Welty's first-short story collection, *A Curtain of Green and Other Stories*,

was published in 1942, followed in the same year by *The Robber Bridegroom*, a novella. "The Wide Net," which had been published in a magazine in 1942, was included as the title story in the collection *The Wide Net and Other Stories* in 1943. The story won the O. Henry Memorial Prize in 1942.

In 1944, Welty worked for the *New York Times Book Review*, and later in that decade she traveled to France, Italy, England, and Ireland, funded by a Guggenheim Fellowship. In 1949, a collection of seven Welty stories was published as *The Golden Apples*, followed by *Bride of the Innisfallen and Other Stories* (1955), which proved to be her final collection of stories. Although her literary reputation rests largely on her short stories, Welty also wrote five novels: *Delta Wedding* (1946), *The Ponder Heart* (1954), *The Shoe Bird* (juvenile) (1964), *Losing Battles* (1970), and *The Optimist's Daughter* (1972), which won the Pulitzer Prize in 1973. Welty's nonfiction includes her best-selling autobiography, *One Writer's Beginnings* (1983).

Welty received many awards, including the National Medal for Literature by the American Academy of Arts and Letters, the Rea Award for the Short Story for her contributions to the American short story, and the PEN/Malamud Award for excellence in the short story. Welty died of pneumonia in Jackson, Mississippi, on July 23, 2001, at the age of ninety-two.

PLOT SUMMARY

I

The story is set in October in Mississippi, near the Pearl River and a natural trail known as the Natchez Trace. William Wallace Jamieson's wife, Hazel, is three months pregnant with their first child. William Wallace thinks that she is acting strangely. She sometimes will not talk to him and runs away or sticks her tongue out at him when he touches her. Frustrated by her behavior, he decides to go out drinking with his friends. He stays out all night, and when he returns, he finds a note from Hazel saying that she can no longer put up with him and intends to drown herself in the nearby river. William is both alarmed and puzzled, since Hazel is afraid of water.

He goes outside and calls for his neighbor, Virgil Thomas, who was one of his two drinking buddies the night before. William Wallace tells Virgil what has happened and says they must drag the river. As they walk down the road

MEDIA ADAPTATIONS

- A recording of Welty reading "The Wide Net" live at a public reading in 1985 is available on YouTube (https://www.youtube.com/watch?v=BO-i31EXSo4).

- The story can also be heard as part of *The Collected Stories of Eudora Welty*, read by various performers and released by Brilliance Audio. The recording is available from https://www.brillianceaudio.com/product?i=5165. The running time is thirty-three hours.

together, William Wallace recalls the first time he met Hazel, who is a very pretty woman. He worries that her mother will come after him, and he regrets having stayed out all night. It is the first time he has misbehaved, he tells Virgil, but he still cannot see how Hazel managed to jump into the water, given her fear of it. Virgil says she must have jumped backwards, without looking.

As they walk along, they see no signs that Hazel has been there. William Wallace stops to catch a rabbit and then lets it go as Virgil reminds him of their purpose. They pause at the top of a hill and decide to get two local families, the Malones and the Doyles, to help them. Six Doyles show up with their dogs, and eight Malones come. Two boys, Grady and Bruce Rippon arrive to help; their father drowned in the Pearl River. Two African American boys named Sam and Robbie Bell also come.

They all go to see Doc, who owns the wide net they need to drag the river. Doc sits in his house high on the hill. William Wallace asks to borrow the net and explains the circumstances. Doc is by no means convinced that Hazel drowned herself, but he allows them to borrow the net and goes along with them. They take a path through the woods. From a high ridge, they watch a freight train passing. Then they arrive at the riverbank, at a point where the river is deep.

II

They stretch the net from bank to bank of the Pearl River, with weights to take it down to the bottom. They begin to drag the river, moving upstream. Doc sits in a rowboat, observing everything. They catch many fish, big and small, in the net, as well as shoes. Seven alligators pass by, and then one alligator is caught in the net. They put the alligator on a sandbank. The Malones say they will take it home with them, although Doc advises them not to.

A string of beads turns up, a heron is sighted, and an eel slides out of the net. At noon, they see a short man with a straw hat who is following them on the other side of the river. No one knows who he is. Virgil swims across the river and speaks to him. Virgil pushes him to the ground, and when the man gets up, he just walks away. When Virgil rejoins the others, he says he warned the man off, even though he said he was harmless.

William Wallace keeps diving to the bottom of the river. At the very depths, it is dark and still. He stays down there for a long time, and when he finally comes back up, he looks dreadfully unhappy. It is as if he has been away from the world for a long time.

By late afternoon, it is time to eat. They start a fire and cook the catfish they caught, eating so much they fall asleep. They do not sleep for long. When William Wallace wakes, he feels good and dances on the sand, laughing, with a big catfish hooked to his belt buckle. Then suddenly, everyone points to the river, where a long snake appears: it is the King of the Snakes, stretching all across the river. William Wallace stares at it until it goes back under the water.

There is a severe thunderstorm with heavy rain. Everyone takes shelter under a tree by the riverbank. Sam and Robbie Bell are nervous because being struck by lightning runs in the family, they say. A large tree is hit by lightning, splits, and falls. Another tree on the opposite side of the river also falls. The river fills with whirlpools. The people are all covered by blown leaves. Virgil points out that they have almost reached the town of Dover and points out that William Wallace has cut his foot on a sharp rock.

III

In Dover, the town looks like new after the thunderstorm. They walk through the town, each carrying their big catch of fish on high. They pass Hazel's mother's house. The townspeople come out and look as the men and boys parade past, wondering at the large amounts of fish on display. Everyone wants to know if they are for sale, but William Wallace says they can have them for nothing. The Malones protest, but William Wallace says he does not want the fish; all he wants is his wife. Hazel's mother emerges from her house, demanding to know what they have done with Hazel. William Wallace turns his back on her and on everyone else, and with that, the party breaks up.

At sunset, Doc sits on his porch. William Wallace returns the net, and he and Virgil exchange some words with Doc. Doc says it was an excellent river dragging, but William Wallace points out that they did not find Hazel. Doc says she was not in the river, and he had never thought she was.

On his way home, accompanied by Virgil, William Wallace angrily complains about Doc, saying he should not have come to the river dragging. William Wallace insists that he himself is the one who knows Hazel. He believes that she would have jumped into the river and that Doc has no business saying otherwise. Virgil tries to calm his friend down but only succeeds in making William Wallace more angry by saying he himself was most essential to the effort. They fight physically for a brief time, until Virgil is forced to say that it was William Wallace's river dragging, not his.

As they walk home, they hear music coming from the grounds of an old church. A young girl is singing a ballad at an event called the Sacred Harp Sing. Virgil bids him goodnight and goes home. William Wallace returns to his own house and is surprised to see that it has not rained. However, he sees a rainbow curving over the roof.

A few moments after entering the house, he hears his name called. Hazel emerges from the bedroom. He asks her how she feels, and she gives a contradictory answer. He shows her the cut he got on his foot while dragging the river. Hazel replies that he should be more careful. She adds that supper is ready, and she has been wondering if he would come home.

After supper, they sit out on the front steps. Hazel says she was hiding close by as he read the letter that morning. William Wallace then puts her across his knee and gives her a not-too-serious spanking, making her promise not to do the same thing again. The good feeling between them is restored, though Hazel says she will do

it again, only in a different way. They go inside, hand in hand.

CHARACTERS

Sam and Robbie Bell

Sam and Robbie Bell are two young African American boys who go on the river drag. They sit in the rowboat with Doc and steer it. During the thunderstorm, they are scared, because both their grandfather and their father died after being struck by lightning.

Doc

Doc lives in a house at the top of a hill. He owns the net that is used in the dragging of the river. Doc appears to be much older than the others, and William Wallace thinks he "is the smartest man around." It is clear from the beginning that Doc doubts whether Hazel drowned herself, but he invites himself to the river dragging all the same. He stands a little apart from the action, watching everything from a small rowboat. At the end of the day, he says to William Wallace and Virgil that he had never believed that Hazel was in the river.

Doyles

Six members of the Doyle family join the river dragging. They are not named or differentiated in any way, other than the fact that they say almost nothing. It is their dogs that make all the noise. During the drag, they swim and push the net from behind as Virgil tells them what to do.

Hazel's Mother

Hazel's mother appears to be a formidable woman. William Wallace says she has the appetite of a man, and he is scared that when she hears about Hazel's disappearance, she will come after him. Later, Hazel's mother comes out of her house in Dover when the river-dragging party parades through the streets. She demands to know what they have done to Hazel.

Hazel Jamieson

Hazel Jamieson is William Wallace's wife. The two have been married for one year, and she is three months pregnant. Everyone thinks she is very attractive and intelligent too. Doc thinks she is the prettiest girl in Mississippi. Hazel and her husband encounter some difficulties in their relationship, and when he decides to stay out all night, she responds by playing a little trick on him, perhaps hoping that she will teach him a lesson. She leaves a note for him saying that she is going to drown herself in the river. Later, when she reveals that she was hiding in the house when he read the note and even watched him reading it, it appears that she has used her ingenuity to reset the balance of power in their relationship and recapture their former love and intimacy.

William Wallace Jamieson

William Wallace Jamieson is a young man who has been married to Hazel for about one year. When she becomes pregnant, he thinks she is acting strangely, and they likely have a quarrel, as a result of which William Wallace stays out all night drinking with his buddies. William Wallace believes that his wife may have deliberately drowned herself, even though he knows she is scared of water, so he rounds up the local men to drag the river. During the dragging, William Wallace does a little bit of everything, but most of the time, he is swimming in the river or diving to the bottom.

Malones

Eight members of the Malone family show up for the drag. They are all large men "with great long black eyelashes." During the drag, they swim and pull near the shore, groaning from the effort. When they catch a baby alligator, they decide to keep him.

Grady and Bruce Rippon

Grady and Bruce Rippon are two small local boys who join the river dragging. Their father drowned in the Pearl River. During the drag, they walk along the sandbars carrying buckets and lines.

Virgil Thomas

Virgil Thomas is a friend and neighbor of William Wallace's. Virgil is one of the men who is with William Wallace when they stay out all night drinking, and it is Virgil whom William Wallace first consults regarding Hazel's disappearance. Together they round up the crew that will drag the river. When Virgil and William Wallace talk, Virgil tends to agree with what his friend says and backs him up in his opinions. He thinks it is indeed likely that Hazel drowned herself in the river. Virgil plays a large role in the dragging of the river, directing operations. On the way home after their expedition, Virgil and William Wallace get into a quarrel, which leads to a brief fight between them, but they soon make peace.

THEMES

Husband-Wife Relationships

Although the details of the relationship between William Wallace and his wife, Hazel, are somewhat sparsely presented, it is clear from the opening paragraph of the story that they have not been getting along well since Hazel became pregnant. They have been married only one year, and Hazel is going through a phase where she struggles to communicate with her husband:

> When he came in the room she would not speak to him, but would look as straight at nothing as she could with her eyes glowing. If he only touched her she stuck out her tongue or ran around the table.

William Wallace is puzzled by her behavior and thinks it might be something to do with her being pregnant. It appears that neither husband nor wife has any idea of how to improve the situation between them. Frustrated, William Wallace decides to go out drinking with his male buddies and stays out all night. This is not the most constructive thing he might have done, and it shows that he is in need of some new way of understanding and dealing with his wife. Hazel's response to the situation is a cunning one: she leaves a note for him saying that she is going to drown herself in the river, which she actually has no intention of doing. Perhaps she wants to test her husband with this note, to see how he reacts and what he will do. It is a testament to the fact that William Wallace does not know his wife very well that when he reads the note he believes that Hazel may indeed have drowned herself, even though he knows she is frightened of water.

When William Wallace rounds up a team of local men to drag the river, he is really going on a symbolic quest for deeper knowledge about life, about Hazel, and about the feminine principle in general. At the literal level of the story, he is not aware of this deeper purpose at all; he organizes the river dragging solely in order to find his wife's body. However, it seems that the mysterious process of life has something else in store for him, and it is through his immersion in the river that he will discover it, although even then he may not consciously be aware of it.

TOPICS FOR FURTHER STUDY

- Give a class presentation in which you examine the role played by Doc in "The Wide Net" and link him to the archetype of the wise old man.

- Choose another story by Welty and write an essay in which you compare and contrast it to "The Wide Net." "A Piece of News," which is also a story about marriage that contains comic elements, might be a suitable story for comparison.

- Go to http://www.easel.ly/ and create an infographic about Welty, including the most important facts about her life and work.

- Write a short story featuring the characters William Wallace Jamieson and his wife, Hazel. Set the story a little while after the incident described in "The Wide Net." How will Hazel react when she and William Wallace next have a disagreement? How will William Wallace respond to her? How will they resolve the situation?

- Consult *Teen Love, on Relationships: A Book for Teenagers*, by Kimberley Kirberger (1999), which is full of useful advice about how to handle romantic relationships, much of it in the form of letters from actual teens. Using information from this book, write a letter to either of the two fictional characters in "The Wide Net," William Wallace or Hazel, giving them some insight into typical male and female behaviors in relationships and how they could improve their marriage.

A clue about the nature of William Wallace's quest is suggested when he unaccountably forgets the name of the river, even though everyone knows it is the Pearl River. Even when he is reminded of the name, he looks "down at the river as if it were still a mystery to him." The river comes to represent the depths of life—about which he has much to learn, it seems. On the surface, then, the river dragging is a great adventure that everyone enjoys, but at a deeper level, William Wallace learns something profound, although if one were to ask him what it was, he would likely be unable to articulate it. It is presented in mysterious, tentative terms, more as a question than an answer. William Wallace keeps diving to the bottom of the river at its deepest point, finding "the dark clear world of deepness." He is gone a very long time:

> Had he suspected down there, like some secret, the real, the true trouble that Hazel had fallen into, about which words in a letter could not speak . . . how (who knew?) she had been filled to the brim with that elation that they all remembered, like their own secret, the elation that comes of great hopes and changes, sometimes simply of the harvest time, that comes with a little course of its own like a tune to run in the head, and there was nothing she could do about it—they knew—and so it had turned into this? It could be nothing but the old trouble that William Wallace was finding out, reaching and turning in the gloom of such depths.

When he surfaces "it was in an agony from submersion," and he looks around "in astonishment, as if a long time had gone by, away from the pale world where the brown light of the sun and the river and the little party watching him trembled before his eyes."

It is clear that something profound has gone on, but it is not all that clear what it might have been. It seems likely that William Wallace is getting the glimmer of an understanding about Hazel's "great hopes and changes," and these are linked to her pregnancy but also to harvest time. The reader is likely to recall that Doc, who fulfills the archetypal role of wise man, comments earlier in the story that it is the "changing-time. . . . Any day now the change will come." He is referring to the fact that it is fall, and nature is in the process of change. "Everything just before it changes looks to be made of gold," Doc says, which makes William Wallace think of Hazel sitting at home "like a piece of pure gold, too precious to touch." Hazel is nurturing an as-yet-unborn life and is therefore part of the changing world that Doc talks about; she is fulfilling her feminine role in the great natural cycle of growth, decay, and rebirth, but William Wallace, intent on his masculine need to go on a heroic quest in search of his lost wife, has not yet made that connection.

Near the end of the story, however, there are clear hints that as a result of his expedition, he has become more attuned to the feminine

After William stays out all night drinking, Hazel leaves a note announcing her intention to drown herself (©alexnika | Shutterstock.com)

voice in life. From the grounds of a church, he hears a Sacred Harp Sing, in which a lady dressed in white plays an organ and a young girl sings. These "sweet sounds of music" make an impression on him. Then, when he reaches his house, he sees curving over the roof a rainbow in the night sky: "In the light of the moon . . . it looked small and of gauzy material, like a lady's summer dress, a faint veil through which the stars showed." This suggests the apprehension on the part of William Wallace of a kind of benevolent, cosmic feminine energy that enfolds his house. When he enters, he finds Hazel there, and they engage in a playful exchange (including a mild spanking administered by William Wallace) that seems to show that they have recovered a healthy balance in their relationship and understand each other better. Hazel may well submit to the spanking but also makes it clear that although she has promised not to write another letter like the one William Wallace found, she has other tricks up her sleeve regarding how to deal with her husband whenever they should be needed.

The last sentence of the story, as they go back into the house from the porch, suggests that Hazel has recovered her feminine power in their relationship, and there is the hint of a benign goddess about her: "She took him by the hand and led him into the house, smiling as if she were smiling down on him." It is likely that because of his deep immersion in the river—the depths of life—William Wallace has become more aware of the power and nature of the feminine, and he is ready to engage with it rather than run away from it, as he did when he stayed out all night drinking.

Chivalry

Chivalry refers to a polite way of behaving, especially in a way that a man behaves toward a woman or women. It also refers to qualities that knights in the Middle Ages were expected to embody, such as courage and honesty, in addition to courtesy to women. In the society depicted in the story, manners play a large role. William Wallace tells Virgil that the first time he met Hazel he "spoke to her with nice manners" and that he has always behaved himself until that one night he went out drinking. There are several references to Hazel as "Lady Hazel," suggesting a medieval lady, and when this particular damsel is in distress, all the male members of the neighborhood join forces in a chivalrous quest to find her. The Doyles and the Malones are like the ranks of medieval knights lining up in formation to do their duty. These southern knights go through trials and tests, as might be expected on a medieval quest adventure. The quest, however, is presented in the form of parody, pointing to and at the same time undermining the masculine ideal. When William Wallace catches a fish, for example, the cry goes up from the Malones, "Rassle with him, son!" which is a parody of knightly or mythic combat, in which the hero might battle a sea monster. In his valiant efforts on behalf of the lady, William Wallace sustains a wound to his foot, which he proudly shows off to Hazel at the end of the story, as a kind of badge of honor.

STYLE

Comic Tone

The story combines realism with elements of myth within an overall comic tone, which undercuts the apparent seriousness of the situation, in which a woman may have drowned herself in the river. There are several hints early on, however, that Hazel did no such thing, and Doc in particular does not believe she did. The leisurely way in which William Wallace and Virgil walk along the road chit-chatting before they round up the river-dragging crew also undermines the ostensible seriousness of the situation. Therefore, when the river dragging yields nothing but a mountain of shoes and fishes (and a string of lady's beads), it is no surprise to the reader, and nor is Hazel's appearance at home, safe and sound, at the end of the story.

In the meantime, the reader can enjoy the comical, fantastical adventure the men experience on the river, with its bizarre incidents, such as when William Wallace, after having feasted with the others on the fish they caught, leaps up, "trampling the sand, up and down, and doing a dance so crazy that he would die." The comic tone is also apparent in other incidents, such as when seven alligators appear in

the river, and Grady says to look at their great teeth, in spite of the fact that "the alligators were not showing their teeth at all." The idea of the Malones keeping the captured baby alligator as a pet is also presented in a comic light.

Myth and Literature

There are several allusions to myth and literature in the story. Virgil, William Wallace's friend who accompanies him on the river dragging, brings to mind Virgil, the ancient Roman poet, who is Dante's guide through hell in *The Divine Comedy*. In Virgil's epic poem *The Aeneid*, which tells the story of Aeneas, a Trojan who traveled to Italy and whose descendants founded Rome, there is an episode set in Carthage, a city in North Africa. Aeneas has a love affair with Dido, queen of Carthage, but eventually leaves her at the behest of the gods, and Dido, grief-stricken, commits suicide. In "The Wide Net," William Wallace spends part of his night out at a carnival at Carthage, which is a real city in Leake County, Mississippi, but has the added advantage of putting the unhappy story of Dido and Aeneas's love affair in the reader's mind. The old story also echoes the fact that William Wallace left his wife (if only for one night) and that Hazel may have taken her own life in response.

HISTORICAL CONTEXT

Natchez Trace

"The Wide Net," is set in the Natchez Trace area in Mississippi. As they walk to the Pearl River, William Wallace, Doc, and Virgil, take the same route they always do: the Old Natchez Trace, which "took them through the deep woods and led them out down below on the Pearl River." Other stories in the collection *The Wide Net*, such as "First Love" and "A Still Moment," share the same setting and also allude to the history of the region, as does Welty's first novel, *The Robber Bridegroom*. In *Understanding Eudora Welty*, Michael Kreyling notes that the Natchez Trace has been important in the history of Mississippi not only to Native Americans for centuries but also since the area was settled by Americans in the late eighteenth century. Covering six hundred miles, by the beginning of the nineteenth century, the Trace had become "the major overland route for emigrants from the trans-Appalachian and trans-Alleghany east to the new territory of the

COMPARE
&
CONTRAST

- **1940s:** Writers of the Southern Renascence are very productive throughout the decade. Notable works include William Faulkner's novel *The Hamlet* (1940), Katherine Anne Porter's collection of short stories *The Leaning Tower* (1944), and Tennessee Williams's play *The Glass Menagerie* (1945).

  Today: Southern writers continue to make a rich contribution to American literature. Richard Ford is known for his novels and short stories, especially the novel *Independence Day* (1995), and Charles Frazier's *Cold Mountain* (1997) won the National Book Award for fiction. Other southern writers who are making their literary mark include Lee Smith, Ron Rash, Jesmyn Ward, and Ann Pancake.

- **1940s:** White people in the South routinely refer to African Americans with a term that is now considered a racial slur, as William Wallace does with Sam and Robbie Bell in the "The Wide Net." Others, such as the story's narrator, use an alternative term, *Negro*.

  Today: The term that was common in the 1940s in reference to African Americans is now completely unacceptable, a remnant of the old racist South.

- **1940s:** There is a reference in "The Wide Net" to "talk of war," and if the story is set around the time of its publication, this must refer to World War II. The United States enters World War II in December 1941, following the Japanese attack on the US naval base at Pearl Harbor.

  Today: The United States is not involved in any full-scale wars but remains engaged in a long-running struggle against global terrorism.

---

lower Mississippi." Kreyling also notes that in the 1930s, plans were under way to build a paved road that would cover the entire distance of the Trace, from near Nashville, Tennessee, to Natchez, Mississippi.

The Southern Renascence

The Southern Renascence (or Renaissance) refers to literature written by southern American writers beginning in the early 1920s and continuing to about 1950. During this time period, writers from the South dominated the American literary scene. The Southern Renascence began with a literary group known as the Nashville Fugitives, an association of poets and critics, including John Crowe Ransom, Allen Tate, Robert Penn Warren, and Donald Davison, who in their writings had a marked influence on how poetry was written in subsequent decades. The Nashville Fugitives, as well as many other southern writers, advocated the preservation of Southern culture as a bulwark against materialism and industrialization, which they believed produced an undesirable homogenizing effect on American culture. Another Southern group, the Agrarians, consisting of novelists, poets, and academics, also wanted to preserve Southern ways and were opposed to industrialization.

The most famous writer associated with the Southern Renascence was William Faulkner. Like Welty, Faulkner was from Mississippi, and he lived most of his life in Oxford, a small town of in the northern part of the state. Faulkner's novels include *The Sound and the Fury* (1929) and *As I Lay Dying* (1930), and he won the Nobel Prize in Literature in 1950. Other southern writers of the period include Thomas Wolfe, Caroline Gordon, Cleanth Brooks, Zora Neal Hurston, Richard Wright, Tennessee Williams, Flannery O'Connor, and Katherine Anne Porter.

As a writer who lived all her life in Mississippi and set her fiction in that state, Welty is a southern writer. When she began to publish in

William asks friends for help, and they get a wide net to drag the river, searching for Hazel's body *(©Love Silhouette / Shutterstock.com)*

the late 1930s, the Southern Renascence was well under way. Some of Welty's early work was linked by reviewers to Southern Gothic, a strain of literature that emphasizes the grotesque and may feature mentally disturbed, socially deviant characters. For example, Diana Trilling, reviewing *The Wide Net* in *Nation*, referred to Welty's having developed "her vision of horror to the point of nightmare." Welty also faced some criticism that in her work she romanticized the South during the days of slavery, although later critics, according to Carol Ann Johnston in *Eudora Welty: A Study of the Short Fiction*, rejected that view and had a greater appreciation for the universality of Welty's work, her strong sense of place notwithstanding.

CRITICAL OVERVIEW

Since its publication, "The Wide Net" has received quite a bit of attention from reviewers and critics. In the *New York Herald Tribune* in

1943, Leo Lerman describes the story as "a rollicking, robust, legend-like saga" that possesses "beauty, wit, deft characterizations, and a gentle irony." It is also "a comment upon man versus woman, and the woman has the last word." For the reviewer in the *Times Literary Supplement*, the story contains

> a rich, racy humour as well as a most sensitive eye for natural beauty in the deep South. . . . The magic of the woods, the wild flowers on the river bank, the golden sandbars, the baby alligator, the fishing, the drowsy and contented peace of it all, is wonderfully well conveyed.

Robert Penn Warren discusses the story in an influential essay on Welty's fiction first published in 1944. He views many of the stories, including "The Wide Net," as embodying "two poles" of existence: "the dream and the world, the idea and nature, innocence and experience, individuality and the anonymous, devouring life-flux, meaning and force, love and knowledge." In "The Wide Net," Hazel was feared to have drowned herself, but the key factor is her pregnancy; she had "sunk herself in the devouring

life-flux, has lost her individuality there." The
river into which William Wallace dives over
and over "is simply force. . . . Man has the definition, the dream, but when he plunges into the
river he runs the risk of having it washed away."
Warren notes, however, that in this story, "there
is not horror at the basic contrast, but a kind of
gay acceptance of the issue."

Of later critics, Michael Kreyling, in *Understanding Eudora Welty*, comments on the ending
of the story, noting that "the divisions between male
and female . . . are smoothed over. The procrea-
tive couple who retreat to their intimacy . . . have
found a way to make their differences complementary." Stephen M. Fuller, in *Eudora Welty and
Surrealism*, identifies elements of "surreal fantasy"
in the story, in terms of both characters and environment. He also notes Welty's "debt to the style of
surrealistic artists," including Salvador Dali. Welty's fiction "testifies to the ordering power of the
irrational in everyday living." In terms of "The
Wide Net," Fuller explains, "the river occupies a
central position because it serves as the site for
Welty's blending of material 'reality' into the flow
of the dream and abstract thought."

CRITICISM

Bryan Aubrey

*Aubrey holds a PhD in English. In the following
essay, he discusses "The Wide Net" in terms of
the opposites of masculine and feminine and
shows how William Wallace develops a deeper
knowledge and appreciation of the latter.*

With extensive use of myth and symbolism,
Welty's "The Wide Net" presents an amusing
but also profound episode in what is sometimes
referred to as the eternal battle of the sexes. The
young couple, William Wallace Jamieson and
his wife, Hazel, married but a year, find themselves immersed in a struggle for power that is
also a search for understanding. In the end,
they reach an understanding, although it is
Hazel who seems to hold the trump card.

The first scene in the story presents a marriage in crisis, largely because husband and wife
are unable to communicate with each other.
Hazel is pregnant, and William Wallace seems
to have little understanding of how his wife's
pregnancy might be affecting her mood and
demeanor. For her part, she appears to have
stopped talking to him altogether. They are at

> AS THE DRAGGING OF THE RIVER GETS
> UNDER WAY, IT BECOMES CLEAR THAT THIS IS NOT,
> IN FACT, A SEARCH FOR A DEAD BODY AT ALL. THE
> MEN DO NOT UNDERTAKE THEIR TASKS WITH A GRIM
> DEMEANOR, FEARING THE WORST; ON THE
> CONTRARY, THEY ALL HAVE A WONDERFUL TIME."

an impasse, but neither seems to have much idea
of how to get beyond it. Their responses are
crude: feeling rebuffed by his wife, William Wallace goes out on an all-night drinking binge with
two of his male buddies, while Hazel, in response
to that, writes him a note falsely saying that she is
going to drown herself in the river. Obviously,
this is a couple who have their work cut out for
them if they are going to restore the love they felt
for each other not too long ago but that appears
to have gone temporarily into hiding.

William Wallace is not helped much by his
friend Virgil as they walk to Doc's house to get
the net to drag the river, because as they chat,
they simply reinforce each other's patronizing
view of women: they agree that Hazel is one of
the prettiest girls around, and Virgil remarks that
it is a pity girls have to grow up to resemble their
mothers. William Wallace adds "She's smart too,
for a girl." When William Wallace says he is
baffled that she could just throw herself into the
river, Virgil has the answer: "It's a woman's
trick," he says. Whimsical tone notwithstanding,
there is a certain amount of casual, ingrained
misogyny here, although likely it is no more pronounced than how most men of that time and
place thought of women—as creatures rather
impossible to understand (since they do not think
in the same rational, straightforward way that all
men do) and needing to be kept in their place.

As the dragging of the river gets under way,
it becomes clear that this is not, in fact, a search
for a dead body at all. The men do not undertake
their tasks with a grim demeanor, fearing the
worst; on the contrary, they all have a wonderful
time. The river dragging may be hard work, but it
is men's work (no women are present), and in the
afternoon they all get to enjoy the fruits of their

WHAT DO I READ NEXT?

- Welty's story "Moon Lake" was first published in her collection *The Golden Apples* in 1949. It can also be found in *The Collected Stories of Eudora Welty*. The story takes place near the fictional town of Morgana, Mississippi, and focuses on the relationships between three girls at summer camp. Each of the girls goes through a difficult experience, including a near drowning. The story explores themes of identity and belonging and the passage from childhood to adolescence.

- *One Writer's Beginnings* (1984) is Welty's brief autobiography, based on three lectures she gave at Harvard University in 1983. Welty explains how her family and the southern environment in which she grew up helped to shape her both as an individual and as a writer.

- Born a decade and a half after Welty, Flannery O'Connor (1925–1964) was also a southerner who became known for her short stories. While Welty set her stories mostly in Mississippi, O'Connor's fictional world was central rural Georgia, where she spent much of her life. O'Connor died young but made a contribution to American literature that is still

valued today. *The Complete Stories* (1971) contains the thirty-one stories she wrote.

- *Eight Men: Short Stories* is a collection by Richard Wright, an African American writer who grew up in the South. These stories feature black protagonists struggling to find a place in a white society that does not accord them equal status. First published in 1960, the year of Wright's death, the collection was reprinted in 2008 in the Harper Perennial Modern Classics series.

- *A Daring Life* (2012), by Carolyn J. Brown, is a biography of Welty for young-adult readers. Brown concisely covers all the important aspects of Welty's life, including her family and her education, how her writing career got started, how she responded to the civil rights era of the 1950s and 1960s, and how by the 1970s she had become a universally acclaimed writer.

- Katherine Anne Porter, like Welty a southern writer, is particularly admired for her short stories. *The Collected Stories of Katherine Anne Porter* (1964, reprinted 1979) contains all her work in this genre, written mostly between the 1920s and 1940s.

---

labors, lazing on a sandbar, building a fire, and cooking and eating the catfish. "There ain't a thing better than fish," William Wallace says, and they all eat so much they fall asleep. When William Wallace awakes, he feels elated. He feels as good as he did the previous night when he went out on the town with his friends. He jumps up and leaps around, "trampling the sand, up and down, and doing a dance so crazy that he would die next." He takes a catfish, attaches it to his belt buckle "and [goes] up and down so that they all hollered." "Tears of laughter" roll down his cheeks in this spontaneous, improvised ritual, which seems to be a joyful assertion of the male life energy.

Robert Penn Warren, in his essay on Welty's fiction, calls William Wallace at this point in the novel a "river-god," and, indeed, he has a certain power, which becomes apparent in the very next paragraph, when the attention of the men is suddenly drawn again to the river, where a huge sea monster rises to the surface, as if called up by William Wallace's ecstatic dance. The cry goes up that it is the "King of the Snakes" and that it is looking William Wallace directly in the eye. William Wallace stares back at it, and the King of the Snakes quickly disappears under the water. It is as if William Wallace, having gone through some transformative ritual, is in command of the river and everything in it. He can face down even the mightiest of the river's life-forms.

William Wallace has also, in his repeated dives to the bottom of the river, amassed some vital knowledge about the feminine element in life—the very opposite of the masculine energy that he and the others are reveling in. The river symbolizes the totality of the flow of life, containing all opposites, including the feminine as well as the masculine elements. If Hazel is not literally at the bottom of the river, she is there symbolically, because in her pregnancy she is a part of the endless transformation of life, which is continually taking on new forms. This may not be an entirely comfortable experience for her; William Wallace intuits the "true trouble that Hazel had fallen into" and perhaps acquires some empathy for her situation. Although at this point William Wallace is still full of masculine bravado and has not yet integrated this new knowledge into his conscious awareness, it nonetheless will exert its influence on him and play a part in the reconciliation he effects with his wife at the end of the story. It is perhaps symbolized by the "little green ribbon of plant, root and all," that he finds himself holding after he comes to the surface of the river for the last time. It represents the fecundity of life, of which his pregnant wife is also an embodiment.

After the revelry with the fish, a thunderstorm blows in, and the men of the river-dragging crew take refuge under a large tree. Then they walk to Dover, which has also had rain, so much so that the town "looked somehow like new"—a hint, perhaps, that some kind of great transformation has been effected by the cleansing downpour. Muddy and tired the men may be, but they swagger into town like a conquering army, stretched out in ranks. William Wallace leads the parade, carrying a string of fish aloft for all to see. Virgil follows, doing the same thing, and then come the Doyles and the Malones, the latter holding up their baby alligator. The townspeople have never seen so many fish before and want to know if they are for sale. William Wallace's mood suddenly changes; he says they can have them for free (much to the Malones' annoyance) because he no longer wants them; what he wants is his wife. It as if William Wallace has had enough of all the masculine revelry and partying; now he must turn to that other pole of life, the feminine realm, and somehow make his peace with it, because by this

point he surely knows that Hazel is likely alive and well somewhere. He immediately comes face to face with one manifestation of the feminine: Hazel's angry mother, who wants to know what he has done with her daughter. He turns his back on her; it is Hazel he must deal with.

On the way home, he encounters signs of the feminine principle at work, beautifying the environment—the female voices that rise from the music festival on the grounds of the old church; the rainbow over his house that appears "of gauzy material like a lady's dress"—although when he gets in the house and hears his name called he reacts in a belligerent way, yelling "What do you want?" The challenge for this young couple is to reestablish their love after their mutual betrayal (he, by staying out all night; she, with her untruthful letter). William Wallace is anxious to show off the fact that he has sustained a wound in his foot searching for her; this is his claim to male heroism, although Hazel's response is rather less than he might have hoped for ("You ought to have been more careful").

After supper, Hazel admits that she was hiding in the house while he read the letter in the morning. William Wallace puts her in her place by spanking her, but no one is fooled here, perhaps not even William Wallace. Hazel is not exactly the chastened wife, corrected by properly exercised male authority. Immediately after promising not to do it again, she says she will do it again, although "next time will be different, too." This is not a woman who is going to be intimidated by a symbolic show of masculine force. It does seem, however, that they have recovered their good feelings for each other. After the spanking, "she lay smiling in the crook of his arm. It was the same as any other chase in the end."

William Wallace and Hazel are not the first couple to discover that underlying the love between a man and a woman, there is always a little tension, a little push and pull, that has to be managed very carefully lest it grow into open hostility or antagonism. They are going to have to continue to work things out between them; their marriage is an ongoing project, never finally resolved one way or another. However, the power, or at least the initiative, after this particular round seems to have shifted to Hazel, as the end of the story makes clear. As they are about to go back into the house from the porch, Hazel looks out across the yard, and her husband stands beside her

The story takes a magical turn when William goes under the water and meets the King of the Snakes
(©Rocksweeper | Shutterstock.com)

with the frown on his face, trying to look where she looked. And after a few minutes she took him by the hand and led him into the house, smiling as if she were smiling down upon him.

Thus does the woman, at this moment calm and authoritative in her goddess mode, lead a for-the-moment subdued man back into their house, into their marriage, peace restored—until next time.

Source: Bryan Aubrey, Critical Essay on "The Wide Net," in *Short Stories for Students*, Gale, Cengage Learning, 2017.

Harriet Pollack

In the following excerpt, Pollack explores literary allusions in "The Wide Net."

. . . "The Wide Net" builds on a generic mixing; it is a vernacular tale about a back-country couple's marital squabble that slips into the mythic tradition of the heroic quest. As she often does, Welty leads a reader to begin making meaning within the context of a "primary framework"—a term borrowed from sociologist Irving Goffman's discussion of the contextuality of interpretation. Then Welty guides a reader to suspect that this initial framing has been a misframing and to readjust that first interpretive strategy. The reader's reworking adds a layer to the interpretation which is still attached to the first frame and its meanings; the layers created by these multiple frameworks may subsequently interact.

A reader meeting "The Wide Net" for the first time begins what appears to be a realistic short story about William Wallace Jamieson's bemused reaction to his wife Hazel's first pregnancy. This father-to-be is troubled by a feeling that he has lost Hazel to some mystery; he feels excluded and resents her acting as though she were about to deliver, although she is only three months pregnant. In response to the situation, he has slipped away to a carnival in Carthage, Mississippi, and then stayed out all night with two boys down the road. But when he returns home, he does not find a chastened, more attentive Hazel. Instead he spots a little letter announcing her intention not to put up with him, but to

> WELTY MAKES WILLIAM WALLACE WANDER INTO A HARMONY WITH NATURE THAT CAUSES HIM TO REJOICE WHEN HE INTENDED TO DRAG THE RIVER FOR HIS WIFE'S BODY."

drown herself. In his distress, William Wallace turns for help to his friend Virgil Thompson, who has sat "on his neck" with him all the previous night, "done as much as he done, and come home at the same time." Together the two organize and conduct a river-dragging party.

Students of mine sometimes say that in their first encounter with the story they loved reading "The Wide Net," but they wonder why the tone of the story eventually seems genuinely celebratory when it might be expected to be full of comic grief. They echo Virgil's question to William Wallace: "Was you out catching cotton-tails, or was you out catching your wife?" It is entirely reasonable that when Hazel's husband gorges himself with fresh-caught fried fish, lapses into a sated sleep and wakes to dance with a catfish hanging from his belt, initial readers may feel startled, and either pleased or puzzled depending on their flexibility and their range of literary experience.

One way to understand the tale's midstream generic transformation from a realistic tale to something else is through its allusions. When it begins, William Wallace has, after all, just spent the night with Virgil. And like Vergil's Aeneas who wandered from his duty and his destiny in Queen Dido's Carthage, William Wallace has strayed from husbandly devotion at a carnival in Mississippi's Carthage.

Welty transforms a realistic short story into one lightly laced with the heroic epic, and then transforms the epic form that she lightly evoked. Susan Gubar has said that while women writers tend to escape their strained relationships with some conventional literary forms through generic amalgamations, she found that in putting together *The Norton Anthology of Women's Literature* she had not come across a woman writing the heroic epic. But it is clear that Welty is revising that form, transforming it precisely as it is gendered.

Vergil's *Aeneid* is not a single, privileged reference that readers must find evoked by the text in order to appreciate it. Nor is it a single key allusion that all studious readers must inevitably find. Michael Kreyling, for example, is helped by memories of Dante taking Vergil as a companion in his search for Beatrice (and later of the attitude of the madonna in Hazel's final gesture) (*Eudora Welty*). It would be inaccurate to claim that Welty's tale recreates any one epic. Rather the story evokes the generic elements of the mythic, heroic quest. Its comic tone is in part the product of a reader's barely conscious awareness of parody and transformation.

Consider, for example, William Wallace's band of men. As if we were in a Homerian epic, we find the clans of Dover represented in it: the eight giant Malones, the Doyles and their noisy dogs, Grady and Brucie Rippen who are tied to this search by their history (their father had drowned in the Pearl River) and two black boys, Sam and Robbie Bell. These troops stomp and paw each other, eager to go, attending while their leaders apply to wise Old Doc for permission to use the wide net; Old Doc himself plays the part of oracle. He is a seer who could foretell the day's outcome, but instead he only obliquely hints at it, not quite revealing fate's decree. He waits patiently for the inevitable to come to pass, and for the order of the universe to become as clear to others as it is to him. As Ruth Vande Kieft points out, there are also the ordeals which the questing hero survives. Like Aeneas who voyaged into the underworld, William Wallace dives to the deepest spot on the Pearl River, a spot "so dark that it was no longer the muddy world of the upper river but the dark, clear world of deepness" and returns from "the gloom of such depths" with an intuition of the "true trouble that Hazel had fallen into." Later he faces the inhabitant of these depths, that river creature, the King of Snakes, and he stares him down. Next he directs his men through a storm which steals the goldenness of the day. Lashing its tail "through the air," this tempest breaks the river "in a wound of silver," and fills the air with fragrance and a mystery reminiscent of Hazel's troubling mystery. Encountering this dragon-tailed storm, our hero founders on a sharp rock, opening a wound he later carries as a trophy of his quest. He reenters that town of Dover not obviously successful in his quest, but oddly triumphant.

Although the story shares several elements with the heroic epic, a reader making full sense of it must know that it also differs from them, and departs from expectations formed on knowledge of that genre. And this need to revise our expectations again, as in so many of Welty's works, brings us to the story's center. William Wallace, triumphant though he seems to be when he returns to Dover, has not in any obvious sense triumphed. That is, he has set out to find Hazel, but returns without her.

Unlike the traditional epic hero whose goal is clear, William Wallace's is not. For William Wallace needs, not to find Hazel, but to gain insight into what has possessed her and caused trouble between them. That is what Hazel, by writing her note, sends William Wallace to discover in the Pearl River. The effect of her suicide note is to send him into the natural world as it approaches its own "changing-time." And so Hazel leaves her husband to observe nature's cycle at this moment when, as Doc puts it, "any day now the change will come":

> It's going to turn from hot to cold, and we can kill the hog that's ripe and have fresh meat to eat. Come one of these nights and we can wander down here and trace a nice possum. Old Jack Frost will be pinching things up. Old Mr. Winter will be standing in the door. Hickory tree there will be yellow. Sweet-gum red, hickory yellow, dogwood red, sycamore yellow. . . . Magnolia and live-oak never die. Remember that. Persimmons will all get fit to eat, and nuts will be dropping like rain all through the woods here. And run, little quail, for we'll be after you too.

Standing on the verge of this ordered change and then immersing himself in the Pearl River, William Wallace intuits what Hazel must feel as she prepares to give birth: "the elation that comes of great hopes and changes, sometimes simply of the harvest time, that comes with a little course of its own like a tune to run in the head." That is, he rediscovers the excitement that nature's changeful cycles can generate. This is what he celebrates finding. Welty has amalgamated the pattern of heroic epic to emphasize the powerful (and mysterious) cycles of nature over a powerful hero's conquest—and made a female revision of a literary form by blending elements of comic realism, pastoral and epic. This accommodation of forms, one to the other, is appropriate to the story's content in which William Wallace comes to accommodate something female and puzzling.

Welty makes William Wallace wander into a harmony with nature that causes him to rejoice when he intended to drag the river for his wife's body. As he returns home from this odd experience, he hears the music of "the Sacred Harp Sing"—female music that seems to evoke an oblique and comic transformation of the Sirens' songs that attracted previous wanderers. William Wallace associates this celestial music permeating the woods with nature's female principle. "He [smiles] faintly, as he would at his mother, and at Hazel, and at the singing women in his life, now all one young girl standing up to sing under the trees the oldest and longest ballads there were." Then in the night sky, he sees a rainbow which looks to him "in the light of the moon . . . small and of gauzy material, like a lady's summer dress, a faint veil through which the stars showed." Affected by his glad knowledge of the Pearl River's depths, the night sky and the mysterious part that women play in mother nature's order, William Wallace walks back into his house. And there he finds Hazel awaiting his return from the ordeal she had conceived. Like some fairy-tale hero who has earned his heart's desire by successfully completing a series of tasks, William Wallace finds his life restored to routine domesticity. He feels relief, but also anger with Hazel who, coolly hidden in the closet, had watched him read her suicide note. Asserting himself against her mysterious and knowing superiority, he turns her upside down and spanks her. And she, responding unpredictably to his challenge, crawls into the crook of his arm. Then as she gazes into "the dark fields where the lightning bugs flickered," he stands beside her with a frown on his face, straining to see what she sees there in the natural world. And when, after a few minutes, she takes him by the hand and leads him into the house, "smiling as if she were smiling down on him," a reader may feel that though William Wallace will never share Hazel's experience entirely, he may now better intuit the source and implication of her mystery.

Return then to the reader's initial notion that somehow in the course of the day William Wallace wandered from his purpose: to recover Hazel. That first impression needed revision, even though Welty appeared to confirm it in Virgil's question "was you out catching cottontails or was you out catching your wife?" As in the case of Aeneas, who to all first appearances was waylaid from his purpose and destiny in Carthage, the wandering of a hero may prove to be his destiny, the path by which he will arrive where he is going—in this case, by way of a river-dragging with the boys from the town. . . .

Source: Harriet Pollack, "On Welty's Use of Allusion: Expectations and Their Revision in 'The Wide Net,' *The Robber Bridegroom*, and 'At the Landing,'" in *The Critical Response to Eudora Welty's Fiction*, edited by Laurie Champion, Greenwood Press, 1994, pp. 314–18.

SOURCES

Fuller, Stephen M., *Eudora Welty and Surrealism*, University Press of Mississippi, 2013, pp. 83–84.

"In the Deep South," in *Eudora Welty: The Contemporary Reviews*, edited by Pearl Amelia McHaney, Cambridge University Press, 2005, p. 47; originally published in *Times Literary Supplement*, May 5, 1945.

Johnston, Carol Ann, *Eudora Welty: A Study of the Short Fiction*, Twayne, 1997, pp. 8–9.

Kreyling, Michael, *Understanding Eudora Welty*, University of South Carolina Press, 1999, pp. 51, 68–69.

Lerman, Leo, "Daughter of the Mississippi," in *Eudora Welty: The Contemporary Reviews*, edited by Pearl Amelia McHaney, Cambridge University Press, 2005, p. 38; originally published in *New York Herald Tribune*, September 26, 1943.

Polk, Noel, "Eudora Welty," Mississippi History Now, http://mshistorynow.mdah.state.ms.us/articles/28/eudora-welty (accessed January 16, 2016).

Trilling, Diana, "Fiction in Review," in *Eudora Welty: The Contemporary Reviews*, edited by Pearl Amelia McHaney, Cambridge University Press, 2005, p. 40; originally published in *Nation*, October 2, 1943.

Warren, Robert Penn, "The Love and the Separateness in Miss Welty," in *Critical Essays on Eudora Welty*, edited by W. Craig Turner and Lee Emling Harding, G. K. Hall, 1989, pp. 47–48; originally published in *Kenyon Review*, Spring 1944, pp. 246–59.

Welty, Eudora, "A Wide Net," in *The Collected Stories of Eudora Welty*, Harcourt Brace Jovanovich, 1980, pp. 169–88.

FURTHER READING

Marrs, Suzanne, *Eudora Welty: A Biography*, Harcourt, 2005.
    This volume is the most thorough and reliable biography of Welty to date.

Polk, Noel, *Faulkner and Welty and the Southern Literary Tradition*, University of Mississippi Press, 2008.
    This is a collection of essays by a senior scholar of southern literature. The first essay, which gives the volume its title, is of particular value in placing Welty's work in the context of her time and place.

Prenshaw, Peggy W., ed., *Conversations with Eudora Welty*, University Press of Mississippi, 1984.
    This is a collection of interviews with Welty conducted over a forty-year period.

Woolf, Sally, *A Dark Rose: Love in Eudora Welty's Stories and Novels*, Louisiana State University Press, 2015.
    Woolf explores the many-sided theme of love and romance in Welty's work and includes a detailed reading of "The Wide Net."

SUGGESTED SEARCH TERMS

Eudora Welty

Welty AND "The Wide Net"

southern literature

Southern Renascence

Natchez Trace

Welty AND Natchez Trace

"The Wide Net" AND symbolism

"The Wide Net" AND myth

Glossary of Literary Terms

A

Aestheticism: A literary and artistic movement of the nineteenth century. Followers of the movement believed that art should not be mixed with social, political, or moral teaching. The statement "art for art's sake" is a good summary of aestheticism. The movement had its roots in France, but it gained widespread importance in England in the last half of the nineteenth century, where it helped change the Victorian practice of including moral lessons in literature. Oscar Wilde and Edgar Allan Poe are two of the best-known "aesthetes" of the late nineteenth century.

Allegory: A narrative technique in which characters representing things or abstract ideas are used to convey a message or teach a lesson. Allegory is typically used to teach moral, ethical, or religious lessons but is sometimes used for satiric or political purposes. Many fairy tales are allegories.

Allusion: A reference to a familiar literary or historical person or event, used to make an idea more easily understood. Joyce Carol Oates's story "Where Are You Going, Where Have You Been?" exhibits several allusions to popular music.

Analogy: A comparison of two things made to explain something unfamiliar through its similarities to something familiar, or to prove one point based on the acceptance of another. Similes and metaphors are types of analogies.

Antagonist: The major character in a narrative or drama who works against the hero or protagonist. The Misfit in Flannery O'Connor's story "A Good Man Is Hard to Find" serves as the antagonist for the Grandmother.

Anthology: A collection of similar works of literature, art, or music. Zora Neale Hurston's "The Eatonville Anthology" is a collection of stories that take place in the same town.

Anthropomorphism: The presentation of animals or objects in human shape or with human characteristics. The term is derived from the Greek word for "human form." The fur necklet in Katherine Mansfield's story "Miss Brill" has anthropomorphic characteristics.

Anti-hero: A central character in a work of literature who lacks traditional heroic qualities such as courage, physical prowess, and fortitude. Anti-heroes typically distrust conventional values and are unable to commit themselves to any ideals. They generally feel helpless in a world over which they have no control. Anti-heroes usually accept, and often celebrate, their positions as social outcasts. A well-known anti-hero is Walter Mitty in James Thurber's story "The Secret Life of Walter Mitty."

Archetype: The word archetype is commonly used to describe an original pattern or model from which all other things of the same kind are made. Archetypes are the literary images that grow out of the "collective unconscious," a theory proposed by psychologist Carl Jung. They appear in literature as incidents and plots that repeat basic patterns of life. They may also appear as stereotyped characters. The "schlemiel" of Yiddish literature is an archetype.

Autobiography: A narrative in which an individual tells his or her life story. Examples include Benjamin Franklin's *Autobiography* and Amy Hempel's story "In the Cemetery Where Al Jolson Is Buried," which has autobiographical characteristics even though it is a work of fiction.

Avant-garde: A literary term that describes new writing that rejects traditional approaches to literature in favor of innovations in style or content. Twentieth-century examples of the literary avant-garde include the modernists and the minimalists.

B

Belles-lettres: A French term meaning "fine letters" or" beautiful writing." It is often used as a synonym for literature, typically referring to imaginative and artistic rather than scientific or expository writing. Current usage sometimes restricts the meaning to light or humorous writing and appreciative essays about literature. Lewis Carroll's *Alice in Wonderland* epitomizes the realm of belles-lettres.

Bildungsroman: A German word meaning "novel of development." The *bildungsroman* is a study of the maturation of a youthful character, typically brought about through a series of social or sexual encounters that lead to self-awareness. J. D. Salinger's *Catcher in the Rye* is a *bildungsroman*, and Doris Lessing's story "Through the Tunnel" exhibits characteristics of a *bildungsroman* as well.

Black Aesthetic Movement: A period of artistic and literary development among African Americans in the 1960s and early 1970s. This was the first major African-American artistic movement since the Harlem Renaissance and was closely paralleled by the civil rights and black power movements. The black aesthetic writers attempted to produce works of art that would be meaningful to the black masses. Key figures in black aesthetics included one of its founders, poet and playwright Amiri Baraka, formerly known as Le Roi Jones; poet and essayist Haki R. Madhubuti, formerly Don L. Lee; poet and playwright Sonia Sanchez; and dramatist Ed Bullins. Works representative of the Black Aesthetic Movement include Amiri Baraka's play *Dutchman*, a 1964 Obie award-winner.

Black Humor: Writing that places grotesque elements side by side with humorous ones in an attempt to shock the reader, forcing him or her to laugh at the horrifying reality of a disordered world. "Lamb to the Slaughter," by Roald Dahl, in which a placid housewife murders her husband and serves the murder weapon to the investigating policemen, is an example of black humor.

C

Catharsis: The release or purging of unwanted emotions—specifically fear and pity—brought about by exposure to art. The term was first used by the Greek philosopher Aristotle in his *Poetics* to refer to the desired effect of tragedy on spectators.

Character: Broadly speaking, a person in a literary work. The actions of characters are what constitute the plot of a story, novel, or poem. There are numerous types of characters, ranging from simple, stereotypical figures to intricate, multifaceted ones. "Characterization" is the process by which an author creates vivid, believable characters in a work of art. This may be done in a variety of ways, including (1) direct description of the character by the narrator; (2) the direct presentation of the speech, thoughts, or actions of the character; and (3) the responses of other characters to the character. The term "character" also refers to a form originated by the ancient Greek writer Theophrastus that later became popular in the seventeenth and eighteenth centuries. It is a short essay or sketch of a person who prominently displays a specific attribute or quality, such as miserliness or ambition. "Miss Brill," a story by Katherine Mansfield, is an example of a character sketch.

Classical: In its strictest definition in literary criticism, classicism refers to works of ancient Greek or Roman literature. The term may also be used to describe a literary work of recognized importance (a "classic") from any time period or literature that exhibits the traits of classicism. Examples of later works and authors now described as classical include French literature of the seventeenth century, Western novels of the nineteenth century, and American fiction of the mid-nineteenth century such as that written by James Fenimore Cooper and Mark Twain.

Climax: The turning point in a narrative, the moment when the conflict is at its most intense. Typically, the structure of stories, novels, and plays is one of rising action, in which tension builds to the climax, followed by falling action, in which tension lessens as the story moves to its conclusion.

Comedy: One of two major types of drama, the other being tragedy. Its aim is to amuse, and it typically ends happily. Comedy assumes many forms, such as farce and burlesque, and uses a variety of techniques, from parody to satire. In a restricted sense the term comedy refers only to dramatic presentations, but in general usage it is commonly applied to nondramatic works as well.

Comic Relief: The use of humor to lighten the mood of a serious or tragic story, especially in plays. The technique is very common in Elizabethan works, and can be an integral part of the plot or simply a brief event designed to break the tension of the scene.

Conflict: The conflict in a work of fiction is the issue to be resolved in the story. It usually occurs between two characters, the protagonist and the antagonist, or between the protagonist and society or the protagonist and himself or herself. The conflict in Washington Irving's story "The Devil and Tom Walker" is that the Devil wants Tom Walker's soul but Tom does not want to go to hell.

Criticism: The systematic study and evaluation of literary works, usually based on a specific method or set of principles. An important part of literary studies since ancient times, the practice of criticism has given rise to numerous theories, methods, and "schools," sometimes producing conflicting, even contradictory, interpretations of literature in general as well as of individual works. Even such basic issues as what constitutes a poem or a novel have been the subject of much criticism over the centuries. Seminal texts of literary criticism include Plato's *Republic,* Aristotle's *Poetics,* Sir

Philip Sidney's *The Defence of Poesie,* and John Dryden's *Of Dramatic Poesie.* Contemporary schools of criticism include deconstruction, feminist, psychoanalytic, poststructuralist, new historicist, postcolonialist, and reader-response.

D

Deconstruction: A method of literary criticism characterized by multiple conflicting interpretations of a given work. Deconstructionists consider the impact of the language of a work and suggest that the true meaning of the work is not necessarily the meaning that the author intended.

Deduction: The process of reaching a conclusion through reasoning from general premises to a specific premise. Arthur Conan Doyle's character Sherlock Holmes often used deductive reasoning to solve mysteries.

Denotation: The definition of a word, apart from the impressions or feelings it creates in the reader. The word "apartheid" denotes a political and economic policy of segregation by race, but its connotations—oppression, slavery, inequality—are numerous.

Denouement: A French word meaning "the unknotting." In literature, it denotes the resolution of conflict in fiction or drama. The *denouement* follows the climax and provides an outcome to the primary plot situation as well as an explanation of secondary plot complications. A well-known example of *denouement* is the last scene of the play *As You Like It* by William Shakespeare, in which couples are married, an evildoer repents, the identities of two disguised characters are revealed, and a ruler is restored to power. Also known as "falling action."

Detective Story: A narrative about the solution of a mystery or the identification of a criminal. The conventions of the detective story include the detective's scrupulous use of logic in solving the mystery; incompetent or ineffectual police; a suspect who appears guilty at first but is later proved innocent; and the detective's friend or confidant—often the narrator—whose slowness in interpreting clues emphasizes by contrast the detective's brilliance. Edgar Allan Poe's "Murders in the Rue Morgue" is commonly regarded as the earliest example of this type of story. Other practitioners are Arthur Conan Doyle, Dashiell Hammett, and Agatha Christie.

Dialogue: Dialogue is conversation between people in a literary work. In its most restricted sense, it refers specifically to the speech of characters in a drama. As a specific literary genre, a "dialogue" is a composition in which characters debate an issue or idea.

Didactic: A term used to describe works of literature that aim to teach a moral, religious, political, or practical lesson. Although didactic elements are often found inartistically pleasing works, the term "didactic" usually refers to literature in which the message is more important than the form. The term may also be used to criticize a work that the critic finds "overly didactic," that is, heavy-handed in its delivery of a lesson. An example of didactic literature is John Bunyan's *Pilgrim's Progress.*

Dramatic Irony: Occurs when the reader of a work of literature knows something that a character in the work itself does not know. The irony is in the contrast between the intended meaning of the statements or actions of a character and the additional information understood by the audience.

Dystopia: An imaginary place in a work of fiction where the characters lead dehumanized, fearful lives. George Orwell's *Nineteen Eighty-four,* and Margaret Atwood's *Handmaid's Tale* portray versions of dystopia.

E

Edwardian: Describes cultural conventions identified with the period of the reign of Edward VII of England (1901–1910). Writers of the Edwardian Age typically displayed a strong reaction against the propriety and conservatism of the Victorian Age. Their work often exhibits distrust of authority in religion, politics, and art and expresses strong doubts about the soundness of conventional values. Writers of this era include E. M. Forster, H. G. Wells, and Joseph Conrad.

Empathy: A sense of shared experience, including emotional and physical feelings, with someone or something other than oneself. Empathy is often used to describe the response of a reader to a literary character.

Epilogue: A concluding statement or section of a literary work. In dramas, particularly those of the seventeenth and eighteenth centuries, the epilogue is a closing speech, often in verse, delivered by an actor at the end of a play and spoken directly to the audience.

Epiphany: A sudden revelation of truth inspired by a seemingly trivial incident. The term was widely used by James Joyce in his critical writings, and the stories in Joyce's *Dubliners* are commonly called "epiphanies."

Epistolary Novel: A novel in the form of letters. The form was particularly popular in the eighteenth century. The form can also be applied to short stories, as in Edwidge Danticat's "Children of the Sea."

Epithet: A word or phrase, often disparaging or abusive, that expresses a character trait of someone or something. "The Napoleon of crime" is an epithet applied to Professor Moriarty, arch-rival of Sherlock Holmes in Arthur Conan Doyle's series of detective stories.

Existentialism: A predominantly twentieth-century philosophy concerned with the nature and perception of human existence. There are two major strains of existentialist thought: atheistic and Christian. Followers of atheistic existentialism believe that the individual is alone in a godless universe and that the basic human condition is one of suffering and loneliness. Nevertheless, because there are no fixed values, individuals can create their own characters—indeed, they can shape themselves—through the exercise of free will. The atheistic strain culminates in and is popularly associated with the works of Jean-Paul Sartre. The Christian existentialists, on the other hand, believe that only in God may people find freedom from life's anguish. The two strains hold certain beliefs in common: that existence cannot be fully understood or described through empirical effort; that anguish is a universal element of life; that individuals must bear responsibility for their actions; and that there is no common standard of behavior or perception for religious and ethical matters. Existentialist thought figures prominently in the works of such authors as Franz Kafka, Fyodor Dostoyevsky, and Albert Camus.

Expatriatism: The practice of leaving one's country to live for an extended period in another country. Literary expatriates include Irish author James Joyce who moved to Italy and France, American writers James Baldwin,

Ernest Hemingway, Gertrude Stein, and F. Scott Fitzgerald who lived and wrote in Paris, and Polish novelist Joseph Conrad in England.

Exposition: Writing intended to explain the nature of an idea, thing, or theme. Expository writing is often combined with description, narration, or argument.

Expressionism: An indistinct literary term, originally used to describe an early twentieth-century school of German painting. The term applies to almost any mode of unconventional, highly subjective writing that distorts reality in some way. Advocates of Expressionism include Federico Garcia Lorca, Eugene O'Neill, Franz Kafka, and James Joyce.

F

Fable: A prose or verse narrative intended to convey amoral. Animals or inanimate objects with human characteristics often serve as characters in fables. A famous fable is Aesop's "The Tortoise and the Hare."

Fantasy: A literary form related to mythology and folklore. Fantasy literature is typically set in non-existent realms and features supernatural beings. Notable examples of literature with elements of fantasy are Gabriel Gárcia Márquez's story "The Handsomest Drowned Man in the World" and Ursula K. Le Guin's "The Ones Who Walk Away from Omelas."

Farce: A type of comedy characterized by broad humor, outlandish incidents, and often vulgar subject matter. Much of the comedy in film and television could more accurately be described as farce.

Fiction: Any story that is the product of imagination rather than a documentation of fact. Characters and events in such narratives may be based in real life but their ultimate form and configuration is a creation of the author.

Figurative Language: A technique in which an author uses figures of speech such as hyperbole, irony, metaphor, or simile for a particular effect. Figurative language is the opposite of literal language, in which every word is truthful, accurate, and free of exaggeration or embellishment.

Flashback: A device used in literature to present action that occurred before the beginning of the story. Flashbacks are often introduced as the dreams or recollections of one or more characters.

Foil: A character in a work of literature whose physical or psychological qualities contrast strongly with, and therefore highlight, the corresponding qualities of another character. In his Sherlock Holmes stories, Arthur Conan Doyle portrayed Dr. Watson as a man of normal habits and intelligence, making him a foil for the eccentric and unusually perceptive Sherlock Holmes.

Folklore: Traditions and myths preserved in a culture or group of people. Typically, these are passed on by word of mouth in various forms—such as legends, songs, and proverbs—or preserved in customs and ceremonies. Washington Irving, in "The Devil and Tom Walker" and many of his other stories, incorporates many elements of the folklore of New England and Germany.

Folktale: A story originating in oral tradition. Folk tales fall into a variety of categories, including legends, ghost stories, fairy tales, fables, and anecdotes based on historical figures and events.

Foreshadowing: A device used in literature to create expectation or to set up an explanation of later developments. Edgar Allan Poe uses foreshadowing to create suspense in "The Fall of the House of Usher" when the narrator comments on the crumbling state of disrepair in which he finds the house.

G

Genre: A category of literary work. Genre may refer to both the content of a given work—tragedy, comedy, horror, science fiction—and to its form, such as poetry, novel, or drama.

Gilded Age: A period in American history during the 1870s and after characterized by political corruption and materialism. A number of important novels of social and political criticism were written during this time. Henry James and Kate Chopin are two writers who were prominent during the Gilded Age.

Gothicism: In literature, works characterized by a taste for medieval or morbid characters and situations. A gothic novel prominently features elements of horror, the supernatural, gloom, and violence: clanking chains, terror, ghosts, medieval castles, and unexplained phenomena. The term "gothic novel" is also applied to novels that lack elements of the traditional Gothic setting but that create a similar atmosphere of terror or dread. The term can also be applied to stories, plays, and poems. Mary Shelley's *Frankenstein* and Joyce Carol Oates's *Bellefleur* are both gothic novels.

Grotesque: In literature, a work that is characterized by exaggeration, deformity, freakishness, and disorder. The grotesque often includes an element of comic absurdity. Examples of the grotesque can be found in the works of Edgar Allan Poe, Flannery O'Connor, Joseph Heller, and Shirley Jackson.

H

Harlem Renaissance: The Harlem Renaissance of the 1920s is generally considered the first significant movement of black writers and artists in the United States. During this period, new and established black writers, many of whom lived in the region of New York City known as Harlem, published more fiction and poetry than ever before, the first influential black literary journals were established, and black authors and artists received their first widespread recognition and serious critical appraisal. Among the major writers associated with this period are Countee Cullen, Langston Hughes, Arna Bontemps, and Zora Neale Hurston.

Hero/Heroine: The principal sympathetic character in a literary work. Heroes and heroines typically exhibit admirable traits: idealism, courage, and integrity, for example. Famous heroes and heroines of literature include Charles Dickens's Oliver Twist, Margaret Mitchell's Scarlett O'Hara, and the anonymous narrator in Ralph Ellison's *Invisible Man*.

Hyperbole: Deliberate exaggeration used to achieve an effect. In William Shakespeare's *Macbeth*, Lady Macbeth hyperbolizes when she says, "All the perfumes of Arabia could not sweeten this little hand."

I

Image: A concrete representation of an object or sensory experience. Typically, such a representation helps evoke the feelings associated with the object or experience itself. Images

are either "literal" or "figurative." Literal images are especially concrete and involve little or no extension of the obvious meaning of the words used to express them. Figurative images do not follow the literal meaning of the words exactly. Images in literature are usually visual, but the term "image" can also refer to the representation of any sensory experience.

Imagery: The array of images in a literary work. Also used to convey the author's overall use of figurative language in a work.

In medias res: A Latin term meaning "in the middle of things." It refers to the technique of beginning a story at its midpoint and then using various flashback devices to reveal previous action. This technique originated in such epics as Virgil's *Aeneid*.

Interior Monologue: A narrative technique in which characters' thoughts are revealed in a way that appears to be uncontrolled by the author. The interior monologue typically aims to reveal the inner self of a character. It portrays emotional experiences as they occur at both a conscious and unconscious level. One of the best-known interior monologues in English is the Molly Bloom section at the close of James Joyce's *Ulysses*. Katherine Anne Porter's "The Jilting of Granny Weatherall" is also told in the form of an interior monologue.

Irony: In literary criticism, the effect of language in which the intended meaning is the opposite of what is stated. The title of Jonathan Swift's "A Modest Proposal" is ironic because what Swift proposes in this essay is cannibalism—hardly "modest."

J

Jargon: Language that is used or understood only by a select group of people. Jargon may refer to terminology used in a certain profession, such as computer jargon, or it may refer to any nonsensical language that is not understood by most people. Anthony Burgess's *A Clockwork Orange* and James Thurber's "The Secret Life of Walter Mitty" both use jargon.

K

Knickerbocker Group: An indistinct group of New York writers of the first half of the nineteenth century. Members of the group were linked only by location and a common theme: New York life. Two famous members of the Knickerbocker Group were Washington Irving and William Cullen Bryant. The group's name derives from Irving's *Knickerbocker's History of New York*.

L

Literal Language: An author uses literal language when he or she writes without exaggerating or embellishing the subject matter and without any tools of figurative language. To say "He ran very quickly down the street" is to use literal language, whereas to say "He ran like a hare down the street" would be using figurative language.

Literature: Literature is broadly defined as any written or spoken material, but the term most often refers to creative works. Literature includes poetry, drama, fiction, and many kinds of nonfiction writing, as well as oral, dramatic, and broadcast compositions not necessarily preserved in a written format, such as films and television programs.

Lost Generation: A term first used by Gertrude Stein to describe the post–World War I generation of American writers: men and women haunted by a sense of betrayal and emptiness brought about by the destructiveness of the war. The term is commonly applied to Hart Crane, Ernest Hemingway, F. Scott Fitzgerald, and others.

M

Magic Realism: A form of literature that incorporates fantasy elements or supernatural occurrences into the narrative and accepts them as truth. Gabriel Gárcia Márquez and Laura Esquivel are two writers known for their works of magic realism.

Metaphor: A figure of speech that expresses an idea through the image of another object. Metaphors suggest the essence of the first object by identifying it with certain qualities of the second object. An example is "But soft, what light through yonder window breaks? / It is the east, and Juliet is the sun" in William Shakespeare's *Romeo and Juliet*. Here, Juliet, the first object, is identified with qualities of the second object, the sun.

Minimalism: A literary style characterized by spare, simple prose with few elaborations. In minimalism, the main theme of the work is often never discussed directly. Amy Hempel and Ernest Hemingway are two writers known for their works of minimalism.

Modernism: Modern literary practices. Also, the principles of a literary school that lasted from roughly the beginning of the twentieth century until the end of World War II. Modernism is defined by its rejection of the literary conventions of the nineteenth century and by its opposition to conventional morality, taste, traditions, and economic values. Many writers are associated with the concepts of modernism, including Albert Camus, D. H. Lawrence, Ernest Hemingway, William Faulkner, Eugene O'Neill, and James Joyce.

Monologue: A composition, written or oral, by a single individual. More specifically, a speech given by a single individual in a drama or other public entertainment. It has no set length, although it is usually several or more lines long. "I Stand Here Ironing" by Tillie Olsen is an example of a story written in the form of a monologue.

Mood: The prevailing emotions of a work or of the author in his or her creation of the work. The mood of a work is not always what might be expected based on its subject matter.

Motif: A theme, character type, image, metaphor, or other verbal element that recurs throughout a single work of literature or occurs in a number of different works over a period of time. For example, the color white in Herman Melville's *Moby Dick* is a "specific" motif, while the trials of star-crossed lovers is a "conventional" motif from the literature of all periods.

N

Narration: The telling of a series of events, real or invented. A narration may be either a simple narrative, in which the events are recounted chronologically, or a narrative with a plot, in which the account is given in a style reflecting the author's artistic concept of the story. Narration is sometimes used as a synonym for "storyline."

Narrative: A verse or prose accounting of an event or sequence of events, real or invented. The term is also used as an adjective in the sense "method of narration." For example, in literary criticism, the expression "narrative technique" usually refers to the way the author structures and presents his or her story. Different narrative forms include diaries, travelogues, novels, ballads, epics, short stories, and other fictional forms.

Narrator: The teller of a story. The narrator may be the author or a character in the story through whom the author speaks. Huckleberry Finn is the narrator of Mark Twain's *The Adventures of Huckleberry Finn.*

Novella: An Italian term meaning "story." This term has been especially used to describe fourteenth-century Italian tales, but it also refers to modern short novels. Modern novellas include Leo Tolstoy's *The Death of Ivan Ilich,* Fyodor Dostoyevsky's *Notes from the Underground,* and Joseph Conrad's *Heart of Darkness.*

O

Oedipus Complex: A son's romantic obsession with his mother. The phrase is derived from the story of the ancient Theban hero Oedipus, who unknowingly killed his father and married his mother, and was popularized by Sigmund Freud's theory of psychoanalysis. Literary occurrences of the Oedipus complex include Sophocles' *Oedipus Rex* and D. H. Lawrence's "The Rocking-Horse Winner."

Onomatopoeia: The use of words whose sounds express or suggest their meaning. In its simplest sense, onomatopoeia may be represented by words that mimic the sounds they denote such as "hiss" or "meow." At a more subtle level, the pattern and rhythm of sounds and rhymes of a line or poem may be onomatopoeic.

Oral Tradition: A process by which songs, ballads, folklore, and other material are transmitted by word of mouth. The tradition of oral transmission predates the written record systems of literate society. Oral transmission preserves material sometimes over generations, although often with variations. Memory plays a large part in the recitation and preservation of orally transmitted material. Native American myths and legends, and African folktales told by plantation slaves are examples of orally transmitted literature.

P

Parable: A story intended to teach a moral lesson or answer an ethical question. Examples of parables are the stories told by Jesus Christ in the New Testament, notably "The Prodigal Son," but parables also are used in Sufism, rabbinic literature, Hasidism, and Zen Buddhism. Isaac Bashevis Singer's story "Gimpel the Fool" exhibits characteristics of a parable.

Paradox: A statement that appears illogical or contradictory at first, but may actually point to an underlying truth. A literary example of a paradox is George Orwell's statement "All animals are equal, but some animals are more equal than others" in *Animal Farm.*

Parody: In literature, this term refers to an imitation of a serious literary work or the signature style of a particular author in a ridiculous manner. Atypical parody adopts the style of the original and applies it to an inappropriate subject for humorous effect. Parody is a form of satire and could be considered the literary equivalent of a caricature or cartoon. Henry Fielding's *Shamela* is a parody of Samuel Richardson's *Pamela.*

Persona: A Latin term meaning "mask." Personae are the characters in a fictional work of literature. The persona generally functions as a mask through which the author tells a story in a voice other than his or her own. A persona is usually either a character in a story who acts as a narrator or an "implied author," a voice created by the author to act as the narrator for himself or herself. The persona in Charlotte Perkins Gilman's story "The Yellow Wallpaper" is the unnamed young mother experiencing a mental breakdown.

Personification: A figure of speech that gives human qualities to abstract ideas, animals, and inanimate objects. To say that "the sun is smiling" is to personify the sun.

Plot: The pattern of events in a narrative or drama. In its simplest sense, the plot guides the author in composing the work and helps the reader follow the work. Typically, plots exhibit causality and unity and have a beginning, a middle, and an end. Sometimes, however, a plot may consist of a series of disconnected events, in which case it is known as an "episodic plot."

Poetic Justice: An outcome in a literary work, not necessarily a poem, in which the good are rewarded and the evil are punished, especially in ways that particularly fit their virtues or crimes. For example, a murderer may himself be murdered, or a thief will find himself penniless.

Poetic License: Distortions of fact and literary convention made by a writer—not always a poet—for the sake of the effect gained. Poetic license is closely related to the concept of "artistic freedom." An author exercises poetic license by saying that a pile of money "reaches as high as a mountain" when the pile is actually only a foot or two high.

Point of View: The narrative perspective from which a literary work is presented to the reader. There are four traditional points of view. The "third person omniscient" gives the reader a "godlike" perspective, unrestricted by time or place, from which to see actions and look into the minds of characters. This allows the author to comment openly on characters and events in the work. The "third person" point of view presents the events of the story from outside of any single character's perception, much like the omniscient point of view, but the reader must understand the action as it takes place and without any special insight into characters' minds or motivations. The "first person" or "personal" point of view relates events as they are perceived by a single character. The main character "tells" the story and may offer opinions about the action and characters which differ from those of the author. Much less common than omniscient, third person, and first person is the "second person" point of view, wherein the author tells the story as if it is happening to the reader. James Thurber employs the omniscient point of view in his short story "The Secret Life of Walter Mitty." Ernest Hemingway's "A Clean, Well-Lighted Place" is a short story told from the third person point of view. Mark Twain's novel *Huckleberry Finn* is presented from the first person viewpoint. Jay McInerney's *Bright Lights, Big City* is an example of a novel which uses the second person point of view.

Pornography: Writing intended to provoke feelings of lust in the reader. Such works are often condemned by critics and teachers, but those which can be shown to have literary value are viewed less harshly. Literary works that have been described as pornographic include D. H. Lawrence's *Lady Chatterley's Lover* and James Joyce's *Ulysses.*

Post-Aesthetic Movement: An artistic response made by African Americans to the black aesthetic movement of the 1960s and early 1970s. Writers since that time have adopted a somewhat different tone in their work, with less emphasis placed on the disparity between black and white in the United States. In the words of post-aesthetic authors such as Toni Morrison, John Edgar Wideman, and Kristin Hunter, African Americans are portrayed as looking inward for answers to their own questions, rather than always looking to the outside world. Two well-known examples of works produced as part of the post-aesthetic movement are the Pulitzer Prize–winning novels *The Color Purple* by Alice Walker and *Beloved* by Toni Morrison.

Postmodernism: Writing from the 1960s forward characterized by experimentation and application of modernist elements, which include existentialism and alienation. Postmodernists have gone a step further in the rejection of tradition begun with the modernists by also rejecting traditional forms, preferring the anti-novel over the novel and the anti-hero over the hero. Postmodern writers include Thomas Pynchon, Margaret Drabble, and Gabriel Gárcia Márquez.

Prologue: An introductory section of a literary work. It often contains information establishing the situation of the characters or presents information about the setting, time period, or action. In drama, the prologue is spoken by a chorus or by one of the principal characters.

Prose: A literary medium that attempts to mirror the language of everyday speech. It is distinguished from poetry by its use of unmetered, unrhymed language consisting of logically related sentences. Prose is usually grouped into paragraphs that form a cohesive whole such as an essay or a novel. The term is sometimes used to mean an author's general writing.

Protagonist: The central character of a story who serves as a focus for its themes and incidents and as the principal rationale for its development. The protagonist is sometimes referred to in discussions of modern literature as the hero or anti-hero. Well-known protagonists are Hamlet in William Shakespeare's *Hamlet* and Jay Gatsby in F. Scott Fitzgerald's *The Great Gatsby*.

R

Realism: A nineteenth-century European literary movement that sought to portray familiar characters, situations, and settings in a realistic manner. This was done primarily by using an objective narrative point of view and through the buildup of accurate detail. The standard for success of any realistic work depends on how faithfully it transfers common experience into fictional forms. The realistic method may be altered or extended, as in stream of consciousness writing, to record highly subjective experience. Contemporary authors who often write in a realistic way include Nadine Gordimer and Grace Paley.

Resolution: The portion of a story following the climax, in which the conflict is resolved. The resolution of Jane Austen's *Northanger Abbey* is neatly summed up in the following sentence: "Henry and Catherine were married, the bells rang and every body smiled."

Rising Action: The part of a drama where the plot becomes increasingly complicated. Rising action leads up to the climax, or turning point, of a drama. The final "chase scene" of an action film is generally the rising action which culminates in the film's climax.

Roman a clef: A French phrase meaning "novel with a key." It refers to a narrative in which real persons are portrayed under fictitious names. Jack Kerouac, for example, portrayed various friends under fictitious names in the novel *On the Road*. D. H. Lawrence based "The Rocking-Horse Winner" on a family he knew.

Romanticism: This term has two widely accepted meanings. In historical criticism, it refers to a European intellectual and artistic movement of the late eighteenth and early nineteenth centuries that sought greater freedom of personal expression than that allowed by the strict rules of literary form and logic of the eighteenth-century neoclassicists. The Romantics preferred emotional and imaginative expression to rational analysis. They considered the individual to be at the center of all experience and so placed him or her at the center of their art. The Romantics believed that the creative imagination reveals nobler truths—unique feelings and attitudes—than those that could be discovered by logic or by scientific examination. "Romanticism" is also used as a general term to refer to a type of sensibility found in all periods of literary history and usually considered to be in opposition to the principles of classicism. In this sense, Romanticism signifies any work or philosophy in which the exotic or dreamlike figure strongly, or that is devoted to individualistic expression, self-analysis, or a pursuit of a higher realm of knowledge than can be discovered by human reason. Prominent Romantics include Jean-Jacques Rousseau, William Wordsworth, John Keats, Lord Byron, and Johann Wolfgang von Goethe.

S

Satire: A work that uses ridicule, humor, and wit to criticize and provoke change in human nature and institutions. Voltaire's novella *Candide* and Jonathan Swift's essay "A Modest Proposal" are both satires. Flannery O'Connor's portrayal of the family in "A Good Man Is Hard to Find" is a satire of a modern, Southern, American family.

Science Fiction: A type of narrative based upon real or imagined scientific theories and technology. Science fiction is often peopled with alien creatures and set on other planets or in different dimensions. Popular writers of science fiction are Isaac Asimov, Karel Capek, Ray Bradbury, and Ursula K. Le Guin.

Setting: The time, place, and culture in which the action of a narrative takes place. The elements of setting may include geographic location, characters's physical and mental environments, prevailing cultural attitudes, or the historical time in which the action takes place.

Short Story: A fictional prose narrative shorter and more focused than a novella. The short story usually deals with a single episode and often a single character. The "tone," the author's attitude toward his or her subject and audience, is uniform throughout. The short story frequently also lacks *denouement*, ending instead at its climax.

Signifying Monkey: A popular trickster figure in black folklore, with hundreds of tales about this character documented since the 19th century. Henry Louis Gates Jr. examines the history of the signifying monkey in *The Signifying*

Monkey: Towards a Theory of Afro-American Literary Criticism, published in 1988.

Simile: A comparison, usually using "like" or "as," of two essentially dissimilar things, as in "coffee as cold as ice" or "He sounded like a broken record." The title of Ernest Hemingway's "Hills Like White Elephants" contains a simile.

Socialist Realism: The Socialist Realism school of literary theory was proposed by Maxim Gorky and established as a dogma by the first Soviet Congress of Writers. It demanded adherence to a communist worldview in works of literature. Its doctrines required an objective viewpoint comprehensible to the working classes and themes of social struggle featuring strong proletarian heroes. Gabriel Gárcia Márquez's stories exhibit some characteristics of Socialist Realism.

Stereotype: A stereotype was originally the name for a duplication made during the printing process; this led to its modern definition as a person or thing that is (or is assumed to be) the same as all others of its type. Common stereotypical characters include the absent-minded professor, the nagging wife, the troublemaking teenager, and the kindhearted grandmother.

Stream of Consciousness: A narrative technique for rendering the inward experience of a character. This technique is designed to give the impression of an ever-changing series of thoughts, emotions, images, and memories in the spontaneous and seemingly illogical order that they occur in life. The textbook example of stream of consciousness is the last section of James Joyce's *Ulysses*.

Structure: The form taken by a piece of literature. The structure may be made obvious for ease of understanding, as in nonfiction works, or may obscured for artistic purposes, as in some poetry or seemingly "unstructured" prose.

Style: A writer's distinctive manner of arranging words to suit his or her ideas and purpose in writing. The unique imprint of the author's personality upon his or her writing, style is the product of an author's way of arranging ideas and his or her use of diction, different sentence structures, rhythm, figures of speech, rhetorical principles, and other elements of composition.

Suspense: A literary device in which the author maintains the audience's attention through the buildup of events, the outcome of which will soon be revealed. Suspense in William Shakespeare's *Hamlet* is sustained throughout by the question of whether or not the Prince will achieve what he has been instructed to do and of what he intends to do.

Symbol: Something that suggests or stands for something else without losing its original identity. In literature, symbols combine their literal meaning with the suggestion of an abstract concept. Literary symbols are of two types: those that carry complex associations of meaning no matter what their contexts, and those that derive their suggestive meaning from their functions in specific literary works. Examples of symbols are sunshine suggesting happiness, rain suggesting sorrow, and storm clouds suggesting despair.

T

Tale: A story told by a narrator with a simple plot and little character development. Tales are usually relatively short and often carry a simple message. Examples of tales can be found in the works of Saki, Anton Chekhov, Guy de Maupassant, and O. Henry.

Tall Tale: A humorous tale told in a straightforward, credible tone but relating absolutely impossible events or feats of the characters. Such tales were commonly told of frontier adventures during the settlement of the west in the United States. Literary use of tall tales can be found in Washington Irving's *History of New York,* Mark Twain's *Life on the Mississippi,* and in the German R. F. Raspe's *Baron Munchausen's Narratives of His Marvellous Travels and Campaigns in Russia.*

Theme: The main point of a work of literature. The term is used interchangeably with thesis. Many works have multiple themes. One of the themes of Nathaniel Hawthorne's "Young Goodman Brown" is loss of faith.

Tone: The author's attitude toward his or her audience maybe deduced from the tone of the work. A formal tone may create distance or convey politeness, while an informal tone may encourage a friendly, intimate, or intrusive feeling in the reader. The author's attitude toward his or her subject matter may also be deduced from the tone of the words he or she uses in discussing it. The tone of

John F. Kennedy's speech which included the appeal to "ask not what your country can do for you" was intended to instill feelings of camaraderie and national pride in listeners.

Tragedy: A drama in prose or poetry about a noble, courageous hero of excellent character who, because of some tragic character flaw, brings ruin upon him- or herself. Tragedy treats its subjects in a dignified and serious manner, using poetic language to help evoke pity and fear and bring about catharsis, a purging of these emotions. The tragic form was practiced extensively by the ancient Greeks. The classical form of tragedy was revived in the sixteenth century; it flourished especially on the Elizabethan stage. In modern times, dramatists have attempted to adapt the form to the needs of modern society by drawing their heroes from the ranks of ordinary men and women and defining the nobility of these heroes in terms of spirit rather than exalted social standing. Some contemporary works that are thought of as tragedies include *The Great Gatsby* by F. Scott Fitzgerald, and *The Sound and the Fury* by William Faulkner.

Tragic Flaw: In a tragedy, the quality within the hero or heroine which leads to his or her downfall. Examples of the tragic flaw include Othello's jealousy and Hamlet's indecisiveness, although most great tragedies defy such simple interpretation.

U

Utopia: A fictional perfect place, such as "paradise" or "heaven." An early literary utopia was described in Plato's *Republic,* and in modern literature, Ursula K. Le Guin depicts a utopia in "The Ones Who Walk Away from Omelas."

V

Victorian: Refers broadly to the reign of Queen Victoria of England (1837-1901) and to anything with qualities typical of that era. For example, the qualities of smug narrow-mindedness, bourgeois materialism, faith in social progress, and priggish morality are often considered Victorian. In literature, the Victorian Period was the great age of the English novel, and the latter part of the era saw the rise of movements such as decadence and symbolism.

Cumulative Author/Title Index

Cumulative Nationality/Ethnicity Index

African American

Baldwin, James
  The Rockpile: V18
  Sonny's Blues: V2
  This Morning, This Evening, So Soon: V44
Bambara, Toni Cade
  Blues Ain't No Mockin Bird: V4
  Geraldine Moore the Poet: V40
  Gorilla, My Love: V21
  The Lesson: V12
  Raymond's Run: V7
  The War of the Wall: V39
Brooks, Gwendolyn
  Home: V35
Butler, Octavia
  Bloodchild: V6
Chesnutt, Charles Waddell
  The Goophered Grapevine: V26
  The Sheriff's Children: V11
Clifton, Lucille
  The Lucky Stone: V34
Collier, Eugenia W.
  Marigolds: V28
  Sweet Potato Pie: V30
Ellison, Ralph
  King of the Bingo Game: V1
Fauset, Jessie Redmon
  Emmy: V43
Hughes, Langston
  The Blues I'm Playing: V7
  Slave on the Block: V4
  Thank You Ma'm: V29
Hurston, Zora Neale
  Conscience of the Court: V21
  Drenched in Light: V42

The Eatonville Anthology: V1
The Gilded Six-Bits: V11
Spunk: V6
Sweat: V19
Lee, Andrea
  New African: V37
Marshall, Paule
  To Da-duh, in Memoriam: V15
McPherson, James Alan
  Elbow Room: V23
Myers, Walter Dean
  The Treasure of Lemon Brown: V31
Petry, Ann
  Like a Winding Sheet: V44
Toomer, Jean
  Blood-Burning Moon: V5
Walker, Alice
  Everyday Use: V2
  Roselily: V11
Wideman, John Edgar
  The Beginning of Homewood: V12
  Fever: V6
  What We Cannot Speak About We Must Pass Over in Silence: V24
Wright, Richard
  Big Black Good Man: V20
  Bright and Morning Star: V15
  The Man Who Lived Underground: V3
  The Man Who Was Almost a Man: V9

American

Adams, Alice
  Greyhound People: V21
  The Last Lovely City: V14

Agüeros, Jack
  Dominoes: V13
Aiken, Conrad
  Impulse: V34
  Silent Snow, Secret Snow: V8
Aiken, Joan
  Lob's Girl: V38
  Sonata for Harp and Bicycle: V33
Alcott, Louisa May
  Back Windows: V41
Alexie, Sherman
  Because My Father Always Said He Was the Only Indian Who Saw Jimi Hendrix Play "The Star-Spangled Banner" at Woodstock: V18
  This Is What It Means to Say Phoenix, Arizona: V36
  What You Pawn I Will Redeem: V44
Allen, Woody
  The Kugelmass Episode: V21
Alvarez, Julia
  Daughter of Invention: V31
  Liberty: V27
Anaya, Rudolfo
  In Search of Epifano: V38
Anderson, Sherwood
  Death in the Woods: V10
  The Egg: V37
  Hands: V11
  Sophistication: V4
Asimov, Isaac
  The Machine That Won the War: V33
  Nightfall: V17
Baida, Peter
  A Nurse's Story: V25

Subject/Theme Index

Subject/Theme Index